"Donnelly and Edquist-Whelan's human rights text combines rich historical detail and deep conceptual engagement with contemporary case studies and practical examples of human rights success and reversal. It is attentive to the contentious politics of human rights and the ways that people and movements struggle for human rights change as well as the domestic and international human rights machinery that has been created to manage their implementation. The result is a comprehensive yet accessible text for students and faculty alike—one that will generate critical engagement and debate over the meaning and practice of human rights in and outside of the classroom."

Carrie Booth Walling, *University of Minnesota Human Rights Program, USA*

"I adopted the previous edition twice after reviewing many alternatives, using it as the primary text for a large, interdisciplinary course introducing first and second-year undergraduates to human rights. It is the most comprehensive, thought-provoking, and accessible book available."

David Cingranelli, *Binghamton University, USA*

"From its inception, *International Human Rights* has been the gold standard of human rights textbooks. The 7th edition not only provides an update of human rights practices, but it will also actively engage students in the material—and the world around them."

Mark Gibney, *University of North Carolina Asheville, USA*

"This book is unique in how it addresses the interdisciplinary field of human rights from an international perspective: situating theories and contemporary practices in their political and historical context. It is elegantly written and clearly organized, with plenty of discussion questions, reading suggestions, and examples of human rights 'problems' that bring the material to life. I'm impressed with the painstaking work that has gone into updating this edition, keeping it fresh and relevant for our changing world order. A great textbook!"

David J Karp, *University of Sussex, UK*

"Daniel Edquist-Whelan and Jack Donnelly have done it again, updating their leading survey for a new present in which human rights are more important than ever."

Samuel Moyn, *Yale University, USA*

International Human Rights

Fully updated, the seventh edition of *International Human Rights* examines the ways in which states and other international actors have addressed human rights since the end of World War II. This unique textbook features substantial attention to theory, history, international and regional institutions, and the role of transnational actors in the protection and promotion of human rights. Its purpose is to explore the difficult and contentious politics of human rights, and how those political dimensions have been addressed at the national, regional, and especially international levels.

Key features include:

- concise yet clearly organized and comprehensive coverage of the topics.
- substantially revised throughout, including a new chapter on rights-conscious business investment.
- new sections on the UN Human Rights Council, including substantive data trends on the distribution and topics of Council resolutions and the changing politics driven especially by the agendas of countries such as China and Russia; the implications of the war in Gaza; and "non-traditional approaches" to human rights.
- in-text features such as discussion questions, fully updated suggested readings, case studies, and "problems" to promote classroom discussion and in-depth examination of topics.
- updated and new case studies on key topics such as the draft International Covenant on the Right to Development.

International Human Rights is essential reading for courses and modules in human rights, politics and international relations, law, criminal justice, sociology, social work, public administration, and international development.

Daniel J. Edquist-Whelan is the Charles Prentiss Hough Odyssey Professor of Politics at Hendrix College, USA.

Jack Donnelly is the Andrew W. Mellon Professor of International Relations at the Josef Korbel School of International Studies at the University of Denver, USA.

International Human Rights

Seventh Edition

DANIEL J. EDQUIST-WHELAN AND JACK DONNELLY

Routledge
Taylor & Francis Group
NEW YORK AND LONDON

Designed cover image: © Getty Images

Seventh edition published 2026
by Routledge
605 Third Avenue, New York, NY 10158

and by Routledge
4 Park Square, Milton Park, Abingdon, Oxon, OX14 4RN

Routledge is an imprint of the Taylor & Francis Group, an informa business

First edition published by Westview Press 1993
Sixth edition published by Routledge 2020

ISBN: 978-1-032-44710-0 (hbk)
ISBN: 978-1-032-44708-7 (pbk)
ISBN: 978-1-003-37352-0 (ebk)

DOI: 10.4324/9781003373520

Typeset in Dante and Avenir
by codeMantra

MIX
Paper | Supporting responsible forestry
FSC® C013056
www.fsc.org

Printed and bound in Great Britain by
TJ Books, Padstow, Cornwall

Contents

List of Figures

List of Tables

List of Boxes

List of Problems

Preface

A Note to the Reader

This is a book about the international politics of human rights since the end of World War II; that is, the ways in which states and other international actors have addressed human rights. The topic, although broad, is narrower than some readers might expect.

Life, liberty, security, subsistence, and other things to which we have human rights may be denied by an extensive array of individuals and organizations. *Human rights*, however, are usually taken to have a special reference to the ways in which states treat their own citizens. For example, domestically, we distinguish muggings and private assaults, which are not typically considered human rights violations, from police brutality and torture, which are. Internationally, we distinguish terrorism, war, and crimes against humanity from human rights abuses, even though all lead to denials of life and security. Although the boundaries are not always clear, the distinction is part of our ordinary language and focuses our attention on an important set of political problems.

No single book can cover all aspects of the politics of human rights. Our concern is with the *international* politics of human rights, a vital and well-established area of policy and inquiry. This does not imply that international action is the principal determinant of whether human rights are respected or violated. In fact, much of this book demonstrates the limits of international action. Ultimately, we argue, human rights are respected and realized at the domestic or national level. Therefore, in contrast to many other discussions of international human rights, we pay ample attention to domestic politics in a number of case studies.

Another distinctive feature of this book is a relatively extensive emphasis on theory and history, which form the heart of Part I. Chapter 1 examines the historical development of international human rights since World War II. Chapter 2 addresses philosophical issues of the nature, substance, and source(s) of human rights; the place of human rights in the contemporary international society of states; and the theoretical challenges posed to the very enterprise of international human rights policy by arguments of radical cultural relativism and political realism (*Realpolitik*, or power politics). Chapter 3 explores the important theoretical issue of the universality (and relativity) of human rights. Chapter 4 explores the unity (indivisibility) of all human rights, with a particular emphasis on the two grand categories of civil/political and economic/social rights.

Part II looks at multilateral, bilateral, and transnational action, both separately and comparatively, with an emphasis on case studies since the end of the Cold War (with a few Cold War-era case studies from earlier editions). The chapters in this section consider global multilateral mechanisms, regional mechanisms, foreign policy action in general, US foreign policy in particular, transnational advocacy, and rights-supportive business investment (new to this edition). All of these chapters have been significantly revised from the sixth edition, including several new case studies that explore recent human rights developments.

Part III turns to three contemporary issues: humanitarian intervention and the responsibility to protect, globalization, and development. As with the chapters in Part II, these chapters have been thoroughly revised and brought up to date with the latest developments in human rights policy and practice.

We then offer a brief conclusion on the future of human rights. Rather than offer our own assessment, though, we seek to identify the kinds of questions and frameworks of analysis readers might consider in making their own judgment of the aims and values of human rights in the contemporary world.

We have tried to write a book that assumes little or no background knowledge. Most readers with an interest in the topic, regardless of age or experience, should find this book accessible, and we have highlighted **in bold** some key terms and concepts that are included in the glossary. However, we have tried not to write a textbook, a term that has justly acquired pejorative overtones. We have taken care not to write "down," either in style or in substance.

Textbook presentations of controversial issues—when they are not entirely avoided—tend to involve bland and noncommittal presentations of "the two sides" to an argument. Although we have made an effort to retain some balance in the discussion, we have not expunged our own views and interpretations. To some readers, it may seem like we often lay out and defend one interpretation and give little attention to alternative views. While we have made great efforts to be accurate and fair, we have no false pretense of objectivity.

With that in mind, we want to draw the reader's attention to the discussion questions for each chapter. There is almost a short chapter's worth of material in these questions, which often frame alternative interpretations and highlight controversial claims (or challenge our own views) in the chapter. They thus provide at least a partial corrective to any "imbalance" in the main text.

We also draw your attention to the nine "Problems" spread throughout the volume. Each is, in effect, a discussion question, followed by our own answer, followed again by further questions or problems. They aim to provoke additional thought and discussion and to illustrate ways in which readers may take the material presented here and go beyond it.

Another central feature of this volume is the nineteen case studies that appear throughout. These include recent as well as historical cases that allow the reader to engage the material in the chapter, adding depth to the discussion and providing points of comparison between earlier periods and more contemporary ones.

Each chapter—as well as each case study and each problem—can be read independently, in any order. Teachers and readers can thus easily customize this book. (We have tried to facilitate this type of flexible reading by providing numerous cross-references to other sections of the text that are relevant to the topic at hand.) Our only strong suggestion is that those without a background begin with Chapter 1. From then on, follow your interests—or the instructions of your teacher. *And approach everything here with a critical mind.*

Our goal is to get you to think about why and how human rights are respected and violated, what can (and cannot) be done about violations through international, regional, and transnational action, why human rights remain such a small part of international politics, and what might be done about that. These are pressing political issues that merit, even demand, thought and attention. This book provides resources to help you think about these issues more broadly, more deeply, and more subtly—and thus to be a more informed, and perhaps even more effective, person and citizen.

Finally, a note on the evolution of the text. Jack published the first edition more than thirty years ago. From the fifth edition on, this has been a completely joint endeavor. Daniel has managed the revision process and has written most of the new material but we have both worked on every single line of the text. At this point, we estimate that each of us has been the initial source of about half of the manuscript. In light of Daniel's continuing managerial role, he is now listed as the first of the co-authors.

Acknowledgments

Over the decades, I have had the help of literally dozens of friends, colleagues, students, research assistants, and editors. Any list would be both too long, losing the individuals in a stream of names, and too short, for I am sure that I would neglect mentioning at least a few people who contributed to this book. Thus, let me simply say: Thanks to all of you. (You know who you are.)

—Jack Donnelly

With the financial support of the Bill and Connie Bowen and Charles Prentiss Hough Odyssey Professorships, which I held in 2023 and 2024, I convened a small team of Hendrix students as research assistants to begin the process of updating this edition: Deuce Carter, Jordan Collins (team coordinator), and Margaret Sampson-Green (who provided additional research assistance through 2025). They provided meticulous updates throughout the manuscript and conducted extensive research for much of the new material that appears in this edition. I am especially grateful for their outstanding support and assistance.

—Daniel J. Edquist-Whelan

And thanks also to the teachers and readers who have kept this book alive—and forced us to keep it up to date. We hope that we have at least a couple more editions in us.

—Daniel and Jack

Abbreviations

ACHR	Arab Charter on Human Rights
AHRD	ASEAN Human Rights Declaration
AI	Amnesty International
AICHR	ASEAN Intergovernmental Commission on Human Rights
ANC	African National Congress
ASEAN	Association of Southeast Asian Nations
AU	African Union
BBC	British Broadcasting Corporation (United Kingdom)
CAT	Convention against Torture
CCI	Community Corporate Investment
CECOT	Centro de Confinamiento del Terrorismo (El Salvador)
CED	Convention on Protection Against Enforced Disappearance
CEDAW	Convention on the Elimination of All Forms of Discrimination Against Women
CEO	chief executive officer
CERD	Convention on the Elimination of All Forms of Racial Discrimination
CERDS	Charter on the Economic Rights and Duties of States
CESCR	Committee on Economic, Social and Cultural Rights
CHRB	corporate human rights benchmark
CIA	Central Intelligence Agency (United States)
CMW	Convention on the Protection of Migrant Workers
CRC	Convention on the Rights of the Child
CRPD	Convention on the Rights of Persons with Disabilities
CSO	civil society organization
CSP	Conference of States Parties
DLR	(Bureau of) Democracy, Labor and Human Rights (United States)
DOGE	Department of Government Efficiency (United States)

DRtD	Declaration on the Right to Development
ECHR	European Convention on Human Rights
ECOSOC	Economic and Social Council (United Nations)
EDG	Expert Drafting Group (United Nations WG-RtD)
ESG	environmental, social, and governance (standards)
EU	European Union
FBI	Federal Bureau of Investigation (United States)
FDI	foreign direct investment
FSLN	Sandinista National Liberation Front (Nicaragua)
G-77	Group of 77 (United Nations coalition)
GDP	gross domestic product
GONGO	government-organized non-governmental organization
HDI	Human Development Index
HRBA	human rights-based approach to development
HRMI	Human Rights Measurement Initiative
HRW	Human Rights Watch
HTS	Hay'at Tahrir al-Sham (Syria)
IACHR	Inter-American Commission on Human Rights
IADC	Inter-American Democratic Charter
ICC	International Criminal Court
ICCPR	International Covenant on Civil and Political Rights
ICE	Immigration and Customs Enforcement (United States)
ICESCR	International Covenant on Economic, Social, and Cultural Rights
ICISS	International Commission on Intervention and State Sovereignty
ICJ	International Court of Justice
IDF	Israeli Defense Forces
IGO	intergovernmental organization
ILO	International Labor Organization
IM	implementation mechanism
IMF	International Monetary Fund
INGO	international nongovernmental organization
ISIL/ISIS	Islamic State (also known as Daesh)
JNA	Yugoslav National Army
KC	King's Counsel
LGBTQ+	lesbian, gay, bisexual, transgender, and queer/questioning (plus others)
LRA	Lord's Resistance Army (Uganda)
MDGs	Millennium Development Goals
MNC	multinational corporation
NATO	North Atlantic Treaty Organization
NED	National Endowment for Democracy (United States)
NGO	nongovernmental organization
NHRIs	national human rights institutions
NIEO	New International Economic Order

NLD	National League for Democracy (Myanmar)
NSS	National Security Strategy (United States)
OAS	Organization of American States
OAU	Organization of African Unity
OECD	Organization for Economic Cooperation and Development
OHCHR	Office of the High Commissioner for Human Rights (United Nations)
OSCE	Organization for Security and Co-operation in Europe
PEPFAR	President's Emergency Plan for AIDS Relief (United States)
PRC	People's Republic of China
PRM	Presidential Review Memorandum (United States)
PSD	Presidential Study Directive (United States)
R2P	Responsibility to Protect (doctrine)
RPF	Rwandan Patriotic Front
RSF	Rapid Support Forces (Sudan)
SDGs	Sustainable Development Goals
SAF	Sudanese Armed Forces
SEAL	Sea, Air, and Land (US Naval Special Force)
SLORC	State Law and Order Restoration Council (Myanmar)
TMB	(human rights) treaty monitoring body (United Nations)
UK	United Kingdom
UN	United Nations
UNAIDS	Joint United Nations Programme on HIV/AIDS
UNAMIR	United Nations Assistance Mission in Rwanda
UNCTAD	United Nations Conference on Trade and Development
UNDP	United Nations Development Programme
UNESCO	United Nations Educational, Social, and Cultural Organization
UNFPA	United Nations Fund for Population Activities
UNICEF	United Nations Children's Fund (the organization was originally the "United Nations International Children's Emergency Fund")
UNPROFOR	United Nations Protection Force in the Former Yugoslavia
UPR	Universal Period Review (United Nations)
URG	Universal Rights Group
US	United States
USAID	United States Agency for International Development
USSR	Union of Soviet Socialist Republics
WG-RtD	Working Group on the Right to Development (United Nations)

Part I

History and Theory

Human Rights in Global Politics

Historical Perspective

1

In the seventeenth century, a system of sovereign states began to emerge in Western Europe, marking the failure of the Spanish and Austrian Habsburgs to establish a continental empire. In the following centuries, through processes of conquest and consolidation, this new system of sovereign states spread across most of the globe. But considerations of human rights emerged as a matter of global concern only in the twentieth century.

Prior to that, only a limited number of specific issues that we today consider matters of human rights were the subject of agreement between sovereign states. For example, the "Westphalia" Treaties of Münster and Osnabrück (1648), which brought the Thirty Years' War to an end, provided limited protection for some Christian minorities; the rights of religious and linguistic minorities were included in treaties recognizing the sovereignty and independence of Belgium (1815), Greece (1832), and Serbia (1878); there were major (and ultimately largely successful) international campaigns against the slave trade and slavery in the nineteenth and early twentieth centuries; and the International Labor Organization, created after World War I, established a system for international protection of workers' rights. The end of World War II and the establishment of the **United Nations**, however, brought two major changes: the language of human rights entered the mainstream of international relations as a major concern and human rights became a matter of international obligation.

Prior to World War II, there was near-universal agreement among states that human rights were *not* a legitimate concern of international relations. For example, the Covenant of the League of Nations, which is usually seen as an expression of the idealism of the immediate post-World War I era, does not even include the term *human rights*. This reflected a particular understanding of the international organizing principle of **sovereignty**.

States, the primary actors in international relations, were seen as supreme authorities in their own territories subject to no higher political authority. The principal duty correlative to the right of sovereignty was **nonintervention**, the obligation not to interfere in matters

DOI: 10.4324/9781003373520-2

essentially within the domestic jurisdiction of other sovereign states (see Chapter 2, Section 9). Human rights, which typically involve a state's treatment of its own citizens in its own territory, were thus seen as such a matter of sovereign domestic jurisdiction—and thus not a legitimate concern in international relations. A major purpose of this book is to chronicle the ways in which, over the past three-quarters of a century, human rights have produced fundamental changes in understandings and practices of state sovereignty, as well as the expansion of the role of nonstate actors in the domestic and international politics of human rights.

1 The Emergence of International Human Rights Norms

The contemporary human rights movement can be traced back to the era between the two world wars. For example, the French *Institut de Droit International*, a public international legal society, adopted a Declaration of the International Rights of Man in 1929. In the 1930s, British novelist and activist H. G. Wells cast much of his advocacy for social reform in terms of a global regime committed to human rights. Such efforts, however, represented only a small fringe of civil society. Even those who believed that all human beings possessed an extensive set of equal and inalienable rights—a distinctly minority idea in an era that had little trouble justifying racism, sexism, and colonialism—did not suggest that other states had obligations with respect to those rights. And not a single state endorsed the idea that governments had *international legal* obligations to their own citizens.

This began to change during World War II. As the United Kingdom and the United States, the principal allied powers, reflected on the nature of their struggle with Hitler's Germany, and on how to justify the war to their own citizens and the rest of the world, respect for human rights became an increasingly central theme. In his January 1941 State of the Union address, nearly a year before the United States entered the war, President Franklin D. Roosevelt framed the Allied war effort in terms of securing four fundamental freedoms: of speech, of religion, from want, and from fear. This initial statement was further elaborated by Roosevelt and British Prime Minister Winston Churchill, who negotiated a statement of Allied war aims in the Atlantic Charter of August 1941. The January 1942 Declaration by United Nations, signed by the twenty-six governments allied against the Axis (Germany, Italy, and Japan), claimed that "complete victory over their enemies is essential to defend life, liberty, independence and religious freedom, and to preserve human rights and justice in their own lands as well as in other lands." From late 1942 on, human rights were an integral part of American and British postwar planning efforts.

The immediate impetus for international action, however, came in 1945 as Allied governments and publics began, finally, to grapple with the Holocaust, Germany's systematic mass murder of millions of innocent civilians, a crime that the Polish lawyer Raphael Lemkin had recently named **genocide**. Before the war, little was done to aid Jews trying to flee Germany and the surrounding countries. Some who escaped were even denied refuge by Allied governments, including the United States. During the war, no effort was made to impede the functioning of the death camps. The Allies did not even target the railway lines that brought hundreds of thousands to the slaughter at Auschwitz and other camps. The world watched—or, rather, turned a blind eye to—the genocidal massacre of 6 million Jews, a half-million Roma, and tens of thousands of communists, social democrats, homosexuals, church activists, and just ordinary decent people who refused complicity in the new politics and technology of barbarism. As the war came to an end, though, Allied leaders and citizens, previously preoccupied with military victory, belatedly began to confront this horror.

The Nuremberg War Crimes Trials, held in Germany in 1945–1946, introduced the novel charge of crimes against humanity. These crimes were distinct from already-recognized violations of the laws of war (**international humanitarian law**). For the first time, officials were held legally accountable to the international community not only for offenses against foreign states and their citizens but also against their own citizens.

These shocking crimes, although crucial in mobilizing broad support for international action, were only the tip of the iceberg. Many organizations and individuals had already recognized that Nazi Germany's wartime atrocities had been preceded by, and built on, years of officially promulgated and systematic violations of fundamental rights. Prior to the instigation of the Final Solution, Jews and others perceived as opponents and "deviants" had been stripped of many of the civil, political, and economic rights they held prior to Hitler's rise to power in 1933. In addition, there was general agreement that the worldwide economic depression and ensuing economic insecurity of the 1930s contributed significantly both to the rise of rights-abusive regimes and to the unraveling of the international system, which precipitated the war. Proposals for the protection of fundamental rights thus become a central focus of postwar international institutions, leading to the incorporation of human rights into the Charter of the United Nations, which was adopted in San Francisco in the summer of 1945.

The Preamble of the UN Charter lists as two of the four principal objectives of the organization "to reaffirm faith in fundamental human rights, in the dignity and worth of the human person, in the equal rights of men and women and of nations large and small," and "to promote social progress and better standards of life in larger freedom." Likewise, Article 1 lists the achievement of "international co-operation in solving international problems of an economic, social, cultural, or humanitarian character, and in promoting and encouraging respect for human rights and for fundamental freedoms for all without distinction as to race, sex, language, or religion" as one of the four purposes of the United Nations.

These statements were in themselves revolutionary. Even more radical was the creation in 1946 of the **Commission on Human Rights** under the auspices of the UN Economic and Social Council (ECOSOC), which quickly began to define these abstract statements of postwar optimism and goodwill. The original Commission was composed of eighteen elected members who were broadly representative of the (then fifty-one) members of the United Nations. Its initial task was to draft an "international bill of human rights." The Commission quickly decided to focus its attention on the first part of the bill, which in 1948 became the **Universal Declaration of Human Rights**.

The initial drafts were written by John Humphrey, a young Canadian member of the Commission's staff, and René Cassin, the French member of the Commission. There was widespread and essential participation, though, by non-Western representatives. The drafting committee included Peng-chun Chang of China (the vice chair of the Commission), Charles Malik of Lebanon (the rapporteur of the Commission), and Hernán Santa Cruz of Chile. Each, along with the chair of both the Commission and of the drafting committee, Eleanor Roosevelt of the United States, played a major role in shaping the Declaration.

2 The Universal Declaration

The UN General Assembly adopted the Universal Declaration of Human Rights on December 10, 1948. (December 10 is thus celebrated globally as Human Rights Day.) The vote was forty-eight in favor, none opposed, with eight abstentions. (Saudi Arabia abstained principally because of provisions that allowed Muslims to change their religion. South Africa abstained because of the provisions on racial equality. The six Soviet-bloc states [USSR, Byelorussian SSR, Czechoslovakia, Poland, Ukrainian SSR, and Yugoslavia] abstained ostensibly because the document was insufficiently detailed, especially with regard to the specific duties of individuals toward their own states.)

Although most of Africa, much of Asia, and parts of the Americas were still under colonial rule, the Universal Declaration had global endorsement. It received the votes of fourteen European and other Western states, nineteen states from Latin America, and fifteen from Africa and Asia. And the countries that later achieved independence were at least as enthusiastic in their embrace of the Declaration as those who voted for it in 1948. It was unanimously endorsed by the representatives of twenty-nine independent Asian and African states who attended the summit held at Bandung, Indonesia, in 1955. In Africa, in particular, the Universal Declaration was liberally referenced and frequently quoted in independence-era constitutions.

Article 1 of the Universal Declaration states its foundation: "All human beings are born free and equal in dignity and rights. They are endowed with reason and conscience and should act towards one another in a spirit of brotherhood." The substantive bookend is Article 28: "Everyone is entitled to a social and international order in which the rights and freedoms set forth in this Declaration can be fully realized."

In between, Articles 2–27 lay out a comprehensive set of rights that have come to define what we mean by internationally recognized human rights. Article 2 recognizes the right to nondiscrimination. An extensive series of **civil and political rights** are recognized in Articles 3–15 and 19–21, including rights to life, liberty, and security of person; an array of legal protections and civil liberties; and the right to political participation. Articles 16–18 and 22–27 recognize a wide range of **economic, social, and cultural rights**, including rights to an adequate standard of living, social security, work, rest and leisure, family, education, and participation in the cultural life of the community.[1]

Even today, the Universal Declaration provides the most authoritative statement of international human rights norms. This vital document, the most translated document in human history, (555 official translations)[2] is reprinted (in English) in the appendix.

3 The Covenants

The Universal Declaration of Human Rights is not *per se* legally binding. (It describes itself as "a common standard of achievement for all peoples and all nations.") The Commission on Human Rights thus moved immediately to drafting a legally binding **treaty** that would spell out general and specific state obligations and measures for monitoring and compliance. The initial 1947 draft "Covenant on Human Rights" was quite short—eighteen articles, focusing exclusively on civil rights. After quite a bit of debate, however, in 1950 the UN General Assembly directed the Commission to include economic, social, cultural, and political rights as well. That work began in the spring of 1951.

By the time the Commission finished in late May, the new draft covenant had grown to an unwieldy 73 articles. There was significant disagreement over monitoring and adjudication mechanisms and a proposed reporting procedure for economic, social, and cultural rights. Many on the Commission—mostly Western states—believed that the new draft should be divided into separate Covenants. Others—mostly from what we today call the Global South—disagreed, arguing that the indivisibility of human rights was paramount (see Chapter 4). After much debate in both the Commission and ECOSOC, the General Assembly in 1952 directed the Commission to draft separate Covenants on civil and political rights and on economic, social, and cultural rights. To underscore the notion of unity, though, the two Covenants, once completed, were to be simultaneously adopted by the General Assembly.

Many accounts of this period in the history of human rights principally blame the East–West ideological divide (the **Cold War**) for the division of the Covenant, with the democratic/capitalist "West" favoring (only) civil and political rights, and the communist "East" favoring (only) economic and social rights. The documentary record, however, tells a different story. There were indeed differences of opinion and ideology between the West and the communist world over the nature of rights. But the more significant divide was between the West and the Third World over monitoring the implementation of the Covenant(s) and adjudicating disputes between states over violations. And although most countries agreed that the United Nations should play more of an advisory rather than an enforcement role, the Soviet Union and its allies rejected any form of monitoring or oversight by the United Nations, no matter how modest.

The Cold War, though, did play a role in debates *within the United States* over different categories of rights and the supranational role of the United Nations (see Chapter 8). A coalition of cold warriors, isolationists, and racists (who did not want additional international scrutiny of legalized racial discrimination in the United States) in 1953 compelled newly elected president Eisenhower to agree not to support any human rights treaty that would emerge from the United Nations. On the Commission, the United States began to argue that perhaps the best way to ensure human rights would be through the provision of technical assistance and support to countries, rather than through binding treaties.

Nonetheless, by 1954, the Commission finished its work on the Covenants and sent them to the UN General Assembly for finalization and adoption. There, the Third Committee (where human rights issues are considered) dithered over the drafts for nearly a dozen years, less because of Cold War wrangling than the wariness of most states—especially in the postcolonial world—of a legally binding treaty. In addition, the delay reflected postcolonial states' prioritization of fighting colonialism and racism, not necessarily protecting and promoting individuals' human rights.

The adoption in 1963 of the Declaration on the Elimination of All Forms of Racial Discrimination, followed by a legally binding Convention two years later, indicated a renewed emphasis on human rights standard setting. A coalition of Third World and Western states, with Soviet-bloc support, pushed the Covenants' drafting process to completion. In December 1966, the UN adopted and opened for signature and ratification the International Covenant on Economic, Social, and Cultural Rights (ICESCR) and the International Covenant on Civil and Political Rights (ICCPR). Although the Covenants make a few substantive revisions to the Universal Declaration, most notably adding a right of self-determination of peoples, they for the most part reaffirm and elaborate on the 1948 Declaration and spell out state obligations in greater detail.

The UN Charter's human rights provisions, the Universal Declaration, and the Covenants are often referred to collectively as the **International Bill of Human Rights**. They state the minimum social and political guarantees recognized by the international community as necessary for a life of dignity in the contemporary world. Table 1.1 summarizes their content.

4 The 1960s and 1970s: From Standard Setting to Monitoring

The comprehensiveness of the **International Human Rights Covenants** meant that further progress on international human rights would now depend primarily on implementing these standards—an area in which the United Nations had been, and still is, far less successful.

The mere existence of international norms does not give the United Nations, or anyone else, the authority to coercively enforce them. By ratifying the Covenants, states agree to comply with certain reporting procedures and to undergo a periodic process of public review of their human rights record. This opens them to multilateral scrutiny. It does not, though, as we will see in some detail in Chapter 5, guarantee that states—even states with the best human rights records—will respect all human rights all of the time. And it gives no other state, international organization, or other kind of actor the right to implement or enforce those rights.

The United Nations is an **intergovernmental organization** (IGO), established by a multilateral treaty (the UN Charter) among sovereign states, which are its members. Delegates to the United Nations represent states, not the international community, let alone individuals whose rights are violated. Like other IGOs, the United Nations has only those powers that states—which are also the principal violators of human rights—give it.

Thus, perhaps more surprising than the limits on its human rights monitoring powers is the fact that the United Nations acquired even these limited powers. This may be of little comfort to victims. We cannot, however, ignore the severe limits imposed by state sovereignty in assessing the human rights achievements of the United Nations and other IGOs.

Table 1.1 Internationally Recognized Human Rights

The International Bill of Human Rights recognizes the rights to:
Equality of rights without discrimination (DI, D2, E2, E3, C2, C3)
Life (D3, C6)
Liberty and security of person (D3, C9)
Protection against slavery (D4, C8)
Protection against torture and cruel and inhuman punishment (D5, C7)
Recognition as a person before the law (D6, C16)
Equal protection of the law (D7, C14, C26)
Access to legal remedies for rights violations (D8, C2)
Protection against arbitrary arrest or detention (D9, C9)
Hearing before an independent and impartial judiciary (D10, C14)
Presumption of innocence (D11, C14)
Protection against ex post facto laws (D11, C15)
Protection of privacy, family, and home (D12, C17)
Freedom of movement and residence (D13, C12)
Seek asylum from persecution (D14)
Nationality (D15)
Marry and found a family (D16, E10, C23)
Own property (D17)
Freedom of thought, conscience, and religion (D18, C18)
Freedom of opinion, expression, and the press (D19, C19)
Freedom of assembly and association (D20, C21, C22)
Political participation (D21, C25)
Social security (D22, E9)
Work, under favorable conditions (D23, E6, E7)
Free trade unions (D23, E8, C22)
Rest and leisure (D24, E7)
Food, clothing, and housing (D25, E11)
Health care and social services (D25, E12)
Special protections for children (D25, E10, C24)
Education (D26, E13, E14)
Participation in cultural life (D27, E15)
A social and international order needed to realize rights (D28)
Self-determination (E1, C1)
Humane treatment when detained or imprisoned (C10)
Protection against debtor's prison (C11)
Protection against arbitrary expulsion of aliens (C13)
Protection against advocacy of racial or religious hatred (C20)
Protection of minority culture (C27)

Note: This list includes all rights that are enumerated in two of the three documents of the International Bill of Human Rights or have a full article in one document. The source of each right is indicated in parentheses, by document and article number. D = Universal Declaration of Human Rights. E = International Covenant on Economic, Social, and Cultural Rights. C = International Covenant on Civil and Political Rights.

Although sovereign states have agreed to these norms and procedures—they participated in drafting them and consented to them by ratifying human rights treaties—they designed them to be weak and highly circumscribed (see Chapter 5).

In the late 1960s, the United Nations began to move, very tentatively and in largely symbolic ways, from merely setting standards to examining how states implement those standards within their own jurisdictions. In 1967, ECOSOC Resolution 1235 authorized the Commission on Human Rights to discuss human rights violations in particular countries. In 1969, the racial discrimination convention came into force, requiring parties to file periodic reports on implementation. In 1970, ECOSOC Resolution 1503 authorized the Commission on Human Rights to conduct confidential investigations of complaints that suggested "a consistent pattern of gross and reliably attested violations of human rights and fundamental freedoms."

Modest progress on monitoring continued in the 1970s. In response to the 1973 military coup in Chile, the United Nations created the Ad Hoc Working Group on the Situation of Human Rights in Chile. In 1976, the International Human Rights Covenants entered into force, leading to the establishment of the **Human Rights Committee**,[3] which monitors implementation of the International Covenant on Civil and Political Rights. (A similar body for the Covenant on Economic, Social and Cultural Rights was established a decade later: see Chapter 4, Section 1.2.2)

Human rights were also explicitly and systematically introduced into the bilateral foreign policies of individual countries in the 1970s, beginning in the United States. Although practice fell short of rhetoric, these bilateral initiatives helped to open space for new ways of thinking about and acting on international human rights concerns, as we will see in some detail in Chapters 7 and 8.

The 1970s also saw substantial growth in the number and range of activities of human rights **nongovernmental organizations** (NGOs), private associations that engage in political activity. Such groups act as advocates for victims of human rights violations by publicizing violations and lobbying to alter the practices of states and international organizations. Best known is Amnesty International (AI), which received the Nobel Peace Prize in 1977 and has more than 7 million members and supporters. Chapter 9 briefly examines transnational human rights advocacy (Table 1.2).

5 The 1980s: Further Growth and Institutionalization

Multilateral, bilateral, and transnational nongovernmental human rights activity continued to increase, more or less steadily, in the following decade. New treaties were adopted on discrimination against women (1979), torture (1984), and the rights of the child (1989). In 1985, ECOSOC established an independent **Committee on Economic, Social and Cultural Rights** that, along with the Human Rights Committee (which oversees implementation of the ICCPR), began to review periodic reports submitted by states (see Chapter 5, Section 3.1). The Commission on Human Rights undertook thematic initiatives on disappearances, torture, and summary or arbitrary executions. A larger and more diverse group of individual countries came under Commission scrutiny.

Table 1.2 Key Dates in the Evolution of Global Human Rights Norms and Institutions

1941	(January): Roosevelt's "Four Freedoms"
1941	(December): Atlantic Charter
1942	Declaration by United Nations
1945	United Nations Charter adopted
1946	Creation of the UN Commission on Human Rights
1948	Adoption of the Genocide Convention and the Universal Declaration of Human Rights
1951	Decision to include economic and social rights in the Covenant on Human Rights
1952	Decision to divide the Covenant into separate treaties
1954	Initial drafting of the Covenants completed by the Commission on Human Rights
1965	Adoption of the Convention on the Elimination of All Forms of Racial Discrimination (CERD)
1966	Adoption of the International Covenants on Economic, Social, and Cultural Rights (ICESCR) and Civil and Political Rights (ICCPR)
1968	International Conference on Human Rights held in Tehran, Iran
1969	CERD enters into force
1970	UN Economic and Social Council adopts 1503 Procedure (petitions mechanism)
1975	Helsinki Accords link human rights protections to security cooperation in Europe
1976	International Human Rights Covenants enter into force
1977	Amnesty International wins Nobel Peace Prize; US State Department makes human rights a foreign policy priority
1979	United Nations adopts Convention on the Elimination of All Forms of Discrimination Against Women (CEDAW)
1981	CEDAW enters into force
1984	United Nations adopts Convention Against Torture (CAT)
1986	United Nations adopts Declaration on the Right to Development
1987	CAT enters into force
1989	United Nations adopts Convention on the Rights of the Child (CRC); enters into force the same year
1993	World Conference on Human Rights held in Vienna, Austria
1993	Establishment of the Office of the High Commissioner for Human Rights
2002	Establishment of the International Criminal Court
2006	UN Human Rights Council replaces the Commission on Human Rights
2006	United Nations adopts Convention on the Rights of Persons with Disabilities (CRPD)
2007	United Nations adopts Declaration on the Rights of Indigenous Peoples
2008	CRPD enters into force
2008	Universal Periodic Review begins
2023	UN Human Rights Council transmits draft International Covenant on the Right to Development to the UN General Assembly

The process of incorporating human rights into bilateral foreign policy also accelerated in the 1980s. The Netherlands, Norway, and Canada developed particularly prominent international human rights policies (see Chapter 8, Section 5). The European Community (predecessor of the European Union [EU]) introduced human rights concerns into its external relations. A few countries in the Global South, notably Costa Rica, also began to emphasize human rights in their foreign policies.

The 1980s also saw a dramatic decline in the fortunes of repressive dictatorships. Throughout Latin America, military regimes that had appeared unshakable in the 1970s crumbled in the 1980s. By 1990, elected governments held office in every continental country in the Western Hemisphere (although the democratic and human rights credentials of some, such as Paraguay, were extremely suspect). In addition, there were peaceful transfers of power after elections in several countries in 1989, including Argentina, Brazil, El Salvador, and Uruguay.

In Asia, the personalist dictatorship of Ferdinand Marcos was overthrown in the Philippines in 1986. South Korea's military dictatorship was replaced by an elected government in 1988. Taiwan ended four decades of imposed single-party rule. In Pakistan, Benazir Bhutto was elected president in December 1988, ending a dozen years of military rule. Asia, however, also presented the most dramatic human rights setback of the decade—the June 1989 massacre in Beijing's Tiananmen Square.

The changes with the greatest international impact, however, occurred in Central and Eastern Europe. Soviet-imposed regimes in East Germany and Czechoslovakia crumbled in late 1989 in the face of peaceful mass protests. In Hungary and Poland, where liberalization had begun earlier in the decade, Communist Party dictatorships also peacefully withdrew from power. Even Romania and Bulgaria ousted their old communist governments (although their new governments included numerous former communists with tenuous democratic credentials). And in the USSR, where *glasnost* (openness) and *perestroika* (restructuring) had created the international political space for these changes, the Communist Party fell from power after the abortive military coup of August 1991. The Soviet Union itself was dissolved four months later.

6 The 1990s: Consolidating Progress and Acting against Genocide

The 1990s was a decade of gradual, but generally positive, change in most regions—punctuated by striking examples of the most retrograde barbarism (see Chapter 11). In Latin America and Central and Eastern Europe, the progress of the 1980s was largely maintained. In many countries, such as El Salvador and Hungary, liberalization substantially deepened. In a few, such as the Czech Republic, Argentina, and Mexico, full democratization was achieved. In most of the former Soviet republics, however, the human rights situation remained—and remains—deeply discouraging.

In sub-Saharan Africa, where one- and no-party states remained the norm throughout the 1980s, political liberalization was widespread in the 1990s. Progress, however, was inconsistent and often not very deep. Nonetheless, the November 1991 electoral defeat of Kenneth Kaunda, Zambia's president for the first twenty-five years of its independence, was an important first for the region. And the end of apartheid in South Africa, which held its first elections under the principle of universal suffrage in 1994, was a dramatic change. More typical, though, was Nigeria, Africa's most populous country, where the military annulled the results of elections in 1992 and 1993 and General Sani Abacha exercised particularly harsh military rule over the country from 1993 to his death in 1998.

In Asia, the picture in the 1990s was also mixed but generally positive. South Korea and Taiwan consolidated democratic, rights-protective regimes. Cambodia, with a substantial assist from the United Nations, cast off Vietnamese occupation and elected a government that was by far the least repressive it had seen in decades. Tentative and partial liberalization occurred in Vietnam. Indonesia saw limited political reform with the expulsion of the Suharto regime in 1998. And India, for all its problems, remained the world's largest multiparty electoral democracy.

China, however, despite its substantial economic opening and political reform, remained a highly repressive, Stalinist party-state. Burma continued to repress its internal democracy movement and rebuff international pressure for liberalization. Afghanistan suffered under the theocratic brutality of Taliban rule from 1996 to 2001. North Korea consolidated its position as the world's most isolated and repressive totalitarian regime. And many Asian governments and elites began to argue that international human rights standards did not apply in their entirety in Asia.

Sadly, though, the mixed picture in Africa and Asia was far more encouraging than that in the Middle East. Hafez al-Assad, Saddam Hussein, and Muammar Gadhafi sustained their personalist dictatorships in Syria, Iraq, and Libya, respectively. Religious intolerance and the suppression of all dissent remained the norm in Iran. The Gulf states remained closed and undemocratic. Increasingly violent Islamic fundamentalist movements occasioned growing repression in Egypt and plunged Algeria into a shockingly brutal civil war. About the only examples of substantial progress in the 1990s were modest liberalization in the monarchies of Jordan, Morocco, and Kuwait.

International action showed a similar pattern of solidifying past gains and modest progress in selected areas. Perhaps most striking was the decisive rebuff of arguments by China and other countries at the World Conference on Human Rights in Vienna in 1993 against the full implementation of internationally recognized human rights in the short and medium terms. The **Vienna Declaration and Programme of Action** constituted a bold restatement of the fundamental tenets of human rights as "universal, indivisible and interdependent and interrelated." The Programme of Action set an ambitious agenda for strengthening the human rights system at the United Nations. And it declared unequivocally that many widespread and overlooked injustices—most notably violence against women—constitute violations of human rights. The long-awaited creation at the end of 1993 of a UN High Commissioner for Human Rights proved to be an important step in expanding both the scope and the depth of multilateral monitoring (see Chapter 5, Section 2). Such events, particularly when coupled with the changes in national practices already noted, signified a deepening penetration of the international consensus on human rights norms.

Human rights also became a more deeply entrenched and less controversial concern of bilateral foreign policy. National nongovernmental human rights organizations and advocates became a significant part of the political landscape in a growing number of countries in the Global South and the former Soviet bloc. Transnational human rights NGOs also increased their prestige and influence.

In one area, however, the 1990s saw not incremental growth but unprecedented change, namely, the development of a practice of legitimate military **humanitarian intervention** against genocide (see Chapter 11). This was a dramatic reversal of Cold War-era (and earlier) practice.

Although the 1948 Genocide Convention established **genocide** as an international crime, the almost universal practice during the Cold War era was international inaction. In places such as Burundi, East Pakistan (Bangladesh), Guatemala, Cambodia, and Uganda, genocide and politicide were met by verbal expressions of concern but little concrete action, except by neighboring states such as India, Vietnam, and Tanzania with strong selfish interests in intervening.

Even with the Cold War at an end, the international community failed to take effective steps to stop the violence that accompanied the disintegration of Yugoslavia in the early 1990s, which included genocide, war crimes, and crimes against humanity. And in 1994 the international community was paralyzed when three-quarters of a million Rwandans—about one-seventh of the population of the entire country (the proportional equivalent of more than 45 million Americans today)—were massacred in a mere hundred days.

These dramatic failures, however, galvanized new efforts. Ad hoc international tribunals for the former Yugoslavia and for Rwanda, created in 1991 and 1994, revived the Nuremberg precedent of bringing to justice individuals responsible for war crimes and crimes against humanity. Perhaps more accurately, these tribunals began a process that transformed Nuremberg from an isolated exception into a precedent. The adoption of the Rome Statute in 1998, which led to the creation of the International Criminal Court (ICC) in 2002, marks an even deeper normative transformation (see Chapter 5, Section 4.1). And the interventions in Kosovo and East Timor in 1999 consolidated an international practice of humanitarian intervention against genocide (see Chapter 11, Section 2.3 (Kosovo) and 5.1 (East Timor)).

7 Human Rights in the Twenty-First Century

Broad trends in the global human rights situation in the twenty-first century reveal both positive developments and significant setbacks and challenges.

The 2000s were largely a time of further advancement of international human rights norms, processes, and institutions. Of special importance was the establishment in 2006 of the UN Human Rights Council, replacing the original Commission on Human Rights. The Council and its new and updated activities have reinvigorated the global political commitment to the promotion and protection of human rights (see Chapter 5, Section 1). The Council has also given greater attention to the rights of marginalized and vulnerable populations, including indigenous peoples, the LGBTQ+ community (albeit with significant pushback from many states in the Global South), people with disabilities, older people, and human rights defenders.

By the mid-2010s, though, particularly following the 2016 election of Donald Trump as president of the United States (and especially since his return to the White House in 2025), many observers were heralding the demise of the "liberal international order" (or the "rules-based order") of global politics that has been in place since 1945. And such concerns intensified after Russia invaded Ukraine in February 2022. But the liberal order—and the place of human rights in global politics—although under significant stress, seems far from finished.

Threats and challenges in broad areas of global concern, such as human migration, gender inequality, global poverty, and climate change, have increasingly been addressed through the lens of human rights. For example, Agenda 2030, which is the UN's plan of action to address global poverty (through the Sustainable Development Goals), is underpinned by a strong human rights framework. Human rights NGOs and civil society actors have expanded in size and scope. It is impossible to go through a week of global news without the subject of human rights coming up, usually often. Awareness of human rights is clearly at an all-time high.

This growing awareness, however, is also an indicator of new and mounting challenges facing the global community in protecting and promoting human rights—challenges that were simply not in evidence at the end of the twentieth century. We see four broad trends that signal significant challenges to human rights as we move into the second quarter of the twenty-first century.

The first is the crisis of democracy. In its most recent report on the Global State of Democracy in 2022,[4] International IDEA, a global think tank, argues that the number of people who believe that "democracy" is the answer to solving global political and economic instabilities—especially in the context of climate change, the effects of COVID-19, and the Ukraine War—is shrinking. Many established democracies are facing populist challenges that, while electorally democratic, have sought to limit human rights in the name of meeting some broader threat or challenge. Striking examples include the rise of far-right parties and movements and the adoption of rights-unfriendly policies in France, Germany, Italy, Israel, Spain, Hungary, Poland, and the United States and crackdowns against civil society protests and activities in places like Russia, Hong Kong, and Iran. The rise of social media, and especially misinformation and disinformation, has contributed to these trends. In regions where democracy was making some inroads in the early part of the century, there have been significant democratic declines, especially in Africa, but also in countries like Brazil, the Philippines, and Hungary—and India under Hindu nationalist rule.

The number of democracies worldwide has stagnated, while at the same time half of the world's democracies are in retreat. Among non-democracies, half are becoming more repressive. And since 2016, the number of countries moving toward authoritarianism is more than double the number moving toward democracy.[5]

A second worrying trend is a rise in the number of barbaric wars involving gross and persistent systematic violations of human rights, crimes against humanity, war crimes, and genocide. As we wrote this in 2024 and 2025, the civil war in Syria finally came to an end after more than a decade, the civil war in Yemen entered into its second decade, a new round of genocidal violence reached tragic proportions in Sudan, and the Israeli-inflicted suffering in Gaza, precipitated by Hamas' heinous massacre of some 1,200 Israelis and kidnapping of 200, entered its third year.

Third, new challenges to the protection and promotion of human rights are being posed by global economic instability (exacerbated by the global COVID-19 pandemic and the Ukraine War) and the increasingly alarming effects of global climate change, which is accelerating human migration, global food insecurity, and negative health consequences.

Finally, many observers have noted increasing polarization within the UN on human rights, with China (and Russia) taking a far more active lead in challenging core human rights principles and global mechanisms. While there have always been divides within the UN on key human rights questions—trade-offs between the imperative of development and the protection of human rights are a prime example—China has become a significant force rallying many countries in the Global South to support its "vision" of human rights. We will examine some of these developments in more detail in Chapter 5.

8 The Global Human Rights Regime

The story we have told in the preceding sections can be described as the story of the rise, consolidation, and new challenges to a normatively robust global human rights regime. (An **international regime** is conventionally defined as a set of principles, norms, and rules, often embedded in international organizations, that states and other international actors accept as authoritative within an issue area.) The global human rights regime, however, does not fundamentally challenge state sovereignty.

Of the hundred or more treaties that address human rights issues, broadly understood, seven are usually taken to provide the core of international human rights law: the two 1966 International Human Rights Covenants; the 1965 Convention on the Elimination of All Forms of Racial Discrimination (CERD); the 1979 Convention on the Elimination of All Forms of Discrimination Against Women; the 1984 Convention Against Torture (CAT) and Other Cruel, Inhuman, or Degrading Treatment or Punishment; the 1989 Convention on the Rights of the Child (CRC); and the 2006 Convention on the Rights of Persons with Disabilities (CRPD).[6] As of December 2025 these treaties had an average of 181 state parties;[7] that is, states that had ratified or acceded to the treaties and thus were bound by them in international law. This represents an astonishing 93 percent ratification rate. We have come a *very* long way from the 1940s.

This extensive and substantively admirable body of international human rights law, however, is not matched by comparably strong international implementation procedures. As we will see in Chapters 5 and 6, states have largely reserved for themselves the right to interpret the meaning of their international human rights obligations and to implement them (or not) as they see fit in their own territories.

International law has established a system of *national implementation of international human rights*. International human rights norms have been fully internationalized. Implementation of international human rights obligations, however, remains almost entirely national.

There is, of course, an immense amount of national and international human rights advocacy. States, international and regional organizations, NGOs, businesses, and private individuals promote human rights every day in every country of the world. Their efforts, however, are focused ultimately on states, which still hold not only the duty but also the right to implement human rights in their own territories.

Later chapters address the shortcomings of this system of national implementation of international human rights. Here we want to emphasize the independent contribution of international human rights norms.

International human rights law has been so widely endorsed because its normative force is seemingly inescapable in the contemporary world. Even states like North Korea and Belarus, which have never given any serious attention to implementing internationally recognized human rights, are parties to at least some core human rights treaties. And even cynical endorsements of these norms are of real practical significance for national and international human rights advocates.

Without an internationally agreed-upon list of human rights, national human rights advocates would be subject to charges of political or cultural bias, inauthenticity, and even treason. But when repressive governments today level such charges at their critics, those critics can reply that all they are doing is advocating rights that the government itself has repeatedly endorsed, including by accepting binding international legal obligations. This decisively shifts the burden of persuasion from the advocates of human rights to the governments that are violating those rights.

Might regularly triumphs over right, especially in the short run. Nevertheless, national human rights advocates are supported by international human rights norms and the institutions created to monitor and support compliance with those norms. This makes a real practical difference in all but the most closed and repressive countries. And in countries with even merely not-too-bad human rights records, these protections are of immense day-to-day value to advocates, activists, and ordinary citizens.

Similarly, when transnational human rights NGOs, foreign states, and regional and international organizations raise concerns about a state's human rights record, targeted states cannot credibly respond that it is none of their business. *All* states in the contemporary world have accepted that human rights are a legitimate subject of international politics—however, much they hate to have their shortcomings brought to the attention of national and international audiences. And all states have agreed that the Universal Declaration of Human Rights and the International Human Rights Covenants provide an authoritative set of international human rights norms. Sovereignty cannot be plausibly invoked as a shield against criticism for human rights violations. And in the case of genocide and comparable severe and systematic violations, as we will see in Chapter 11, there is a growing recognition that sovereignty is *conditional* rather than absolute.

International human rights law has taken off the table debates over whether there really are human rights and what belongs on a list of human rights. The scarce resources of human rights advocates thus can be focused on the real work of implementing internationally recognized human rights. And this fundamental redefinition of the terms of national and international political legitimacy is the principal legacy, and the vital continuing contribution, of the global human rights regime.

9 The Plan of This Book

The rest of this book expands upon many of the themes and issues touched on in this historical overview. Chapters 2–4 explore in some depth key philosophical and historical questions. Chapter 2 examines foundational theoretical issues such as the sources and justifications for human rights, the nature of obligations to respect and protect human rights, and the problems posed by state sovereignty. Chapter 3 explores the universality of human rights; the idea that all human rights are held equally by all humans, everywhere. Chapter 4 looks at the indivisibility, interrelatedness, and interdependence of different categories of human rights, providing a different perspective on the universality of human rights.

Part II explores how human rights goals are achieved through international institutions at the global and regional levels (in Chapters 5 and 6), bilateral state action through their foreign policies (in Chapters 7 and 8), transnational nongovernmental actors through research and advocacy work (in Chapter 9), and businesses and rights-conscious investing (in Chapter 10).

Finally, Part III looks at three contemporary challenges for international human rights: humanitarian intervention against genocide and other crimes (Chapter 11), globalization (Chapter 12), and development (Chapter 13). We conclude (Chapter 14) with a brief discussion of the future of human rights.

Discussion Questions

1. What explains the changes in human rights norms and practices over time? Consider the following possibilities:
   - Changing moral sensibilities. Are our moral views all that different from those of other generations? If so, what does that suggest about the universality of human rights? Or is it that we now feel freer to act on these values? If so, why? What is the relationship between changes in ideas and changes in policy?
   - Changes in the character of international relations. Have peace and prosperity changed our views of human rights? Growing international interdependence? The end of the Cold War? Decolonization? Contemporary challenges, such as poverty and climate change?
   - Changes in national human rights practices. Or is it that we are now doing better at home and thus want to project that progress abroad? Are we still doing better at home after 9/11?
2. How deeply have these changing views toward international human rights penetrated? We often talk about international human rights, but action regularly falls far short of rhetoric. Why? Is it due to a lack of real interest? Constraints on our ability to achieve our objectives? Competing objectives?
3. What accounts for the weakness of international human rights enforcement? What would be required to overcome the existing impediments? How costly—economically, politically, and in human terms—would this be? Would these costs be worthwhile? Do

you think that change is likely in the next few years? The next few decades? In your lifetime? What factors would lead you to expect continuity? What factors suggest change?

4. What kind of actor is best suited to pursue the protection and promotion of international human rights: individuals, NGOs, states, IGOs, or businesses? How do your assessments vary with the nature of the target of action? What are the strengths and weaknesses of each type of human rights advocate?

Suggested Readings

David P. Forsythe, *Human Rights in International Relations*, 4th ed. (Cambridge University Press, 2017), Michael Freeman, *Human Rights*, 3rd ed. (Polity Press, 2017), and Michael E. Goodhart, ed., *Human Rights: Theory and Practice*, 4th ed. (Oxford University Press, 2022) provide good introductory overviews of international human rights. Micheline Ishay, *The History of Human Rights* (University of California Press, 2008), Paul Gordon Lauren, *The Evolution of International Human Rights: Visions Seen*, 3rd ed. (University of Pennsylvania Press, 2011), Peter N. Stearns, *Human Rights in World History*, 2nd ed. (Routledge, 2023), and Jean Quataert and Lora Wildenthal, eds., *The Routledge History of Human Rights* (Routledge, 2019) will be of interest to those looking for a historical bent. Samuel Moyn's *Last Utopia: Human Rights in History* (Harvard University Press, 2010) argues that the contemporary human rights era did not really begin until the 1970s.

The standard international law textbook is Philip Alston, *International Human Rights* (privately published, 2025). It is available at no charge from https://humanrightstextbook.org/digital-book. This revised version of Philip Alston and Ryan Goodman, *International Human Rights* (Oxford University Press, 2013), although directed principally at law students, contains much of interest to those with little or no interest in international law. See also Daniel Moeckli et al., eds., *International Human Rights Law* 4th ed. (Oxford University Press, 2022) and Hurst Hannum et al., eds., *International Human Rights: Problems of Law, Policy, and Practice*, 7th ed. (Aspen Publishing, 2023). Stephen Wheatley's, *The Idea of International Human Rights Law* (Oxford University Press, 2019) is also interesting (and much briefer).

Patrick Hayden, ed., *The Philosophy of Human Rights* (Paragon House, 2001), includes a large and excellent selection of international documents, extensive excerpts from important historical and contemporary theorists, and excellent (if now somewhat dated) essays on a wide range of contemporary human rights issues. Even after twenty years it remains a fine book and a great value. Micheline Ishay, ed., *The Human Rights Reader*, 3rd ed. (Routledge, 2023) is also wide-ranging and excellent (and up to date).

The website of the Office of the UN High Commissioner for Human Rights (www.ohchr.org/en/ohchr_homepage) comprehensively covers international human rights law and the activities of the UN system. The websites of Amnesty International (www.amnesty.org), Human Rights Watch (www.hrw.org), Minority Rights Group (www.minorityrights.org), and Freedom House (www.freedomhouse.org) have much useful current information on human rights situations in individual countries.

On the Universal Declaration of Human Rights, Johannes Morsink, *The Universal Declaration of Human Rights: Origins, Drafting, and Intent* (University of Pennsylvania Press, 1999), is the standard study, offering a theoretically informed history of the drafting of the Declaration and a thoughtful analysis of its content. Readers who want a more digestible account that highlights the Declaration's contemporary relevance may prefer Morsink's, *Article by Article: The Universal Declaration of Human Rights for a New Generation* (University of Pennsylvania Press, 2022). Mary Ann Glendon, *A World Made New: Eleanor Roosevelt and the Universal Declaration of Human Rights* (Random House, 2001), is excellent and immensely readable (although, as its title indicates, somewhat more limited in scope). John P. Humphrey, *Human Rights and the United Nations: A Great Adventure* (Transnational, 1984), is a memoir by the most senior human rights official in the early years of the United Nations Secretariat. On the role of the smaller states in the drafting process, see Susan Waltz, "Universalizing Human Rights: The Role of Small States in the Construction of the Universal Declaration of Human Rights," *Human Rights Quarterly* 23 (February 2001): 44–72; and Mary Ann Glendon, "The Forgotten Crucible: The Latin American Influence on the Universal Declaration of Human Rights Idea," *Harvard Human Rights Journal* 16 (2003): 27–39. For a detailed account of the drafting of the two Covenants, see Daniel J. Whelan, *Indivisible Human Rights: A History* (University of Pennsylvania Press, 2010), Chapters 3–5.

For critical perspectives on international human rights that see the entire enterprise as, at best, seriously distorted by hegemonic American dominance, see two books and one edited collection by Tony Evans, *U.S. Hegemony and the Project of Universal Human Rights* (Macmillan Press, 1996); *The Politics of Human Rights: A Global Perspective*, 2nd ed. (Pluto Press, 2005); and *Human Rights Fifty Years On: A Reappraisal* (Manchester University Press, 1998). See also David Chandler, ed., *Rethinking Human Rights: Critical Approaches to International Relations* (Palgrave Macmillan, 2002). The examples in these books may seem out of date but the criticisms remain relevant. More recently, see Samuel Moyn, *Not Enough: Human Rights in an Unequal World* (Belknap Press, 2018). Briefer classic critiques still worth reading include Makau Mutua, "Savages, Victims, and Saviors: The Metaphor of Human Rights," *Harvard International Law Journal* 42 (Winter 2001): 201–245 and David Kennedy, "The International Human Rights Movement: Part of the Problem?," *Harvard Human Rights Journal* 15 (2002):101–125.

Stephen Hopgood, Jack Snyder, and Leslie Vinjamuri, eds., *Human Rights Futures* (Cambridge University Press, 2017), is a wide-ranging survey of past achievements and future challenges. Useful reappraisals of the overall effectiveness and legitimacy of the global human rights project include Emilie M. Hafner-Burton, *Making Human Rights a Reality* (Princeton University Press, 2013), Stephen Hopgood, *The End-Times of Human Rights* (Cornell University Press, 2015), Bardo Fassbender and Knut Traisbach, eds., *The Limits of Human Rights* (Oxford University Press, 2019), Hurst Hannum, *Rescuing Human Rights: A Radically Moderate Approach* (Cambridge University Press, 2019), and Gentian Zyberi et al., eds., *Reflections on the Future of Human Rights* (Routledge, 2023). Alison Brysk and Michael Stohl, eds., *Expanding Human Rights: 21st Century Norms and Governance* (Edward Elgar, 2017), emphasizes the need to expand the range and focus on contemporary human rights advocacy, a theme that is also thoughtfully explored in Alison Brysk's *Human Rights and Private Wrongs: Constructing Global Civil Society* (Routledge, 2005).

Notes

1 Article 29 indicates that people also have duties to their community that set parameters for the exercise of rights. Article 30, the final article, states that nothing in the Declaration may be interpreted as justifying any act that aims at the destruction of any of the enumerated rights in the Declaration.

2 According to the Guinness Book of World Records, the Universal Declaration achieved this distinction in 1999, at 370 official translations. See www.guinnessworldrecords.com/world-records/most-translated-document/. The current figures are at www.ohchr.org/en/human-rights/universal-declaration/universal-declaration-human-rights/about-universal-declaration-human-rights-translation-project.

3 The name of this monitoring body is a bit of a misnomer; an artifact of the original draft "Covenant on Human Rights." It really ought to be called the "Committee on Civil and Political Rights" to match other treaty monitoring bodies, which take their name from their respective treaties.

4 International IDEA, The Global State of Democracy 2022: Forging Social Contracts in a Time of Discontent. Available at www.idea.int/publications/catalogue/global-state-of-democracy-2022, which documents the trends noted in this and the following paragraph.

5 See V-Dem Institute, Democracy Report 2025 https://www.v-dem.net/documents/60/V-dem-dr__2025_lowres.pdf.

6 The UN Office of the High Commissioner for Human Rights also considers the treaties on migrant workers and enforced disappearances to be core treaties. We leave them off our list because of their relatively narrow scope and low ratification rate (barely 30 percent of the average of the other seven treaties).

7 While there are 193 member-states of the UN, an additional four "observer states" may ratify UN treaties. The least ratified of the core treaties is the Covenant on Economic, Social, and Cultural Rights, with 173. The most ratified, the children's rights treaty, has 196 of a possible 197 parties (excluding only the United States).

Theories of Human Rights 2

The preceding chapter reviewed major developments in the international politics of human rights over the past several decades. This chapter examines three sets of theoretical issues. Sections 1–7 consider philosophical theories of human rights. Sections 8 and 9 address the place of human rights in international society. Section 10 considers political realism, which challenges the very idea of international human rights policies. The following two chapters extensively address the universality and unity (indivisibility) of human rights.

1 Right and Rights

Right in English has two principal senses: *being* right and *having* a right.

We often speak of something being right; that is, in accord with a standard of righteousness. What *is* "right" thus depends on what standard we are using.

Something may be right in the sense that it is fair or equitable. The resulting outcome, though, may not be equal—and thus, according to another standard, *not* right. For example, most of us think that it is right that the rich be taxed at a higher rate than the poor, who may, rightly, pay no income taxes at all.

A decision or outcome may also be right or wrong because a particular procedure was or was not followed properly. The standard of righteousness here is procedural. And this procedural standard may or may not conflict with substantive standards (which themselves may also conflict).

For example, is it right that one can lose the popular vote but still be elected (by the Electoral College) President of the United States? It depends on the standard of "right" being applied—in this case, democracy, or the intentionally nondemocratic Electoral College (in which Wyoming, with a population of nearly 584,000, has three electoral votes and California, with a population of almost 39 million, has 54 electoral votes, giving the

DOI: 10.4324/9781003373520-3

average Wyomingite almost four times the impact on the outcome of the election as the average Californian).

We also speak of some*one having a right* to something; that is, being *entitled* to that thing. These two senses often overlap. For example, that someone has a right to something is itself a standard of righteousness that makes it right that they have it. Here, however, we will emphasize the divergences between having a right and being right.

Not everything that *is* right is something to which anyone *has* a right. For example, it may *be* right (good, desirable) that everyone be loved. But no one *has a righ*t to be loved—and not just because some people are unlovable. Even the lovable *have no right* to be loved.

Conversely, many things to which people have rights are not right under every standard of righteousness. For example, it may be wrong—that is, not right—that some people have immense wealth while others can barely survive. But, assuming that they obtained their wealth legally, even the unjustly wealthy have a right to their property.

2 The Practice of Rights

Rights create special relationships between people and things. "A has a right to x with respect to B." This paradigmatic statement of a right indicates that a right-holder (A) stands in a special relationship to a duty-bearer (B) with respect to the object(s) of A's right (x). Conversely, with respect to x, B has special duties to A.

Theories of rights generally emphasize the entitlement of the right-holder or the special claims that arise from having a right. Claims and entitlements, though, are linked by the fact that they specially empower right-holders.

If A has a right to x, they are *entitled* to x. It is not merely good, desirable, or right that they have x. X belongs to them, in a particular and special way. They suffer a special harm if denied x. It is not merely unjust (wrong; not right). Their rights have been violated. They have been deprived of something to which they are entitled.

Having a right also makes available to the right-holder special claims and related practices that seek to guarantee their enjoyment of x. Rights claims ordinarily take prima facie priority over—that is, they "trump"—other types of claims. And, when rights are violated, the remedial claims of right-holders also have a special force.

In fact, a principal purpose of rights is to take things out of the domain where decisions are appropriately based on calculations of what is right, good, desirable, or otherwise acceptable. Appeals to rights, as it were, (1) stop discussion, at least for the moment; (2) shift the burden of proof to those who would infringe on a right; and (3) raise that burden substantially. Only rarely, when something else of relatively great importance is at stake, is it right to override a right.

3 Human Rights

The term **human rights** indicates both their nature and their source: they are the *rights* that one has simply because one is *human*. They are held by all human beings, irrespective of any differences that human beings have—for example, age, race, ethnicity, gender, religion, or residence—and regardless of any other rights or duties they may (or may not) have as members of states, families, or other public or private groups.

If all human beings have human rights simply because they are human, then human rights are held equally by all.[1] One cannot renounce, lose, or forfeit one's humanity. Therefore, human rights are also inalienable. Even the cruelest torturer and the most debased victim are still human beings.

Not all people are able to *enjoy* all their human rights, let alone enjoy them equally. But all human beings *have* the same human rights, which they hold equally and inalienably.

Human rights are a special type of rights. They are paramount moral rights. They are also rights recognized in international law. Most countries also recognize many of these rights in their national legal systems. The same thing—for example, food or protection against discrimination—thus is often guaranteed by several different types of rights.

We need *human* rights principally when they are not effectively guaranteed by national law and practice. If you can secure food through markets or equal treatment through national legal processes, you are unlikely to claim these as human rights. You still *have* those human rights, but they are not likely to be *used* (as human rights).

For example, in the United States, both constitutional and federal statutory laws prohibit discrimination based on national origin, race, color, religion, disability, sex, and familial status. And in recent years, "sex" has usually been understood to include sexual orientation. However, similar protections for people based on *gender identity* exist nationwide only in a few narrow contexts, such as employment. Indeed, many states have moved to prohibit or deny access to essential support and health services for transgendered people. Therefore, transgender activists frequently claim a human right to nondiscrimination. Racial minorities, by contrast, usually claim legal or constitutional civil rights. Similarly, the name of one of America's leading LGBTQ+ advocacy groups, the Human Rights Campaign, reflects its founding at a time when discrimination against gender minorities was permitted, and sometimes embedded, in American law.

Human rights is the language of victims and the dispossessed. Human rights claims usually seek to alter legal or political practices. Claims of human rights thus aim to be self-liquidating. To assert one's human rights is to attempt to change political practices (and ultimately political structures) so that it will no longer be necessary to claim those rights as *human* rights. For example, the struggle against apartheid in South Africa was a struggle to change South African laws and practices so that nonwhite South Africans could turn to the legislature, courts, or the bureaucracy should they be denied, for example, their human right to equal protection of the laws or political participation.

Human rights thus provide an internationally endorsed and recognized moral standard of national political legitimacy. (The **Universal Declaration of Human Rights** describes itself as "a common standard of achievement for all peoples and all nations.") Human rights are also emerging as an international political standard of legitimacy. More precisely, regimes that grossly and systematically violate human rights are widely seen as compromising their full legitimacy—although they continue to be fully sovereign as a matter of international law.

4 The Source or Justification of Human Rights

One common way to classify rights is according to the mechanism by which they are created and the domain within which they operate. Legal rights, for example, arise from, and operate within the domain of, the law. Constitutional rights arise from the constitution. Human rights, following this paradigm, arise from humanity.

Philosophically, it is not at all clear how humanity gives rise to rights. Nonetheless, international human rights law is clear and insistent that human rights are grounded in our shared humanity, often understood as a matter of inherent human dignity. The Universal Declaration of Human Rights refers to "the inherent dignity ... of all members of the human family." The International Human Rights Covenants proclaim that "these rights derive from the inherent dignity of the human person." The **Vienna Declaration** adopted at the 1993 World Conference on Human Rights likewise claims that "all human rights derive from the dignity and worth inherent in the human person."

Whatever the philosophical problems with such claims, we will take them here as given. This simply is how human rights are generally understood today. Humanity or inherent dignity is presented as a "natural" attribute of all human beings; a feature of our nature as human beings. (What we today call human rights were, in the seventeenth, eighteenth, and nineteenth centuries, usually called natural rights.)

The human nature that underlies human rights is sometimes explained in terms of (basic) human needs. But any list of needs that can plausibly claim to be empirically established provides an obviously inadequate list of rights: life, food, protection against cruel or inhuman treatment, and perhaps companionship. Science simply is incapable of providing the appropriate theory of human nature. (As we will see in Section 3.5, an anthropological approach that seeks to ground human rights on cross-cultural consensus faces similar problems.)

We have human rights not to what as animals we need naturally for survival. We have human rights to what as *human* beings we need to live a life of dignity. The human nature that is the source of human rights is a moral account of human possibility. It reflects what human beings might become (not what they "are" in some scientifically determinable sense or what they have been historically). Human rights rest on an account of a life of dignity to which human beings are "by nature"—by their *moral* nature—suited.

In particular, international human rights reflect a vision of human dignity in contemporary economic, political, and social circumstances—a world of states, markets, and other social structures and actors capable of impeding or preventing individual human beings from living a life of dignity. If the rights specified by the underlying theory of human nature are implemented and enforced, they should help to bring into being the envisioned type of person who is worthy of such a life. The effective implementation of human rights thus resembles a self-fulfilling moral prophecy.

But however one understands the source of human rights, in what follows we will simply assume that there are human rights. This theoretical evasion is justified by the fact that almost all states acknowledge the existence of human rights. The assumption that there are human rights thus is relatively unproblematic for our purposes here, namely, studying the international politics of human rights.

5 Equal Concern and Respect

We will also take the core list of rights in the Universal Declaration and the Covenants (see Table 1.1) as given and unproblematic. The principal justification for this is practical: to act internationally based on a different list would risk the charge of imposing one's own preferences rather than supporting widely accepted international standards.

This list, however, can also be derived from a plausible and attractive philosophical account, namely, the requirement that the state treat each person with equal concern and respect. Consider the Universal Declaration (the full text is in the Appendix).

One must be recognized as a person (Article 6) to be treated with any sort of concern or respect. Personal rights to nationality and to recognition before the law, along with rights to life and to protection against slavery, torture, and other inhuman or degrading practices, (Articles 3–5, 15) can be seen as legal and political prerequisites to recognition and thus respect. And rights to equal protection of the laws and protection against racial, sexual, and other forms of discrimination (Articles 1, 2, 7) are essential for *equal* respect.

Equal respect for all persons, though, is likely to be at most a hollow formality without the freedom to choose and act on one's own ideas of the good life. Freedoms of speech, conscience, religion, and association, along with the right to privacy, (Articles 12, 18–20) guarantee a private sphere of personal autonomy. The rights to marry and found a family, to education, and to participate in the cultural life of the community (Articles 16, 26, 27) provide a social dimension to personal autonomy. The rights to vote and to freedom of speech, press, assembly, and association (Articles 18–21) guarantee political autonomy.

Rights to food, clothing, housing, health care, and social insurance (Article 25) make equal concern and respect a practical reality rather than a mere formal possibility. The right to work (Article 23) is a right to economic participation very similar to the right to political participation. A (limited) right to property (Article 17) also may be justified in such terms.

Finally, the special threat to personal security and equality posed by the modern state requires legal rights to constrain the state and its functionaries. These include rights to the presumption of innocence until proven guilty; due process; fair and public hearings before an independent tribunal; and protection from arbitrary arrest, detention, or exile (Articles 8–11). Anything less would allow the state to treat citizens with differential concern or respect.

The idea of equal concern and respect certainly is philosophically controversial. It does, however, have a certain inherent plausibility. It is closely related to the basic fact that human rights are equal and inalienable. And it offers an attractive extension of the claim that internationally recognized human rights "derive from the inherent dignity of the human person."

6 The Unity of Human Rights

The Universal Declaration, which, as we have seen, presents itself as "a common standard of achievement for all peoples and all nations," understands the rights that it enumerates as indivisible parts of an organic whole. As the 1993 Vienna Declaration puts it, "All human rights are universal, indivisible and interdependent and interrelated" and the goal of international human rights action is "universal respect for, and observance and protection of, all human rights and fundamental freedoms for all."

In the next two chapters, we will examine in some detail the ways in which we can think about the universality and indivisibility of human rights, in theory and practice. In general, though, the conclusion that all human rights are essential to a life of human dignity reflects the idea that we are complex and multifaceted creatures who live in complex and multifaceted economic, social, and political situations. We thus require access to a relatively wide range of goods, services, opportunities, and protections in order to live a life of dignity. International human rights thus are regularly described as interdependent and indivisible.

Unless (nearly) *all* internationally recognized human rights are respected and protected, a life of dignity is unlikely to be a realistic possibility. For example, a person is denied a life of dignity if they have enough to eat but are prevented from freely exercising their religion or faith. From this standpoint, the unity of human rights begins with the simultaneous multiplicity and unity of human experience and human dignity.

We can also, though, think of the interdependence or interrelatedness of rights functionally. One is much less likely to be able to enjoy a right to x if one does not also enjoy a right to y. For example, a person who has the right to vote and assemble probably cannot effectively exercise those rights if their freedom of movement is severely restricted. A person's freedom to seek out and receive information is hindered if their right to education has been violated to the extent that he is illiterate. The rights of poor rural children to education are often undermined by the needs of their families for their labor.

There is also an essential unity or interdependence of rights and their correlative obligations. Having a right to x is undermined if the duty-bearer is undefined or if the content of the obligations required to effectively fulfill the right is unclear or insecure.

For example, a few philosophers, and a substantial segment of conservatives in the United States, have expressed skepticism about whether economic and social rights (other than the right to property) are really rights at all. Such arguments usually reflect the idea that only rights that have correlative duties that are negative—that require only inaction that avoids directly infringing the right—ought to be recognized as universal human rights. And, it is argued, such negative rights—"freedom from" rights—are restricted to civil and political rights (plus the right to property). Conversely, economic and social rights are held to be positive rights that require (often extensive) actions and expenditures to discharge the obligations that they impose.

The implied moral distinction here, however, is problematic. Is there really much difference between intentionally killing someone and intentionally leaving him to die? But even if we accept the moral distinction, many civil and political rights are in fact positive rights, and in many instances duties of forbearance (that is, the state refraining from taking an action) are sufficient to realize some economic and social rights.

Consider the right to "a fair and public hearing by an independent and impartial tribunal" or the right to "periodic and genuine elections." Providing for courts and elections are very positive, and expensive, endeavors that require significant action by the state, not mere inaction. Even the right to freedom from torture requires extensive and costly training and monitoring of police and prison personnel. Similarly, the right to property can only be protected by a robust legal system that assigns, registers, and adjudicates disputes over property rights as well as a criminal justice system to protect those rights.[2]

Conversely, the right to housing imposes both negative and positive obligations on the state, such as an obligation not to evict people onto the street without due process. The right to education obligates the state to refrain from preventing students (e.g., women or members of minority groups) from attending school. And, in some rural areas, the best way to protect the right to food is for the government not to permit (let alone encourage) land that is used for subsistence agriculture to be turned to the production of cash crops for export.

There are, of course, differences between economic and social rights and civil and political rights (see Chapter 4, Section 4). But there are equally significant differences within each broad class of rights. And there are important similarities across these classes. For example, the (civil and political) right to life and the (economic and social) right to food can be seen as different means to protect the same value. Categorical substantive distinctions simply do not withstand scrutiny.

Internationally recognized human rights represent a comprehensive vision of a set of goods, services, opportunities, and protections that are necessary in the contemporary world to provide the preconditions for a life of dignity. No *systematic* deviations from the list of internationally recognized human rights can be theoretically justified.

7 Duties and Duty-bearers of Human Rights

Rights in general and human rights in particular, as we have seen, have correlative duties that typically are both positive and negative. Extending a distinction originally drawn by Henry Shue, we can distinguish three types of duties: to avoid depriving, to protect from deprivation, and to aid the deprived.[3] We can also rephrase this in terms commonly used in international discussions as obligations to *respect*, to *protect*, and to *fulfill*.

However we describe them, these different types of duties can be (and usually are) differentially allocated to different actors.

All social actors, including all individual human beings, are obligated to respect the human rights of every human being, in the sense of not depriving them of the enjoyment of those rights. In this sense, human rights are not merely held universally (by all human beings) but also apply universally (to all actors).

Nonetheless, most actions by individuals that deny someone the enjoyment of their human rights are not ordinarily thought of or talked about as human rights violations. For example, if your neighbor shoots and kills you, we ordinarily would not say that they have violated your human right to life. We call it murder, an ordinary crime.

Human rights are largely concerned with the duties and obligations that fall on those *in organized society* that have special responsibilities not to deprive someone of the enjoyment of a human right. The state is probably the first such agent that comes to mind. Others, though, are sometimes at least as important: for example, parents, families, daycare centers, hospitals, airlines, private employers, and markets.

The duty not to discriminate provides a striking example of the importance of duties of "private" actors. For example, employers (with respect to the right to work), landlords and homeowners (with respect to the right to housing), and many other social groups (in their special spheres of social action) typically *are* considered to be violating human rights by engaging in invidious discrimination against members of protected classes of people. In areas such as housing and employment, "private" actors (in the public sphere) are the primary duty-bearers of the obligation to *respect* the right to nondiscrimination in these areas—and are the principal violators.

Both states and "private" actors also have duties to promote and ultimately to *fulfill* the enjoyment of particular human rights. The state has an international legal obligation to ensure, for example, that everyone is housed, fed, and employed (or compensated for unemployment) and has access to health care. But in most societies, these rights are guaranteed by a combination of public and private provision in which families and markets play a central role. In fact, in most societies, most people enjoy their right to work by participating in markets and their right to food through the mechanisms of markets and families.

Nonetheless, there are good reasons why when we think of human rights obligations we do tend to think first of the state. And the state, in our contemporary world, is the principal bearer of duties to *protect* human rights through legal recognition and enforcement in the territory that it governs. For example, the state has a special obligation to prohibit invidious discrimination in housing and employment and to provide legal redress for those who are discriminated against. In many cases, the state is the exclusive actor with duties to protect. Consider "the right to an effective remedy by the competent national tribunals for acts violating the fundamental rights granted him by the constitution or by law" (Universal Declaration, Article 8).

The resulting *systems of provision* can be quite complex.

Consider health care in the United States. Most children get their health care through their families, most of whom purchase it (indirectly by buying insurance) with their own money, often combined with a financial contribution made by their employer (or the government). There is thus a substantial element of what might be called self-provisioning. But there are also special government healthcare programs for children, especially the Children's Health Insurance Program (CHIP). Most elderly people, however, get most of their health care from the government through Medicare. Many low-income children and working adults also receive health care from the government (primarily through Medicaid). And the state is obliged to ensure access for everyone and to regulate markets (for example, by prohibiting and preventing discrimination and other practices that deny equal access or equal treatment).

Mixed systems of provisioning can be found in other areas of human rights concern. For example, in India, Israel, Singapore, and Taiwan, adult children have certain legal obligations to support their aged parents. Employer-provided housing has sometimes proved successful. Privately funded schools are an important part of the educational system of many countries. Churches and charities are a significant part of the welfare systems of some states.

Turning to civil and political rights, legal services are in most countries obtained both by purchase on the market and through the state. Police protection is sometimes substantially augmented by private security firms. Much of the burden of protecting property lies with property owners.

Different countries may choose different mixes of public and private provision for different rights or at different times. The state, however, has ultimate responsibility for the *system* of provision, based on its special duties to protect and provide internationally recognized human rights and to aid the deprived.

Finally, there is the question of whether duties and obligations for respecting, protecting, and fulfilling human rights exist beyond states. For example, does an American clothing company have a duty to respect the workplace rights of garment workers in Bangladesh, who are working for a third or fourth party within a complex global supply chain? (And if it does have such a duty, to what extent is it a *human rights* duty and to what extent is it a matter of righteousness?) Do wealthier countries have a positive obligation to provide better terms of trade, or aid and other forms of financial assistance, to poorer countries? What duties and obligations do international organizations, such as the United Nations, have to ensure that human rights are respected, protected, or fulfilled? What about the international community as a whole? We will return to these questions in different contexts throughout the book.

8 Human Rights and Related Practices

Human rights, as we have seen, are a particular type of social practice, founded on a particular conception of human dignity, implemented by particular kinds of mechanisms. They must not be confused with other values and practices.

Not all good things are human rights. People do not have a right to many good things: for example, charity, respect, talent, and beauty. Many things to which we do have rights arise not from mere humanity but from our actions (e.g., contractual rights) or from particular relationships in which we stand (e.g., the rights of members of families or of citizens). And many actors other than individual human beings hold rights (e.g., states, corporations, and clubs).

Human rights do not even provide a comprehensive account of social justice. Justice is particular as well as universal. And it is not entirely a matter of rights.

Human rights are the minimum set of goods, services, opportunities, and protections that are widely recognized today as essential prerequisites for a life of dignity. No more. But no less.

9 Sovereignty and International Society

We turn now from philosophy to a broad theoretical consideration of the place of human rights in international relations. The modern international system is often dated to 1648, when the "Westphalia" Treaties of Münster and Osnabrück ended the Thirty Years' War. As we saw in Chapter 1, though, human rights have been an explicit issue in international relations for barely seventy-five years. The absence of human rights from the first three centuries of modern international relations reflected an international order based on sovereignty.

A sovereign is subject to no higher authority (except those that the sovereign has voluntarily acknowledged, for example, by ratifying an international treaty). In early modern Europe, **sovereignty** was a personal attribute of rulers. In many other times and places, though, no (earthly) power was considered to be sovereign over all others. For example, in medieval Europe, various secular and ecclesiastical actors exercised different kinds of authority with respect to a variety of aspects of civic and religious life. At any one time, a person might be subject to multiple powers—for example, the Pope, the Holy Roman Emperor, a king, a duke, a bishop, and a village lord—exercising authority in complex, often overlapping, and sometimes even crosscutting, ways.

In contemporary international relations, however, the sovereignty of territorial states is a central legal and political organizing principle.[4] International relations is structured around the legal premise that states initially have exclusive jurisdiction over their territories, their occupants and resources, and the events that take place there. Furthermore, states have the right to pursue their own interests in their relations with other states. And all states, being equally states, are equally sovereign.

Practice regularly falls far short of precept, as usually is the case with legal and political principles. Nonetheless, the fundamental norms, rules, and practices of contemporary international relations rest on state sovereignty and the formal legal equality of (sovereign) states.

If the norm of sovereignty gives states a right to national independence and autonomy then **nonintervention** is the duty correlative to the right of sovereignty. Other states are obliged not to interfere with the *internal* (and thus sovereign) actions of a sovereign state. Because human rights principally regulate the ways states treat their own citizens within their own territories, international human rights policies thus might seem to involve unjustifiable interference in their domestic affairs.

A principal function of international law, however, is to overcome the *initial* exclusive allocation of sovereign jurisdiction. International law, including international human rights law, is largely the record of the exercises of sovereignty to create international obligations (including restrictions on how a state treats its own nationals on its own territory).

A **treaty** is a contract between states to accept reciprocal obligations. It is an exercise of sovereignty that restricts the freedom of action of the (still-sovereign) states in question. For example, a treaty of alliance may oblige a state to aid an ally that is attacked. Such a state is no longer (legally) free to choose whether to go to war. Through the treaty, it has voluntarily relinquished some freedom of action. The same is true of international human rights treaties.

A system of sovereign states is, literally, anarchic—without *arkhē* (rule) or an *arkhos* (ruler); a political arena without official hierarchical relations of central authority. But **anarchy**, the absence of hierarchical political rule, does not imply chaos or the absence of order. In addition to international law, states regulate their interaction through institutionalized practices such as diplomacy, balance of power, and recognition of spheres of influence. There is no international government. There is, however, rule-governed order; rule in the absence of a ruler.

International relations takes place within an anarchical **society of states**; that is, an international society in which states are the principal (although not sole) actors or agents.[5] And in many societies of states, there is considerable *governance* despite the absence of a government. (Many also see an emerging cosmopolitan world society. See Section 10 immediately below.)

During the eighteenth, nineteenth, and early twentieth centuries, the international society of states gave punctilious respect to the sovereign prerogative of each state to treat its own citizens as it saw fit. Today, however, as we have seen, there is a substantial body of international human rights law. States have become increasingly vocal in expressing, and sometimes even acting on, their international human rights concerns. In addition, human rights NGOs, which seek to constrain the freedom of action of rights-violating states, have become more numerous and more active (see Chapter 9).

This reflects (and has helped to create) a transformed understanding of the place of individuals in international relations. States traditionally were the sole subjects of international law; the only actors with international legal standing. The rights and interests of individuals were traditionally protected in international law only by states acting on their behalf. The International Bill of Human Rights does not empower individuals (or even other states) to act against states to coercively enforce human rights protection. Contemporary international human rights law, however, has given individuals, or at least their rights, a significant standing in international relations.

It has also introduced a new conception of international legitimacy. Traditionally, a government was considered legitimate if it exercised authority over its territory and accepted the international legal obligations that it and its predecessors had contracted. What it did at home was irrelevant. Today, human rights provide a standard of moral legitimacy that has been (very incompletely) incorporated into the rules of the international society of states.

Consider the almost universal negative reaction to the Tiananmen Square massacre in 1989, when Chinese troops fired on unarmed demonstrators and brutally crushed China's emerging democracy movement. China's diplomatic isolation reflected this new human rights-based understanding of legitimacy. However, that isolation lasted only a year or two. Even the strongest supporters of sanctions were not willing to allow Chinese brutality to interfere with long-term economic and security interests – even when China was far less powerful than it is today.

A similar dynamic is evident in the case of the brutal assassination of Saudi dissident and journalist Jamal Khashoggi at the Saudi Embassy in Istanbul in October 2018. Even though the US Central Intelligence Agency (CIA) and the United Nations concluded that Saudi Crown Prince Mohammad Bin Salman had ordered the execution, the Saudi kingdom did not suffer any significant sanctions. Even President Joe Biden, who during the 2020 presidential campaign said he would make Saudi Arabia a "pariah," later visited Bin Salman in 2022 to patch up relations (largely to counter growing Chinese influence in the region). And in 2025 President Trump berated a journalist for even bringing up the subject.

This tension is characteristic of the current state of international human rights. The future of international human rights activity can be seen as a struggle over balancing the competing claims of sovereignty and international human rights—and the competing conceptions of legitimacy, political community, and political order that they imply. And this balancing becomes even more complicated, as the two preceding examples show, when other interests of states are taken into account (as they ought to be in national foreign policies; see Chapters 7 and 8).

10 Three Models of International Human Rights

The universality of human rights fits uncomfortably with a political order structured around the absolute supremacy of the rights of sovereign states. Universal moral rights seem better suited to a cosmopolitan conception of world politics, which sees individuals more as members of a global political community (*cosmopolis*) than as citizens of states. Instead of thinking of inter-national relations (the relations between nation-states), a cosmopolitan thinks of a global political process in which individuals and other nonstate actors are important direct participants. We thus have three competing theoretical models of the place of human rights in international relations, each with its own conception of the character of the international community.

The traditional **statist** (or pluralist) model sees human rights as principally a matter of sovereign national jurisdiction. Statists readily admit that human rights are no longer the exclusive preserve of states and that the state is no longer the sole significant international actor (if it ever was). They nonetheless insist that human rights remain *primarily* a matter of sovereign national jurisdiction and (ought to continue to be) a largely peripheral concern of international (interstate) relations. For statists, "the international community" is a thin, largely interstate, international society.

A **cosmopolitan** model starts with individuals rather than states—which are often "the problem" for cosmopolitans. Cosmopolitans see the state challenged both from below, by individuals and NGOs, and from above, by the truly global (not merely international or interstate) community. International action on behalf of human rights is relatively unproblematic in such a model. In fact, cosmopolitans largely reverse the burden of proof, requiring justification for *non*intervention in the face of gross and persistent violations of human rights. International society, in other words, is seen as a global or world society.

The space toward the center of the continuum defined by statism and cosmopolitanism is occupied by **internationalist** models. The international community is seen as a society in which states have a central role but in which NGOs, IGOs, individuals, firms, and other "private" actors also have been formally and informally incorporated into international political processes. International human rights activity is permissible to the extent authorized by the norms of international society. These norms, however, may vary considerably across particular international societies. Therefore, we need to distinguish between (relatively) strong internationalism and (relatively) weak internationalism.

Each of these three models can be read as making descriptive claims about the place that human rights have in international relations or prescriptive claims about the place they ought to have. For example, a statist might argue (descriptively) that human rights are in fact peripheral in international relations or (prescriptively) that they ought to be peripheral, or both.

Cosmopolitanism, however, even in this era of globalization, has little descriptive power. States and their interests still dominate world politics. The international political power of individuals, NGOs, firms, and other nonstate actors is real and growing but is still relatively small—and power is a relative notion. The global political community—world society as opposed to (a more or less statist) international society—is at best rudimentary. The cosmopolitan model, if more than a prescription about what is desirable, predicts a direction of change in world politics.

If the world envisioned by cosmopolitans has yet to come into being, that envisioned by statists is at least in part a thing of the past. Although accurate even into the 1970s, the statist model of international human rights today is at best a crude and increasingly deceptive first approximation. Furthermore, it directs attention away from decades of significant, cumulative changes that typically go under the label of globalization.

Some sort of internationalist model (or a very heavily hedged statism) provides the most accurate depiction of the place of human rights in contemporary international relations. (The chapters of Parts II and III provide extensive evidence to support this conclusion.) Current descriptive power, however, is no guarantee of future accuracy. And it does not mean that internationalism is the best, or even a good, way to treat human rights in international relations. Nevertheless, the international human rights reality that we face today, as later chapters show in some detail, is one of state sovereignty modestly limited by a still-significantly-statist international society.

11 The Realist Challenge to Human Rights

Before leaving the discussion of theory, we need to consider a common theoretical challenge to even this limited concern with international human rights, namely, political **realism** or *Realpolitik* (power politics). The realist view stands in contrast to liberal, institutionalist, constructivist, and many other theories of international relations, which emphasize that, despite international **anarchy**, there are various mechanisms that allow states and other international actors to cooperate, often quite effectively.

Most of what we have described above accords with a broadly liberal and **constructivist** conception of politics, which gives considerable emphasis to the formation of norms, law, and institutions in a great variety of areas in international relations, including trade and finance, peace and security, economic and social development, and protecting the environment—and also, of course, international human rights. Realists, in contrast, emphasize the fear and uncertainty, bred of anarchy (lack of an international government), that leads to conflict between states.

Realpolitik is an old and well-established theory of international relations, typically traced back to figures such as Niccolò Machiavelli (in the early sixteenth century) and Thucydides, whose *History of the Peloponnesian War* chronicles the great wars between Athens and Sparta in the final decades of the fifth century BCE. Realism stresses "the primacy in all political life of power and security."[6] Because people regularly are egoistic (and sometimes evil) and because international anarchy requires states to rely on their own resources even for defense, realists argue that "universal moral principles cannot be applied to the actions of states."[7] Thus to pursue a moral foreign policy would not only be foolishly unsuccessful but also leave one's country vulnerable to the power of (other) self-interested states.

Realists argue that only considerations of the national interest should guide foreign policy. And the national interest, for the realist, must be defined, largely if not entirely, in terms of power and security. For example, George Kennan, one of the architects of the postwar US foreign policy of **containment** of the Soviet Union and one of the most respected post-World War II realist writers, argued that a government's "primary obligation is to the *interests* of the national society it represents ... its military security, the integrity of its political life and the well-being of its people." "The process of government ... is a practical exercise and not a moral one." As for international human rights policies,

> it is difficult to see any promise in an American policy which sets out to correct and improve the political habits of large parts of the world's population. Misgovernment ... has been the common condition of most of mankind for centuries and millennia in the past. It is going to remain that condition for long into the future, no matter how valiantly Americans insist on tilting against the windmills.[8]

Such arguments do contain a kernel of truth. The demands of morality do often conflict with the national interest defined in terms of power. But *all* objectives of foreign policy, not just moral ones, may compete with the national interest thus defined. For example, arms races may contribute to the outbreak of war. Alliances may prove dangerously entangling. Realists, however, rightly refuse to conclude that we should eschew arms or allies. They should also abandon categorical attacks on morality in foreign policy. A valuable caution against moral*istic* excess too often has been wildly exaggerated into a general principle of politics.

Realist arguments against morality in foreign policy also appeal to the special office of the statesman. For example, Herbert Butterfield argued that although a man may choose to sacrifice himself in the face of foreign invasion, he does not have a "right to offer the same sacrifice on behalf of all his fellow-citizens or to impose such self-abnegation on the rest of his society."[9] But nonmoral objectives as well may be pursued by statesmen with excessive zeal—and equally deadly consequences. In any case, most moral objectives can be pursued at a cost far less than national survival. This certainly is true of many international human rights goals.

In addition, there is no reason that a country cannot, if it wishes, include human rights or other moral concerns in its definition of the national interest. (The national interest is a matter of what the nation is interested in.) Security, independence, and prosperity may be necessities of national political life. Governments, however, need not limit themselves to those necessities. Even if the primary obligation of governments must be to the national interest defined in terms of power, this need not be their sole, or even ultimate, obligation.

Finally, using the anarchic structure of international relations as a rationale will not rescue realist amoralism. For example, Robert Art and Kenneth Waltz claimed that "states in anarchy cannot afford to be moral. The possibility of moral behavior rests upon the existence of an effective government that can deter and punish illegal actions."[10] But even if we set aside the confusion of morality and law, this logic is clearly faulty. Just as individuals may behave morally without government to enforce moral rules, so moral behavior is possible in international relations.

The costs of moral behavior are typically greater in an anarchic than in a hierarchical system. Nonetheless, states often can act on moral concerns without harm, and sometimes with success. There may be good policy reasons to pursue amoral, or even immoral, policies *in particular instances*. There are, however, no good theoretical reasons for requiring amoral policies or even accepting them as the norm.

Problem 2.1 Democracy and Human Rights

The Problem

Americans typically describe their form of government as a democracy committed to protecting basic human rights (especially those rights specified in the Constitution). Across the globe as well, the terms *democracy* and *human rights* are often used somewhat interchangeably. The analysis offered in this chapter, which emphasizes the differences between human rights and other moral, legal, and social practices, challenges this understanding.

One standard conception of democracy is government of, by, and for the people. This fits with the etymology of the Greek term *dēmokratia*: the power (*kratos*) and thus rule of the people (*dēmos*). But the people can, and regularly do, choose to do some very nasty things to some segments of the national population, including systematically violating their human rights. Think about the history of legalized racism, sexism, and religious discrimination in the United States.

Human rights require that democratic governments, no less than other forms of government, respect human rights. But they do not assume that democratically elected governments necessarily advance or guarantee rights-respecting outcomes. Human rights require a rights-protective regime. And that often requires acting in opposition to the will of the people.

How should we resolve the conflicts between democracy and human rights?

A Solution

Human rights set boundaries of democratic decision-making. A rights-protective regime will be democratic both for instrumental reasons (other forms of government, such as theocracy, aristocracy, monarchy, and vanguard party dictatorship have all proved to be systematically incapable of providing sustained protection of human rights) and for intrinsic reasons (self-rule is an important part of the conception of human dignity underlying internationally recognized human rights). But democratic government is desirable only to the extent that the rule of the people realizes the rights of all citizens (and in particular guarantees every citizen equal concern and respect).

Political scientists often describe such governments as "liberal democracies." Democracy operates within the constraints of the liberties (human rights) of the citizenry, which provide the justification and standard of legitimacy for any government. (The language of *democratic rights-protective regime* is clearer and more accurate—*democracy* is the adjective rather than the noun—but clumsy and unlikely to gain wide acceptance.)

Whatever the verbal formula, though, human rights trump democracy when they conflict. (In the American legal context, the more limited set of constitutional rights performs exactly this role.) Even when elections are free, fair, and open—and especially when they are not—"democratic" regimes may fall far short of the demands of human rights. Elected governments are, on average, better than unelected governments. But human rights demand that all governments provide all their citizens (and others under their jurisdictions) with all the goods, services, opportunities, and protections required by internationally recognized human rights.

Further Problems

How should we respond to governments that plausibly claim that their rights-abusive actions reflect the will of the people?

In 2022, the State of Florida enacted the Parental Rights in Education Act (which critics have dubbed "Don't Say Gay"). It prohibits public schools from teaching or allowing classroom discussions about sexual orientation or gender identity. (The prohibition was originally only from kindergarten through third grade, but the Florida Department of Education later expanded the probation through twelfth grade.) The law was passed by solid majorities in both houses of the Florida legislature. From the standpoint of human rights (and perhaps even American constitutional law), this law clearly violates a number of rights including freedom of speech and expression and rights to nondiscrimination. It has also paved the way for other infringements of rights, including book bans by public and school libraries.

For the sake of argument, let us assume that this is a case where human rights ought to take priority over democracy. How, then, do we deal with arguments that it is more important to protect children from potentially dangerous ideas and that taxpayers should have a say over what their children are taught in public schools?

When dealing with such conflicts of rights and fundamental interests, there are no general rules—or, rather, the rules (in this case, about democracy and human rights) conflict with one another. We must balance costs and benefits, in the context of particular cases.

Here, the crucial issue is balancing the harms to children and families whose identities and family structures are excluded from schools against the harms to families and children who consider nontraditional family structures, sexual orientations, and gender identities immoral (or otherwise unfit for mention in school). The harm to nonbinary individuals and nontraditional families, however, is both imposed by the state and reflects a particular substantive vision of morality and family life. (In the language of American constitutional law, it is not "content neutral.") And they have been singled out for invidious discrimination; only *their* identities and ways of life are disparaged by being excluded from the schools. This, at the very least, gives substantially enhanced weight to the harms created by Florida law. (Traditional binary conceptions of gender are (somehow) not considered "gender identities."). Furthermore, from a human rights perspective, the rights of minorities—including, and especially, despised minorities—ought to be a central political concern.

Public schools, as agencies of the government, may neither advocate nor disparage any race, religion, or creed. Analogously, we would argue, they may not advocate nor disparage any (legal) form of family. ("Men and women of full age, without any limitation due to race, nationality or religion, have the right to marry and to found a family." Universal Declaration, Article 16[1].) Declaring and teaching that there is only one proper form of family is no less indoctrination because it is the view of the majority. And it is quite intentionally "grooming" boys and girls for a particular way of life.

Similarly, public schools may not teach only one system of sexual orientation and gender identity—at least when there are members of the community and students in the school who have, live with, or acknowledge "nonconforming" orientations and identities. "Not teaching sexual orientation or gender identity" in practice means teaching traditional "hetero-normative" orientations and identities. Only references to families with two moms or two dads or nonbinary parents and to individuals who do not identify with the traditional male-female binary are prohibited. (Or, were the law to be strictly interpreted, teaching about or discussing *any* form of family arrangement or romantic interaction between any people of any orientation or identity would run contrary to the law—a preposterous outcome.)

The *preferences* of the majority must give way to the fundamental *rights* of the minority. And if members of the majority are uncomfortable with the results, that is perhaps unfortunate but unavoidable. They must find a way to deal with it—just as they must deal with any discomfort they may have with sending their students to public schools that acknowledge the existence and equal rights of atheists, Satanists, practitioners of Santaria, and other often-despised religious minorities.

As we will see, the conflict between democracy and human rights is only one of many such fundamental conflicts. Human rights and the demands of development often conflict in the short run. How should we deal with that conflict? With the conflicts between human rights and broader conceptions of social justice? Human rights and environmental protection? Such questions similarly call for balancing, recognizing the special weight of human rights.

Human rights rarely provide the whole answer to issues of political controversy. But they *ordinarily* trump other concerns. And in all cases, they shift the burden to those who would infringe them to show that other concerns are unusually weighty and thus ought to take priority.

Discussion Questions

1. We emphasize differences between rights and other sorts of moral principles and practices. Do we overemphasize the differences? What are the ways in which rights are *similar* to considerations of righteousness?
2. Should we prefer to protect human rights when doing so conflicts with social utility? Should the rights of the individual or the few take priority over the happiness of the many? (Try thinking about different rights in answering this question.) In particular, should *governments* act on any principle other than social utility?
3. We assume that some sort of justification of human rights is possible. But doesn't it matter *why* people believe that there are human rights? For what purposes might it matter?
4. Why are many Americans reluctant to consider economic and social rights as fully legitimate human rights? Are the reasons philosophical? Are they a reflection of the generally poor performance of the United States in ensuring these rights? How different are such arguments from those made by some developing countries that civil and political rights are luxuries that first require the fulfillment of economic, social, and cultural rights?
5. Is there a moral dimension to the positive-negative distinction? Is there really no difference between killing someone and refusing to help someone who is dying? Does your answer differ when you move from personal behavior to the activities of governments?
6. Many countries (not just authoritarian ones) have claimed that their sovereignty is paramount to global human rights norms. Is that really such a bad thing? Do you want other countries and international organizations inquiring into the human rights practices of your country? International anarchy has its obvious drawbacks, but do you *really* want an outside political authority telling your country how it ought to behave or publicly condemning it for its human rights failures?
7. Which of the three models of international human rights—statist, cosmopolitan, or internationalist—do you find most attractive (issues of their current descriptive accuracy notwithstanding)? Why? What are the greatest strengths of your preferred model? Why might others find it defective?
8. Even if realists overstate their case, don't they have a legitimate one? How often do states have the political space and resources to be successful in pursuing international human rights concerns? Have the rise of China, the complications of globalization, or political instabilities in key regions of the world that are of strategic importance to the United States made it harder or easier to defend human rights? (In answering this question, consider a range of different rights.)
9. How often do states use realism as an excuse for not doing what they know they ought to do but don't want to be bothered with? Imagine personal moral relations if realist arguments were allowed. Are the differences between interpersonal and international relations really so great that we can allow radically different standards to apply? Conversely, are the similarities so great that we can apply the same standards without major modifications across the two realms?

Suggested Readings

Steven Lukes, "Five Fables about Human Rights," in Stephen Shute and Susan Hurley, eds., *On Human Rights* (Basic Books, 1993), https://stevenlukes.files.wordpress.com/2012/06/3-sl-five-fables-about-human-rights.pdf, provides a brilliant brief discussion of the difference that having human rights makes. If you are looking for a place to begin further reading, this is probably it.

The chapters in Part 3 of Patrick Hayden, ed., *The Philosophy of Human Rights* (Paragon House, 2001), are also well worth consulting. We have found that students particularly enjoy Martha Nussbaum's 1997 *Fordham Law Review* article, "Capabilities and Human Rights," https://www.palermo.edu/Archivos_content/2015/derecho/pobreza_multidimensional/bibliografia/Sesion3_doc1.pdf, which argues for rooting human rights in a notion of human capabilities (rather than the broader and vaguer idea of human dignity).

For an excellent book-length discussion that emphasizes the similarities between rights and other grounds of action (in contrast to our emphasis on the special features of rights), see James W. Nickel, *Making Sense of Human Rights: Philosophical Reflections on the Universal Declaration of Human Rights*, 2nd ed. (University of California Press, 2006).

A powerful but brief and readily accessible version of the realist argument against pursuing moral issues, including human rights, in foreign policy is presented in George F. Kennan, "Morality and Foreign Policy," *Foreign Affairs* 63 (Winter 1985–1986): 205–218. A rather more nuanced version of a similar argument is provided in Chapter 4 of Hedley Bull, *The Anarchical Society*, 3rd ed. (Columbia University Press, 2002). For a counter-argument, see Chapter 6 of Jack Donnelly, *Realism and International Relations* (Cambridge University Press, 2000).

Henry Shue's *Basic Rights: Subsistence, Affluence, and U.S. Foreign Policy*, 2nd ed. (Princeton University Press, 1996), provides a subtle and powerful argument for the equal and overriding priority of rights to security, subsistence, and liberty; an extended discussion of the duties that flow from these rights; and a sensitive (if now rather dated) application of these theoretical ideas to U.S. foreign policy. A shorter version of the core of the argument is available in Shue's essay "Rights in the Light of Duties," in Peter G. Brown and Douglas MacLean, eds., *Human Rights and U.S. Foreign Policy: Principles and Applications* (Lexington Books, 1979). For attacks on the idea of economic and social rights, see Maurice Cranston, "Are There Any Human Rights?" *Daedalus* 112 (Fall 1983): 1–18 and Hugo Adam Bedau, "Human Rights and Foreign Assistance Programs," in the Brown and MacLean reader. Sandra Fredman, eds., *Human Rights Transformed: Positive Rights and Positive Duties* (Oxford University Press, 2008), is an interesting philosophical discussion.

Daniel J. Whelan and Jack Donnelly, "The West, Economic and Social Rights, and the Global Human Rights Regime: Setting the Record Straight," *Human Rights Quarterly* 29(4) (2007): 908–949, provides a detailed empirical refutation of the often-encountered idea that the West resisted including economic and social rights in the Universal Declaration and the Covenants. Whelan, *Indivisible Human Rights: A History* (University of Pennsylvania Press, 2010), traces the history of the ideas of interdependence and indivisibility in discussions in the United Nations.

Notes

1 This is not exactly correct. Although children are human beings, they usually are not thought to have, for example, a right to vote, on the grounds that they are not fully developed. Once they reach a certain age, however, they must be recognized as holding all human rights equally. Similarly, those who suffer from severe mental illness are often denied the exercise of many rights—but only until they regain full use and control of their faculties. Furthermore, both children and those with severe mental disabilities still have, and must be allowed to enjoy equally, all other human rights. And the 1989 Convention on the Rights of the Child and the 2006 Convention on the Rights of Persons with Disabilities seek to clarify this special status and specify a variety of rights to special protections.

2 We can also note that other standard arguments for recognizing only this one economic right fail to stand up to scrutiny. For example, there are many ways other than a right to property to guarantee economic security and economic participation in society (e.g., rights to work, social insurance, and old-age pensions). In fact, those other mechanisms are vastly more important for most people in modern societies.

3 Henry Shue, *Basic Rights: Subsistence and Affluence in U.S. Foreign Policy* (Princeton University Press, 1996; originally published 1980), 51–64.

4 In what follows, we focus on the "external" dimensions of sovereignty; that is, sovereignty as it appears in the relations of states, where the emphasis is on the absence of any superior (sovereign) above the state and thus on the sovereign equality of states. The "internal" dimensions of sovereignty concern the supreme authority of the state within its territory. Here, the focus is on the legal and political superiority of the state over other actors. In the contemporary world, internal sovereignty is usually seen as resting on the state acting in the name and interests of the people: "popular sovereignty."

5 For an extended discussion of this idea, see Hedley Bull, *The Anarchical Society* (Columbia University Press, 1977).

6 Robert Gilpin, "The Richness of the Tradition of Political Realism," in *Neorealism and Its Critics*, edited by Robert O. Keohane (Columbia University Press, 1986), 305.

7 Hans Morgenthau, *Politics Among Nations*, 2nd ed. (Alfred A. Knopf, 1954), 9.

8 George F. Kennan, "Morality and Foreign Policy," *Foreign Affairs* 64 (Winter 1985–1986): 206; George F. Kennan, *Realities of American Foreign Policy* (Princeton University Press, 1954), 48; George F. Kennan, *The Cloud of Danger: Current Realities of American Foreign Policy* (Little, Brown, 1977), 45.

9 Herbert Butterfield, *Christianity, Diplomacy, and War* (Epworth Press, 1953), 11.

10 Robert J. Art and Kenneth N. Waltz, "Technology, Strategy, and the Uses of Force," in *The Use of Force*, edited by Robert J. Art and Kenneth N. Waltz (University Press of America, 1983), 6.

3 The Relative Universality of Human Rights

Human rights are understood today to be universal rights, held by every human being, everywhere in the world. The foundational international legal instrument is the *Universal* Declaration of Human Rights. The first operative paragraph of the Vienna Declaration and Programme of Action adopted at the 1993 World Conference on Human Rights insists that "the universal nature of these rights and freedoms is beyond question." The universality of human rights is a central theme in diplomatic, political, popular, and academic discussions alike.

As we discussed in Chapter 1, though, the idea of moral and political claims against states and other actors available to every human being simply because they are human is relatively recent. How can such historically particular ideas and practices reasonably purport to be universal? And how does this purported universality relate to the undeniable cultural, political, economic, and historical diversity of our contemporary world?

The answer proposed here is that human rights are *relatively universal*, a notion that, although initially paradoxical, captures the essential universality *and* the essential particularity of internationally recognized human rights.

1 Universality and Relativity

Human rights are often presented as either universal or relative. In fact, though, they are both. And this duality is built into the very notion of universality.

The first definition of *universal* in the *Oxford English Dictionary* is "extending over, comprehending, or including the whole of something." *Universal*, in this sense, is "relative" to a particular class or group; the "something" that is encompassed. *Universal*, in this most basic sense, means "applies across all of a particular domain." For example, universal health care, universal primary education, and universal suffrage involve making health care, primary education, and voting rights available to all citizens, nationals, or residents of a country—not

DOI: 10.4324/9781003373520-4

everyone on the globe (let alone anywhere in the universe). A universal remote control neither controls all possible entertainment devices nor works everywhere in the universe—only in the movie *Independence Day* are alien spaceships designed so that a Mac can be effortlessly plugged into the command console—but controls only those devices that are standard for us here and now. Some American "universal remotes" won't even work in Europe.

There is a second sense of *universal*: "Of or pertaining to the universe in general or all things in it; existing or occurring everywhere or in all things." In this sense, though, little if anything in the empirical world is universal. Thus, the *Oxford English Dictionary* goes on immediately to indicate that this sense is "chiefly poetic or rhetorical," to which we would add "or philosophical or theological." Human rights are definitely *not* universal in this "occurring everywhere" sense.

They are, however, universal in at least three important "across a class" senses. We will call these international legal universality, overlapping consensus universality, and functional universality.

2 International Legal Universality

Human rights are universal in the sense that they have been accepted by almost all states as establishing obligations that are binding in international law. As we saw in Chapter 1, the seven core international human rights treaties—the two **International Human Rights Covenants** plus the conventions on racial discrimination, torture, and the rights of women, children, and persons with disabilities—have, on average, a 93 percent ratification rate. In this important sense, we can say that despite all the cultural, political, regional, and economic diversity in the contemporary world, there is near-universal agreement on both the existence and the substance of internationally recognized human rights.

International legal universality, however, is bounded. Although states have agreed that they have obligations with respect to these rights, there are, as we will see in more detail in later chapters, no significant international enforcement mechanisms. International legal universality is a universality of possession. It does not entail universal implementation, enforcement, or enjoyment.

Furthermore, international legal universality depends on the decisions of states, international organizations, transnational actors, and various national groups to treat human rights treaties as authoritative statements of internationally recognized human rights. International actors may in the future no longer give as much weight to, or even continue to accept, such principles and practices. Today, however, they have chosen, and are continuing to choose, human rights—making those rights, for us, today, effectively universal *for the purposes of international law and politics*.

3 Overlapping Consensus Universality

The second kind of universality—overlapping consensus universality—relies on a useful distinction drawn by the American political philosopher John Rawls. "Comprehensive doctrines," in Rawls' terminology, are sets of beliefs rooted in foundational philosophical, moral, religious, or ideological perspectives or worldviews. These are distinguished from what Rawls calls "political conceptions of justice:" narrower, constitutional accounts of the basic elements of political legitimacy, specified largely without reference to any specific comprehensive doctrines.

Proponents of very different, and even irreconcilable, comprehensive doctrines may reach an overlapping consensus on a political conception of justice. This consensus is only partial; it is overlapping, not complete. It is restricted to a political conception of justice. But it can be real and important.

Human rights can be readily grounded in a variety of moral theories. For example, they can be seen as encoded in natural law, called for by divine commandment, political means to further human good or utility, or institutions designed to produce virtuous citizens. Since the end of World War II, and especially since the end of the Cold War, more and more proponents of more and more comprehensive doctrines from more and more regions of the globe have come to see in human rights a political expression of their deepest values. Christians, Muslims, Jews, Buddhists, Confucians, atheists, Kantians, utilitarians, neo-Aristotelians, Marxists, social constructivists, and postmodernists, and many others as well—all for their own very different reasons—have come to participate in an overlapping consensus on the rights enumerated in the Universal Declaration.

We are quite familiar with this process within Western liberal democracies. For example, **Thomists** and **utilitarians** disagree about just about everything at the level of foundational moral theory. Thomists do not even consider utilitarianism to be a moral theory. Furthermore, both doctrines have throughout their history emphasized universal standards of righteousness rather than rights. (Jeremy Bentham, the founder of utilitarianism, famously described the idea of imprescriptible natural rights as "nonsense upon stilts.") Nonetheless, today most Thomists and most utilitarians endorse human rights *as a political conception of justice*. And much the same process is occurring today globally.

The implication of this argument is that human rights have no *single* philosophical or religious foundation. Rather, they have *multiple* foundations. And this multiplicity of foundations is essential to human rights (as we understand them).

Human rights *are* a (Rawlsian) *political* conception of justice. Human rights are a category of political, legal, and social theory—not moral theory. Human rights are not a moral "primitive" or foundation, an irreducible core that defines in the most basic possible sense what is right and wrong. They are one level removed from such foundations.

This removal however, strengthens, rather than weakens, human rights—as they actually function in the world. Multiple, diverse foundations make human rights much more strongly rooted. They provide a wide-ranging, complex, interlocking network of roots that supports and grounds international human rights far more effectively than any single taproot could.

Besides its intrinsic interest and importance, overlapping consensus universality also helps to explain international legal universality. The striking extent of the formal international legal endorsement of human rights reflects the fact that adherents of most leading comprehensive doctrines across the globe do, in fact, endorse internationally recognized human rights.

Again, we must carefully specify the limits of this universality. Not all the comprehensive doctrines that today endorse human rights have done so throughout all or even much of their history. Quite the contrary. Consider the West.

The ancient Greeks distinguished between civilized Hellenes (Greeks) and barbarians and, within Hellenic societies, made a variety of categorical moral and political distinctions based largely on birth and virtue—both of which were understood in deeply inegalitarian ways. The Romans may have had a somewhat wider conception of who was capable of being civilized. For legal and political purposes, however, a sharp line was drawn between civilized and barbarian peoples. And both class distinctions and slavery were central to Roman society.

During the medieval era, Europeans drew a comparable distinction between Christians and heathens, practiced slavery and serfdom, and regularly ranked men by their birth (noble or common) or their work (ruling and fighting, praying, or working to provide sustenance for the community). And, of course, *men* meant males. Everyone in both the ancient and medieval worlds "knew" that women of whatever status were not entitled to the same rights as men of similar status.

Therefore, if we date Western history to the Persian Wars in the first half of the fifth century BCE, then the West, for its first two millennia, had neither the idea nor the practice of human rights (understood as equal and inalienable rights that all human beings have and may exercise against society and the state). And, as we will see below, we cannot find much of an idea of human rights—or even a real hint of the practice—in early modern Europe either.

Much the same is true of all the great non-Western civilizations and almost all but the simplest nonstate societies. The international overlapping consensus on human rights largely emerged after World War II.

This does not make the contemporary consensus any less real or important. It does, however, point to its historical particularity.

4 Functional Universality

The emergence of overlapping consensus universality can itself be explained, in part, by global social changes over the past three centuries that provide the basis for the functional universality of human rights. Human rights represent a set of best practices to respond to certain standard threats to human dignity posed by modern markets and modern states.

Natural (or human) rights ideas first developed in the modern West. Early inklings are clear in Britain by the 1640s. A full-fledged natural rights theory is evident in John Locke's *Second Treatise of Government*, published in 1689 in support of Britain's so-called Glorious Revolution of 1688. A century later, the American and French Revolutions used these ideas as the basis for constructing new political orders.

The essential point here, however, is that human rights ideas and practices developed in response to the conditions of modernity, not out of a cultural "Westernness." Nothing in the West's classical or medieval culture made it unusually conducive to the development of human rights ideas. Quite the contrary, in the eleventh and twelfth centuries, parts of the

Islamic world, most notably the Fatimid Caliphate (909–1171), provided a much more tolerant cultural and religious environment that would on its face seem to have been more conducive to the development of human rights ideas and practices.

The Catholic Counter-Reformation and the intolerance of most ruling Protestant regimes in the sixteenth and seventeenth centuries suggest that early modern Europe was in many ways a particularly *un*supportive cultural milieu for developing human rights ideas, even setting aside European support for slavery and colonialism. The late sixteenth and early seventeenth centuries, it is important to remember, were an era of violent, often brutal, internecine and continental religious warfare. No widely endorsed reading of Christian scriptures before the late-seventeenth century supported the idea of a broad set of equal and inalienable individual rights held by all Christian men—let alone all men everywhere.

To grossly oversimplify, the emergence of states and markets lies behind both the "modernization" of Western economies, societies, polities, and cultures and the rise of human rights ideas and practices. Ever-more-powerful (capitalist) markets and (sovereign, bureaucratic) states disrupted, destroyed, or radically transformed traditional communities and their systems of mutual support and obligation—with traumatic consequences. Rapidly expanding numbers of (relatively) separate families and individuals faced a growing range of increasingly unbuffered economic and political threats to their interests and quality of life. New kinds of "standard threats" to human dignity[1] provoked a variety of remedial responses. By the late seventeenth century, claims of natural rights began to become a preferred mechanism for securing new visions of human dignity in these new social, economic, and political conditions.

In parallel with the early rise of states and markets, the Protestant Reformation disrupted the unity of Christian Europe, often quite violently. By the middle of the seventeenth century, however, states, due more to exhaustion than conviction, began to stop fighting over religion. (The Westphalia settlement of 1648 is conventionally presented as the start of modern international relations.) Although full religious equality remained very far off, limited religious toleration for selected Christian sects became the European norm and provided an important foundation for broader ideas of human rights (and state sovereignty). If individual choice was permitted on the salvation of one's immortal soul, the most important of all issues, why not allow it on issues of lesser magnitude as well? And where religious conformity was enforced, it was done by sovereign rulers (not a "universal" Church).

Add to this the growing possibilities for physical and social mobility and we have the crucible in which contemporary human rights ideas and practices were formed. Privileged ruling groups faced a growing barrage of demands from an ever-widening range of dispossessed groups—first for relief from particular legal and political disabilities and eventually for full inclusion on the basis of equality. Such demands took many forms, including appeals to scripture, church, morality, tradition, justice, natural law, order, social utility, and national strength. But as we moved into the eighteenth and nineteenth centuries, claims of equal and inalienable natural/human rights became increasingly common.

These processes of threat and response first occurred in modern Europe. Modern markets and states, however, have spread to all corners of the globe, bringing with them roughly the same threats to human dignity—creating a functional universality for human rights. Human rights represent the most effective response yet devised by human ingenuity to a wide range of threats to human dignity that have become nearly universal across the globe.

Westerners, as we have already noted, had no special preexisting cultural proclivity toward human rights. Rather, they had the (good or bad) fortune to be the first to experience the indignities of modern markets and states. These new forms of suffering and injustice called forth new remedies. One increasingly popular and effective response was claims of equal and inalienable individual human rights. And nothing better has yet been devised for coping with the vulnerabilities created by markets and states.

Human rights remain the only proven-effective mechanism for ensuring human dignity in societies dominated by markets and states. The nearly universal spread of the idea of human rights is rooted in the fact that they represent the record of a process of social learning about protections needed as preconditions for a life of dignity in a world of modern markets and states.

Although this universality is rooted in a particular time and place—or, more precisely, in a particular kind of social structure—human rights are (relatively) universal for us now. And by *us*, we mean virtually everyone on this planet. Almost all of us live in a world of modern markets and modern states, which need to be tamed by human rights if those powerful institutions are to be made compatible with a life of dignity for all human beings.

5 Anthropological or Historical Relativity

The preceding sections clearly show that human rights are *not* universal either historically or anthropologically. Although it is often claimed that most cultures and civilizations have long-standing indigenous ideas and practices of human rights, such arguments lack empirical support. We have just seen that the idea and practice of human rights is historically relatively recent in the West. The same is true of other areas of the world.

As we saw in Chapter 2, rights—entitlements that ground claims with a special force—are one mechanism for realizing social and political values. Human rights—equal and inalienable entitlements held by all individuals that may be exercised against the state and society—are a very distinctive way to seek to realize social values such as justice and human flourishing. But they are not the only way.

The literature on so-called non-Western conceptions of human rights regularly confuses values such as limited government or respect for personal dignity with the practice of equal and inalienable individual human rights to realize such values. For example, Dunstan Wai argues that traditional African beliefs and institutions "sustained the 'view that certain rights should be upheld against alleged necessities of state.'"[2] This confuses human rights with limited government. Government has been limited on a variety of grounds other than human rights, including divine commandment, tradition, legal rights, and extralegal checks such as a balance of power or the threat of popular revolt.

Similarly, Hung-Chao Tai, discussing traditional Chinese views, argues that

> the concept of human rights concerns the relationship between the individual and the state; it involves the status, claims, and duties of the former in the jurisdiction of the latter. As such, it is a subject as old as politics.[3]

Not all political relationships, however, are governed by, related to, or even consistent with human rights. What the state owes to those over whom it rules is indeed a perennial question of politics. Human rights provide one answer. Other answers include divine-right monarchy, the dictatorship of the proletariat, the principle of utility, aristocracy, theocracy, and democracy.

Much the same confusion is evident in the extensive literature claiming that "Islam has laid down some universal fundamental rights for humanity as a whole, which are to be observed and respected under all circumstances ... fundamental rights for every man by virtue of his status as a human being."[4] For example, the scriptural passages that Khalid M. Ishaque argues establish a "right to protection of life" are in fact divine injunctions not to kill and to consider life inviolable.[5] The "right to justice" proves to be instead a duty of rulers to establish justice. The "right to freedom" is a duty not to enslave unjustly (not even a general duty not to enslave). "Economic rights" turn out to be duties to help to provide for the needy. And the purported "right to freedom of expression" is actually an obligation to speak the truth.

Even the claim that because "different civilizations or societies have different conceptions of human well-being ... they have a different attitude toward human rights issues" is misleading.[6] Other societies may have (similar or different) attitudes toward issues that we consider today to be matters of human rights. But without a widely understood concept of human rights advocated by some important segment of that society, it is hard to imagine that they could have *any* attitude toward human rights. And it is precisely the idea of equal and inalienable rights that one has simply because one is a human being that was missing in traditional Asian, African, Islamic, Latin American, and (as we saw above) Western societies.

Most arguments of anthropological universality are rooted in an admirable desire to show cultural sensitivity, respect, or tolerance. In fact, however, they impose an alien analytical framework that misunderstands and misrepresents the foundations and functioning of those societies.

Just to be clear, we are *not* claiming that Islam, Confucianism, or traditional African ideas cannot support internationally recognized human rights. Quite the contrary, as we saw in Section 3.3, they not only logically can but in practice increasingly do. The point here simply is that Islamic, Chinese, and African societies, *like Western societies*, did not endorse human rights ideas or practices until rather recently.

6 Cultural Relativism

We have already seen that human rights are historically relative to the modern era and that their foundations are relative to a number of comprehensive doctrines that participate in the contemporary overlapping consensus on internationally recognized human rights. Human rights, however, are *not* culturally relative in any strong sense of that term. Their justification is not based on any particular culture. Neither is their endorsement or practice tied to a particular culture or set of cultures.

In particular, as we saw above, there is nothing special about the West or Western culture that made it particularly suited for human rights. For example, Christianity throughout most of its history has supported deeply hierarchical forms of social and political life that organized people according to divisions—of culture, religion, gender, race, and occupation—rather than drawing political attention to what bound all human beings (or even all Christian men). And although Christian ideas have regularly inspired mass movements from below, such movements were effectively repressed in the name of Christianity throughout almost all of Christian history.

Nonetheless, when men and women faced new social conditions—when traditional hierarchies were destroyed and modern ones built—these Christian and other Western cultural resources increasingly came to be appropriated by new groups, in new ways, on behalf of the idea of universal human rights. And today, most Christians draw attention to biblical texts that point in a universalistic and egalitarian direction.

If the medieval Christian world of crusades, serfdom, and hereditary aristocracy could become today's world of liberal and social democratic welfare states, then it is hard to imagine a place where a similar transformation would be impossible. For example, Gandhi took Hinduism—on its face perhaps the least likely comprehensive doctrine to support human rights, given its traditional emphasis on qualitative caste differences and its denial of the moral significance of the category of human being—and transformed it into a powerful force in support of human rights.

No culture or comprehensive doctrine is by nature either compatible or incompatible with human rights. It is a matter of what particular people and societies make of and do with their cultural resources. Cultures are immensely malleable, as are the political expressions of comprehensive doctrines. Most if not all cultures have in their past denied human rights, both in theory and in practice. But that stops none of them from today finding human rights to be a profound expression of their deepest cultural values.

Denying that human rights derive from or are defined by culture implies neither the irrelevance of culture to human rights nor cultural homogenization. Quite the contrary, an overlapping consensus approach emphasizes the importance of people using their own cultural resources on behalf of their own human rights.

The problems that human rights were designed to remedy are today universal—as is the now almost hegemonic global endorsement of human rights as the best remedy. But people and peoples across the globe have come to universal human rights by a great variety of paths. And a central purpose of human rights is to protect the right of different individuals, groups, and peoples to make those choices of paths.

7 Universal Rights, Not Identical Practices

Although culture is not particularly relevant to the *definition* of human rights, it may be central to their *reception*. Different places at different times will draw on different cultural resources to provide support for human rights. And the different cultural idioms within and by which human rights are justified and explicated are of immense local importance. Therefore, effective advocacy of human rights requires knowledge of and sensitivity to how human rights fit with local cultures—and histories, and economies, and ecologies, and social structures.

Culture is also important for the details of implementation. We can think of three levels of universality and relativity.[7]

- Human rights are relatively universal at the level of the *concept*, the broad formulations characteristic of the Universal Declaration such as the claims in Articles 3 and 22 that everyone has "the right to life, liberty and security of person" and "the right to social security."
- Particular rights concepts, however, usually have different defensible *conceptions* (more detailed specifications of the overarching concept), introducing a very real element of relativity among universal human rights.
- Furthermore, any particular conception is likely to have many defensible *implementations*. At this level—for example, the design of electoral systems to realize the claim in Article 21 of the Universal Declaration that "everyone has the right to take part in the government of his country, directly or through freely chosen representatives"—the range of legitimate variation and relativity is substantial.

Functional and overlapping consensus universalities lie primarily at the level of human rights concepts. (The arguments that support these kinds of universality usually operate at a high level of abstraction that rarely reaches very far into the level of conceptions, let alone implementations.) The quite substantial range of legitimate variability at the levels of conceptions and implementations, however, means that substantial second- and third-level variations, by country, region, or other grouping, are fully compatible with the relative universality of internationally recognized human rights.

Striking legitimate variations exist even within regions. For example, conceptions and implementations of many economic and social rights differ dramatically between the United States and the countries of Western Europe. Important variations exist even within Europe. For example, Robert Goodin and his colleagues demonstrated important systematic differences between the welfare states of Germany and the Netherlands.[8]

Even here, though, we should be careful not to overstate the significance of culture, which is not the only, or even obviously the most important, source of diversity in justifications and implementations of human rights. There are often immense philosophical and religious differences *within* a culture that are absolutely central to how human rights are understood and practiced. And historical, political, economic, and simply accidental factors are no less important than culture in explaining the different ways that societies implement human rights.

Problem 3.1 on hate speech (at the end of this chapter) provides some pertinent examples of applying the ideas of comprehensive doctrines and concepts and conceptions of human rights to working through practical problems of human rights.

8 Universalism Without Imperialism

The universality of internationally recognized human rights clearly does not encourage, let alone require, global homogenization or the sacrifice of valued local practices. Quite the contrary, (relatively) universal human rights protect people from imposed conceptions of the good life, whether those visions are imposed by local or foreign actors.

The underlying purpose of human rights is to allow human beings, both individually and in groups that give meaning and value to their lives, to pursue their own vision of the good life. Such choices deserve our respect so long as they are consistent with comparable rights for others and reflect a plausible vision of human flourishing to which we can imagine a free people freely assenting. Understanding human rights as a political conception of justice supported by an overlapping consensus *requires* us to allow human beings, individually and collectively, considerable space to shape (relatively) universal rights to their particular purposes—within the constraints at the level of the concept established by functional, international legal, and overlapping consensus universalities.

The legacy of colonial imperialism does demand that Westerners in particular show special caution and sensitivity when advancing arguments of universalism in the face of opposing cultural values. Caution, however, must not be confused with inaction. Even if we are not entitled to impose our values on others, they are our values. They may demand that we act on them even in the absence of agreement by others, especially when that action does not involve force. If the practices of others are particularly objectionable, even strongly sanctioned traditions may deserve neither our respect nor our toleration. (Remember that slavery and sexism have been central parts of all the world's great civilizations throughout most of their histories.)

Such concerns are especially relevant to American foreign policy, which often confuses American interests with universal values. This particular variant of "American exceptionalism" is reflected in the view of many Americans that what's good for the United States is good for the rest of the world (see Chapter 8, Section 3).

The proper solution to the false universalism of a powerful actor mistaking its own interests for universal values, however, is not relativism but *relative universalism*. Without authoritative international standards, what is there to hold the United States (or any other power) accountable to? If international legal universality has no force, it is hard to find a ground for saying that human rights are not whatever the United States (or China) says they are. This is especially true in international relations, where normative disputes that cannot be resolved by rational persuasion tend to end up being resolved by political, economic, and cultural power—of which the United States today has more than any other country.

The relative universality of human rights can be a significant resource for calling the powerful, including the United States, to account—especially because the principal problem with American foreign policy is not where it does raise human rights concerns but where it does not, or where it allows them to be subordinated to other concerns. And although universal human rights are hardly a panacea for the world's problems, they do fully deserve the prominence they have received in recent decades. The world is a better place than it would have been without the spread of universal human rights ideas and practices. And, for the foreseeable future, universal human rights are likely to remain a vital resource in national, international, and transnational struggles for social justice and human dignity.

9 The Relativity *and* the Universality of Human Rights

Are human rights universal? Yes and no; it depends on the sense of *universal*. Are human rights relative? Yes and no; it depends on the sense of *relative*.

Sometimes the relativity of particular human rights practices and justifications deserves emphasis. Other times, the universality of internationally recognized human rights deserves emphasis. But both relativity and universality are essential to international human rights. There is danger both in treating the universal as if it were relative and in falsely universalizing contingent practices.

Human rights empower free people to build for themselves lives of dignity, value, and meaning. To build such lives anywhere in the contemporary world requires internationally recognized universal human rights. But one of the central purposes of universal human rights is to protect the free decisions of free people to justify and implement those rights in ways rooted in their own histories and experiences.

It is an empirical, not a logical, matter whether the legitimate demands of universality and relativity conflict or coordinate. Perhaps the most striking fact about the universality of human rights in the contemporary world, however, is how infrequently there is a truly fundamental—rather than contrived or disingenuous—conflict. And when there is indeed a real conflict, it is almost always restricted to a particular right or even just one part of an internationally recognized human right.

For example, one of us (Donnelly) has for more than four decades lectured overseas on issues of human rights and cultural relativism. He has often asked audiences to name the rights in the Universal Declaration that their society, culture, or religion rejects. Never has an audience objected to more than parts of two or three rights. For example, many Muslims reject the provision of Article 18 that allows anyone to change their religion. (Islam is ordinarily interpreted to prohibit Muslims from renouncing their faith.) But this is only one relatively small part of the internationally recognized right to freedom of religion, a right that Muslims strongly endorse. Another commonly encountered example involves some of the details of Article 16, which deals with family rights, especially the equal rights of women with respect to marriage. But, again, the basic right to marry and found a family is always strongly endorsed by those who challenge details of the conception elaborated in the Universal Declaration.[9]

It is common to talk about universality and relativity as the end points of a continuum. We think, though, that a multidimensional conception of universality and relativity is both more accurate and more conducive to constructive dialogue. For example, international legal, overlapping consensus, and functional universalities are probably better seen not as parts of a single entity called "universality" but as qualitatively different dimensions of the universality of internationally recognized human rights. This formulation encourages us to appreciate the multiple forms that both universality and relativity take—and the fact that, in different contexts, different dimensions of both appropriately come to the fore.

However we conceptualize it, the universality of human rights is relative to the contemporary world. The particularities of implementation are relative to history, politics, and contingent decisions. But at the level of the concept, as specified in the Universal

Declaration, human rights are universal. The formulation *relatively universal* is thus apt. Relativity modifies—operates within the boundaries set by—the universality of the body of interdependent and indivisible internationally recognized human rights.

Problem 3.1 Hate Speech

The Problem

Article 4(a) of the International Convention on the Elimination of All Forms of Racial Discrimination requires parties not just to prohibit violence and incitement to violence but also to "declare an offence punishable by law all dissemination of ideas based on racial superiority or hatred." When the US Senate ratified the Convention in 1994, it officially declared that the obligations of Article 4 were in direct conflict with the First Amendment to the US Constitution and therefore would not be accepted. In the past several years, Americans have been forced to contend with this dilemma in myriad instances—consider, for example, the significant blowback many colleges and universities have experienced over allowing pro-Palestinian groups to protest Israel's war against Hamas in Gaza, often chanting phrases ("From the [Jordan] River to the [Mediterranean] Sea, Palestine will be free!") that invoke the destruction of the State of Israel and possibly encourage genocide. How should Americans respond to this conflict between rights? What is the appropriate response for outsiders?

A Solution

Dealing with cases of conflicts between internationally recognized human rights can be facilitated by some general principles. In addition to the distinction among concepts, conceptions, and implementations introduced above (Section 3.7), we suggest the following.

1. Important differences in the character of the threats being faced are likely to justify variations. For example, countries with a recent history of violent ethnic conflict might reasonably choose to deal with issues of discrimination in general, and hate speech in particular, differently than would countries with different histories.
2. Variations that appeal to important principles or precepts in underlying comprehensive doctrines involved in the overlapping consensus deserve special consideration. The case of apostasy in Muslim countries, mentioned above, may fall under this principle.
3. Arguments claiming that a particular conception or implementation is, for cultural or historical reasons, deeply embedded within or of unusually great significance to some significant group in society deserve, on their face, sympathetic consideration (but cannot be treated as decisive and may not even be genuine).

4. Variations (or even deviations) from international standards are likely to be more acceptable the lower the level of legal and political coercion used to support them (which suggests both a greater degree of popular support, or at least acquiescence, and relatively limited damage to those who suffer as a result of these practices).

How do these criteria apply to the case of hate speech in the United States? The first two are not particularly relevant, but the last two do seem to imply some toleration for this American peculiarity.

Free speech has an especially important place historically among constitutional rights in the United States. And there is a long legal history of allowing even hate speech (or what used to be called "fighting words"), so long as it is restricted to speech that does not incite violence. Furthermore, even targets of hate speech are legally protected against not only violence but also incitement to violence. Many local and state jurisdictions have even increased the penalties for hate crimes (while leaving hate speech uncriminalized).

Hate *speech*, in other words, has been very narrowly understood and has been protected only so long as it remains unconnected to otherwise criminal activity. And part of the underlying justification for the American practice is that prohibiting speech because of its content harms those whose speech is prohibited and involves inegalitarian state support for particular viewpoints.

It thus seems relatively unproblematic for Americans to support this particular deviation from international human rights norms—especially because in ratifying the racial discrimination convention, the United States, as was its legal right, explicitly included a **reservation** that it would not be bound by this provision.

What about the views of those outside the United States? Although they ought to have some appreciation for American arguments, there is no compelling reason for them to accept them. Verbal pressure to criminalize hate speech is entirely appropriate. And those with a particular concern for the suffering it creates or an especially strong commitment to the general cause of international human rights standards may rightly feel compelled to draw critical attention to this internationally deviant American practice and to press for its change.

Further Problems

Suppose that we are talking about hate speech in, say, Rwanda or Bosnia, only a couple decades after genocide. Or in Singapore, half a century after racial violence against Chinese helped to lead to its independence from Malaysia? These societies do in fact prohibit hate speech. But what if they were to move to allow it?

This example points to a very general problem, namely, different human rights regularly conflict with one another. (It also suggests that one of the ways in which societies differ is in how they handle such conflicts.)

What are some of the more prominent examples of conflicting human rights that you are familiar with? What are the implications of such regular and important conflicts for our understanding of the universality and relativity of human rights? Do such conflicts, when combined with the forms of relativity already noted above, leave much *as a practical matter* to the universality of human rights? Be careful to consider different types of countries (and different rights) in thinking about your answer.

Problem 3.2 Discrimination Based on Sexual Orientation and Gender Identity

The Problem

Many countries have in recent years undertaken more or less strenuous efforts to remedy discrimination based on sexual orientation or gender identity. In fact, LGBTQ+ (lesbian, gay, bisexual, transgender, queer, and others) rights have been a major focus of human rights activism in all Western and many non-Western countries. But gender and sexual minorities are not explicitly protected in international human rights law. And many countries are strongly opposed to prohibiting discrimination against them. How should international human rights advocates respond given the silence of international human rights law?

A Solution

Established nondiscrimination norms provide a strong prima facie case for international action on behalf of LGBTQ+ rights. Article 2 of the Universal Declaration reads, "Everyone is entitled to all the rights and freedoms set forth in this Declaration, without distinction of any kind, such as race, color, sex, language, religion, political or other opinion, national or social origin, property, birth or other status." The language clearly says *everyone* is entitled to *all* human rights *without distinction of any kind.* And several articles in the Declaration typically begin "Everyone is entitled ...," "Everyone has the right ...," or "No one shall be...." *Everyone*, it seems, would include those with minority sexual or gender identities.

But "without distinction of any kind" does not really mean what it seems to say. For example, children and the mentally incompetent are, appropriately, excluded from the exercise of many rights. Those incarcerated for crimes are not permitted full personal liberty (as guaranteed in Article 3). In many countries, those who have not registered to vote may not exercise the right to participate in government through elected representatives (Article 21). And in many countries certain felons do not have equal access to public service (Article 21).

Furthermore, the phrase "such as race, color, ..." has typically been taken as something like an authoritative list of impermissible grounds. More precisely, it is widely held that all countries are required only to specify these grounds as impermissible—although they are, of course, free to add additional grounds.

In addition, had the drafters of the Declaration (and the Covenants) been asked, they almost certainly would have said that sexual orientation was *not* an impermissible ground for discrimination—and certainly the governments that voted to adopt the Universal Declaration would have agreed. For example, when Article 16 states "Men and women of full age, without any limitation due to race, nationality or religion, have the right to marry and to found a family," it was unquestionably assumed that this meant that men could marry women, and vice versa. Period.

Finally, we must consider the importance of consensus in the development of international human rights law. In the 1940s, 1950s, and 1960s, there was a clear and strong international consensus that discrimination based on sexual orientation was permissible. In some parts of the world, mostly in the West, such a consensus has collapsed. But there is nothing even close to a consensus on positive protections for gender or sexual minorities. Therefore, advocacy for LGBTQ+ rights is *not* advocacy for *internationally recognized* human rights.

This does not mean that *all* advocacy for protections for sexual minorities is problematic from the perspective of international human rights law. In many countries, LGBTQ+ people are subjected to private *violence* that is not prosecuted by the authorities, who sometimes even condone it. Such treatment is a clear violation of basic internationally recognized human rights. The **Human Rights Council** (see Chapter 5, Section 1) recognized that violence against people on the basis of their sexual orientation or gender identity was a grave concern and in 2011 commissioned a study on the problem (see below). Denial of rights to vote, education, health care, or social security simply because one has a minority gender identity is similarly prohibited by international human rights law. ("Everyone has a right to ..."). Even if we were to accept, as some argue, that homosexuality is a moral abomination, people cannot be denied the enjoyment of their human rights on the basis of their private (immoral) behavior.

Where to draw the line between permissible and impermissible discrimination will be a matter of considerable controversy. But the criminalization of consenting same-sex sexual activity is clearly *not* prohibited by international human rights law. And this is a powerful wedge that could be used to justify further discrimination.

Conversely, though, there is no reason that advocates of LGBTQ+ rights—individuals, NGOs, firms, states, and even regional and international organizations—should not campaign on their behalf. But they should be careful to differentiate these activities from the defense of internationally recognized human rights.

Consider the recent efforts at the United Nations Human Rights Council to move more deeply into this area. Based on reporting on the situation of violence against LGBTQ+ people by the secretary-general, in 2016 the Council debated a draft resolution that would have appointed an independent expert (see Chapter 5, Section 5) to continue this work. There was significant backlash, though, from conservative states around the world. The vote was twenty-three (yes) to eighteen (no) with six abstentions.[10] The independent expert was barely appointed.

What kept the six abstainers from voting "no" was a series of amendments to the resolution, which repeated, in particular, the importance of respecting "regional, cultural and religious value systems on matters associated with historical, cultural, social and religious sensitivities." Perhaps more importantly, the resolution "deplores" the use of external pressure and coercion to influence what are essentially domestic matters and "is concerned" with attempts to "undermine the international human rights system" by "imposing concepts … that fall outside of the internationally agreed human rights legal framework." Although these are in principle legitimate concerns and perhaps even legitimate grounds for opposing the development of new norms, suspicions that they are merely a pretext for protecting already prohibited discrimination and human rights violations also seem legitimate.[11]

We are far from comfortable with this "solution." But if we take seriously the commitment to international human rights law *as it is*, there seems to be no alternative, at least for the moment. The norms surrounding sexual orientation and gender identity are changing—but very slowly in many places.

The Council renewed the mandate of the Independent Expert in 2019, 2022, and 2025.[12] The 2019 renewal stripped the 2016 language reaffirming "social and cultural sensitivities." And the 2022 resolution took additional measures to extend the normative reach of the resolution beyond simply extending the Independent Expert's mandate. Its third operative clause called upon states

> to amend or repeal laws and policies that discriminate against persons on the basis of their sexual orientation and gender identity, and to take effective measures to prevent, investigate, and, where applicable, to prosecute acts of violence and discrimination based on those grounds…

The *issue* of discrimination based on sexual orientation and gender identity now seems pretty firmly embedded in the international human rights agenda. But there is nothing even close to serious discussions about, let alone consensus on, international norms specifying impermissible forms of discrimination and special protections such as those that have been established with respect to race, gender, and disability.

LGBTQ+ activists may chafe at this. But the normative power of international human rights rests in large measure on their universality—which is guaranteed by consensus. And, linking up to our earlier discussion of democracy and human rights, neither in international organizations nor in states do we want the fate of human rights to be decided by majority (or even supermajority) vote.

Further Problems

Can human rights advocates really allow systematic discrimination and suffering to be consistent with international human rights norms simply because within living memory most people denied the full humanity of a particular group?

How are LGBTQ+ people different from disabled persons, women, or members of racial minorities, who secured their own human rights convention? They did so, however, through the process of building international consensus. What should LGBTQ+ people and others concerned with their plight do until such consensus is achieved? (We suspect that the "right" answer is national action, supported by friendly and allied international actors, acknowledging a revision of human rights standards to better conform to contemporary conceptions of justice and equality.)

Given all of these questions, do we really have a *human rights* issue here for which international human rights law provides no adequate solution? Just how authoritative should we take the list of human rights accepted in international human rights law? What are the benefits and risks of talking of human rights that are not internationally recognized?

Discussion Questions

1. Make a list of all the arguments you can think of that can be made for cultural relativism. Which of these actually involve *cultural* factors? Which involve political, economic, or ideological factors? Are arguments of political relativism as persuasive as arguments of cultural relativism? Why? What about economic relativism? Is the distinction among culture, politics, and economics helpful or revealing? Why?
2. *Are* human rights ideas truly universal today? Are the differences between contemporary cultures and countries really primarily concerned with secondary or peripheral human rights issues? Many state governments insist on more fundamental disagreements. How should we deal with those arguments? How much force do they have?
3. Do recent changes in international relations have anything to tell us about the universality of human rights? Consider, for example, the fall of the communist bloc and democratization in much of the Third World. Then consider Islamic fundamentalism and the rise of nationalist ethnic hostilities. Now consider the rise of populist parties and illiberal democracies—and the global rise of China.
4. Why do so many people, in every region of the world, insist that their cultures have had human rights ideas and practices at times when they clearly have not? How much of this can be attributed to the notion that the legitimacy of cultures is somehow dependent on their conformity with "modern" Western ideas?
5. With respect to human rights (or any other notion of justice), is the achievement of consensus morally important? Politically important? Why or why not?
6. What are some of the principal threats to human dignity that are *not* connected with markets and states? How important is their absence from the list of internationally recognized human rights? If they are very significant, how much does this undermine the claim for even the relative universality of human rights?
7. Just how malleable is culture? Even if it is immensely malleable across extended periods, is it relatively static over a few decades? Is that not the time frame of politics?
8. Should the United States be held to the same standards as everyone else? If not, how can Americans justify holding others to human rights standards?

Suggested Readings

The literature on human rights and cultural relativism is immense—although most of the major work was done in the 1980s, 1990s, and 2000s. Excellent short overviews can be found in Ann-Belinda S. Preis, "Human Rights as Cultural Practice: An Anthropological Critique," *Human Rights Quarterly* 18 (May 1996): 286–315; Andrew J. Nathan, "Universalism: A Particularistic Account," in Lynda Bell, Andrew J. Nathan, and Ilan Peleg, eds., *Negotiating Culture and Human Rights* (Columbia University Press, 2001), 349–368; Abdullahi A. An-Na'im, "Towards a Cross-Cultural Approach to Defining International Human Rights Standards," in Abdullahi A. An-Na'im, ed., *Human Rights in Cross-Cultural Perspectives* (University of Pennsylvania Press, 1992), 19–43; and Onuma Yasuaki, "Toward an Intercivilizational Approach to Human Rights," in Joanne Bauer and Daniel Bell, eds., *The East Asian Challenge for Human Rights* (Cambridge University Press, 1999), 103–123. See also Bhikhu Parekh, "Non-Ethnocentric Universalism," in Tim Dunne and Nicholas J. Wheeler, eds., *Human Rights in Global Politics* (Cambridge University Press, 1999), 128–159.

Classic statements of radical relativism are Adamantia Pollis and Peter Schwab, "Human Rights: A Western Construct with Limited Applicability," in Adamantia Pollis and Peter Schwab, eds., *Human Rights: Cultural and Ideological Perspectives* (Praeger, 1979), 1–19; and Alison Dundes Rentlen, "The Unanswered Challenge of Relativism and the Consequences for Human Rights," *Human Rights Quarterly* 7 (November 1985): 514–540. For a sharp response to such views, see Rhoda E. Howard, "Cultural Absolutism and the Nostalgia for Community," *Human Rights Quarterly* 15 (May 1993): 315–338.

Two superb books that treat the complexities of rights and related ideas in Chinese philosophy and political practice are Stephen C. Angle, *Human Rights and Chinese Thought: A Cross-Cultural Inquiry* (Cambridge University Press, 2002); and Marina Svensson, *Debating Human Rights in China* (Rowman and Littlefield, 2003). Both are extremely sympathetic to the similarities and the differences between Chinese and Western ideas and their significant changes over time. Even for readers with no special interest in China, these books are well worth reading. They offer careful and detailed understandings of complex issues that are far too often handled in glib generalities. Zhang Yongjin and Barry Buzan, "China and the Global Reach of Human Rights," *The China Quarterly* 241 (2020): 169–190, although they do not directly address issues of relativism, explore the complicated engagement of China with the global human rights regime.

Ann Elizabeth Mayer, *Islam and Human Rights: Tradition and Politics*, 5th ed. (Westview Press, 2013), does much the same for the Islamic world. Nader Hashemi and Emran Qureshi, *Islam and Human Rights: Critical Concepts in Islamic Studies* (Routledge, 2022) is a four-volume compendium that provides a comprehensive and dispassionate understanding of the relationship between Islam, Muslim societies and human rights.

The following are among the most interesting arguments in support of indigenous non-Western conceptions of human rights: Adbul Aziz Said, "Precept and Practice of Human Rights in Islam," *Universal Human Rights [Human Rights Quarterly]* 1, no. 1 (1979): 63–80; Fouad Zakaria, "Human Rights in the Arab World: The Islamic Context," in *Philosophical Foundations of Human Rights* (UNESCO, 1986), 227–242; Majid Khadduri, "Human Rights in Islam," *Annals* 243 (January 1946): 77–81; Dunstan M. Wai, "Human Rights in

Sub-Saharan Africa," in Schwab and Pollis, eds., *Human Rights*, 115–144; Kwasi Wiredu, "An Akan Perspective on Human Rights," in Patrick Hayden, ed., *The Philosophy of Human Rights* (Paragon House, 2001), 298–314; Timothy Fernyhough, "Human Rights and Precolonial Africa," in Ronald Cohen, Goran Hyden, and Winston P. Nagan, eds., *Human Rights and Governance in Africa* (University Press of Florida, 1993), 39–73; Asmarom Legesse, "Human Rights in African Political Culture," in Kenneth W. Thompson, ed., *The Moral Imperatives of Human Rights: A World Survey* (University Press of America, 1980), 123–136; Yougindra Khushalani, "Human Rights in Asia and Africa," *Human Rights Law Journal* 4, no. 4 (1983): 403–442; Ralph Buultjens, "Human Rights in Indian Political Culture," in Thompson, ed., *Moral Imperatives of Human Rights*; James C. Hsiung, "Human Rights in an East Asian Perspective," in James C. Hsiung, ed., *Human Rights in an East Asia: A Cultural Perspective* (Paragon House, 1985), 1–30; and Lo Chung-Sho, "Human Rights in the Chinese Tradition," in UNESCO, ed., *Human Rights: Comments and Interpretations* (Columbia University Press, 1949), 186–190.

Three recent works in various ways challenge contemporary relativist arguments. Using evidence from CEDAW and the European Court of Human Rights, Frederick Cowell's, *Defensive Relativism: The Use of Cultural Relativism in International Legal Practice* (University of Pennsylvania Press, 2022) argues that the practice of defensive relativism is not about alternative legal theories, concepts, or practices but a tactic that states use to circumvent international human rights law. Santino Ayuel Longar Dau, *International Human Rights in Post-Colonial Africa* (University of Wales Press, 2024) argues that "collectivist" relativist arguments in Africa are increasingly irrelevant to modern African states, advancing legal and moral justifications for the universality of human rights standards. Kriangsak Kittichaisaree, *International Human Rights Law and Diplomacy* (Edward Elgar, 2022) investigates the idea of human rights relativism and allegations of hypocrisy and double standards, as well as illuminating the diplomatic methods employed by nations wishing to evade human rights obligations.

Finally, one of us (Donnelly) has written extensively on questions of universality and relativism. This chapter summarizes views that are developed in more detail in Part 2 of *Universal Human Rights in Theory and Practice*, 3rd ed. (Cornell University Press, 2013).

Notes

1 Henry Shue, *Basic Rights: Subsistence, Affluence, and U.S. Foreign Policy* (Princeton University Press, 1996; originally published 1980), 29–34.

2 Dunstan M. Wai, "Human Rights in Sub-Saharan Africa," in *Human Rights: Cultural and Ideological Perspectives*, edited by Adamantia Pollis and Peter Schwab (Praeger, 1979), 116.

3 Hung-Chao Tai, "Human Rights in Taiwan: Convergence of Two Political Cultures?," in *Human Rights in East Asia: A Cultural Perspective*, edited by James C. Hsiung (Paragon House, 1985), 77, 79.

4 Fouad Zakaria, "Human Rights in the Arab World: The Islamic Context," in *Philosophical Foundations of Human Rights*, edited by UNESCO (UNESCO, 1986), 228. Cf. Abul A'la Mawdudi, *Human Rights in Islam* (Islamic Foundation, 1976), 10.

5 Khalid M. Ishaque, "Human Rights in Islamic Law," *Review of the International Commission of Jurists* 12 (1974): 32–38.

6 Manwoo Lee, "North Korea and the Western Notion of Human Rights," in Hsiung, *Human Rights in East Asia*, 129, 131.
7 This scheme is developed in greater detail in Jack Donnelly, *Universal Human Rights in Theory and Practice*, 3rd ed. (Cornell University Press, 2013), pp. 99–105.
8 Robert E. Goodin et al., *The Real Worlds of Welfare Capitalism* (Cambridge University Press, 1999).
9 Other examples, such as pornography and homosexuality, miss the mark. Tolerance of neither is required by international human rights norms (although the Human Rights Council has begun to make some headway on the issue of sexual orientation and gender identity; see below in this chapter). Where they are allowed, they involve particular conceptions of the rights to free speech and nondiscrimination that are permitted but not mandated by international human rights norms.
10 The resolution adopted was A/HRC/32/2, July 15, 2016.
11 Incidentally, when the report of the Human Rights Council came up for a vote in the UN General Assembly's Third Committee in November 2016, a block of states led by the African group attempted to "defer consideration" of the appointment of the independent expert "in order to allow time for further consultations to determine the legal basis" of the mandate (UN Doc A/C.3/71/L.46). That provision was stripped out by an amendment to the draft resolution (A/C.3/71/L.52), but the vote on the amendment was exceedingly narrow: 84–77–17. The attempt to thwart a decision of the Human Rights Council was itself unusual. That the vote was so close reinforces our main argument.
12 The 2025 extension was by a vote of 29 in favor, 15 opposed (Algeria, Bangladesh, Burundi, China, Côte d'Ivoire, Democratic Republic of the Congo, Ethiopia, Gambia, Indonesia, Kuwait, Malawi, Maldives, Morocco, Qatar, Sudan), with 3 abstentions (Benin, Ghana, Kyrgyzstan).

The Unity of Human Rights 4

The universality of human rights, discussed in Chapter 3, is closely connected to the unity or indivisibility of internationally recognized human rights.

The most authoritative statement of the international community's understanding of the unity of human rights is found in Paragraph 5 of the Vienna Declaration and Programme of Action, adopted by consensus at the conclusion of the 1993 World Conference on Human Rights:

> All human rights are universal, indivisible and interdependent and interrelated. The international community must treat human rights globally in a fair and equal manner, on the same footing, and with the same emphasis. While the significance of national and regional particularities and various historical, cultural and religious backgrounds must be borne in mind, it is the duty of States, regardless of their political, economic and cultural systems, to promote and protect all human rights and fundamental freedoms.

All types or categories of human rights are to be treated as equally fundamental. And differences of history, culture, or development may not be used to justify treating different categories of human rights differently. All states must protect and promote *all* human rights *equally*.

Paragraph 5 has been reaffirmed in literally thousands of UN resolutions and other documents adopted over the past three decades. The rhetoric of "indivisibility," however, has shifted over time, reflecting changing priorities that emerged as a result of the end of colonialism, the uneven pace of economic development, and the global political context of the Cold War. Only in the immediate post-Cold War period did this particular understanding of indivisibility emerge.

1 Interdependent and Interrelated Rights

Despite the ubiquitous repetition of the formula "indivisible, interdependent, and interrelated," there is no agreed-upon definition of these terms. The terms often are treated as

DOI: 10.4324/9781003373520-5

interchangeable. But why, then, use three words instead of one? And on closer examination, it becomes clear that the terms describe different aspects of and approaches to the *unity* of internationally recognized human rights.

1.1 Interdependent Rights

To say that rights are interdependent suggests that their effective enjoyment requires (is dependent on) other rights—and vice versa. Furthermore, this interdependence crosses categories. For example, the civil right to freedom of movement is necessary for the full enjoyment of some other civil rights (such as freedom of assembly), some political rights (such as the right to vote), and many economic and social rights (the right to work, for example).

The language of interdependence emphasizes that particular human rights are parts of a larger whole. And that whole is more than the sum of its parts. Denial of one right impedes enjoyment of other rights. Conversely, enjoying one right can improve the enjoyment of others. The language of interdependency also underscores that states are not free to merely pick and choose from the catalog of internationally recognized human rights.

1.2 Interrelated Rights

The idea that rights are interrelated emphasizes their connectedness. (Early UN resolutions used the term *interconnected*.) This suggests a certain permeability of rights and categories of rights.[1]

Relatedness also suggests similarity—that they share common characteristics. In particular, when the UN General Assembly voted in 1952 to divide the "Covenant on Human Rights" into separate treaties dealing with civil/political and economic/social/cultural rights, it insisted that the two Covenants have "as many similar provisions as possible." This helps to explain, for example, their identical preambles and nondiscrimination provisions and the inclusion of a right to self-determination in both treaties.

As they were originally drafted and adopted, however, the two Covenants exhibited significant differences. Here we will address two: differences in states' legal obligations and the design of institutions for monitoring implementation of those obligations. (In the next section, we will consider some more political and symbolic differences.)

1.2.1 The Covenants: "Immediate" vs. "Progressive" Obligations

Each Covenant's second article outlines the general obligations states have with respect to the treaty as a whole.

Article 2 of the **International Covenant on Civil and Political Rights** (ICCPR) requires states (a) "to adopt such laws or other measures as may be necessary to give effect to the rights recognized in the present Covenant;" (b) to provide "effective remedy" in the case of violations; and (c) to ensure that those remedies are enforced by the state.

In contrast, Article 2 of the **International Covenant on Economic, Social and Cultural Rights** (ICESCR) only requires states to "take steps ... to the maximum of its available resources, with a view to achieving progressively the full realization of the rights recognized in the present Covenant." It also allows developing countries the option not to guarantee these rights to "non-nationals."

This differentiation between what are often called "immediate" and "progressive" obligations was for many years interpreted by critics of economic and social rights to imply that civil and political rights were more important or fundamental—and that economic and social rights were largely programmatic aspirations. This highly partisan reading, however, confuses importance with ease of implementation. (And, even then, why not say that the more difficult-to-implement rights are the more important ones?) This reading also ignores the crucial fact that the ICESCR establishes *obligations* "to the maximum of [a state's] available resources." It also ignores the fact that in practice *full* implementation of the political, legal, and judicial reforms necessary for civil and political rights usually takes quite a long time. And the ICCPR in fact does *not* specify that its obligations are "immediate."

1.2.2 Institutions and Mechanisms for Monitoring

The second major difference between the Covenants concerns their monitoring procedures and mechanisms (see Chapter 5, Section 3). The ICCPR established the **Human Rights Committee**: a monitoring body of independent experts empowered to review the reports of states-parties, consider disputes between states about compliance, and, where authorized by the state in question, investigate petitions by individuals or groups alleging violations. The Committee created for itself a third function: interpretation of the text of the Covenant through the elaboration of "General Comments."

The ICESCR, however, created no such committee. While states were required to submit periodic reports (as with the ICCPR), those reports were sent to an ad hoc committee of the UN's Economic and Social Council (ECOSOC) for review. And there were no procedures for handling disputes between states or receiving individual or group petitions.

After the Covenants entered into force, though, the international community began to appreciate that these differing procedures had no basis in the nature of the rights themselves and were fundamentally incompatible with the unity of human rights. In 1985, ECOSOC established a new **Committee on Economic, Social, and Cultural Rights** (CESCR) to review periodic reports by states and issue general comments (see Chapter 5, Section 3.2), parallel to the Human Rights Committee. And in 2011, an **optional protocol** to the ICESCR allowed the CESCR to adjudicate state-to-state complaints, receive individual and collective petitions, and initiate inquiries into alleged violations of the Covenant. This move toward greater institutional interrelatedness also strengthened the principle of the unity of all internationally recognized human rights.

2 The Indivisibility of Human Rights

Indivisibility as it relates to human rights is more difficult to define precisely. And it carries especially great conceptual and symbolic weight. The word itself, in the dictionary definition sense of "incapable of being divided, in reality or thought," conjures powerful symbolic imagery. For example, the American Pledge of Allegiance declares that Americans constitute "one nation, indivisible." Or consider the Catholic belief in the indivisibility of the Holy Trinity—God the Father, the Son, and the Holy Spirit. There is one God but in three instantiations: all are God.

The words *interdependent* and *interrelated* suggest separability—although at a cost when kept separate. *Indivisibility* emphasizes that division, if it occurs, harms the thing in question.

International understandings of indivisibility, however, have changed over time. Below we focus on four significant nodes in this evolution, in which the concept of unity was articulated by the international community: two fundamental UN General Assembly resolutions and two global human rights conference declarations. Each had a distinct understanding of indivisibility, both conceptually and politically. Although the following discussion may at times seem overly skewed towards "UN nerds," we think it is important for students to deeply engage some of the more subtle theoretical and practical implications of "indivisibility." It also illustrates the difficulties and complexities of seeking consensus.

2.1 UN General Assembly Resolution 421 (V) (1950)

In 1949 and 1950, the Commission on Human Rights began to draft a legally binding treaty to give effect to the Universal Declaration, then called the "Covenant on Human Rights." The original draft (proposed by the United Kingdom), however, was limited to core civil rights. Many delegations in the Commission and General Assembly raised objections to the absence of economic, social, cultural, and political rights as "anachronistic" and "retrograde" and threat to the universality of the Universal Declaration.[2] A delegate from Argentina remarked that the United Nations should not attempt to "divide the indivisible."[3]

Therefore, the UN General Assembly instructed the Commission in Resolution 421 (V) to include "a clear expression of" those rights in the Covenant. The preamble to this section of the resolution[4] included the following preamble which helps us to understand their motivations and aims.

> *Whereas* the Covenant should be drawn up in the spirit and based on the principles of the Universal Declaration of Human Rights,
>
> *Whereas* the Universal Declaration regards man as a person to whom all civil and political freedoms as well as economic, social and cultural rights indubitably belong,
>
> *Whereas* the enjoyment of civic and political freedoms and the economic, social and cultural rights are interdependent and interrelated,
>
> *Whereas* when deprived of economic, social and cultural rights, man does not represent the ideal of the free man…

Declaring economic, social, and cultural rights "interdependent and interconnected" with civil and political rights reflected the "spirit" of the Universal Declaration. Moreover, depriving human beings of these rights (by not including them in the Covenant) would violate the fundamental ideal of human freedom that the Declaration envisions.

In 1951, the Commission, following these instructions, drafted several articles addressing the economic, social, and cultural rights in the Declaration (but excluding the right to property) as well as a reporting procedure for monitoring the implementation of those rights (rather than a complaints procedure, which was already included in the draft Covenant but only applied to civil and political rights).

In 1952, these differences in reporting procedures led the General Assembly to instruct the Commission to draft separate Covenants but emphasized that they should contain "as many similar provisions as possible" and be open simultaneously for ratification and signature in order to "emphasize the unity of the aim in view."[5] And in December 1966, the two Covenants were adopted simultaneously and presented together for signature and ratification by states.

2.2 The Proclamation of Teheran (1968)

Nevertheless, many concerns that economic, social, and cultural rights were sufficiently underemphasized persisted, especially in the post-colonial world. And when the United Nations convened an international conference on human rights in Tehran, Iran, in 1968 (to commemorate the twentieth anniversary of the Universal Declaration) the UN's membership had expanded dramatically, shifting the balance in the General Assembly toward the post-colonial Third World. The Proclamation of Teheran,[6] which was adopted by consensus, reflected their concerns, especially about ongoing colonialism, the "repugnant policy" of *apartheid* and related racial discrimination, and the slow pace of economic development, which now dominated the UN's agenda. With respect to human rights, we see this reflected in Paragraphs 12 and 13 of the Proclamation:

> 12. The widening gap between the economically developed and developing countries impedes the realization of human rights in the international community…
>
> 13. Since all human rights and fundamental freedoms are indivisible, the full realization of civil and political rights without the enjoyment of economic, social and cultural rights is impossible. The achievement of lasting progress in the implementation of human rights is dependent on sound and effective national and international policies of economic and social development.[7]

Paragraph 12 sets the (under)development context for Paragraph 13. The concept of indivisibility thus provides a fundamental normative foundation to the related imperative of development policies (at both the national and international levels). (We return to the topic of human rights and development in Chapter 13.)

This emphasis, however, can be read as a one-sided suggestion that economic, social, and cultural rights are *more* fundamental or foundational than civil and political rights. And in practice a growing number of states argued that civil and political rights, as important as they might be, can never be realized unless (or perhaps until) economic and social development is achieved (first). Therefore, the UN's adoption of the ICESCR was not enough. More was needed to address the problematic *global* economic situation facing developing countries.

2.3 UN General Assembly Resolution 32/130 (1977)

By the 1970s, the Global South had leveraged its majority in the UN General Assembly to call for the establishment of a "New International Economic Order" (NIEO), a sweeping (in the minds of some, radical) set of proposals designed to challenge the Global North's hegemony over global development, trade, and finance policies. This was accompanied by the UN's adoption of the "Charter of the Economic Rights and Duties of States" (CERDS), which was hailed by Global South leaders as a new type of charter, on par with the Universal Declaration. Although not explicitly human rights documents—only CERDS has a passing reference to "respect for human rights" as a general principle—they rhetorically reflected the contention of the majority of Third World states that their access to resources for economic development (including better terms of trade, aid, and financing) was a necessary *precondition* for the achievement of human rights. Therefore, economic rights must be realized first, followed (ostensibly) by civil and political rights.

In 1976, the Covenants finally garnered the minimum number of ratifications (thirty-five) to enter into force. The following year, spurred on by its delegates from the Global South (especially Senegal and Iran), the Commission on Human Rights convinced the General Assembly to adopt resolution 32/130, which sought to re-prioritize the UN's human rights agenda, placing more emphasis on economic and social rights understood within the framework of the NIEO and CERDS vision of development.

On the one hand, the older language of interdependence and indivisibility is repeated in the first operative paragraph of resolution 32/130:

> 1(a). All human rights and fundamental freedoms are indivisible and interdependent; equal attention and urgent consideration should be given to the implementation, protection and promotion of both civil and political, and economic, social and cultural rights...
>
> 1(b). (repeats verbatim the passage cited above from the Proclamation of Teheran)

On the other hand, the context for this statement is found in the eighth preambulatory paragraph of the resolution, which stipulates that,

> in accordance with the Universal Declaration of Human Rights, the ideal of free human beings enjoying freedom from fear and want can only be achieved if conditions are created whereby everyone may enjoy his economic, social and cultural rights as well as his civil and political rights.

What is evident is resolution 32/130's emphasis on addressing *global conditions* rather than the human rights situations within states. Subsequent operative clauses of 32/130 bear this out. They insisted that all human rights questions should be examined "globally, taking into account both the overall context of the various societies in which they present themselves..." and that the Commission should *prioritize* solutions to "mass and flagrant violations" stemming from *apartheid*, racial discrimination, colonialism, foreign domination and occupation, aggression and threats against national sovereignty, and the "refusal" (of states in the Global North) to recognize self-determination and permanent sovereignty over natural resources.[8] The resolution also noted that the realization of the NIEO was an "essential element" to the realization of human rights and should be "accorded priority."

Even in the shadow of 32/130's adoption, however, other forces were already beginning to push back against this reorientation of priorities. A greater emphasis on civil and political rights was beginning to reappear, especially in Cold War Europe. The Helsinki Final Act (1975), which settled many Cold War political and territorial issues left unresolved since the end of World War II, also compelled the Soviet Union and its Eastern European satellites to accept minimal monitoring of their compliance with basic (civil and political) human rights norms. The mid-1970s also saw Amnesty International receive the Nobel Peace Prize (in 1977); the emergence of new NGOs like Helsinki Watch (today, Human Rights Watch); the rise of dissident movements in Eastern Europe (for example, Charter 77, founded by Czech writer and later statesman Václav Havel); and the election (in 1978) of Karol Wojtyła of Poland as Pope John Paul II. In Latin America, national and transnational secular and religious civil society groups were instrumental in publicizing crimes committed during the "dirty wars" in the Southern Cone (Argentina, Uruguay, and Chile), prompting the Inter-American Commission on Human Rights to begin challenging repressive regimes in Latin America over enforced **disappearances** and torture. Furthermore, governments in the Global North began to include human rights in their foreign policy priorities.

2.4 The Vienna Declaration (1993)

The tension between a statist and developmental approach to human rights and a vision of interdependent and indivisible universal rights persisted through the 1980s. The end of the Cold War and the collapse of the Soviet Union, however, fundamentally altered this discourse. When a second global conference was held in Vienna in 1993 to chart a new and reinvigorated course for the advancement of human rights, the unity of human rights again became a central principle.

Recall Paragraph 5 of the Vienna Declaration, which we quoted at the beginning of this chapter.

> All human rights are universal, indivisible and interdependent and interrelated. The international community must treat human rights globally in a fair and equal manner, on the same footing, and with the same emphasis. While the significance of national and regional particularities and various historical, cultural and religious backgrounds must be borne in mind, it is the duty of States, regardless of their political, economic and cultural systems, to promote and protect all human rights and fundamental freedoms.[9]

Consider also Paragraph 8, which addresses the relationship between democracy, development, and human rights:

> Democracy, development and respect for human rights and fundamental freedoms are interdependent and mutually reinforcing. Democracy is based on the freely expressed will of the people to determine their own political, economic, social and cultural systems and their full participation in all aspects of their lives. In the context of the above, the promotion and protection of human rights and fundamental freedoms at the national and international levels should be universal and conducted without conditions attached. The international community should support the strengthening and promoting of democracy, development and respect for human rights and fundamental freedoms in the entire world.[10]

These restatements of basic principles rebalanced the relationship between civil and political and economic and social rights, decisively reaffirming their fundamental equality and equal importance. Paragraph 5 clearly states that countries cannot use underdevelopment, past colonialism, or different cultural values as pretexts for failing to promote and protect *any* category of human rights. Paragraph 8 reminds us that only truly participatory democracy and development policies are consistent with human rights and that protecting and promoting human rights must not be subject to (any) "conditions."

The strength of these assertions of universality reflected both the relative weakness of both China, which was still something of an international pariah following the Tiananmen massacres of democracy protestors on June 4, 1989, and post-Soviet Russia, as well as the growing attention to democracy in much of the Global South (especially in Latin America) and Central and Eastern Europe. The vision of development as a prerequisite to the full implementation of internationally recognized human rights did not die. It did, however, recede into the background. We will return to this issue in Chapter 13.

3 Politics, History, Theory, and Consensus

This book takes the body of international human rights law as establishing the meaning of *human rights* for the purposes of international action. The preceding sections, however, show that this body of law was shaped amidst political controversy and historical circumstances that were no less important than conceptual and theoretical reflection. Therefore, given the central role of politics and history in shaping international human rights law, we need to ask whether we really *should* take international law as an authoritative statement of the meaning of human rights. We suggest that although the making of laws, like the making of sausages, is not a pretty sight, the results in this case stand up rather well to theoretical scrutiny.

An important reason has been the centrality of the principle of **consensus** in the development of international human rights law. In the United Nations and other multilateral organizations, consensus procedures require the acquiescence (although not the active positive endorsement) of all participants. In principle, any single participant can prevent action. In practice, any single major actor or significant group of minor actors have a veto.

This usually slow and often difficult process insists that political conflict, although it probably cannot be fully overcome, must at least be reduced to "acceptable" levels. Consensus ensures that decisions are accepted rather than imposed. (We thus should expect the high ratification rates of international human rights treaties that we in fact see.)

But many states have no intention of implementing their international human rights obligations. Why then would they agree to the treaties in the first place? Largely, we suggest, because of the deep attraction of the idea of human rights in the contemporary world.

Few states are in a position simply to reject the idea of human rights. (North Korea is the exception that proves the rule.) Most feel a need to appear to support human rights, even as they go about systematically violating them. Hypocrisy is the compliment paid by vice to virtue. In the language that we introduced in the preceding chapter, international legal universality is rooted in overlapping consensus and functional universality.

This in turn reflects the significant achievement of the Universal Declaration of Human Rights. A remarkable group of individuals, working in a moment of historical optimism following the most destructive conflict in human history, was able to craft an unusually good statement of the most progressive vision of human rights best practices. And this firm foundation, buttressed by the principal of consensus, has continued to set the parameters for the development of international human rights law.

Contemporary international human rights law elaborates and updates the Universal Declaration. It fills in a few gaps. But it continues to follow the Universal Declaration. And, in practice, the consensus principle has always—eventually—brought the international community back to the Universal Declaration.

The process of developing international human rights law thus has managed to transcend partisan politics and maintain considerable substantive and theoretical integrity. And, as the preceding sections have shown, an important part of retaining that integrity has been the insistence that human rights are interdependent, interrelated, and indivisible—an insistence on the unity of human rights that was first embedded in the Universal Declaration.

4 An Alternative View of Unity? Three Generations of Human Rights

Another approach to the unity of human rights that is widely cited by scholars and activists attempts to construct an historical synthesis of different "generations" of human rights. This approach was first articulated in 1977 by Czech jurist Karel Vašák, then a lawyer at the United Nations Educational, Scientific and Cultural Organization.[11] Vašák envisioned three generations of rights that, he argued, had been fully recognized by the international community by the late 1970s. Table 4.1 reflects our reading and elaboration of this formula.

Each generation is based on one of the philosophical ideals of the French Revolution: liberty, equality, and fraternity, corresponding to civil and political rights (from classical

Table 4.1 "Generations" of Human Rights

	First Generation	*Second Generation*	*Third Generation*
Principle reflected	Liberty	Equality	Fraternity
Types of rights	Civil/political	Economic/social	Solidarity/group
Target of claims	Anti-state	Anti-market	Anticolonial
Prioritized by	First World	Second World	Third World

liberalism), economic and social rights (from socialism/Marxism), and, finally, solidarity or group rights, such as the right to self-determination, sovereignty over natural resources, and the right to development. Not coincidentally—and central to the attractiveness of this Cold War-era model—each generation was associated with one of the three principal geopolitical blocs of the era.

Table 4.1 also adds an additional dimension to Vašák's original formula, indicating the principal "enemy" of rights within each generation. First-generation rights view the state as the primary violator of rights. Second-generation rights seek to combat the power of capitalist markets. Third-generation rights were initially anticolonial but increasingly have become focused on the globalization of markets (see Chapter 12).

There are, however, at least three serious problems with this three-generations model.

First, it is historically inaccurate. From the beginning, Western conceptions of natural (human) rights included economic rights. For example, John Locke's short and iconic list included life, liberty, and estates (property). Thomas Jefferson similarly emphasized rights to life, liberty, and the pursuit of happiness. The nineteenth-century development of more robust conceptions of economic and social rights, especially for working men who had little or no property, initially predated socialism and continued to proceed largely independently of (although sometimes in alliance with) socialism. (For example, the foundations of the German welfare state were laid by the archconservative Otto von Bismarck.) And in the interwar and post-World War II periods, when modern welfare states were consolidated and new ones created, Western states not only took the lead in elaborating and implementing economic and social rights but also achieved results far surpassing those of socialist bloc states.

Second, the three-generations formulation gives wildly excessive emphasis to so-called third-generation rights, which make up only a tiny fraction of internationally recognized human rights—and, with the crucial exception of self-determination, have had little practical impact. Self-determination was an essential addition to the body of internationally recognized human rights. It is indeed qualitatively different from other human rights. And the Third World did play a central role in pressing for its recognition. (Although even here we should note that the right was in fact first introduced to international law by Westerners for application in Europe.) The idea of a coequal third generation, however, has little basis in either theory or practice.

Third, and most immediately relevant to the issue of the unity of human rights, the three-generations model is fundamentally in tension with the ideas of interdependence, interrelatedness, and indivisibility. Political practice by states in the socialist bloc systematically denigrated civil and political rights (and did not even treat economic and social rights as inalienable entitlements of citizens). Similarly, leading advocates of solidarity rights often advanced them as prerequisites for, if not alternatives to—rather than additions to—civil and political rights. In addition, the language of historically periodized generations risks driving permanent wedges between contemporary human rights categories. The generations approach also makes it difficult to consider the development of particular rights, their extension to wider segments of the population, and the development of institutions (especially the modern regulatory welfare state) in which interdependent rights and freedoms take on new and important meanings.

We thus come back, again, to the idea that "all human rights are universal, indivisible and interdependent and interrelated." Or, phrased as an imperative for policy: all human rights for all.[12]

Problem 4.1 Human Rights: Hierarchical or Indivisible?

The Problem

Imagine that someone is speaking about human rights violations in some country but does not specify which rights are being violated. What pops into your mind? In our experience, most Americans tend to think of violations of what human rights theorists often call "personal integrity rights," such as torture, arbitrary arrest and detention, police brutality, enforced disappearances, or arbitrary executions. If the person clarified that they had in mind the lack of educational opportunities for girls or high maternal mortality rates, this would, we think, strike most Americans as odd. That's just not what Americans ordinarily mean when we talk about "human rights violations."

Even those of us convinced by the theoretical argument of indivisibility and deeply wary of the practical problems of the abuse of categorical distinctions between human rights often find ourselves falling into hierarchical thinking. For example, many human rights advocates simply do not treat unemployment or even homelessness as if they were as significant violations of human rights in comparison with torture, enforced disappearances, or arbitrary executions. However deep our commitment to the maxim "all human rights for all," we are still reluctant to accept, in our unthinking practice, that all internationally recognized human rights really are equal.

How can we resolve such hierarchical thinking about human rights with the theoretically central idea of interrelated, interdependent, and indivisible human rights? Here we will focus on the argument for hierarchy most commonly encountered in our own country, namely, the prioritization of civil and political rights.

One Solution

We suggest shifting attention from *violations* to *obligations* and applying the conceptual distinctions developed in Chapter 2. There we saw that categorically dividing civil and political rights from economic and social rights as "negative" and "positive" rights, respectively, is deeply problematic. Most internationally recognized human rights impose both positive and negative duties (although not always on the same social actors). Furthermore, *all* internationally recognized human rights are subject to progressive implementation. For example, what counts as adequate legal representation in criminal proceedings will vary at least as dramatically with the level of resources available in a society as will what counts as free and universal primary education.

In Chapter 2 we also noted that states have duties to respect, protect, and promote or fulfill human rights. The duty to respect often is primarily negative—but even then it requires the state to positively enact prohibitions on its own actions. But duties to protect and to promote or fulfill are fundamentally positive. And they clearly underscore the necessarily progressive realization of *all* human rights.

In other words, focusing on state obligations draws us away from haggling over the content of different categories of human rights. Instead, it focuses on the mechanisms and structures of making the state and society more just and more conducive to realizing the human dignity that underlies internationally recognized human rights. Interdependent and indivisible human rights reappear in the form of interdependent and indivisible state duties to allow people to live a life of dignity, respect, autonomy, and self-determination—across the full range of internationally recognized human rights.

Going Further

Although every violation of every right is significant, not every violation is equally important. But the importance of a violation is largely a matter of the circumstances of implementation—not the content of the right.

Again, let us focus on civil and political rights and economic and social rights in the United States. Most Americans, we suspect, would consider torture and arbitrary arrest and detention more serious violations of human rights than unemployment and homelessness. Such evaluations, though, depend on certain assumed circumstances in which these violations present themselves. Imagine, however, a middle-income country in which the state arbitrarily detains and tortures a very small number of people targeted for their political views but in which one-third of the adult population cannot find gainful work and half the population lives in temporary housing or on the streets. Here, the more serious violations would seem to concern economic and social rights.

Again, we need to focus on the impact of violations on human dignity, both of particular individuals and of the members of society collectively. And *that* has little to do with the particular content of the right. It depends on contingent historical, material, and political circumstances.

More generally, the interdependence and indivisibility of human rights is a claim about the essential character of internationally recognized human rights. The gross and systematic denial of *any* of these rights is an unacceptable denial of human dignity.

One cannot live a life of dignity unless one has at least some degree of enjoyment of nearly all these rights.

This is not incompatible with temporary and contingent decisions to prioritize progress on some rights rather than others. Quite the contrary, such decisions are inescapable in a world of limited material and political resources. And different societies, as well as the same society at different times, may legitimately make different decisions about priorities. (This is particularly true as we move down the levels identified in Chapter 3 toward detailed matters of implementation.)

The interdependence and indivisibility of human rights prohibit *categorical* priorities among rights. It does not deny that some human rights in some particular circumstances demand greater social and political attention than other human rights *in those particular circumstances.*

Much of the day-to-day struggle for human rights involves choosing to prioritize progress in one area over other (equally important, in principle) areas, both because of limited resources and because of variations in the nature, intensity, or scope of the threats to human dignity. Such contingent practical priorities, however, must not be confused with categorical hierarchies of human rights. And, in the long run, the interdependence and indivisibility of human rights require all states and all societies to strive to realize all human rights for all.

Discussion Questions

1. Even if you accept that economic and social rights are just as important as civil and political rights, is there still a difference between them? If so, what?
2. Why do we continue to talk about these two categories of rights? Is it about the nature of the rights themselves (what they try to protect with respect to individuals) or are the differences rooted in what states' obligations are with respect to their protection? If it is about their nature as rights, can you say what that nature is? If it is about the obligations, what are the differences? Are those differences qualitatively important? Or is it all basically a matter of politics? Or habit?
3. We have argued here that the historical generations approach to understanding human rights is problematic. Are you convinced? Why or why not?
4. Following from Question 3, would it make sense to talk about contemporary economic and social rights (guaranteed by the state), such as those related to work, working conditions, education, health, and social security, in the context of the eighteenth century (when core civil and political rights first emerged)? (In this sense, the three-generation idea points to the fact that the particular rights implications of "life" and "liberty" were elaborated before the rights implications of "the pursuit of happiness." And then the social solidarity underlying all human rights came to receive greater emphasis.)

5. The principle of indivisibility argues that civil/political and economic/social rights are fundamentally equal, no matter the details about how any specific right or rights must be respected or guaranteed. Yet some have also argued that one set of rights was more fundamental and therefore needed to be secured before the other. Do you think there is any logic to either prioritization (i.e., that civil/political rights need to come first or that economic/social rights need to come first)? What is the reasoning behind each argument? How convincing is each?

Suggested Readings

This chapter is largely distilled from the work of one of this volume's coauthors (Edquist-Whelan), whose book *Indivisible Human Rights: A History* (University of Pennsylvania Press, 2010) explores these issues and the history in much greater detail. As we mention in the chapter, a major focal point about indivisibility has centered on the status of economic and social rights relative to civil and political rights. The literature reflecting those discussions began to emerge in the late 1980s, when the ICESCR's weak and ineffective reporting procedure was reformed and the UN Committee on Economic, Social, and Cultural Rights was established. These works are still worth reading, for they established the terms of the debates that we explore in this chapter.

Generally, in the realm of theory, philosophy, and the general politics of these questions, see David Beetham, "What Future for Economic and Social Rights?" *Political Studies* 43 (1995): 41–60; Antonio A. Cancado Trindade, "The Interdependence of All Human Rights—Obstacles and Challenges to Their Implementation," *International Social Science Journal* 50 (1998): 513–523; Isfahan Merali and Valerie Oosterveld, eds., *Giving Meaning to Economic, Social and Cultural Rights* (University of Pennsylvania Press, 2001); Craig Scott, "The Interdependence and Permeability of Human Rights Norms: Towards a Partial Fusion of the International Covenants on Human Rights," *Osgoode Hall Law Journal* 27 (1989): 769–875; and "Reaching Beyond (Without Abandoning) the Category of 'Economic, Social and Cultural Rights," *Human Rights Quarterly* 21 (1999): 633–660; and James Nickel, "Rethinking Indivisibility: Towards a Theory of Supporting Relations between Rights," *Human Rights Quarterly* 30 (2008): 984–1001.

On the legal obligations of the ICESCR and the establishment of the Committee on Economic, Social, and Cultural Rights, see Philip Alston and Gerard Quinn, "The Nature and Scope of States Parties' Obligations Under the International Covenant on Economic, Social and Cultural Rights," *Human Rights Quarterly* 9 (1987): 156–229; International Commission of Jurists, "The Limburg Principles on the Implementation of the International Covenant on Economic, Social and Cultural Rights," *Human Rights Quarterly* 9 (1987): 122–135; and Robert E. Robertson, "Measuring State Compliance with the Obligation to Devote the 'Maximum Available Resources' to Realizing Economic, Social and Cultural Rights," *Human Rights Quarterly* 16 (1994): 693–714.

On the adoption of "violations approaches" for economic, social, and cultural rights and the establishment of a petitions procedure for the ICESCR, see Audrey R. Chapman, "A 'Violations Approach' for Monitoring the International Covenant on Economic, Social and Cultural Rights," *Human Rights Quarterly* 18 (1996): 23–66; Scott Leckie, "Another Step towards Indivisibility: Identifying the Key Features of Violations of Economic, Social and Cultural Rights," *Human Rights Quarterly* 20 (1998): 81–124; International Commission of Jurists, "The Maastricht Guidelines on Violations of Economic, Social and Cultural Rights," *Human Rights Quarterly* 20 (1998): 691–704; Victor Dankwa, Cees Flinterman, and Scott Leckie, "Commentary to the Maastricht Guidelines on Violations of Economic, Social and Cultural Rights," *Human Rights Quarterly* 20 (1998): 705–730; Michael J. Dennis and David P. Stewart, "Justiciability of Economic, Social and Cultural Rights: Should There Be an International Complaints Mechanism to Adjudicate the Rights to Food, Water, Housing and Health?," *American Journal of International Law* 98 (2004): 462–515; and Catarina de Albuquerque, "Chronicle of an Announced Birth: The Coming into Life of the Optional Protocol to the International Covenant on Economic, Social and Cultural Rights—The Missing Piece of the International Bill of Rights," *Human Rights Quarterly* 32 (2010): 144–178.

Finally, the following four volumes cover current trends and research on the economic, legal, and political status of economic, social, and cultural rights: Katherine G. Young, *Constituting Economic and Social Rights* (Oxford University Press, 2012); Lanse Minkler, ed., *The State of Economic and Social Human Rights* (Cambridge University Press, 2013); Sakiko Fukada-Parr, Terra Lawson-Remer, and Susan Randolph, eds., *Fulfilling Social and Economic Rights* (Oxford University Press, 2015); and Christina Binder, Jane Hofbauer, Flávia Piovesan, and Amaya Úbeda de Torres, eds., *Research Handbook on International Law and Social Rights* (Edward Elgar, 2020).

Notes

1 Craig Scott, "The Interdependence of Permeability of Human Rights Norms: Towards a Partial Fusion of the International Covenants on Human Rights," *Osgoode Hall Law Journal* 27 (1989): 769–875.
2 UN Doc. A/C.3/SR.297, p. 174; A/C.3/SR.390, p. 254.
3 UN Doc. A/C.3/SR.299, p. 188.
4 The subject of the resolution was the "future work of the Commission on Human Rights" and contained several directives besides the inclusion of economic, social, and cultural rights in the Covenant.
5 UN General Assembly Resolution 543 (VI) (February 1952).
6 Included as Section II of the Final Act of the International Conference on Human Rights, UN Doc. A/CONF.32/41 (1968).
7 Included as Section II of the Final Act of the International Conference on Human Rights, UN Doc. A/CONF.32/41 (1968), p. 4, paragraph 13.
8 UN General Assembly Resolution 32/130 (December 1977), operative clause 1(e).
9 UN Doc A/CONF.157/23, paragraph 5.
10 UN Doc A/CONF.157/23, paragraph 8.
11 Karel Vašák, "A 30-Year Struggle: The Sustained Efforts to Give Force of Law to the Universal Declaration of Human Rights," *UNESCO Courier* (Volume XXX.11, November 1977), 28–29, 32.
12 This was the motto adopted by the United Nations to mark the fiftieth anniversary of the Universal Declaration in 1998.

Part II

Multilateral, Bilateral, and Transnational Action

Global Multilateral Mechanisms

5

This chapter examines the multilateral global institutions and procedures designed to facilitate greater compliance by states with international human rights law. We first consider the "Charter-based bodies"; that is, those that draw their authority from the **UN Charter**, with a particular focus on the UN Human Rights Council and the Office of the UN High Commissioner for Human Rights. This is followed by an exploration of the work of the "treaty monitoring bodies," whose authority derives from the various human rights treaties. We also briefly note the work of other global multilateral actors. We conclude with a case study on the special procedures of the UN human rights system. The following chapter then turns to regional human rights regimes.

1 The Human Rights Council

The **Human Rights Council**[1] is the institutional centerpiece of the global human rights regime. It was created in 2006 to replace the Commission on Human Rights, which despite its fine work in developing the body of international human rights law, not only had made little progress on monitoring the implementation of internationally recognized human rights but had in its final decade become hopelessly politicized (as symbolized by the election in 2003 of Muammar Gaddafi, the longtime military dictator of Libya, as its chair).

The Human Rights Council holds three regular sessions each year (in February-March, June-July, and September-October), for a total of at least ten weeks. (In the 2020s, it has met on average for 13.5 weeks.). The Council also can call special sessions to address serious human rights situations, often in the context of an armed conflict. As of December 2025, the Council had held thirty-eight special sessions (on average, about two a year, usually lasting only a single day).[2] Fully one-third of these sessions have focused on the situation in Israel/Palestine. Other situations that have been the subject of more than one special

DOI: 10.4324/9781003373520-7

session have included Syria (five), Sudan/South Sudan (five), Myanmar (three), and Democratic Republic of the Congo (DRC) (two).

The Council is composed of forty-seven states elected by secret ballot in the UN General Assembly. Members serve staggered three-year terms and may be re-elected once (but may serve again if elected in another nonconsecutive cycle). Seats on the Council are distributed proportionally by region.

Although elections are supposed to take into account the candidate-state's contribution to the promotion and protection of human rights, several states with poor human rights records (e.g., Burundi, China, Cuba, Democratic Republic of the Congo, Ethiopia, Sudan, and Vietnam) currently sit on the Council. But most members that are regularly elected to the Council (e.g., Chile, Japan, India, and the Netherlands have each served four or five terms each) have much better human rights records. And the Human Rights Council is widely perceived as a largely nonpartisan forum for the consensual development of new international human rights norms and for promoting the national implementation of the extensive body of international human rights law.

Although some countries have, for political reasons, received more attention than their human rights records warrant (e.g., Israel) and many (e.g., China) have received less, the Universal Periodic Review (UPR) process (see immediately below) has been relatively even-handed. Furthermore, states targeted for criticism in the Council's resolutions always are guilty of well-documented systematic violations.

1.1 Universal Periodic Review

The most important task of the Council is the nearly continual process of the UPR, under which all 193 UN member-states undergo scrutiny of their human rights records every four to five years.[3] Prior to each of the three regular annual sessions, the Council reviews thirteen or fourteen countries. In preparation, states under review submit national reports on their efforts to promote and protect internationally recognized human rights. In addition, a wide variety of information is gathered from independent human rights experts and groups both within and outside the UN system, including national human rights institutions and NGOs.

In the UPR process, all forty-seven members of the Council form a Working Group to review these documents and engage in a conversation with the state under review. Typically, this involves questions and comments leading to a series of recommendations. Generally, after the process is concluded, reviewed states formally "support," "note," or "reject" each recommendation—sometimes with an explanation. These recommendations (and responses) become important data points for the next review (typically four and a half years later).

At the end of each review round, a group of three members (a "troika") prepares an outcome report for each country, which summarizes discussions with the state under review. The report is then sent to the Council to be adopted (following any clarifications, additional comments or questions, and comments or questions from observer states or NGOs present).

The fourth UPR round began in November 2022 and will conclude in February 2027. As all 193 UN member-states have been reviewed at least three times, we have enough evidence to consider the character of the impact of the UPR mechanism. Following an analysis by the Universal Rights Group (URG), a Geneva-based human rights think tank,[4] we look at three measures of effectiveness.

1.1.1 Quality of State Reports

The Council's guidelines specify that national reports should be prepared through a "broad consultation process" with relevant national stakeholders (especially elements from civil society) to ensure that the reports are as objective and reliable (accurate) as possible. In practice, though, only a small minority of states take this directive seriously. Most national reports are drafted by ministries of foreign affairs, often with little or no input from other groups (even within the government).

1.1.2 Quality of Working Group Peer Review

The participatory nature of the UPR mechanism is in many ways remarkable. More important, though, is the quality of that review. Here, the record is mixed.

The time allotted to review each country permits each member only two or three minutes of question-and-answer. Working Group sessions thus tend to be scattered, formulaic, and superficial, often amounting to a "rapid, almost metronomic delivery of recommendations by reviewing States ... [followed by] a valedictory speech by the [State under review] to mark the end of the session."[5]

Nevertheless, the number of recommendations has increased dramatically, from 430 at the very first (2008) Working Group session in Cycle 1 (an average of about twenty-five per country) to 1,804 by the fourth (2009) session of that cycle (an average of more than a hundred per country). During the third (2017–2022) cycle, there were 43,229 recommendations (an average of more than 200 per country). Furthermore, the URG analysis shows that seven-eighths of the recommendations made in the second cycle were specific and salient or germane and measurable, greatly facilitating the opportunities for follow-up in the next round. (The percentage of *specific* recommendations that were accepted by the state under review was around 71 percent; those that were *nonspecific* or general were accepted at a rate of nearly 90 percent.)

1.1.3 Implementation of Recommendations

Perhaps the most important measure of the effectiveness of the UPR is the extent to which states implement the recommendations they have accepted. The URG analysis, which examined seventy-four countries from all regional groups, covering more than 5,000 recommendations, found that:

- Nearly half of all accepted recommendations were implemented; another fifth were partially implemented. In some countries, the implementation rate of accepted recommendations was as high as 82 percent.
- Recommendations concerning women's rights and children's rights enjoy high levels of implementation (54 percent and 62 percent, respectively).

- Levels of implementation varied by the type of recommendation. For example, recommendations to accede to international human rights agreements or institutions had higher levels of implementation compared to those focusing solely on domestic-level reforms. This suggests that as easily implemented recommendations are implemented, the overall level of implementation may begin to shrink.
- Even 30 percent of recommendations that were "noted" by states under review (i.e., neither accepted nor rejected) resulted in some domestic-level reforms.

This success is most likely due to the peer-to-peer, state-centric model of self-assessment embedded in the UPR—both because states are more likely to respond to their peers and because state peers are more likely to avoid embarrassing or confronting their peers. Furthermore, although the other "compilation reports" (by the UN system and other stakeholders) are part of the review dossier, *only the national report is presented to the Working Group*. This often wildly skews the review and almost certainly leads to an overestimate of the effectiveness of the recommendation process. Conversely, though, by including a topic in its report, a state often implies that it is willing to address that issue.

In sum, it seems fair to say that a multilateral political process that produces not merely often-constructive dialogue but considerable (if limited) positive impact is a significant achievement. The Human Rights Council has unquestionably become a valuable institution in the global human rights regime.

1.2 Other Activities of the Human Rights Council

Although the UPR is its signature endeavor, the Human Rights Council engages in many other important activities (most of which were begun under the Commission for Human Rights).

The Council continues to create and promote international human rights norms. For example, at its 55th regular session, from February to April 2024, the Council adopted thirty-two resolutions on a variety of topics (including the rights to food and work, support systems for persons with disabilities, the negative effects of unilateral coercive measures and foreign indebtedness on the enjoyment of economic and social rights, countering disinformation, and discrimination and violence against intersex persons) and situations (in Iran, Myanmar, North Korea, Syria, and Belarus) and on technical assistance programs for Haiti, Mali, and South Sudan. Furthermore, several Working Groups remain actively engaged in developing new legal instruments and recommendations on topics including the rights to development, the human rights obligations of transnational corporations and other business enterprises, the activities of private military and security companies, and the rights of indigenous peoples.

The Council also receives research and advice from a number of subsidiary mechanisms. The Advisory Committee serves as a "think tank" for the Council—a role that was previously fulfilled by the former Sub-Commission on the Promotion and Protection of Human Rights.[6] There are also two Expert Mechanisms, on the Rights of Indigenous Peoples (established in 2007) and the Right to Development (established in 2019). Four forums provide a platform for dialogue and cooperation on specific topics: the Forum on Minority Issues, the Social Forum (an annual meeting that brings together civil society actors, states, and intergovernmental organizations (IGOs) to address a particular theme—in 2025, the theme was "the contribution of education to the respect, promotion, protection and fulfillment of all human rights for all"), the Forum on Business and Human Rights, and the Forum on Human Rights, Democracy, and the Rule of Law.

In addition, the Council has an extensive set of "special procedures" on particular topics and situations. (See Section 5 below) It engages in its own fact-finding and investigatory missions. (As of January 2026, the Council had undertaken forty-two investigations and was carrying out active inquiries in Belarus, Iran, the Democratic Republic of the Congo, Myanmar, Nicaragua, the Occupied Palestinian Territory and Israel, Sudan, South Sudan, Syria, Ukraine, and Venezuela.) There is also a complaint procedure but it has not been used since 2014.

1.3 Trends and Politics within the Human Rights Council

1.3.1 Agenda Items

The Council organizes its work under ten standing agenda items. Item 3 (Promotion and Protection of Human Rights; "thematic" issues) is the most important and accounts for more than half of the work of the Council. Institutional and procedural agenda items and

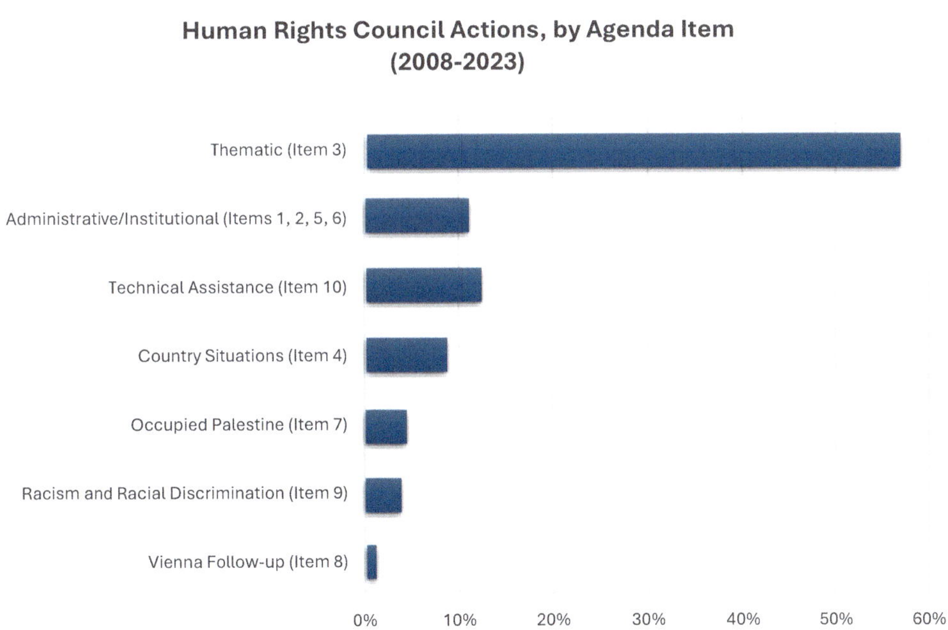

Figure 5.1 Human Rights Council Actions, by Agenda Item (2008–2023)

Source: Universal Human Rights Group

technical assistance and capacity building each also accounted for about an eighth of the Council's work from 2008 to 2023.[7] Figure 5.1 shows the distribution of action from 2008 to 2023.

1.3.2 Resolutions and Decisions: General Trends

During its three annual sessions, the Council adopts, on average, about ninety-five resolutions per year.[8] (In 2025, ninety-two resolutions were adopted.) Roughly two-thirds of all actions taken by the Council are by consensus; that is, adopted without a formal vote. Most of the floor action during a typical Council session is devoted to the delivery of reports, focused discussions, and interactive dialogues between Special Mandate holders and member-states. Off the floor, delegations are working to draft resolutions with the aim of achieving adoption by consensus. Differences between delegations thus are, whenever possible, worked out ahead of time.

For more contentious resolutions, delegations are free to table amendments. But such amendments, which were not accepted during the drafting process, usually are considered "hostile" (that is, significantly altering the core text of a resolution) and are rarely adopted. Only two percent of the 362 amendments tabled between 2017 and 2022 were adopted. (Two-thirds were defeated and the remainder were withdrawn.[9])

As Figure 5.1 shows, most resolutions adopted by the Council are thematic (Agenda Item 3). In 2023, the Council adopted sixty-three resolutions under Item 3. Figure 5.2 shows that nearly a third were on civil and political rights. A quarter addressed economic and social rights (including development and extreme poverty). The remainder dealt with "cross-cutting"

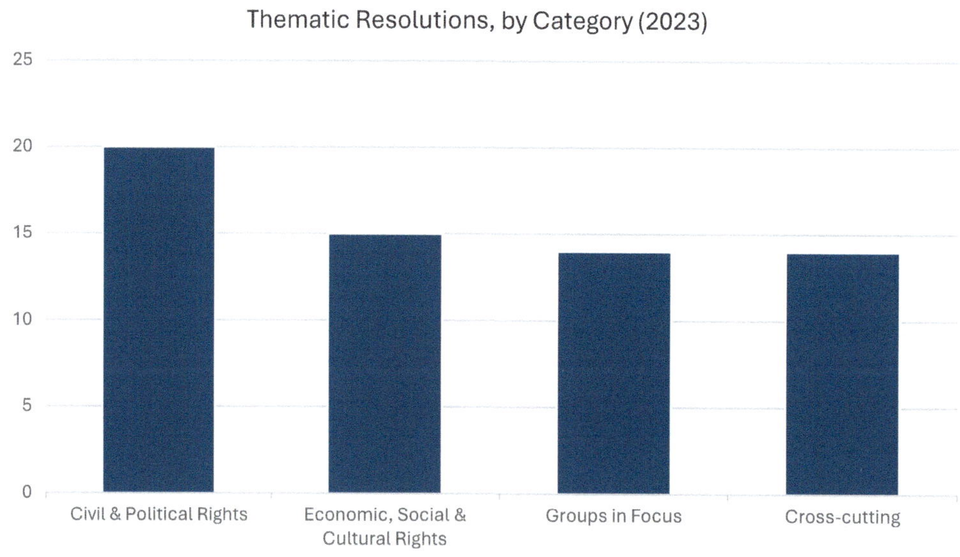

Figure 5.2 Thematic Resolutions by Category (2023)

Source: Universal Human Rights Group

themes, such as "international solidarity," "unilateral coercive measures," business and human rights, education, and "groups in focus," such as women, children, migrants, and indigenous peoples.[10]

1.4 China and the Global South in the Council

Many countries in the Global South have held distinctive perspectives on human rights, beginning with India (which achieved independence 1947) and accelerating after the independence of the Gold Coast (as Ghana) in 1957. The rise of China as a global power over the past three decades—since the Council's establishment in 2006, China has held a seat every year except two—has given these states a powerful champion that shares many of their concerns about human rights. They have also received growing support from Russia, which under President Vladimir Putin (first elected in 1999), has turned increasingly nationalist and anti-Western.

Thematic (Agenda Item 3) resolutions sponsored by the Global South tend to focus on three broad areas of concern: (1) discrimination, especially racism and the rights of minorities, women, and children; (2) global or systemic norms, especially in economic and financial affairs, including the right to development (see Chapter 13), the promotion of "international solidarity," debt relief, and economic sanctions, and (3) limiting or pushing back against the universal ambit of human rights in order to support "traditional values" and families, give greater emphasis to the cultural contexts of societies, protect religions (especially Islam) against defamation, and rejecting the idea that gender-related rights include sexual orientation and gender identity.[11]

The 2020s have seen more public political contention at the Council. For example, at the 48th Session in 2021, which the URG defined as "the most acrimonious in the Council's history,"[12] 28 percent of resolutions were targeted by hostile amendments. Furthermore, a draft amendment on Yemen,[13] which would have renewed the mandate of a group of international experts investigating the civil war, was defeated in a vote of 18-21-7. Saudi Arabia mobilized this outcome by placing significant pressure on African delegations on the Council: out of the thirteen African members, nine voted "no" and the remainder abstained. Similarly, at the 51st Session, in 2022, on a procedural vote (a "decision") to open a formal discussion of the situation of the Uyghur people in China's Xinjiang Province,[14] the Council rejected the draft by a vote of 17-19-11 following intense lobbying by China. All the "no" votes and abstentions were from the Global South.[15]

This new authoritarian assertiveness does not seem to have fundamentally reshaped the character or work of the Council. It does, however, merit close attention—and concern to the extent that it presents a real challenge to the post-Cold War consensus on the relative universality of internationally recognized human rights.

1.4.1 China's "Normfare"

"Normfare" refers to the diffusion of norms for strategic purposes—in this case, China's stated goal of cementing a China-led global order by mid-century.[16]

The Chinese view of human rights resonates with many countries in Africa, the Middle East, and Asia. In particular, China emphasizes sovereignty understood as "non-interference"—deployed as a shield against "meddling" human rights criticism. China uses the language of "cooperation" and "common but differentiated responsibilities." In this view, each state has a distinctive history, development trajectory, and political system and is entitled to determine its own "understanding" of human rights (and to prioritize those rights that most align with its interests).

In the Chinese view, the foundation of human rights is the responsibility of individuals and all social actors to promote national and social harmony and stability. The rights of individuals can only be realized in a context where individual and social duties have been fulfilled. This understanding makes the state itself the most important holder of human rights, effectively flipping the meaning of "human rights" inside-out. "Human rights" becomes a means to protect authoritarian states from their own citizens (and criticism from other states and international actors).

This vision, which many had hoped had been decisively subordinated (if not entirely limited) in the 1990s, has been increasingly advocated by dictators, authoritarian rulers, and would-be autocrats around the world.[17] To the extent that China and its allies can reshape fundamental understandings of the nature and substance of internationally recognized human rights, they will have created a shield against both internal and external criticism. This is a much more serious threat to human rights than political contention over individual issues. But, so far at least, this remains a minority view in the Council. And such debates have not seriously undermined or displaced the Council's generally nonpartisan work both in elaborating and supporting internationally recognized human rights and in the UPR process.

1.4.2 China's Behavior in the Council

A 2023 study by Alexander Dukalskis[18] of China's political behavior in the Council found four general patterns.

First (and this should not be surprising), China uses its influence to deflect the spotlight away from its own human rights record. Resolutions critical of China have been prevented from coming to a vote. And China has even been able to undermine attempts to investigate. For example, on the high-profile visit of High Commissioner Michelle Bachelet in 2022 to investigate the situation of Uyghurs in Xinjiang Province, the authorities blocked her access to many sites. Even more troubling, Bachelet's public statements while in China largely parroted official government talking points. And she refused to release her report on the situation until literally minutes before her term ended. Then, as noted above, China successfully lobbied to defeat a draft decision to discuss the Uyghur situation. And all of this was hailed as a victory in Chinese state-run media.[19]

Second, China regularly votes against country-specific (Item 4) resolutions. On sixty-three such resolutions, China has voted no forty-four times and abstained twice. When they have voted "yes" (fifteen times), nearly all targeted Israeli actions in the Occupied Palestinian Territories.[20] This pattern reflects China's long-standing advocacy of "non-interference" and "dialog over naming-and-shaming."

Third, China usually supports resolutions on development, an equitable international order, mutually beneficial cooperation, solidarity, and multilateralism. They see themselves as the natural leader of the Global South, espousing a widely held stance that the Council should encourage "dialogue without confrontation." Consider China's response to a questionnaire sent by the Human Rights Advisory Committee in 2019:

> The trend of politicization of human rights is rising and double standards prevail. Some countries engage in open confrontation and 'name calling and shaming.' They use human rights issues to attack others and interfere in the internal affairs of other countries, thus poisoning the global atmosphere of human rights governance .... The international community should stand at the height of all mankind, firmly establish the concept of mutually beneficial cooperation, strengthen dialogue and cooperations on the basis of equality and mutual respect, and jointly promote the cause of international human rights.[21]

The terms that China deploys have very specific meanings to Chinese policy makers. As Dukalskis nicely puts it:

> '[m]utual respect' implies acceptance of China's nondemocratic political system as legitimate. A 'multilateral' world of 'mutual respect' and 'cooperation' in the human rights realm is thus one with few binding standards or mechanisms of scrutiny, legitimacy for nondemocratic political systems, and human rights dealt within the context of state-to-state reciprocity.[22]

Finally, China tends to vote no or abstain on certain categories of resolutions, especially those dealing with civil and political rights. It tends to oppose resolutions to protect human rights defenders, abolish or limit the death penalty, and strengthen civil society as well as resolutions on sexual orientation and gender identity. China generally abstains on resolutions dealing with torture, the internet and digital technology, climate change, HIV, and terrorism.[23]

Turning to *how* China uses its diplomacy to secure its goals, Dukalskis again finds four broad strategies.

First, China works to mobilize support from about fifty "like-minded" undemocratic and antidemocratic countries. For example, when China came up for review during the UPR process in 2018, it "flooded the speakers list with representatives from friendly countries."[24] And after twenty-two mostly Western countries issued a "Joint Statement on Xinjiang" to High Commissioner Michelle Bachelet in July 2019, calling on China to uphold its human rights commitments, thirty-seven countries sent a response letter four days later that commended China on its "remarkable achievements in the field of human rights," especially through its development policies. The letter also claimed that China's policies in Xinjiang were "successful counter-terrorism operations." Of the thirty-seven states that signed the letter, only Nepal was above the median score on the Liberal Democracy Index of the V-Dem project.[25] More broadly, there is both qualitative and quantitative evidence that the presence of China in the Council is consequential; that a small but significant number of states switch their votes when China is a member.[26]

Second, China regularly uses economic statecraft to persuade other states to support China's positions in the Council. It has even directly threatened trade relations for supporting, for example, Hong Kong democratic activists, the Dalai Lama, or Taiwan.

Third, China employs "tactical deception" to take advantage of the Council's long-standing commitment to allow civil society actors (NGOs) to interact directly with the Council. Chinese "NGOs" are really state-sponsored groups of academics, headed up by Communist Party officials—GONGOs (government organized nongovernmental organizations)—who parrot Beijing's line in the Council under the auspices of "civil society" support. (The China Society for Human Rights Studies[27] is the most notable.).

Finally, China regularly represses its domestic critics. It blocks dissident Chinese citizens from engaging with the Council, denying them exit visas, for example, or arguing that such people are terrorists or criminals. Hong Kong activists have received official police inquiries for writing to the High Commissioner. (Few Chinese outside of Hong Kong would even consider taking such an action.) Many individuals and groups are silenced by the threat of police retaliation. And a general atmosphere of fear regularly produces "self-censorship." China also uses its frequent seat on Economic and Social Council (ECOSOC's) Committee on NGOs to block the accreditation of observer status (which enables NGOs to participate at the United Nations) of groups that are critical of China and pressures other countries to support their blocking maneuvers.[28]

1.4.3 An Emerging Shift?

In its most recent report on the Human Rights Council in 2023, the URG noted that while the power balance in the Council continued to see a shift favorable to China and "like-minded" states and groups of states (such as the Organization of Islamic Cooperation and the Non-Aligned Movement), it appears that China has begun to moderate its "wolf-warrior" style of diplomacy. This is due in part to a new human rights team within the PRC's Permanent Mission to the United Nations in Geneva. China refrained from sponsoring or supporting contentious resolutions targeted at the West (addressing, for example, colonialism) and tabling hostile amendments. China has also worked with the High Commissioner to fund more human rights advisors (albeit focused solely on economic, social, and cultural rights) and has helped to secure the adoption, by consensus, of a resolution on inequality.[29]

With respect to the Global South, URG also points out that members of the Western Group of states do not do themselves any favors by undermining their relationships, especially with the Organization of Islamic Cooperation and the African Group. In 2023, some Western states voted against resolutions on the human rights situation in Occupied Palestinian Territories, on religious intolerance (especially Quran burning), and failed to support resolutions on racism sponsored by the African Group. While there were principled human rights reasons for these votes, it is possible that a more strenuous effort to achieve consensus might bear fruit and encourage the recent Chinese turn toward more moderate advocacy of its views.

2 The Office of the UN High Commissioner for Human Rights

The Council's (and earlier the Commission's) activities reflect an information–advocacy model of human rights implementation. It seeks to acquire and disseminate authoritative information on violations to encourage (and if necessary, shame) governments to improve their practices. It relies on the desire of states to be respected—by their peers, their citizens, and international publics—and on the damage to a state's reputation that can be caused by well-publicized systematic human rights violations.

The UN Office of the High Commissioner for Human Rights (OHCHR), created after the 1993 Vienna World Conference, also employs the information–advocacy approach. The High Commissioner, who is directly accountable to (and appointed by) the UN Secretary-General, has the global reach of the Council but without its cumbersome procedures and the complications and roadblocks that result from the fact that members of the Council are states, not independent human rights experts. The High Commissioner may deal directly with governments, any of whom they may approach, at their discretion, on any issue.

The second High Commissioner, Mary Robinson (the former president of Ireland), turned the Office into a major force during her tenure (from 1997 to 2002). The quality of the secretarial support work was brought to a higher level, the budget increased substantially, and Robinson became a well-known public figure across the globe as a result of her difficult-to-resist intellectual brilliance, moral commitment, and hard work, combined with an unusual mix of diplomatic skill and a constant willingness to push the bounds of what her targets were willing to tolerate from an international public servant.

Robinson's successor, Sérgio Vieira de Mello of Brazil, was among the victims of the bombing of the UN offices in Baghdad in August 2003. The acting High Commissioner, Bertrand Ramcharan of Guyana, a career UN official and scholar of international human rights law, was succeeded in 2004 by Louise Arbour of Canada. Arbour, who had previously served as the chief prosecutor for the International Criminal Tribunal for the former Yugoslavia and the International Criminal Tribunal for Rwanda, aggressively exercised her mandate on behalf of human rights and victims of violations.

In 2008, Navanethem (Navi) Pillay of South Africa, a former judge of the International Criminal Court (ICC) and former president of the International Criminal Tribunal for Rwanda, became High Commissioner. She was succeeded in 2014 by Prince Zeid Ra'ad Zeid Al Hussein of Jordan, the first Asian, Muslim, and Arab High Commissioner.

In 2018, Michele Bachelet, the former president of Chile and the first Executive Director for UN Women, became the High Commissioner. Bachelet came under fire from many human rights NGOs after her high-profile visit to China in 2022. She issued a press statement that critics characterized as "soft" with respect to violations of the rights of Uyghurs in Xinjiang province. Soon thereafter, Bachelet announced she would not seek a second term as High Commissioner and had been delaying the release of a Council study on Xinjiang. The report was finally released on her last day in office—but without her signature.

In October 2022, Volker Türk of Austria became the UN's eighth High Commissioner for Human Rights. An advocate for refugees and stateless persons, Türk had previously served as the UN's Under-Secretary for Policy in the Executive Office of the

Secretary-General and played a key role in the development of the landmark Global Compact on Refugees.

Although the public activities of the High Commissioner draw the most attention, the significance of the behind-the-scenes work of the Office is also notable. The OHCHR website[30] is a model of clarity and comprehensive coverage that is of great value to activists, scholars, ordinary citizens, and victims. The Office also provides direct administrative support for the Council and the treaty bodies (which are discussed in the next section), engages in original research (with special attention to the Vienna Programme of Action and the right to development), and provides capacity-building and advisory services to governments seeking to improve their national practices.

The OHCHR staffs and maintains seventeen country offices (in Burkina Faso, Cambodia, Chad, Colombia, Guatemala, Guinea, Honduras, Liberia, Mauritania, Mexico, Niger, the State of Palestine, Syria (based in Lebanon), Sudan, Tunisia, Uganda, and Yemen) and regional offices for East Africa (Addis Ababa), Southern Africa (Pretoria), West Africa (Dakar), Central America (Panama City), South America (Santiago de Chile), Europe (Brussels), Central Asia (Bishkek), Southeast Asia (Bangkok), the Pacific (Suva), and the Middle East and North Africa (Beirut). It also supports a Regional Center for Human Rights and Democracy for Central Africa (Yaoundé, Cameroon) and a Training and Documentation Centre for South-West Asia and the Arab Region (Doha, Qatar). In 2021, the Office of the High Commissioner deployed nearly 900 international human rights officers and national staff placed in eleven separate peace missions, as well as resident human rights advisers and/or mainstreaming projects in fifty-five countries—more than triple the number deployed in 2010.[31]

In 2024, the total funding available to OHCHR was $450.1 million. (About 40 percent of that amount comes from the regular UN budget, with the remainder raised from voluntary contributions, most of which come from UN member-states.)[32] The regular OHCHR budget, however, represents a mere 4.3 percent of the overall UN budget. By comparison, in 2024, the World Bank made lending commitments totaling more than $117 billion. Its administrative budget request for 2024 was $3.17 billion—seven times the total budget of the Office of the High Commissioner.[33] Nevertheless, the OHCHR has continued to expand its range of activities.

3 Treaty-Reporting Systems

An important cluster of global human rights institutions derive their authority from multilateral human rights treaties (see Table 5.1). The principal activity of the committees created by these treaties (**treaty monitoring bodies** [TMBs]) is to review reports on compliance submitted by states-parties. Many also consider individual communications or petitions from alleged victims of violations. In addition, TMBs regularly review the scope of their respective treaty's provisions and issue "general comments" that attempt to advance international human rights jurisprudence.

Unlike the Human Rights Council, whose members are representatives of their governments, the members of the TMBs are individual experts who serve in their personal and

Table 5.1 Treaty Monitoring Bodies

Committee (Treaty Supervised)	*Parties to Treaty*	*Established*	*Allows Petitions?*	*Year First Petition Received*
Human Rights Committee (ICCPR)	175	1976	Yes, for the 117 that have ratified the Optional Protocol	1976
Committee on Economic, Social, and Cultural Rights (ICESCR)	173	1985	Yes, for the twenty-six states that have ratified the Optional Protocol	2013
Committee on the Elimination of Racial Discrimination (ICERD)	182	1969	Yes, under Article 14 of ICERD	1982
Committee on the Elimination of Discrimination Against Women (CEDAW)	189	1981	Yes, for the 115 states that have ratified the Optional Protocol	2003
Committee Against Torture (CAT)	175	1987	Yes, for the seventy states that have made a declaration under Article 22 of CAT	1987
Committee on the Rights of the Child (CRC)	196	1990	Yes, for the fifty states that have ratified the Optional Protocol	2013 (one petition; declared inadmissible)
Committee on Migrant Workers (CMW)	60	2004	Yes, for states that have made a declaration under Article 77 of the CMW (only four have done so; requires ten for the procedure to enter into force)	N/A
Committee on the Rights of Persons with Disabilities (CPPD)	192	2009	Yes, for the 104 states that have ratified the Optional Protocol	2010
Committee on Enforced Disappearances (CED)	77	2011	Yes, for the twenty-four states that have made a declaration under Article 31 of the ICED	2013

Source: Data from UN Human Rights Office as of July 2025. (See indicators.ohchr.org/)

professional capacity (although their governments may be instrumental in their nomination or election). They are expected to be impartial experts in the subject matter of the treaty and of "high moral character." The membership of the ten TMBs ranges from ten to twenty-five, with most (five) having eighteen members.

3.1 Reporting

The principal and most important activity of the treaty bodies is to review periodic reports on compliance that states-parties are required to submit, usually every four or five years. Based on the report and additional information gathered by the members of the committee, questions are prepared and submitted to the state in writing. A state representative participates in the committee's public discussion of the report. A follow-up written exchange often ensues.

The reporting process is an exchange of information that provides limited, noncoercive monitoring. The extent of state participation, beyond submitting its report, ranges from active cooperation to largely nonresponsive presence. There are no sanctions of any sort associated with the reporting procedure, even for refusing to submit its report (as some countries do).

Reporting systems aim not to provide coercive enforcement but to encourage and facilitate compliance. Judged in these terms, reporting often has a significant positive effect. The most constructive part of the process often is the preparation of the report. Much like the UPR, periodic reviews of national practice, if undertaken with any degree of conscientiousness, require states, agencies, and officials to step back from their day-to-day work and reflect on their processes, procedures, and institutions.

Reporting is especially valuable in countries with an active civil society. Issue-specific NGOs are sometimes directly involved in preparing the national report. They often lobby the officials who draft the report. And they can use preparation of the report and its public review by the treaty body as occasions for campaigning. NGOs may also participate indirectly in the committee review through contacts with individual members. And the public hearing and comments by the committees often provide an occasion for amplified publicity.

Paradoxically, then, reporting is most likely to have an impact where it is not critically needed: that is, where human rights records are relatively good. Nevertheless, any victim who is helped is a victory for international action, wherever that person resides.

One might even argue that the greatest virtue of treaty-reporting systems is their ability to address violations that are not sufficiently severe to merit scrutiny by the Council or a special procedure. Particularly for countries and violations that do not have a high international profile, reporting may actually provide greater scrutiny.

Furthermore, small-scale incremental progress, which is a realistic possibility in the case of any state that takes its reporting obligation seriously, is not to be sneered at—especially when we consider the typically modest impact of higher-profile inquiry or petition procedures. And even if stronger mechanisms are available, the periodic self-study that reporting requires is a valuable contribution.

The positive effects of reporting, however, depend ultimately on the willingness of the state to change—either because of a positive desire to improve or because of an openness or vulnerability to criticism (which all but the most repressive of regimes possess to some degree). Therefore, changes produced by such mechanisms are limited and incremental.

States typically engage in (massive) human rights violations only when they believe something of great importance is at stake. The national and international political costs of negative publicity and advocacy campaigns are almost never sufficient to overcome the political incentives to continue gross and persistent systematic violations. But where the violations are relatively minor or narrowly circumscribed—for example, particular rules on the treatment of prisoners, activities of a single part of the government bureaucracy, particular nondiscrimination policies, or the treatment of a single individual—all but the worst governments may be willing to consider improvements.

For all their limits, such modest improvements are not insignificant. And, over time, they may accumulate. This is especially true as the process is repeated in multiple treaty bodies—and as the reporting process interacts with other national, transnational, bilateral, and multilateral monitoring and advocacy.

3.2 General Comments

Treaty bodies also regularly review the scope and content of their treaty and issue general comments. This practice, first developed and most effectively employed by the Human Rights Committee (which monitors implementation of the International Covenant on Civil and Political Rights),[34] attempts not only to improve the reporting process but also to influence the progressive development of international human rights law by offering quasi-authoritative interpretations of the obligations under the treaty.

Consider a more or less arbitrarily chosen example: General Comment 20 of the Human Rights Committee, adopted in 1992.[35] It interprets Article 7 of the International Covenant on Civil and Political Rights, which states (in its entirety), "No one shall be subjected to torture or to cruel, inhuman or degrading treatment or punishment. In particular, no one shall be subjected without his free consent to medical or scientific experimentation." This pithy statement certainly could benefit from some elaboration, which General Comment 20 seeks to provide.

Paragraph 2 states that the aim of the article "is to protect both the dignity and the physical and mental integrity of the individual"—offering a relatively expansive reading that links this provision to the foundational claim in the Preamble of the Covenants that "these rights derive from the inherent dignity of the human person." Paragraph 2 also explicitly links this article to the provision in Article 10 that "all persons deprived of their liberty shall be treated with humanity and with respect for the inherent dignity of the human person." And it explicitly applies these obligations to agents of the state not just when acting in their official capacity but also when operating "outside their official capacity or in a private capacity."

Paragraph 3 draws attention to the fact that no exceptions are permitted in times of emergency. (Along similar lines, Paragraph 15 expresses concern over amnesties for torturers that have been granted by some states.) And, in holding that "no justification or extenuating circumstances may be invoked to excuse a violation of Article 7 for any reasons, including those based on an order from a superior officer or public authority," the committee in effect applies the provisions of the 1984 Convention Against Torture to the interpretation of the Covenant. (The prohibition of the use of evidence obtained by torture, advanced in Paragraph 12, does much the same thing.)

Paragraph 4 holds that it is neither necessary nor productive to draw up a list of prohibited acts. Nonetheless, Paragraph 5 emphasizes that mental suffering falls within the acts prohibited by Article 7 and that its protections extend to certain forms of corporal punishment, including protection of "children, pupils and patients in teaching and medical institutions." Paragraph 6 explicitly places prolonged solitary confinement within the coverage of Article 7.

Paragraph 8 claims that the obligation of the state is not simply to legislatively prohibit such actions but also to take positive steps of protection. Paragraphs 10–13 specify some of those steps, including widely disseminating information on the ban on torture, systematically reviewing interrogation practices, and prohibiting incommunicado detention.

Such observations and interpretations are not formally binding. They do, however, have considerable informal authority—and are especially useful for human rights lawyers and advocates who are seeking authoritative legal grounding for their representation and advocacy.

3.3 Communication/Petition Procedures

The core international human rights treaties also allow individual communications (sometimes called petitions): four within the text of the treaty (but states are required to opt in or opt out of these procedures) and the remainder in the form of an **optional protocol** (see Table 5.1). Depending on the treaty, between one-third and two-thirds of states-parties do not allow individual petitions. Not surprisingly, some of the worst violators choose not to participate. In addition, the number of cases considered is tiny. And, in the end, petition procedures are not even binding in international law.

Although the details differ from body to body, there is a general pattern. Communications from individuals or groups are screened by the UN Secretariat. Those that show potential merit are registered. Registered petitions are then screened carefully for admissibility. (The principal requirements are that the alleged violations fall under the scope of the treaty and that local remedies have been exhausted.)

Once the initial procedural hurdles have been surmounted, the relevant committee corresponds with the government in question and sometimes with the petitioner (or their representative). It also often carries out inquiries into public records and independent sources of information. It then states its views as to whether there has been a violation of the treaty and makes recommendations as to remedies.

These findings are, explicitly, merely the view of the committee. They are not binding in international law (let alone national law). In fact, the state has no obligation even to respond to the committee's views. Nonetheless, many states, especially those with an active civil society, do take the findings seriously. Individuals often receive remedy as a result of their petitions. In some cases—prominent examples include complaints of discrimination on the basis of sexual orientation in Australia and against indigenous women in Canada—national legislation has been changed in response to the recommendations of the committee.

4 Additional Global Multilateral Actors

At least four other global multilateral actors merit note: the International Criminal Court (ICC), the UN Security Council, the International Labor Organization (ILO), and the United Nations Educational, Scientific, and Cultural Organization (UNESCO). Each has a functional mandate that centrally includes, but is not limited to, human rights.

4.1 International Criminal Court

The ICC was established by the Rome Statute, which was adopted in 1998 and entered into force in 2002. It is a permanent international tribunal that adjudicates individual criminal liability for genocide, crimes against humanity, war crimes, and the crime of aggression.[36]

At the end of 2025, the Court had, since its first indictment in 2005 (of Joseph Kony of Uganda), indicted seventy-four individuals[37] and begun proceedings in thirty-four cases[38] that have resulted in seven convictions[39] and four acquittals.[40] (Four individuals remained under trial.[41]). In its early years, the Court was sometimes criticized for focusing only on African cases. Defenders replied that the Court was simply going where the crimes were. Today, however, the reach of the Court now seems close to global. In addition to several African cases, the Court in 2025 was investigating situations in Georgia, Bangladesh/Myanmar, Afghanistan, Palestine, the Philippines, Venezuela, and Ukraine.[42] And prominent individuals indicted included Vladimir Putin, Benjamin Netanyahu, and Rodrigo Duterte. (The proceedings against Mohammed Diab Ibrahim Al-Masri (Deif), the commander of the military wing of Hamas, were terminated after his death.)

The ICC, however, has jurisdiction only over a narrow range of human rights issues. And the focus on individual violators, while in many ways attractive—it ends the international impunity of leaders whose crimes fall within the jurisdiction of the Court—at best provides symbolic justice rather than practical remedy—and then only in a very small number of cases. (In recent years, there have been about five or six indictments a year.)

Furthermore, states must agree to recognize the Court's jurisdiction,[43] which only 124 out of 193 UN member-states have chosen to do. Therefore, a third of the world's countries, containing half the world's population, are not subject to the ICC's jurisdiction—including the world's five most populous countries (China, India, the United States, Indonesia, and Pakistan) and Russia. And these nonmembers often present the Court as a threat to their sovereignty. For example, the United States has pressured allies that are members to commit to not turning indicted Americans into the ICC.

Like many other multilateral human rights institutions, the fairest overall assessment of the ICC probably is "mixed but modestly positive." And the symbolic significance of the Court is immense.

4.2 UN Security Council

The UN Security Council regularly addresses human rights issues, which since the 1990s have become a part of most peacekeeping and peace-building operations. It also has the authority to authorize the threat or use of force, which it has occasionally exercised in response to genocide—although with a timidness that has provoked considerable controversy. We will look more closely at humanitarian intervention against genocide in Chapter 11.

4.3 International Labor Organization

The ILO is the granddaddy of multilateral human rights organizations, founded in 1919.[44] Eleven "fundamental" ILO conventions (treaties) have dealt with freedom of association, the right to organize and bargain collectively, forced labor, discrimination, child labor, migrant workers, equal pay for equal work, working conditions, and workplace safety. Even nonbinding ILO recommendations provide an important international reference point for national standards.

ILO monitoring procedures, which date back to 1926, have been the model for international human rights reporting systems. The Committee of Experts meets annually to review periodic reports submitted by states on their implementation of ratified conventions. If apparent problems are uncovered, the committee may issue a direct request for information or for changes in policy. Over the past two decades, more than a thousand such requests have brought changes in national policies. If the problem remains unresolved, the committee may make "observations," that is, authoritative determinations of violations of the convention in question.

The Conference Committee, which is made up of ILO delegates (rather than independent experts), provides an additional level of scrutiny with greater political backing. Each year it selects cases from the report of the Committee of Experts for further review. Government representatives are called upon to provide additional information and explanation. Special complaint procedures also exist for violations of the right to freedom of association and for discrimination in employment.

No less important than these inquisitorial or adversarial procedures is the institution of "direct contacts," a program of consultations and advice, often initiated by a government concerned about improving its performance with respect to a particular convention. The ILO is a leader in the cooperative resolution of problems before they reach international monitoring bodies.

Part of the ILO's success can be attributed to its unique tripartite structure. Intergovernmental organizations typically are made up solely of state representatives. NGOs often participate in deliberations but have no decision-making powers. In the ILO, however, workers' and employers' representatives from each member-state are voting members of the organization, making it much more difficult for states to hide behind the curtain of sovereignty. The trans-ideological appeal of workers' rights has also been important to the ILO's success. In addition, the Committee of Experts, the ILO's central monitoring body, deals principally with technical issues such as hours of work, minimum working age, workplace safety, and identity documents for seamen. In monitoring such technical conventions, the committee develops and confirms expectations of neutrality that can help to moderate controversy when more contentious political issues do arise.

4.4 United Nations Educational, Scientific, and Cultural Organization

UNESCO has addressed a variety of human rights issues.[45] Its 1960 Convention on Discrimination in Education was an important normative instrument during the doldrums while the Covenants languished in the General Assembly (see Chapter 1, Section 3). Its 2005 Declaration on Bioethics and Human Rights has helped to globalize the discussion of this important topic. And UNESCO has done important normative and programmatic work on cultural rights, especially connected with preserving cultural heritages and languages.

A striking example is the close cooperation of UNESCO with the ICC to bring charges against Ahmad al-Faqi al-Mahdi, who was indicted on charges of orchestrating the destruction of ancient mausoleums, medieval shrines, tombs of Sufi saints, and a fifteenth-century mosque in Timbuktu, Mali, in 2012. In issuing the indictment, ICC prosecutor Fatou Bensouda declared these acts to be war crimes under the Rome Statute. Al-Mahdi surrendered and was transferred to The Hague for trial in September 2015 and in September 2016 was sentenced to nine years in prison.

5 Case Study: Special Procedures

The special procedures (also called "special mandates") established by the Human Rights Council involve either a single individual or a five-member Working Group of independent human rights experts tasked to report to and advise the Council on "thematic" (issue-specific) or country-specific human rights issues. As of January 2025, there were forty-six thematic mandates and fourteen country mandates. Examples of thematic mandates include Working Groups on arbitrary detention, enforced/involuntary disappearances, human rights and transnational corporations and other business enterprises, and discrimination against women and girls. The Council has appointed special rapporteurs on topics such as cultural rights, the rights of disabled persons, the right to food, the situation of human rights defenders, and the protection of human rights in the context of climate change. Independent experts have been appointed to investigate matters such as the rights of older persons; the impact of foreign debt on the enjoyment of economic, social, and cultural rights; and violence and discrimination based on sexual orientation and gender identity (LGBTQ+ persons). The country-specific mandates in 2025 were Belarus, Burundi, Cambodia, the Central African Republic, North Korea, Eritrea, Iran, Mali, Myanmar (Burma), Nicaragua, Palestine, Russian Federation, South Sudan, and Syria.

Mandate holders submit annual reports to the Human Rights Council. Many also report to the General Assembly. The Human Rights Council reviews country-specific mandates every year and thematic mandates every three years. Some mandates (such as the Working Group on Enforced or Involuntary Disappearances) have operated continuously since the 1980s.

Mandate holders work in their own capacity as independent experts. As such, they are not considered to be UN staff, receive no financial remuneration, and are expected to remain impartial. Individuals appointed are limited to a tenure of six years for each assignment.

Mandate holders are empowered to undertake a wide range of activities in support of their mandate. They can visit countries, communicate with states regarding alleged violations, conduct thematic studies, convene expert consultations, engage in advocacy and raise public awareness, give advice on technical operations, receive information from individuals and civil society organizations, and overall contribute to the betterment of international human rights standards.

The stature of the mandate-holder can also be used to increase the impact of these special procedures. For example, Juan Mendez (from Argentina), who served as the special rapporteur on torture from 2010 to 2016, is the former head of Human Rights Watch and the International Center for Transnational Justice. Between 2005 and 2011, John Ruggie (from the United States) was the special representative of the secretary-general on human rights and transnational corporations and other business enterprises. Ruggie (who died in 2021) was one of the world's leading scholars of international relations (teaching at Harvard and having previously been a dean at Columbia), a former assistant secretary-general of the United Nations, and the founder of the Global Compact (a leading international actor in the field of corporate responsibility in the areas of human rights, labor, environment, and corruption). The groundbreaking work that Ruggie undertook as special representative prompted the Council to establish the Working Group on Business and Human Rights in 2011.

5.1 Growth and Development of the Special Procedures

In 1963—in response to alleged human rights violations in South Vietnam—the South Vietnamese government invited UN representatives to investigate the situation directly.[46] Although the subsequent mission to South Vietnam does not resemble the special procedures we have today, it was the first example of a country visit to assess human rights conditions.

In 1965, states from Africa, Asia, and the Middle East called for a UN response to human rights violations related to colonialism, racism, and apartheid. This prompted the Commission on Human Rights to establish the first two special procedures mandates for a Working

Group on the state of South Africa and for a special rapporteur on the South African practice of apartheid.

In 1980, the first *thematic* special procedure was established by creating the Working Group on Enforced or Involuntary Disappearances. A thematic mandate was chosen in response to arguments that a country-specific mandate would be discriminatory, insofar as enforced disappearances plagued nations around the world. Over the next ten years, additional Working Groups were established to address extrajudicial, summary, or arbitrary executions; religious intolerance; mercenaries; torture; and the sale of children.[47] By the time the Human Rights Council replaced the Commission on Human Rights (in 2006), there were forty special procedure mandates. In May 2014, the number of active special procedure mandates reached fifty for the first time. It now hovers around sixty.

Despite their somewhat narrow scope, thematic mandate-holders can investigate their topic in any country (and usually with little further authorization). The relative abundance of thematic mandates reflects the current preference of the United Nations. Country mandates have proven more difficult to both establish and fulfill, both because of the impression that they are more political and because they are reviewed every year (instead of every three years).

5.2 Impact of the Special Procedures

The special procedures mechanism has become a core component of UN human rights protection and promotion and is perhaps the most important multilateral mechanism (along with the High Commissioner) for addressing human rights violations on the ground. The steady expansion of the special procedures suggests that the United Nations as an institution believes the system has been and will continue to be effective in shaping state behavior regarding human rights. But has this mechanism actually initiated positive change in state behavior?

A 2014 report by the URG does not find that numerical expansion has improved efforts to shape or change state behavior. Instead, the URG nevertheless identified six core "determinants of influence" that UN policy makers must strive to strengthen and improve: independence and accountability; expertise and standing; flexibility, reach, and accessibility; cooperation; implementation and follow-up; and availability of resources and secretariat support.

In another assessment, Surya Subedi stated that most mandate-holders are overloaded with responsibility, as they are "expected simultaneously to become a human rights activist, a rallying point for human rights, an international diplomat, an academic, and a government adviser."[48] This work is also done without financial compensation and on the mandate-holder's own time. Subedi also believes that the support that the OHCHR provides to its mandate-holders is meager (e.g., only providing one assistant and recommending only two country visits per year). Although mandate-holders who are based at academic institutions often receive university support, this arrangement favors selecting mandate holders from relatively wealthy universities and research centers in the Global North.[49] Subedi also cited the lack of effective follow-up procedures and overlaps in mandate duties (particularly between country and thematic mandates) as hindering the effectiveness of mandate-holders.

Rosa Freedman and Jacob Mchangama have reached similarly pessimistic conclusions. They found that the increase in mandates has not been paired with an appropriate increase in resources and funding, resulting in fewer country visits, fewer reports, and overall less time for mandate-holders to conduct their activities. They also found that new mandates are diverting resources away from other activities and increasingly focus not on individual cases but on criticizing state policy programs and foreign relations.[50] (One might argue, though, that even though it is often easier to provide remedies in individual cases of violations, state policies are usually the cause of individual violations and thus a more fundamental problem.)

Whatever their limitations, though, the special procedures can make a real difference for individuals suffering from human rights violations.

Consider the Working Group on Enforced or Involuntary Disappearances. After examining communications detailing a disappearance, the Working Group transmits the case to the government in question. If necessary, reminders are sent, at least once a year. More than 19,000 were handled in the group's first decade of work. According to its latest report (from July 2025), the Working Group has since its inception in 1980 inquired into the fate of 62,904 individuals in 115 countries around the world. In the preceding year it had initiated 1,278 new cases in thirty-eight states and "clarified" (that is, identified the fate of) 233.[51]

In more than one in five cases, the whereabouts or fate of the individual has been clarified. Special urgent-action procedures for disappearances within the three months preceding the communication, when most victims suffer torture or execution but also when they are most likely to reappear, have resolved a somewhat higher percentage of cases. There is good reason to believe that a significant number of those identified by this procedure owe their lives to it.

The immediate impact of these bodies is ultimately a matter of the willingness of governments to engage in conversations with them, allow them to visit their countries, and listen to their concerns and advice. But particularly when either the body or the mandate holder has a prominent international reputation, many states are willing to make improvements in the treatment of particular individuals. And some of the reports by these experts are important sources of information about abuses, used by national and transnational advocates.

Discussion Questions

1. Several UN TMBs have an interstate complaints mechanism where a state can report another state for an alleged human rights violation. However, this mechanism remains unused. Why might this be? Do you think states will continue to refrain from its usage? What are the potential effects of one state reporting another?
2. TMBs can conduct inquiries into a state's actions upon the body's own discretion. However, a state can opt out of this process by not recognizing the competence of the

TMB. Does this render the inquiries mechanism useless? Can you think of instances where an opt-out might be justifiable?

3. We have suggested that international human rights procedures are likely to have their greatest impact where human rights abuses are less egregious. What does this suggest about the most effective forms of international action? Are you comfortable with the idea of writing off the worst cases (which some may conclude is the central policy implication of this argument)? Is there a practical alternative?
4. Membership on the Human Rights Council has included states with traditionally good human rights records, like the Netherlands, as well as states with deeply defective human rights records, like China. Is it better to attempt to include all states in this mechanism or selectively exclude states with troublesome records? *All* states with dismal records? In your view, is there anything like a clear cutoff of acceptability?
5. Both special procedures and treaty bodies have a seemingly disproportional emphasis on civil and political rights. What are the reasons for this? (Bias? Tradition? The character of the rights/violations? Possibility for impact?). Is this a defensible allocation of resources and attention? What would have to change to bring about a more comprehensive system of international human rights monitoring?
6. As stated in this chapter, the number of thematic UN mandates has proliferated in recent decades, especially when compared to country-specific mandates. Why might this be? Are thematic mandates more likely to safeguard human rights, or are they simply easier to establish because they are not focused on a specific country? What are the potential pros and cons of this emphasis on thematic special procedures?

Suggested Readings

Primary source information on most of the bodies considered in this chapter is available on the comprehensive and easy-to-use Office of the High Commissioner for Human Rights website. The websites for all the individual treaty bodies can be accessed through www.ohchr.org/EN/HRBodies/Pages/HumanRightsBodies.aspx.

Among the extensive published scholarly literature, special note should be made of the second edition of Frédéric Mégret and Philip Alston, eds., *The United Nations and Human Rights: A Critical Appraisal* (Oxford University Press, 2020). Also excellent is the *Research Handbook on Compliance in International Human Rights Law*, edited by Rainer Grote, Mariela Morales Antoniazzi, and Davide Paris (Edward Elgar, 2021). Two older wide-ranging readers are Gundmundur Alfredsson, Jonas Grimheden, Bertrand D. Ramcharan, and Alfred Zayas, eds., *International Human Rights Monitoring Mechanisms: Essays in Honour of Jakob Th. Möeller*, 2nd ed. (Martinus Nijhof, 2009); and Geoff Gilbert, ed., *The Delivery of Human Rights: Essays in Honour of Professor Sir Nigel Rodley* (Taylor & Francis, 2010).

The standard work on treaty monitoring is Philip Alston and James Crawford, eds., *The Future of UN Human Rights Treaty Monitoring* (Cambridge University Press, 2000). It covers the full range of venues and issues. A more recent article on the subject is Dinah Shelton, "The Development of Human Rights Law and Challenges Faced by UN Treaty Bodies 1969–2022," in the *Max Planck Yearbook of United Nations Law Online* 25 (2022): 682–717.

Christof Heyns and Frans Viljoen, *The Impact of United Nations Human Rights Treaties on the Domestic Level: Twenty Years On* (Brill | Nijhoff, 2024) provides considerable illustrative material on the domestic impact of international human rights treaties—and this latest edition is available as a free, open-source e-book. A less recent yet comprehensive examination of the treaty system is Helen Keller and Geir Ulfstein, eds., *UN Human Rights Treaty Bodies: Law and Legitimacy* (Cambridge University Press, 2012). A recent analysis of how self-reporting to treaty monitoring bodies can be associated with better human rights practices, see Cosette D. Creamer and Beth A. Simmons, "The Proof is in the Process: Self-Reporting under International Human Rights Treaties," *American Journal of International Law* 114 (2020): 1–50.

The literature on individual bodies is immense. The following books provide a good start for those interested in more details:

Yogesh Tyagi, *The UN Human Rights Committee: Practice and Procedure* (Cambridge University Press, 2011); Alex Conte, *Defining Civil and Political Rights: The Jurisprudence of the United Nations Human Rights Committee* (Ashgate, 2009); Patricia Schulz, Ruth Halperin-Kaddari, Beate Rudolf, and Marsha A. Freeman, eds., *The UN Convention on the Elimination of All Forms of Discrimination Against Women and its Optional Protocol: A Commentary*, 2nd ed. (Oxford University Press, 2022); Hanna Beate Schöpp-Schilling and Cees Flinterman, eds., *The Circle of Empowerment: Twenty-Five Years of the UN Committee on the Elimination of Discrimination against Women* (Feminist Press at the City University of New York, 2007); Andrew Byrnes and Jane Connors, *The International Bill of Rights for Women: The Impact of the CEDAW Convention* (Oxford University Press, 2008); Meena Shivdas and Sarah Coleman, eds., *Without Prejudice: CEDAW and the Determination of Women's Rights in a Legal and Cultural Context* (Commonwealth Secretariat, 2010); Fleur van Leeuwen, *Women's Rights Are Human Rights: The Practice of the United Nations Human Rights Committee and the Committee on Economic, Social, and Cultural Rights* (Intersentia, 2010); John Tobin, *The UN Convention on the Rights of the Child: A Commentary* (Oxford University Press, 2019); Catherine Rutgers, ed., *Creating a World Fit for Children: Understanding the UN Convention on the Rights of the Child* (International Debate Education Association, 2011); Trevor Buck, *International Child Law*, 2nd ed. (Taylor & Francis, 2010); and Manfred Nowak, Moritz Birk, and Giuliana Monina, *The United Nations Convention Against Torture: A Commentary*, 2nd ed. (Oxford University Press, 2019). For an authoritative introduction to the International Criminal Court, see William A. Schabas, *An Introduction to the International Criminal Court*, 6th ed. (Cambridge University Press, 2020) Finally, Joel E. Oestreich, *Power and Principle: Human Rights Programming in International Organizations* (Georgetown University Press, 2007), examines human rights in the work of UNICEF, the World Bank, and the World Health Organization.

Notes

1 Comprehensive information on the activities of the Council is available at www.ohchr.org/en/hr-bodies/hrc/about-council.

2 The Council also has held nine "urgent debates," for example, on the situations in Syria, Ukraine, and Gaza.

3 The main UPR gateway page is at www.ohchr.org/en/hr-bodies/upr/upr-main. For more information, see www.ohchr.org/en/hr-bodies/upr/basic-facts.
4 Subhas Gujadhur and Marc Limon, *Towards the Third Cycle of the UPR: Stick or Twist (Lessons Learned from the First Ten Years of the Universal Periodic Review)* (Universal Rights Group, July 2016).
5 Gujadhur and Limon, *Towards the Third Cycle of the UPR*, 4.
6 Created in 1947, it was originally called the Sub-Commission on the Prevention of Discrimination and Protection of Minorities. It was renamed in 1999.
7 Universal Rights Group/yourHRC.org, *The Human Rights Council in 2023*. Online at https://www.universal-rights.org/urg-policy-reports/the-human-rights-council-in-2023/, p. 17.
8 Universal Rights Group/yourHRC.org, *The Human Rights Council in 2022*. Online at https://www.universal-rights.org/urg-policy-reports/the-human-rights-council-in-2022/, p. 17.
9 Universal Rights Group/yourHRC.org, *The Human Rights Council in 2022*. Online at https://www.universal-rights.org/urg-policy-reports/the-human-rights-council-in-2022/, p. 23.
10 Universal Rights Group/yourHRC.org, *The Human Rights Council in 2023*. Online at https://www.universal-rights.org/urg-policy-reports/the-human-rights-council-in-2023/, p. 19.
11 Michael Joel Voss, "The Global South and Norm Advocacy at the United Nations Human Rights Council," *International Journal on Minority and Group Rights* 27 (2020): 728–764, at 731.
12 Universal Rights Group/yourHRC.org, *The Human Rights Council in 2022*. Online at https://www.universal-rights.org/urg-policy-reports/the-human-rights-council-in-2022/, p. 23.
13 UN Doc. A/HRC/48/L.11.
14 UN Doc. A/HRC/51/L.6.
15 Universal Rights Group/yourHRC.org, *The Human Rights Council in 2022*. Online at https://www.universal-rights.org/urg-policy-reports/the-human-rights-council-in-2022/, p. 9. See also the Report of the Human Rights Council on its fifty-first session, UN Doc. A/HRC/51/2, p. 19.
16 Tanner Larkin, "China's Normfare and the Threat to Human Rights," *Columbia Law Review* 122/8: 2285–2322 (December 2022), p. 2295.
17 Larkin, "China's Normfare and the Threat to Human Rights" p. 2298.
18 Alexander Dukalskis, "A Fox in the Henhouse: China, Normative Change, and the UN Human Rights Council," *Journal of Human Rights* 22, no. 3 (2023): 334–350.
19 Dukalskis, "A Fox in the Henhouse" p. 339.
20 Dukalskis, "A Fox in the Henhouse" p. 339.
21 Dukalskis, "A Fox in the Henhouse" p. 340.
22 Dukalskis, "A Fox in the Henhouse" p. 340.
23 Dukalskis, "A Fox in the Henhouse" p. 340.
24 Andréa Worden, "China at the UN Human Rights Council: Conjuring a 'Community of Shared Future for Humankind?'" in *An Emerging China-Centric Order: China's Vision for a New World Order in Practice*, edited by N. Rolland (2020), 33–48. National Bureau of Asian Research Special Report #87. Online at https://www.nbr.org/publication/china-at-the-un-human-rights-council-conjuring-a-community-of-shared-future-for-humankind/.
25 Dukalskis, "A Fox in the Henhouse," p. 340–341. The V-Dem dataset is at https://v-dem.net/data/the-v-dem-dataset/.
26 Gino Pauselli, Francisco Urdinez, and Federico Merke, "Shaping the Liberal International Order from the Inside: A Natural Experiment on China's Influence in the UN Human Rights Council" (December 10, 2022). Available at SSRN: https://ssrn.com/abstract=4299087 or http://doi.org/10.2139/ssrn.4299087.
27 Dukalskis, "A Fox in the Henhouse," p. 343–344.
28 Dukalskis, "A Fox in the Henhouse," p. 345.
29 Universal Rights Group/yourHRC.org, *The Human Rights Council in 2023*. Online at https://www.universal-rights.org/urg-policy-reports/the-human-rights-council-in-2023/, p. 3.
30 See www.ohchr.org/en/ohchr_homepage.
31 Located in Argentina, Bahrain, Bangladesh, Barbados, Belize, Bosnia Herzegovina, Brazil, Bolivia, Burkina Faso, Burundi, Republic of Congo, Costa Rica, Dominican Republic, Ecuador, El

Salvador, Equatorial Guinea, Eswatini, Gambia, Georgia/South Caucasus, Guinea-Bissau, Guyana, Jamaica, Jordan, Kazakhstan, Kenya, Lesotho, Madagascar, Malawi, Malaysia, Maldives, Moldova, Mongolia, Montenegro, Mozambique, Myanmar, Nepal, Nigeria, the Republic of North Macedonia, Papua New Guinea, Paraguay, Peru, the Philippines, Russian Federation*, Rwanda, Samoa, Serbia, Sierra Leone, Sri Lanka, Suriname, Tajikistan, Timor-Leste, Trinidad and Tobago, Uruguay, Zambia, and Zimbabwe.

32 See https://www.ohchr.org/en/about-us/funding-and-budget.

33 See https://www.wbgalumni.org/world-bank-budget-increases-by-6-in-real-terms-in-fy25-for-more-country-engagement-and-supervision-support/.

34 The name of this committee is a historical artifact from the early draft of the then-single "International Covenant on Human Rights," before it was split into the ICCPR and ICESCR. The United Nation never bothered to change the name to Committee on Civil and Political Rights, which would put it in line with the other TMBs.

35 Full text of the Comment is available at https://www.refworld.org/docid/453883fb0.html.

36 See www.icc-cpi.int.

37 https://www.icc-cpi.int/defendants.

38 https://www.icc-cpi.int/cases.

39 https://www.icc-cpi.int/cases?f%5B0%5D=accused_states_cases%3A358.

40 https://www.icc-cpi.int/cases?f%5B0%5D=accused_states_cases%3A359. In addition, six individuals had their charges vacated, withdrawn, or not confirmed. https://www.icc-cpi.int/cases?f%5B0%5D=accused_states_cases%3A356.

41 https://www.icc-cpi.int/cases?f%5B0%5D=state_of_%3A131.

42 https://www.icc-cpi.int/situations-under-investigations.

43 The Security Council has exercised its authority to refer a situation to the Court in 2005 concerning Sudan and in 2011 concerning Libya.

44 See https://www.ilo.org/.

45 See https://unesco.org/.

46 This section draws heavily on Marc Limon and Hilary Power, *History of the United Nations Special Procedures Mechanism: Origins, Evolution and Reform* (Universal Rights Group, 2014).

47 See www.ohchr.org/en/special-procedures-human-rights-council/special-procedures-human-rights-council.

48 Surya Subedi, "Protection of Human Rights through the Mechanism of UN Special Rapporteurs," *Human Rights Quarterly* 33, no. 1 (February 2011), p. 212.

49 Subedi, "Protection of Human Rights through the Mechanism of UN Special Rapporteurs," p. 218.

50 Rosa Freedman and Jacob Mchangama, "Expanding or Diluting Rights? The Proliferation of United Nations Special Procedure Mandates," *Human Rights Quarterly* 38, no. 1 (February 2016): 164–193.

51 "Enforced or Involuntary Disappearance: Report of the Working Group on Enforced or Involuntary Disappearances," UN Doc. A/HRC/60/35.

6 Regional Human Rights Regimes

Regional human rights regimes run the gamut from a system of authoritative judicial enforcement in Europe to barely nascent regimes in Asia and the Arab Middle East. This chapter reviews these regimes and assesses their contributions to the multilateral promotion and protection of human rights. The chapter concludes with case studies on the Inter-American Commission and the African Commission.

1 The European Regional Regime

1.1 The Council of Europe System

The forty-six-member Council of Europe operates a strong system of regional human rights enforcement.[1] Its normative core is the 1954 Convention for the Protection of Human Rights and Fundamental Freedoms (commonly known as the European Convention on Human Rights, or ECHR), which covers mostly civil and political rights, and the European Social Charter, which addresses a wide range of economic and social rights in considerable detail. The Council of Europe Commissioner for Human Rights (Michael O'Flaherty, an Irish human rights lawyer, became the fifth commissioner in 2024) has extensive powers to investigate and publicize human rights issues on either a thematic or a country basis. Special procedures exist for torture, including the right of the European Committee for the Prevention of Torture to visit all places of detention in any member-state.

The 1954 European Convention, which is mandatory for the members of the Council of Europe, addresses core civil and political rights. In 2010, fifteen protocols were added to deepen and extend the list of rights protected by the Convention.

The original European Social Charter of 1961 includes nineteen enumerated rights. In 1996, the Revised European Social Charter greatly extended the range of recognized rights. Parties to the Revised Charter are bound by at least six out of nine core rights, of their own

DOI: 10.4324/9781003373520-8

selection, and no fewer than sixteen articles total. Forty-two of the forty-six member-states of the Council are parties to one of the Charters.

The European Court of Human Rights exercises mandatory jurisdiction over the European Convention and its decisions create binding legal obligations.[2] (The European Social Charter is not subject to judicial enforcement.) Since the reorganization and expansion of the Court in 1998, individuals in any member country have had direct access to the Court, subject to minimal procedural restrictions (most notably the requirement that local remedies have been exhausted).

Since its founding in 1959, the European Court of Human Rights has issued more than 28,000 judgments.[3] Some of its more prominent decisions have led to significant changes in national law. About two-thirds of its decisions are in favor of the petitioner and most of those have brought relief, including monetary damages. The system, however, has become a victim of its own success. In 2024, 28,400 applications were received and 13,373 "priority applications" were pending (along with more than 46,000 other applications).[4]

A small number of states find themselves continually before the Court, with more than a third of the Court's judgments involving just four member-states: Russia (which both attempted to withdraw and was expelled from the Council in March 2022), Turkey, Italy, and Romania. Nearly two-thirds of pending cases involve petitioners in Greece, Romania, Russia, Turkey, and Ukraine.

One of the most important features of the Court has been its adoption of the principle of "evolutive interpretation." Treaty provisions are interpreted not according to the understandings at the time of drafting (which is the norm in international law and many national legal systems) but in light of current understandings and practices. The Court thus serves as an important mechanism for the progressive evolution of regional human rights obligations.

The European Committee of Social Rights[5] supervises implementation of the rights of the Social Charter, principally through a state reporting procedure similar to those in the UN system (see Chapter 5, Section 3.1). Reports focus on four thematic areas: employment, training, and equal opportunities; health, social security, and social protection; labor rights; and children, families, and migrants. Each year, states-parties must report on one area. After the completion of a four-year cycle, the Committee issues its findings and recommendations to the member-state. Under a 1998 optional protocol, the Committee created a collective, rather than an individual, complaints procedure. Petitions or complaints may be filed only by "representative" organizations, such as trade unions and specific NGOs who have been officially recognized by the Committee to file petitions.[6]

1.2 The European Union and the OSCE

The twenty-seven-member European Union (EU), although not primarily a human rights body, has further strengthened the European regime in at least three important ways. First, the 2007 Lisbon Treaty, a major constitutional revision of the EU that amended the earlier Rome (1957) and Maastricht (1993) Treaties, made the Charter of Fundamental Rights of the EU (adopted in 2000) legally binding on all member-states. Second, the Lisbon Treaty gave the Union's supreme judicial organ, the Court of Justice of the EU, the power to interpret the Charter of Fundamental Rights and to hear cases arising under its guarantees. (The United Kingdom (before Brexit) and Poland secured protocols of dubious legal effect to exempt themselves from some aspects of this provision.) Third, the Lisbon Treaty committed the EU *as an intergovernmental organization* to accede to the ECHR, thus making the Union itself and its institutions subject to the decisions of the European Court of Human Rights.

The post of the EU Special Representative for Human Rights was created in 2012 to promote the EU's human rights interests. The Special Representative's responsibilities include meeting with governments about the human rights conditions in their countries, chairing formal dialogues about human rights between the EU and other countries, meeting with members of civil society, and speaking at the United Nations and the Human Rights Council. Eamon Gilmore of Ireland, a former leader of the Irish Labour Party and Minister of Foreign Affairs and Trade, was appointed in 2018 and served until February 2024. During his two terms, Gilmore was responsible for ensuring the implementation of the EU's Action Plan on Human Rights and Democracy which was adopted in November 2020. After the brief tenure of Olof Skoog of Sweden, Kajsa Ollongren of the Netherlands was appointed Special Representative in June 2025.

At the UN Human Rights Council, the EU is a recognized caucusing bloc, often organizing a common position for its member-states (only a few of which serve on the Council). As a recognized observer with enhanced status, the EU can make statements on behalf of all of its members, engage in negotiations, and present proposals.

Important European regional mechanisms also exist under the Organization for Security and Co-operation in Europe (OSCE),[7] a group of fifty-seven states from Europe, Central Asia, and North America. Its work on minority rights has been especially significant: the OSCE High Commissioner on National Minorities is a leading regional actor on this topic of immense historical and contemporary importance. The OSCE also has notable programs to support free elections and rule of law (through the Office for Democratic Institutions and Human Rights) and media freedom (through the OSCE Representative on Freedom of the Media) and to combat human trafficking (through the Office of the Special Representative and Coordinator for Combating Trafficking in Human Beings).

The citizens of Europe thus have a considerable array of regional multilateral mechanisms available to them not just to encourage their governments to implement their obligations but in many instances to make legally binding findings of violations. And given the context of extensive and intensive regional cooperation, most states usually comply with most decisions.

2 The Inter-American System

2.1 Regional Norms

The American Declaration of the Rights and Duties of Man was adopted by the General Assembly of the Organization of American States (OAS) in April 1948. Like the Universal

Declaration, it is not legally binding. The 1969 American Convention on Human Rights, which is a legally binding instrument, came into force in 1978. It has been ratified by twenty-five of the thirty-five OAS members, including all Central and South American states (except Belize).[8] The United States, Canada, and several Caribbean states, however, have not ratified the Convention.

The American Convention largely parallels the International Covenant on Civil and Political Rights, although it contains a few unusually robust guarantees. For example, Article 13 specifies that freedom of thought and expression includes the right to seek, receive, and impart information and Article 14 grants journalists and the media the right of reply. In its decisions and rulings, the Inter-American Commission and the Inter-American Court of Human Rights (discussed below) have ruled that transitional governments have an affirmative duty to investigate and prosecute human rights violations of prior governments, thus establishing a "right to truth" and the illegality of **amnesty** policies.

The 1988 Protocol of San Salvador addresses economic and social rights. It has been ratified by only half (eighteen) of the OAS member-states. There are also regional conventions on torture, violence against women, disappearances, and discrimination against persons with disabilities. And the OAS has adopted resolutions and declarations on a variety of topics, including freedom of expression, indigenous peoples, and racism and discrimination.

The other major regional normative instrument is the 2001 Inter-American Democratic Charter (IADC), which has become arguably as important as the Declaration and the Convention. Unlike the American Convention, the IADC is legally binding on all thirty-five OAS member-states. It defines democracy and the obligations of states when democratic rule appears to be under threat and aims to promote and defend democracy in the Americas.

The power of the IADC is well illustrated by its invocation by fourteen OAS heads of state in 2002, when elements of the Venezuelan military attempted to remove Hugo Chavez from power in a coup d'état, inhibiting even the United States, which was strongly opposed to Chavez, from recognizing the coup. In July 2009, the OAS General Assembly suspended Honduras after its elected government was deposed by a military coup. In late 2016, the OAS used the Democratic Charter to push for dialogue in the political crisis that was emerging in Venezuela. By January 2019, the OAS Permanent Council agreed not to recognize Nicolas Maduro's presidency given that it was the result of an illegitimate electoral process.[9] Although Maduro remained in power until January 2026, this reflects not only the ultimate weakness of the system (to remove a non-democratic regime) but also its strength (in impeding the United States from intervening to remove the dictator—and in the near universal regional condemnation of his removal by US military forces).

2.2 The Inter-American Commission and Court

The Inter-American Commission on Human Rights (IACHR) was established in 1959.[10] Much like the UN's Human Rights Council, it operates independently of any human rights treaty, in this case as an autonomous organization within the OAS (whose thirty-five members include all the independent states of the Western Hemisphere). Its seven members are elected by secret ballot by the OAS General Assembly and serve in a personal capacity.

The Inter-American Commission conducts country studies and examines thematic issues of regional concern. During the 1970s and 1980s, the Commission aggressively used its independent authority to pressure repressive governments. Its reporting on Chile under military rule was particularly important to both internal and international human rights advocates (see the historical case study 6.1 below).

As the overall regional human rights situation has improved in the post-Cold War world, the reports of the Commission have become less prominent. Nonetheless, they remain significant. For example, Commission reports on Honduras in 2009 and 2010 drew attention to serious problems. And at the end of 2009, it issued an important report on citizen security and human rights. More recently, the Commission has published thematic reports on childhood, freedom of expression, and the media (2021); environmental human rights defenders in Northern Central America (2022); and two reports on the impact of organized crime—on children and youth and on women (2023).[11] In 2025, the Commission issued a major report on the human rights situation in Guatemala.[12]

The Commission is active in a variety of areas. In 2024 it had eleven thematic rapporteurs;[13] made investigatory visits to Colombia and Guatemala and working, technical, or promotional visits to Costa Rica, Honduras, Colombia, Chile, Bolivia, Guatemala, the Dominican Republic, Barbados, and Belize;[14] responded to more than eighty requests for information (from all of the OAS members except Cuba, whose membership is suspended);[15] and held 279 promotion and training events;[16]

The Commission also plays a central role in processing individual petitions, which recently have numbered about 2,400 a year. After an initial procedural screening, the Commission conducts its own fact-finding and typically attempts to facilitate a friendly settlement between the petitioner and her government.[17] If this is not successful, it issues a report, indicating its findings and recommendations. And if the state does not accept those recommendations, the Commission may refer the case to the Inter-American Court of Human Rights (for the twenty states that have recognized its jurisdiction). In 2022, the Commission participated in the largest number of hearings before the Court (fifty-two) and presented 213 legal briefs on both active cases and others under supervision.

The Inter-American Court of Human Rights sits in San José, Costa Rica.[18] Its seven members are elected by state parties to the Convention (although nationals of any OAS member-state may serve, even if their state is not a party to the convention). Twenty-three of the twenty-five states-parties to the American Convention are also parties to the Court, and twenty of those recognize its **contentious jurisdiction**, meaning its power to declare a state-party to the Convention in breach of its treaty obligations and to order reparations. Individuals do not have direct access to the Court. Only the Commission and parties to the Convention can submit cases. One of the more interesting and innovative procedures of the Court is the use of (more than seven hundred) provisional measures to attempt to protect persons in danger of irreparable harm or death. The Court also tries to serve as an active source of the progressive development of regional human rights law through its advisory opinions (thirty-two of which had been issued through July 2025).[19]

The Court, however, has faced considerable criticism. Through late 2025, it had issued only 564 judgments.[20] Furthermore, as with most international judicial institutions, the Court lacks the power to enforce its rulings. (By the Court's own reckoning, fewer than half of its decisions finding violations have been fully implemented.) A handful of states—Trinidad and Tobago, the Dominican Republic, Peru, and Venezuela—have quit paying their dues, recalled their ambassadors, threatened to leave, or suspended membership to protest judgments. (The bright side of this behavior is that it signals the Court's judicial independence.) The Court also faces a funding problem that prevents it from taking on a more robust role in the region. Finally, until recently, the Court tended to focus on remedying the violations of military or authoritarian governments. It thus has been criticized for not covering a wide enough range of human rights violations, including such politically sensitive issues as indigenous rights, access to abortion, and LGBTQ+ rights (although the Court has often weighed in on these types of matters by handing down advisory opinions).

This disappointingly small number of cases heard by the Court indicates the relative weakness of the Inter-American regime compared to its European counterpart. But we should be careful not to confuse cause and effect. As we will see in more detail below, strong multilateral measures are largely a consequence, not a cause, of a high level of national practice throughout the region.

3 The African Regional Regime

The African regional human rights regime is based on the 1981 African Charter on Human and Peoples' Rights (also known as the Banjul Charter). It includes the African Commission on Human Rights and the African Court of Peoples' and Human Rights. Although the regime is substantively much weaker than its European and American counterparts, the African Union (AU) has attempted to at least strengthen the institutional mechanisms for human rights on the African continent. Despite its shortcomings, the African system carries great symbolic significance in the region and has provided considerable encouragement and support to national activists in their struggle for human rights.

The African regime operates under the auspices of the fifty-five-member AU, of which every state on the continent is a member. All members are subject to the African Charter on Human and People's Rights. (Europe is the only other region in which all members of the regional organization are bound by the regional human rights treaty.)[21] In addition, Article 4(h) of the Constitutive Act of the AU empowers the Union to intervene in a member-state if the AU Assembly has made a finding of war crimes, genocide, or crimes against humanity. This is a significant departure from the AU's predecessor, the Organization of African Unity, which adhered to a rigid and extreme principle of nonintervention that was regularly used as a shield by governments that committed grievous violations of human rights.[22]

The African Charter, which entered into force in 1986, is unique in several ways. It is the only regional instrument to include a full array of civil, political, economic, social, and cultural rights in a single document. It includes group rights as well as individual rights. Article 29 outlines a number of individual duties, such as "not compromising the security of the

State" and "to preserve and strengthen social and national solidarity," which may clash significantly with individual (and group) rights claims. Furthermore, and most significantly, many articles of the African Charter contain "clawback clauses" that weaken its protections.[23] For example, Article 6 states, "No one may be deprived of his freedom except for reasons and conditions previously laid down by law." In other words, so long as a government bothers to pass a law first, it can deprive people of their freedom for pretty much any reason it chooses.

These departures from other regional systems are rooted in Africa's experience with imperial colonialism, which remained a powerful presence in the region into the 1970s (when nine of the AU's fifty-four members finally achieved independence, following thirty-three of their colleagues who achieved independence in the 1960s). That experience fostered an unusual sense of solidarity and a strong focus on issues of self-determination and racism (see also Section 12.3). And independence-era African governments regularly stressed the importance of the social unit and society, rather than the individual, in African cultures.

The Charter purports to combine different systems of justice, both individual and collective, and to balance rights with obligations toward the community and the state. Furthermore, newly independent African governments, like their eighteenth- and nineteenth-century Western counterparts, gave perhaps understandable priority to state building and national consolidation over internationally recognized human rights.

The result, however, was increasingly dismal human rights records across the continent, with nearly all African states suffering under personalist or military dictatorships in the 1970s and 1980s. The post-Cold War era, however, has brought substantial (although quite uneven) democratic progress. And even the relatively weak institutions of the African regional regime have made a real if modest contribution to an improved regional attitude toward human rights.

The African Commission on Human and Peoples' Rights was established to protect, promote, and interpret the African Charter. It is primarily a promotional and advisory body. Members of the Commission are elected by the Assembly of Heads of State and Government of the AU from a slate of nominees put forth by member-states.[24] Prior to 2005, the Commission's eleven members often held high political posts within their respective governments, thus making them far less independent than their European and American counterparts. In 2005, the Commission issued a *note verbale* emphasizing that members are supposed to serve as experts in their own capacity and urging AU member-states to exclude senior civil servants and diplomats from nomination. The reporting system is plagued by poor reports—a reflection of both lack of resources in most states and lack of interest by many—and the Commission's chronic lack of funding. As for the investigation of complaints, few states cooperate and the decisions of the Commission have been criticized for their vagueness with respect to suggested remedies. In addition, the Commission's members work under confidentiality clauses that prevent the public's awareness of its work.[25]

The African Court of Peoples' and Human Rights sits in Arusha, Tanzania, and is composed of eleven judges elected by secret ballot from nominees put forth by member-states. The African Court resembles its Inter-American counterpart in that its jurisdiction is optional. (Thirty states have accepted its jurisdiction.) The protocol establishing the Court stipulates that the Court may (only) hear cases brought to it by the Commission, other states-parties, and African intergovernmental organizations. Individuals may bring cases to the Court only if the state involved has made a "special declaration" (under Article 34.6) that it will allow such petitions. (Only eight states have done so.)

The Court first met in July 2006. After a slow start, by March 2023, the Court had received 355 applications, finalized 230 cases, and issued 85 orders for provisional measures. It had also issued fifteen advisory opinions.[26] The Court has also embarked on "sensitization visits" to AU member-states to promote the Court's activities and to lobby states to adopt the Court's protocol and especially the special declaration allowing for individual and group petitions.

The African Commission and Court are leading regional voices for human rights. The meetings of the Commission provide the occasion for valuable networking by NGOs from across the continent. Its activities have helped to socialize African states to the idea that their human rights practices are legitimately subject to regional scrutiny—a not insignificant achievement given the radical notions of sovereignty and nonintervention that dominated the continent in the 1970s and 1980s. And there is an infrastructure in place that African states can build on in the future.

4 Asia

In Asia there is no legally binding convention on human rights and no formal monitoring or enforcement mechanisms. Part of the reason for this is that Asia is largely a geographical entity, not a cultural, economic, or political region.

Even at the subregional level, however, organizations that might include a human rights dimension to their mandates are rare. Only the Association of Southeast Asian Nations (ASEAN) enjoys region-wide participation and has a long tradition of collective multilateral consultation.

ASEAN is notorious for its extreme deference to state sovereignty, understood in almost absolutist terms. Nevertheless, building on more than a decade of advocacy by the Working Group for an ASEAN Human Rights Mechanism, member-states in the region finally agreed to the creation of the ASEAN Intergovernmental Commission on Human Rights (AICHR) in 2009. (Note, however, the clear designation of the body as an *intergovernmental* commission.)

The first task of the Commission was to draft the ASEAN Human Rights Declaration (AHRD), which member-states unanimously adopted in 2012. Despite this watershed achievement, the AHRD was heavily criticized not only by human rights NGOs but even by the UN High Commissioner for Human Rights.[27] Many of the Declaration's provisions, which were drafted without collaboration with the public or nongovernmental organizations, act as a shield for ASEAN member-states against already established international human rights standards. It does not include fundamental rights such as freedom of association or protection against enforced disappearance. Many of the rights it does recognize are subordinated to national law. The Declaration is heavily skewed toward group rights and limitations on human rights demanded by "Asian culture." And in many cases, the enjoyment of rights is secondary to the fulfillment of duties to the community or the state.

The AICHR uses the ASEAN Charter and its own Terms of Reference as its core governing documents. The AICHR is a consultative organ—it has no power to investigate human rights violations or monitor the human rights situations within the region. Its Terms of Reference promote principles such as the "independence, sovereignty, equality, territorial integrity and national identity of all ASEAN Member States," "non-interference in the internal affairs of ASEAN Member States," and "respect for the right of every Member State to lead its national existence free from external interference, subversion and coercion." State preferences are prioritized over human rights.

The activities of AICHR are decidedly low key. They do keep the topic of human rights in play in the broader regional context. And in a few instances, there is real substance to the work, especially with respect to the rights of women, children, the elderly, and persons with disabilities. For example, the AICHR recently adopted the ASEAN Enabling Masterplan 2025: Mainstreaming the Rights of Persons with Disabilities.[28] Its focus, however, is on gentle encouragement of better practice. No attention is given to shortcomings, let alone violations.

More generally, AICHR prefers to address human rights topics that do not involve state responsibility, such as business and human rights. Also illustrative are the adoption in 2025 of the ASEAN Declaration on the Right to a Safe, Clean, Healthy and Sustainable Environment[29] and the ASEAN Declaration on Promoting the Right to Development and the Right to Peace Towards Realising Inclusive and Sustainable Development,[30] which shift attention from the rights of individuals and the responsibilities of states to broad contextual issues.

Or consider the AICHR approach to torture. The focus has been, as it put it in 2013, on building a torture-free ASEAN community[31]—rather than the persistence of torture in many member states. And in 2024 it held still another ASEAN Dialogue on Realising Southeast Asia as a Torture-Free Region[32] that was largely restricted to publicizing standards. The best that one can say is that persistent reference to the importance of a right and the existence of international and regional standards is better than nothing.

And ASEAN does have a (sub)regional human rights mechanism. Nothing like this exists elsewhere in Asia.

5 The Arab World

We turn finally to human rights in the Arab Middle East.

The League of Arab States (known commonly as the Arab League) created the Permanent Arab Commission on Human Rights in 1968, largely in response to the 1967 occupation of Palestinian territory in the West Bank and Gaza. The League adopted the Arab Charter on Human Rights in 2004, which entered into force in 2008. The Charter includes a full array of civil, political, economic, social, and cultural rights. The monitoring mechanism is the Arab Human Rights Committee, which is composed of seven members who serve in their own capacity. Each is elected by secret ballot from a slate of candidates nominated by states-parties to the Charter.

As of 2025, sixteen of the twenty-two member-states of the League have ratified the Arab Charter. The Charter does not include a complaints or petitions mechanism. And its state-reporting procedures are unusually weak and rarely involve the participation of civil society organizations.

In the last three editions of this book, we described the Arab League's website as "atrocious" (with respect to its confusing and quite archaic structure) and noted that the English language version link did not work. That has since been remedied (and Google Translate helps as well). Nevertheless, the site remains enormously difficult to navigate and largely out of date. For example, in June 2024, there was no information on meetings of the Permanent Committee after 2015 and only the first reports of states, from 2012, were available. In a region of the world that is home to some of the wealthiest countries on Earth (in per-capita terms), the abject lack of attention to even basic documentation is reflective of the region's lack of political commitment to human rights.

Optimists might suggest that there are possibilities for improvement. For example, the General Secretariat of the Arab League proclaimed 2016–2026 the Decade of Arab Civil Society Organizations. It is difficult, though, to discern what specific activities related to this initiative have been undertaken (there is some indication that this is rolled into some of the civil society engagement goals related to the UN's "Agenda 2030" and achievement of the Sustainable Development Goals). There has also been an effort to establish a human rights court for members of the Arab League in accordance with the Arab Charter on Human Rights.[33] Only Saudi Arabia has ratified the statute of the Court—six other states will need to ratify before it can come into existence. It also appears that the Committee has been actively engaged in promotional activities with respect to the war in Gaza, in the form of regular condemnations of Israeli violations of human rights and humanitarian law.

Pessimists, however, are likely to conclude that the Committee is only interested in the human rights of Arabs when they are violated by Israel. Arab state violations of the human rights of their Arab citizens are not addressed.

6 Assessing Regional Human Rights Regimes

Strong regional human rights regimes are more an effect than a cause of good human rights performance. If a state has a good human rights record then not only will a strong regime appear relatively unthreatening but the additional support it provides for national efforts is likely to be welcomed. Conversely, states with bad records are unlikely to support strong regional monitoring mechanisms, let alone systems of authoritative legal remedy.

Several states in Central and Eastern Europe, however, have poor human rights records and yet agree to subject themselves to the strong regional procedures. Part of the explanation is the normative and emotional significance of being part of "Europe." (This active sense of regional identity also supports the Inter-American and African regimes and helps to explain the ASEAN exception in Asia.) And for EU members there is a strong financial incentive. But even in Europe, the European Court of Human Rights deals only with individual cases. A finding of a violation only requires the state to provide restitution to the individual victim, not change the law or administrative practice that produced the violation. (Russia, before its expulsion, appears to have had a more or less regular budget item for paying judgments of the European Court.)

This brings us back to the importance of national commitment and political will. States with a real commitment to human rights usually will take the findings of a court, committee, commissioner, or expert to heart. Those without such a commitment can get by nicely, even in the European system, with formalistic compliance with a reporting process, court decision, or visits by monitors. Thus, the impact of the European and Inter-American regimes varies greatly among countries within the region.

Regional mechanisms, however, do have the special advantage of greater cultural community. This may give the organization special credibility. And it undercuts arguments about the imposition of inappropriate alien standards. Furthermore, the expectation that there should be regional human rights regimes may exert some modest but perhaps not entirely insignificant pressure for progress even in Asia and the Arab world.

Regional regimes can also be valuable simply by providing another set of eyes. This additional scrutiny, because it is regional rather than global, may even be better attuned to or better able to address some issues. And, in practice, there is considerable synergy, and even interaction, between regional and global multilateral mechanisms. Regional human rights regimes thus are significant players in the global human rights regime.

7 Case Studies

7.1 Chile and the Inter-American Commission (Historical)

In Chile, military rule had been rare since the mid-nineteenth century. After World War II, a stable three-party democratic system emerged. In 1970, Salvador Allende became the world's first freely elected Marxist president. Allende dramatically intensified the economic and social reforms begun under his Christian Democratic predecessor, Eduardo Frei. Large agricultural estates were expropriated. Key private industries and banks were nationalized, including Chile's (largely US-owned) copper industry. Social services were expanded. These changes were both lavishly praised and reviled, both within Chile and abroad. The resulting ideological polarization helped to set the stage for a military coup in September 1973, which installed a repressive military regime under the dictatorial rule of Augusto Pinochet, who remained in power until 1990.

Within a week of the coup on September 11, 1973, the Inter-American Commission cabled Chile expressing its concern and asking for information. In October, its executive secretary, Luis Reque, visited Chile. His report advised a formal onsite visit by the Commission, which took place July 22–August 2, 1974.

During its visit, the Inter-American Commission interviewed government authorities, received 575 new communications, and took statements from witnesses to support previously submitted communications. Commission members also observed military tribunals, studied trial records of military and civil courts, and gathered information on the junta's legislation. Their visits to detention centers led to some minor changes and helped to identify facilities where torture was being practiced.

The Commission's report concluded that the government of Chile was guilty of a wide range of human rights abuses, including systematic violations of the rights to life, liberty, personal security, due process, and civil liberties. In October 1974, this was hardly news. Nonetheless, the report was thorough and tough. It also provided authoritative confirmation of the charges that had been made against the Chilean junta. This made it much more difficult for sympathetic foreign governments to dismiss the complaints of exiles and human rights activists as partisan or unsubstantiated. For example, the report was a standard source of information in US congressional hearings.

Over the next two years, the Commission focused on individual communications. In 1975, it considered more than 600 cases of torture and 160 disappearances. The government, however, was uncooperative. Furthermore, as noted earlier, individual communications are not well suited to handling systematic, gross violations. Not much came of these investigations—beyond added publicity and greater detail on individual violations.

The Commission's second report on Chile, in 1976, applied new pressure on the Pinochet regime. Although noting a decline in some violations, it documented continuing systematic abuses and concluded that government actions and policies continued to be an impediment to the restoration of respect for human rights in Chile. This helped to undercut arguments made by and on behalf of Chile that the situation was returning to normal.

The political organs of the OAS, however, refused to follow the Commission's lead. The first report on Chile provoked an innocuous resolution that did little more than ask for additional information. The OAS was so little moved that in 1975 the members overwhelmingly accepted Chile's offer to host the next session of the OAS General Assembly. Following the Commission's second report, Chile was asked "to continue adopting and implementing the necessary procedures and measures for effectively preserving and ensuring full respect for human rights in Chile." By implying more progress than had in fact occurred, this resolution was in some ways worse than nothing. And after the third report, in March 1977, the OAS General Assembly did not even extend the formal courtesy of asking for a further study.

This icy reception underscores the limits of even aggressive and independent monitors in an organization with little concern for human rights. Nonetheless, the Commission persisted. Its annual reports for 1977, 1978, and 1979–1980 included sections on Chile. The reports for 1980–1981 through 1982–1983, in a concession to the generally hostile organizational environment, contained no references to particular countries. But the 1983–1984 report returned to a tougher stand, with a chapter on violations in several states (including Chile).

In May 1984, in response to the worsening situation in Chile, the Commission began work on a new country report, issued in 1985. A resolution criticizing Chile by name failed by a single vote in the OAS General Assembly in December 1985. And the IACHR continued to pressure the Pinochet government until it was finally removed from office.

What can we conclude from all this? A cynic can point to the bottom line, namely, the persistence of military rule in Chile. If a state is willing to accept the costs to its reputation, which rarely exceed strained relations and reduced foreign aid, it can flout international human rights regimes.

But to expect recalcitrant states to be forced to mend their ways is wildly unrealistic. The Inter-American Commission, like most other multilateral human rights agencies, works primarily with the power of publicity. It can promote the regional implementation of human rights norms. It can monitor and publicize violations and try to persuade states to improve their practices. But it cannot—and is not intended to be able to—force a state to do anything. Sovereignty remains the overriding norm in the Inter-American human rights regime—as in all other international human rights regimes (except Europe).

Nonetheless, in summarizing the Commission's work on Chile, Cecilia Medina, who herself was forced into exile by the military government, has argued that in a situation of gross, systematic violations, the constant attention of the international community is of the highest importance; it serves as a support and encouragement for those suffering and opposing repression within the country, and at the same time prompts and serves as a basis for further international action by other governmental and nongovernmental international organizations.[34]

This is particularly true when a state is subject to scrutiny in multiple intergovernmental organizations and by several national and international NGOs.

Perhaps the strongest evidence for the importance of international publicity is the diplomatic effort states exert to avoid it. In the late 1970s and early 1980s, both Argentina and Chile devoted much of their diplomacy—in the United Nations, the OAS, and the United States—to avoiding public criticism. If rights-abusive regimes take international condemnation seriously enough to struggle to avoid it, the work of international human rights agencies is unlikely to be entirely pointless.

We must also remember that the bottom line includes individuals who are helped. States often respond to international pressure by releasing or improving the treatment of prominent victims. These small victories for international action are victories nonetheless—and of immense significance to individual victims.

In rare cases, there may even be a systematic impact. For example, the 1978 IACHR report on Nicaragua increased the pressure on the dictatorial Somoza government. Furthermore, the OAS call for Somoza to resign in June 1979 shook his political confidence and seems to have hastened his departure.

Reports, though, are only reports. Decisions on individual cases are only nonbinding resolutions. Real change requires additional action by states. This is an inherent shortcoming of almost all international human rights regimes.

Nonetheless, the Inter-American Commission has aggressively exploited its powers to at least some effect. Its activities have improved the treatment of many thousands of victims of human rights violations. If we compare it not to Europe but to global mechanisms discussed in Chapter 5, the record of the Inter-American regime, even in the difficult environment of the Cold War, appears in a relatively good light.

7.2 The African Commission and LGBTQ+ Human Rights

As we discussed in Problem 3.2, discussions of human rights in relation to sexual orientation and gender identity are slowly evolving. Whereas significant strides have been made in some countries and regions, others are literally worlds apart. Africa nicely illustrates some of this diversity and the extremely controversial nature of change.

Prior to the colonial era, many African cultures showed some toleration for homosexuality and sexual/gender diversity. Under colonialism, however, homophobic European legal norms became deeply embedded in most African societies. And in the 1980s and 1990s, nearly all African states—post-apartheid South Africa was the exception that proved the rule—more or less harshly repressed even modest efforts to protect LGBTQ+ individuals not just from discrimination but from targeted violence.

By 2018, however, homosexuality had been decriminalized or provided some limited legal protection in twenty-two African states. Among these, South Africa boasts the most robust protections, having legalized same-sex marriage and adoption by same-sex couples in 2006. But even South Africa faces major hurdles in overcoming homophobia and hate. In 2023, the Pew Research Center reported that 58 percent of South Africans do not believe homosexuality should be accepted by society. In Kenya, Uganda, and Nigeria, the figure was 90 percent or more. These negative attitudes are reflected in increasing hostility toward LGBTQ+ persons and organizations, which makes advocacy work incredibly difficult.

Indeed, thirty-two countries in Africa continue to criminalize consensual same-sex sexual practices. Prescribed prison terms vary from a few months to several years and in Mauritania, Sudan, and some states in northern Nigeria homosexuality is punishable by death. Uganda's 2023 Anti-Homosexuality Act is a particularly striking example. Modeled on a 2014 law that the Ugandan high court had invalidated on procedural grounds, the Act calls for life imprisonment for sex between two people of the same biological sex and the death penalty for what it calls "aggravated homosexuality" (this includes "repeat offenders," sex with someone over the age of seventy-five or with a disabled person). Anyone found guilty of the "normalization" of homosexuality may be imprisoned for up to twenty years. Similar legislation has been proposed or is pending in several more African countries. Furthermore, "private" violence against LGBTQ+ persons is common in many countries—and even encouraged by political authorities in a few.

In the mid- and late-2010s, the African Commission on Human and Peoples' Rights had begun to take steps toward including LGBTQ+ rights in the human rights conversation. In 2014, the Commission adopted Resolution 275, condemning violence "targeting persons on the basis of their imputed or real sexual orientation or gender identities." This resolution came at a time when many states in Africa were experiencing a rise in intolerance and violence directed toward LGBTQ+ individuals, including Uganda's extreme 2014 Anti-Homosexuality Act.

At its 60th Ordinary Session in 2017, the African Commission actively addressed the issue of discrimination against LGBTQ+ individuals, including harassment, threats, and even death, primarily in its "soft law instruments," including general comments, resolutions, and guidelines. For example, the Commission's comment on torture of May 8, 2017 observes that "corrective rape" and forced anal testing amount to acts of sexual and gender-based violence that can be defined as torture and/or ill-treatment under the African Charter. Although not legally binding, such statements attempt to provide a baseline for individual states and provide support for activists and local organizations that support LGBTQ+ rights and protections.

More recently, though, the Commission has begun to backpedal in the face of a growing number of African countries that have doubled down on anti-LGBTQ+ legislation. Most notoriously in 2023, the African Commission refused to grant observer status applications from three pro-LGBTQ+ NGOs—Alternative Côte d'Ivoire, Human Rights First Rwanda, and Synergía-Initiatives for Human Rights—on the grounds that "sexual orientation is not an expressly guaranteed right or freedom under the African Charter" and is "contrary to the virtues of African values." A statement signed by nineteen human rights NGOs operating in Africa pointed out that the Commission's ruling contradicted its own (fairly recent) jurisprudence found in Resolution 275, Resolution 376 (from 2017, on the protections afforded to human rights defenders under the Charter) as well as the Commission's previous judgments in a number of petitions around LGBTQ+ rights.

7.3 Indigenous Human Rights, Guatemala, and the Inter-American Commission

The establishment of a military dictatorship in Guatemala in 1952 sowed the seeds for the outbreak of civil war in 1960. While Guatemalans of all sorts suffered grievously from human rights violations over more than three decades, indigenous communities, which make up more than four-tenths of the population, were special targets of the military regime, especially during the 1980s. According to the Guatemalan Commission for Historical Clarification, Mayan communities constituted 83 percent of the approximately 200,000 who lost their lives in the civil war.

In addition to often-horrendous massacres and forced disappearances, indigenous people were forced to flee their homes and villages. Although the 1996 agreement that ended the civil war included a promise to promote cultural and social rights for indigenous peoples, severe discrimination continues today. While the Guatemalan government has pursued reconciliation policies regarding deaths and forced disappearances during the civil war, a number of these cases continue to be processed by the Inter-American Commission for Human Rights.

No less importantly, the Commission is examining contemporary instances of discrimination and other human rights violations. Such appeals reflect the fragile state of the rule of law in Guatemala. Indigenous activists who seek justice in Guatemalan courts regularly find their rulings to be inadequate or even ineffective.

Activists have thus begun to invoke the idea of the "right to truth" in cases brought before the IACHR. This right is not codified in any treaty. Nonetheless, it began to emerge in the 1990s as democratization swept across Latin America and recently democratized countries began to grapple with issues of transitional justice and reconciliation processes. Although originally focused on forced disappearance, the right to truth has come to include judicial guarantees and protections—and, importantly in the Guatemalan case, reparations for violations of human rights.

Indigenous activists in Guatemala face the lack of a clear legal framework dealing with the human rights of indigenous people. Both the UN and the OAS have adopted declarations on the rights of indigenous peoples (and in both cases, Guatemala voted for their adoption). Neither of these declarations, however, is legally binding.

Indigenous rights activists nevertheless still bring a number of cases to the Inter-American Commission each year. In fact, the 2017 report from the IACHR on the situation of human rights in Guatemala found that indigenous communities experience the highest amount of "social exclusion" in Guatemalan society and that there are a number of barriers that impede access to justice for these communities. It further notes that the United Nations Rapporteur on the Rights of Indigenous Peoples estimated that only 10 percent of indigenous people have adequate access to justice in the country.

For example, in 2013 Guatemalan indigenous organizations filed a suit in the Inter-American Commission over a 1997 Mining Law. The suit alleges that the law infringes on the right of indigenous people to consult with the government and consent to such legislation. In addition, there are allegations of forced eviction and persecution of communities by mining companies. This suit specifically referenced a mine operated by the company Goldcorp in the Northwestern part of Guatemala. The Inter-American Commission even called for the suspension of operations at this mine until it could issue a ruling on the case. In 2016, the Guatemalan government ordered the mine to be closed, a move that surprised many insofar as the government had previously been all in favor of the mining operation.

Other suits continue to be filed by indigenous activists from Guatemala, often involving land rights and justice for crimes committed during the Guatemalan Civil War. These cases often contend that the Guatemalan justice system has been inadequate or even unable to resolve complaints by indigenous groups about violations of their human rights. As the IACHR reported in 2017, many of the violations and subsequent suits stem from the relative impunity of perpetrators and a justice system that is still struggling to achieve efficiency, independence, and universal access. The IACHR has made a number of recommendations on how the Guatemalan state might improve the human rights situation of indigenous people, particularly focusing on establishing consultation practices with indigenous communities regarding projects that would utilize natural resources in ancestral lands.

Guatemala has made some progress in addressing some recommendations put forth by the IACHR; nevertheless, its most recent report on Guatemala from December 2025 cited ongoing discrimination against indigenous peoples, their lack of access to basic services (including legal services to remedy violations), and misappropriation of ancestral lands. The continuing use of the Inter-American system by local activists testifies to a real, if limited, value as part of a broader advocacy strategy. Nonetheless, it remains an understatement to say that much work remains to be done to ensure that indigenous communities in Guatemala do not suffer substantial systematic discrimination.

Discussion Questions

1. The ASEAN human rights declaration allows member-states to circumvent certain rights. Is such a rights framework be preferable to no framework at all? Could faulty frameworks cause harm to international human rights fulfillment overall?
2. More generally, is there a risk that regional human rights bodies could subvert inter-

national human rights bodies? Or do regional human rights conventions have the capability to complement international human rights law? Is the answer to these, and most other, questions about regional mechanisms "It depends on the region"?
3. What differences stand out when comparing the different regional organizations? What about when compared to global mechanisms?
4. Are states are more likely to follow a global or regional human rights framework? Why?
5. Is it better to have a stronger system where countries threaten to leave, such as the Inter-American system, or a weaker system, like the African example, that might have greater participation by all states?
6. A number of the regional treaties that serve as the normative cores for regional human rights mechanisms include provisions that reflect unique regional conceptualizations of human rights. What are the positives or negatives of this approach? How does this relate to international human rights mechanisms?
7. What explains the African Commission's seeming turnabout with respect to LGBTQ+ rights, and the recent, somewhat dramatic shift in attitudes among a small but growing number of African states with respect to these rights? Are the states that have not legalized (or decriminalized) homosexual behavior or identity pushing the Commission in that direction, or is the Commission pushing states toward reform?
8. As discussed above, the European Union has put forth serious effort to become a party to the European Convention on Human Rights. Should this be a model for other IGOs? What implications might this have for the international system?

Suggested Readings

Dinah Shelton and Paolo G. Carozza, *Regional Protection of Human Rights*, 2nd ed. (Oxford University Press, 2013) is the standard (although increasingly outdated) legal text comparing regional human rights regimes. See also Basak Cali, Mikael Rask Madsen, and Frans Viljoen, eds., *Comparative Regional Human Rights Regimes: Defining a Research Agenda* (Oxford University Press, 2018). More up to date material is available in several of the chapters in Rainer Grote, Mariela Morales Antoniazzi, and Davide Paris, eds., *Research Handbook on Compliance in International Human Rights Law* (Edward Elgar Publishing, 2021).

The Council of Europe website (https://www.coe.int/en/web/portal) is superb. Books worth consulting include Fiona de Londras and Kanstantsin Dzehtsiarou, *Great Debates on the European Convention on Human Rights* (Palgrave, 2018), Janneke Gerards, *General Principles of the European Convention on Human Rights* (Cambridge University Press, 2019), Angelika Nussberger, *The European Court of Human Rights* (Oxford University Press, 2020), and Helmut Aust and Esra Demir-Gürsel, eds., *The European Court of Human Rights: Current Challenges in Historical Perspective* (Edward Elgar, 2021). Lauri Mälksoo and Wolfgang Benedek, eds., *Russia and the European Court of Human Rights: The Strasbourg Effect* (Cambridge University Press, 2017) provides a fascinating look at one of the most important and difficult situations faced by the European regional regime. William A. Schabas, *The European Convention on Human Rights: A Commentary* (Oxford University Press, 2015) is the standard source on the European Convention.

Good recent works on the Inter-American regime include Thomas M. Antkowiak and Alejandra Gonza, *The American Convention on Human Rights: Essential Rights* (Oxford University Press, 2017), James L. Cavallaro et al., eds., *Doctrine, Practice, and Advocacy in the Inter-American Human Rights System* (Oxford University Press, 2019), Per Engstrom and Courtney Hillebrecht, eds., *The Inter-American Human Rights System: The Law and Politics of Institutional Change* (Routledge, 2019), and Natalia Zuniga, *The Inter American Court of Human Rights* (Routledge, 2023). Finally, Ludovic Hennebel and Hélène Tigroudja, *The American Convention on Human Rights: A Commentary* (Oxford, 2022) offers the first comprehensive and systematic article-by-article treatment of the American Convention.

On the African regime, we would suggest beginning with three articles in Rainer Grote, Mariela Morales Antoniazzi, and Davide Paris, eds., *Research Handbook on Compliance in International Human Rights Law* (Edgar Elgar, 2021): Gaye Sowe and Eric Bizimana, "Implementation of Human Rights Decisions in the African Human Rights System;" Kounkinè Augustin Somé, "A Pick and Pay Approach: Burkina Faso's Compliance with International Human Rights Law;" and Debra Long,. "Compliance with International Human Rights Decisions in Cameroon: Mechanisms in Place But a Lack of Transparency." On the Court, see Charles C. Jalloh, Kamari M. Clarke, and Vincent O. Nmehielle, eds., *The African Court of Justice and Human and Peoples' Rights in Context: Development and Challenges* (Cambridge University Press, 2019). Rachel Murray, *The African Charter on Human and Peoples' Rights: A Commentary* (Oxford University Press, 2019) is the standard source on the Charter

Alison Duxbury and Hsien-Li Tan, *Can ASEAN Take Human Rights Seriously?* (Cambridge University Press, 2019) offers a critical but sympathetic assessment of the ASEAN human rights mechanism. Dwi Ardhanariswari Sundrijo, *Regionalizing Global Human Rights Norms in Southeast Asia* (Palgrave Macmillan, 2020) explains how the AICHR was created and why it functioned with a promotional rather than protection mandate, by positioning itself within a sizable literature on norm diffusion. See also Kevin Y. L. Tan, David Cohen, and Aviva Nabahan eds., *Human Rights and ASEAN: Indonesian and International Perspectives* (World Scientific Publishing, 2021).

Notes

1 For more information about the Council of Europe, see www.coe.int/.

2 The European Court website is at www.echr.coe.int.

3 The case law and jurisprudence of the European system can be searched through the powerful Human Rights Documentation (HUDOC) database at https://hudoc.echr.coe.int/eng#{%22documentcollectionid2%22:[%22GRANDCHAMBER%22,%22CHAMBER%22]}.

4 https://www.echr.coe.int/documents/d/echr/stats-analysis-2024-eng and https://www.echr.coe.int/d/annual-report-2024-eng.

5 https://www.coe.int/en/web/european-social-charter/european-committee-of-social-rights is the portal for information on the European Committee of Social Rights.

6 By late 2025, nearly two hundred and fifty collective complaints had been filed. See https://www.coe.int/en/web/european-social-charter/activity-reports

7 See www.osce.org/.

8 Venezuela, an original signatory, denounced the Convention in 2012, only to re-ratify the Convention in 2019.

9 www.oas.org/en/media_center/press_release.asp?sCodigo=E-001/19 and https://www.reuters.com/world/americas/latin-americas-left-raises-pressure-venezuelas-guaido-oas-2022-10-06/.

10 See www.oas.org/en/iachr/.

11 See https://www.oas.org/en/IACHR/jsForm/?File=/en/iachr/reports/thematic.asp.

12 When we went to press, only the Spanish-language report was available. https://www.oas.org/es/cidh/informes/pdfs/2025/Informe_Guatemala_ES.pdf For an English-language summary, see https://www.oas.org/en/iachr/jsForm/?File=/en/iachr/media_center/preleases/2025/245.asp&utm_content=country-gtm&utm_term=class-ip#:~:text=Washington%2C%20DC%E2%80%94The%20Inter%2D,an%20instrument%20for%20selective%20persecution.

13 https://www.oas.org/en/iachr/docs/annual/2024/IA2024_ENG.pdf p. 390.

14 https://www.oas.org/en/iachr/docs/annual/2024/IA2024_ENG.pdf pp. 391–403.

15 https://www.oas.org/en/iachr/docs/annual/2024/IA2024_ENG.pdf pp. 415–422.

16 https://www.oas.org/en/iachr/docs/annual/2024/IA2024_ENG.pdf pp. 423–469.

17 www.oas.org/en/iachr/reports/pdfs/ImpactFriendlySettlement-2018.pdf surveys the development and impact of the friendly settlement mechanism in the Inter-American system.

18 https://www.oas.org/en/iachr/mandate/basics/statutecourt.asp#:~:text=The%20Inter%E2%80%91American%20Court%20of,Convention%20and%20the%20present%20Statute is the web portal for the Court. The Court's 2024 Annual Report is available at https://www.oas.org/en/IACHR/reports/IA.asp?Year=2024. (Changing the Year value in the URL should bring up more reports for other years.)

19 https://www.corteidh.or.cr/opiniones_consultivas.cfm?lang=en.

20 See https://www.corteidh.or.cr/casos_sentencias.cfm?lang=en.

21 Obviously there is a distinction here: Europe is "organization-rich" compared to nearly every other region of the world, as we see in the preceding section of the chapter. Not every country in Europe is a member of the EU, and members of the Council of Europe (whose membership is also not universal) are not required to adhere to the European Social Charter.

22 Paul D. Williams, "From Non-Intervention to Non-Indifference: The Origins and Development of the African Union's Security Culture," *African Affairs* 106, no. 423 (2007): 253–279, www.jstor.org/stable/4496441.

23 These should not be confused with derogation clauses, which permit the suspension of a right under certain limited circumstances for a defined period of time. A clawback clause allows national or local law to supersede the guarantees of the right, without any procedural requirements or other limitations. See Richard Gittleman, "The Banjul Charter on Human and People's Rights: A Legal Analysis," in *Human Rights and Development in Africa*, edited by Claude E. Welch and Ronald I. Meltzer (State University of New York Press, 1984), pp. 152–176, at 157–158.

24 For more information, see https://achpr.au.int/.

25 Nsongurua J. Udombana, "Toward the African Court on Human and Peoples' Rights: Better Late Than Never," *Yale Human Rights and Development Journal* 3, no. 1 (2000): Article 2.

26 https://www.african-court.org/cpmt/statistic.

27 See, for example, Human Rights Watch, "Civil Society Denounces Adoption of Flawed ASEAN Human Rights Declaration," November 19, 2012, www.hrw.org/news/2012/11/19/civil-society-denounces-adoption-flawed-asean-human-rights-declaration and "UN Official Welcomes ASEAN Commitment to Human Rights, but Concerned over Declaration Wording," November 19, 2012, www.un.org/apps/news/story.asp?NewsID=43536#.V1cfLZMrIdW.

28 https://aichr.org/wp-content/uploads/2019/01/ASEAN-Enabling-Masterplan-2025-Mainstreaming-the-Rights-of-Persons-with-Disabilities.pdf.

29 https://asean.org/asean-declaration-on-the-right-to-a-safe-clean-healthy-and-sustainable-environment/.

30 https://asean.org/asean-declaration-on-promoting-the-right-to-development-and-the-right-to-peace-towards-realising-inclusive-and-sustainable-development/.

31 https://aichr.org/news/building-a-torture-free-asean-community/#:~:text=Moreover%2C%20the%20ASEAN%20Heads%20of,Convention%20against%20Torture%20(CAT).

32 https://aichr.org/news/aichr-hosts-dialogue-on-realising-southeast-asia-as-a-torture-free-region/#:~:text=BANTEN%2C%2022%20August%202024%20%E2%80%93%20The,achieving%20a%20world%20without%20torture.

33 www.icnl.org/research/monitor/las.html.

34 Cecilia Medina Quiroga, *The Battle of Human Rights: Gross, Systematic Violations and the Inter-American System* (Martinus Nijhoff, 1988), p. 312.

7 Human Rights and Foreign Policy

The preceding chapters examined how the international community collectively addresses human rights and how states interact within multilateral and regional human rights mechanisms and institutions. This chapter looks in general at how states include human rights concerns in their relations with other states. Chapter 8 explores human rights in US foreign policy (and in lesser detail the policies of the so-called "like-minded states"). We consider both the ways that human rights concerns interact with other foreign policy goals and the means available to states for acting bilaterally on their international human rights obligations and objectives. We also consider undesirable unintended consequences of human rights foreign policies and criticisms of states that target other states' human rights practices.

In the contemporary world, states of different capabilities have varied and often complex bilateral relationships. Security is typically at the heart of national foreign policy—and thus of many bilateral relationships. This is especially true of the United States, which (not implausibly) considers itself to be the leading global power. For example, the United States is especially concerned about the growing influence of China, both in Asia and globally. Therefore, it maintains and has tried to strengthen its ties and influence with other nations in the region such as Vietnam and Malaysia along with traditional allies such as Japan and South Korea.

Economic ties are also often important in bilateral relationships. We live in a globalized world economy (see Chapters 12 and 13). Most states rely on trade with other states to access the resources they need for their own economic welfare, growth, and development. Whether trade and investment relationships are balanced or lopsided, they often color the ways in which states will consider the importance of other foreign policy priorities, including human rights.

Virtually all states, however, also pursue a great variety of other interests in their bilateral foreign policies. This is where human rights enter the picture: as one of many interests that states pursue in their foreign policies.

DOI: 10.4324/9781003373520-9

1 Human Rights and the National Interest

We have come a long way since the 1970s and 1980s, when discussions about human rights and foreign policy often centered on *whether* states ought to have international human rights policies—and when the answer given to that question was as often no as yes. Today, it is largely uncontroversial (and often even expected) that states pursue human rights objectives in their bilateral and multilateral foreign policies. In liberal-democratic countries in particular, the questions have become what should be included in a country's human rights foreign policy, where should it be pursued, and how aggressively. Such a change reflects a fundamental redefinition of the national interest.

In an earlier era, a distinction was often drawn between the "high politics" of security and other international concerns of states ("low politics"). The theoretical and policy perspective of *Realpolitik*—political realism, power politics—largely considers *any* interests beyond military, political, and economic security to be at best unimportant and often undesirable (see Chapter 2, Section 11). In such a world, human rights are a (merely) moral concern. Although states may choose to pursue international human rights objectives out of a sense of compassion or justice, they must be rigorously subordinated to vital national and economic security interests.

In fact, though, the national interest is whatever states and their citizens are interested in. If states consider it in their interest to expend some of their foreign policy resources and attention on the rights of foreigners, there is no categorical reason that they should not. And the reasons for doing so need not be instrumental (e.g., the idea that rights-protective regimes are more peaceful or better trading partners). An intrinsic interest in living in a more just world fully justifies including international human rights in a country's definition of its national interest. And, in fact, many countries have done precisely that.

Today, most liberal-democratic countries in all regions of the world have more or less ambitious international human rights objectives in their bilateral foreign policies. Most nondemocratic regimes at least tolerate the multilateral global and regional mechanisms discussed in Chapters 5 and 6. But with very few exceptions, nondemocratic regimes do not include human rights concerns as part of their bilateral relations with other states (but see Chapter 5, Section 1.4).

The inclusion of human rights in the foreign policy agendas of democratic states has both internal and international dimensions. Democracies tend to identify themselves internally with the pursuit of human rights. Carrying this pursuit over into their foreign policies thus seems natural. It also gives expression to a sort of universal solidarity based on a common humanity (without challenging the system of national implementation of international human rights).

Democratic regimes, though, long predate the development of international human rights norms. Bilateral human rights policies emerged along with the maturing of the global human rights regime. The expression of a "natural" internal inclination to pursue human rights in foreign policy was in fact greatly facilitated, and in some senses even created, by changes in international norms.

Foreign policy is in large measure driven by how a state sees itself, the world around it, and its place in that world. The global human rights regime has created a world in which a government's commitment to human rights is seen as essential to full national and international legitimacy. That has not only enabled the expression of existing tendencies to address human rights in national foreign policies but also created additional support for such policies. The transformation of the national interest represented by the rise of bilateral human rights policies is thus both a cause and a consequence of the domestic preferences of states and the global human rights regime's mutual interactions with one another to push policy in a particular direction.

2 Means and Mechanisms of Bilateral Action

As an objective of foreign policy, human rights can be legitimately pursued using all the means of foreign policy—short of the threat or use of force, which contemporary international law reserves for self-defense (but see Chapter 11). We can think of policy responses along a continuum, with persuasion through "quiet diplomacy" at one end and military, economic, and political sanctions at the other.

We should not, though, think of a simple persuasive–coercive dichotomy. For example, diplomatic measures often are primarily persuasive but may sometimes serve to signal coming coercion. Sanctions, by contrast, tend to be relatively coercive. When they involve carrots rather than sticks, though, they are fundamentally persuasive. And action may be neither coercive nor persuasive but primarily expressive: for example, passing judgment, supporting values, or taking a stand with no significant expectation of altering the world.

2.1 Persuasion through Diplomacy

Human rights diplomacy tends to have three principal areas of concern: the treatment of specific individuals (usually dissidents and political prisoners), particular policies, and the character of the regime (with a focus on patterns of gross and systematic violations of internationally recognized human rights). These objectives are pursued through both public and private means.

Although most attention is rightly focused on public human rights diplomacy, private diplomatic initiatives—**quiet diplomacy**—can be important. This is particularly true when dealing with individual victims or attempting to change laws, policies, or practices. Nonetheless, private action alone, without at least the plausible threat of public action, rarely helps even in the most limited cases. And when gross and systematic violations are at issue, rarely is quiet diplomacy an adequate response.

Public human rights diplomacy has at least three important dimensions: gathering and disseminating information, communicating criticisms of violations and support for improvements in human rights practices, and mobilizing pressure. Although mobilizing pressure certainly is of central importance, we should not underestimate the importance of information gathering and the diplomatic exchange of views.

The international politics of human rights is often a matter of mobilizing shame. Reliable information about national human rights practices thus is essential to human rights advocacy of any sort. Professional diplomats are well positioned to develop and disseminate such information, both through their own direct inquiries and through contacts with human rights advocates in their host country.

The United States in particular has made a major contribution through its annual Country Reports on Human Rights Practices.[1] Especially since the end of the Cold War, these reports have become a major source of reliable information about national human rights practices that are used not only by foreign policy decision-makers in numerous countries but also by national and transnational human rights advocates across the globe.

The private and public exchange of views, especially among friendly countries, is a frequently underestimated means of exerting influence. This is often particularly effective in countries that have fair to good human rights records and where foreign policy initiatives support the work of local activists. Knowing that one's international allies—especially powerful friends—are watching and will raise an issue sometimes influences a government's actions. This is rarely the case when addressing gross and systematic violations. But when dealing with particular individuals or practices, it can be of considerable help. Especially when undertaken in concert with other national, international, and transnational action, persuasive diplomacy can make a difference. Sometimes it may even provide the decisive element that tips the balance.

But, just as quiet diplomacy depends on the possibility of escalation to public pressure, the efficacy of exchanging partially diverging and partially converging views often depends on the public mobilization of shame. Escalation to direct public criticism may be used as a threat. No less importantly, though, the retreat to less publicly contentious means may allow a country to save some face. It may also facilitate the often-difficult internal and international negotiations associated with changes in policy.

2.2 Coercive Diplomacy

Diplomacy, however, can be, and often needs to be, coercive, not merely persuasive. Rarely will the privately expressed views of other countries, or even polite public disagreements among friends, be sufficient to improve even very specific human rights practices. States in their relations with other states often may reasonably choose to allow other actors, both national and transnational, to bear the burden of voicing public criticism. But such criticism is almost always necessary to win even incremental improvements in human rights practices. And when confronting severe and systematic violations, anything less than public criticism will appear to be, if not complicity, then at least acquiescence to practices that simply should not be borne in silence.

Words are the principal tool of bilateral human rights policy. The same is true of multilateral action, as we saw earlier, and of transnational action, as we will see in Chapter 9. States, however, typically have more material means at their disposal that can be utilized on behalf of internationally recognized human rights than most multilateral human rights actors and transnational human rights NGOs.

One strategy that has often been employed is to link foreign aid to the human rights practices of recipients. Two different kinds of strategies have been pursued. Many countries have reduced aid in response to human rights violations (and, to a somewhat lesser extent, increased aid to reward improved human rights performance). However, as we will explore in Chapter 8, "like-minded" "middle powers" such as Canada, the Netherlands, and the Nordic countries have gone further, choosing aid recipients in significant measure on the basis of good or improving human rights records.

2.3 Sanctions

States also have a variety of other relations that they can manipulate to support their bilateral human rights policies. At the lowest level, which shades into diplomacy, states may engage in symbolic gestures, such as recalling an ambassador for consultations or delaying the nomination of a new appointee to a vacant ambassadorial post. Cultural contacts can be expanded or curtailed, as can joint military or political actions. Trade relations have occasionally been curtailed. Very rarely, diplomatic relations may be broken.

The use of material means of persuasion and coercion, however, is often problematic. For example, cutting development assistance, assuming that it had previously been effectively employed, perversely punishes people for being oppressed by their government. Wide-ranging economic sanctions, although relatively rare, have also typically had such perverse results. (South Africa under apartheid is the one clear exception, in part because there was considerable support from the majority of South Africans for the sanctions but also because sanctions proved, in the end, not to be particularly punishing.)

Therefore, sanctions today are almost always "targeted." For example, rather than seek to block investment in a country, the overseas bank accounts of rights-abusive foreign leaders and officials are targeted. In rare cases, though, such as North Korea, where a brutal government has insinuated itself in all areas of the economy and society, suspending all but the most narrowly defined humanitarian aid may prove the right course, all things considered.

But even—or, rather, especially—in these cases, the coercive power of sanctions is limited. Where human rights violations are so severe and systematic that material sanctions seem appropriate, or even demanded, they are unlikely to have much effect. Governments like North Korea's, Assad's Syria, or Myanmar under the generals need little from the outside world—because they are willing to make their people suffer the consequences of isolation. Comprehensive sanctions thus are likely to have little direct or immediate impact on changing the behavior of the most abusive regimes. Some evidence even suggests that economic sanctions sometimes lead to *greater* repression in target countries, although the underlying causal mechanisms are not well understood.[2]

Nonetheless, most human rights advocates still see *targeted* sanctions as an appropriate, and often necessary, course of action even where they have little prospect of altering the behavior of the target government. This raises the important question of what we expect international human rights policies to achieve.

2.3.1 Case Study: Sanctions against Myanmar (Burma)

Myanmar (Burma) presents a particularly interesting case study of the complex possibilities and limits of human rights sanctions.

Burma, which achieved independence from Britain in 1948, ended twelve years of multiparty elections in 1962 when the military (under General Ne Win) staged a coup d'état and established a "socialist" regime under the direction of a Revolutionary Council. The 1977 constitution did little more than place a legal cloak over a system of military rule.

Growing dissatisfaction, however, resulted in widespread pro-democracy demonstrations in 1988. Security forces responded by killing thousands of demonstrators. Military rule, though, was reordered (under the direction of General Saw Maung) through the State Law and Order Restoration Council (SLORC), which declared martial law and changed the country's official name to the Republic of the Union of Myanmar. (Burman or Burmese is the name of the predominant ethnic group in the country.)

The SLORC did, however, permit free elections in 1990 in which the National League of Democracy (NLD) won four-fifths of the seats in Parliament. But the generals refused to cede power, instead placing the NLD's leader, Aung San Suu Kyi, under house arrest. Her notoriety as a prisoner of conscience helped to earn her the Nobel Peace Prize in 1991, which in turn helped to keep Myanmar in the international spotlight over the following two decades.

After the military failed to recognize the results of the 1990 elections, the United States cut off military and economic assistance and recalled its ambassador. In 1997, it prohibited American investments in Myanmar and imposed a number of other (minor) sanctions. In 2003, after a government attack on members of the NLD, Congress passed the Burmese Freedom and Democracy Act, which imposed harsher sanctions, including import restrictions and asset freezes targeted at members of the ruling regime. These sanctions were expanded again in 2007 and 2008. And, in 2008, George W. Bush nominated Suu Kyi to receive a congressional medal "in recognition of her courageous and unwavering commitment to peace, nonviolence, human rights, and democracy in Burma." Congress unanimously agreed. (All of these actions were supported by numerous civil society organizations and supplemented by local boycotts and divestment campaigns.)

The European Union imposed more modest but still significant sanctions. Beginning in 1990, it expelled members of the military from Myanmar's diplomatic missions and imposed an arms embargo and a suspension of nonhumanitarian aid. In 1996, it banned entry visas for and froze certain assets of SLORC officials and some members of the military (and their families). It also suspended all high-level contacts. In 2003, the EU expanded the visa bans and asset freezes and extended the arms embargo to include technical training and assistance. (These efforts were supported by a number of national advocacy campaigns, such as the Burma Campaign UK.)

Australia also independently imposed sanctions beginning in 1991, reflecting both its own international human rights policy and its attempt to position itself as a significant regional actor in post-Cold War Southeast Asia. Norway and Canada imposed sanctions as well, partly for independent reasons and partly in conjunction with their neighbors.

Immediately after taking office, however, the Obama administration adopted a new tack, combining economic sanctions with pragmatic engagement with Myanmar's military leaders. (Carrots were added to the sticks that were still being wielded.) High-level visits ensued. In 2011, Secretary of State Hillary Clinton visited Myanmar and promised humanitarian aid from the United States and economic assistance through the International Monetary Fund and the World Bank (which the United States had previously blocked) in return for reforms.

It would appear that this combination of international sanctions and incentives may have helped to strengthen the hand of those in the regime who saw personal, institutional, or national advantages to liberalization. In 2011, Myanmar embarked on some limited political reforms and began negotiating with the opposition. In response, international sanctions began to be loosened incrementally in tandem with continued liberalization. By 2015, Suu Kyi was released from house arrest, a National Human Rights Commission had been created, political prisoners received amnesty, overt censorship of the media was ended, and labor unions were legalized and obtained the right to strike. In November 2015, the NLD won a supermajority in parliamentary elections. In October 2016, Obama formally terminated all remaining American sanctions.

Up to that point, Myanmar presented a fairly straightforward and unquestionable example of successful international human rights sanctions. Although the shift in policy under Obama reflected geopolitical no less than human rights considerations—the United States was unhappy with growing Chinese influence in Myanmar and this reorientation was part of a broader "Asian pivot" in American foreign policy aimed at balancing against China—this is no reason for cynicism. Foreign policy, as we noted above, is appropriately about much more than human rights. And in this case, a broader strategic reorientation seems to have facilitated new thinking about human rights that proved fruitful. It does, however, underscore the fact that when other foreign policy objectives support, or at least do not interfere with, human rights policies, the likelihood of their success is increased.

Unfortunately, liberalization in Myanmar did not produce a democratic, let alone deeply rights-protective, regime. The 2015 elections were far from free and fair. Many new governmental positions were held by former military officers. And the military, which as an institution still controlled (and today continues to control) the country, was, at best, unwilling to permit further liberalization.

The aim of the intensely nationalist military government seems to have been to play external powers off against each other to create an autonomous space of action independent of both Western and Chinese pressure. And the limits of change have been tragically illustrated by the brutal campaign against the minority Rohingya community in Rakhine State (in the west of the country) that began at the end of 2016.

The Muslim Rohingya have historically suffered systematic discrimination in this officially Buddhist nation. These new attacks, though, were much more severe. And they increased in early 2017, including arbitrary arrests, extrajudicial killings, gang rape, looting, and wholesale destruction of villages, producing a massive flow of refugees into neighboring Bangladesh. A second wave of genocidal atrocities began in August 2017, when government forces and Buddhist extremists began a campaign of mass killings, burning of villages, and other brutalities aimed at "ethnic cleansing" of the region. One study estimates that at least 24,000 Rohingya were killed and 18,000 women and girls suffered from gang rape and other forms of sexual violence. Hundreds of thousands more were subject to various abuses and more than half a million were forced out of the country.[3]

In response, limited international sanctions, largely targeting military leaders, were imposed by both the United States and the European Union. And, in a very unusual move, The Gambia brought a case to the International Court of Justice (ICJ)— not to be confused with the International Criminal Court (ICC)—claiming state responsibility under the 1948 Genocide Convention. In late January 2020 the Court imposed "provisional measures," ordering the Myanmar government to cease all actions that might constitute genocide against the Rohingya as well as to preserve any evidence of such prior activity. The proceedings of the case are ongoing. (In 2025, it appeared that the phase of written submissions was coming to an end and oral arguments were likely to begin in 2026.)

These events led to a dramatic reversal in the reputation of Aung San Suu Kyi. At the outset of the atrocities, she remained silent. Her few comments since have been largely dismissive or exculpatory. And in December 2019, she defended the campaign as little more than a "counter-terrorism" operation at a hearing before the ICJ. A human rights icon had, in a few short years, become an apologist for genocide.

If Suu Kyi adopted this stance to maintain her political position, that did not work either. The NLD won the 2020 parliamentary elections by a landslide—a huge embarrassment to the military's proxy party, which eked out a paltry 6 percent of the seats. On February 1, 2021, the day the new parliament was set to convene, the military staged a coup and arrested Suu Kyi and other NLD officials, leading to a fresh round of Western sanctions.

The NLD and other opposition parties and regional groups formed militias and began a campaign of armed insurgency that has led to a brutal civil war, in which the military government continues to enjoy a modicum of diplomatic and material support from countries such as India, China, and Russia. As of May 2024, more than 50,000 have been killed and 2.3 million are internally displaced. In March 2024, the UN Special Rapporteur on Human Rights in Myanmar stated that 18.6 million were in need of humanitarian assistance.

In November 2024, ICC prosecutor Karim A.A. Khan (KC) filed an application to seek an international arrest warrant for Senior General and Acting President Min Aung Hlaing, stating that he "bears criminal responsibility for the crimes against humanity of deportation and persecution of the Rohingya, committed in Myanmar, and in part in Bangladesh…" Khan suggested more such applications were forthcoming.

As we have emphasized, the kinds of pressure available to external actors rarely are sufficient to produce more than incremental changes in the policies of a repressive regime. Even in Myanmar, where sanctions facilitated what can fairly be called regime change in the early and mid-2010s, the military as an institution remained in control, and many of the same individuals and their families retained positions of power.

During the period of reform, the overall state of human rights in Myanmar undoubtedly improved—significantly for the majority Buddhist and Burman populations. But a commitment to respecting internationally recognized human rights was never institutionalized. Although it is certainly desirable that repressive rulers be induced to reduce human rights violations, we should be careful not to overestimate the nature of such changes or what they imply for the future of human rights. Where human rights conditions are bad enough to provoke significant international sanctions, unless there are wide-ranging structural political reforms, the best that usually can be hoped for in the short and medium term is for a dismal human rights situation to become less bad, or perhaps even not too bad.

This poses real questions for international human rights policies. At what point is change "enough" to merit a lessening of sanctions? (Conversely, if change is not forthcoming, at what point is it time to abandon ineffective sanctions? Or is symbolic action demanded even in the face of instrumental failure?) What happens to the capacity of external actors to exert influence as sanctions are reduced or eliminated? (Was it a coincidence that the campaign against the Rohingya did not begin until after Western sanctions were ended?)

Both the example of the Rohingya and the broader limits to liberalization in Myanmar also illustrate the practical divisibility of "interdependent and indivisible" human rights. In good conditions, improvements in one area of human rights practice are likely to spill over into, support, or be supported by improvements in other areas. But positive spillover and cascading progress is not "natural," and certainly not inevitable.

Finally, the case of Aung San Suu Kyi, who is currently serving a twenty-seven-year sentence for "corruption," illustrates the limits to human rights strategies that depend on individual leaders. A charismatic leader can be a great force for progressive change, especially when she can draw on considerable independent political resources (in Suu Kyi's case, a politically prominent family in a political system that remains deeply patrimonial). A rights-protective regime, though, requires institutionalization of a commitment to human rights. A single leader cannot provide that—even if she stays the course in her commitment to human rights.

3 The Aims and Effects of Human Rights Policies

The most obvious aim of international human rights policies and initiatives is to improve the human rights practices of the targeted government. This is indeed an important objective. But it is not the only aim. In fact, sometimes it is not even the principal purpose.

International human rights policies that do not eliminate or even reduce the violations directly addressed may nonetheless be important in preventing further deterioration or deterring similar future violations. States may be reluctant to appear to be bowing to external pressure. That pressure, though, may be factored into calculations in the future, especially if there is a reasonable prospect that pressure will be repeated. For example, in El Salvador in the 1980s (see Chapter 8, Section 4.1.1) American pressure did not eliminate violations but did help to moderate them.

Even human rights initiatives that bring no direct change in a government's practices may have positive effects by supporting local human rights advocates or delegitimating repressive regimes. By subtly altering the local human rights environment that a rights-abusive regime faces, human rights initiatives may have significant long-term effects.

Another common goal of international human rights policies is altering the broader normative environment. For example, the 1975 Helsinki Accords, which sought to reduce tensions in Europe between the West and the Soviet Union, included a set of human rights provisions that the Soviet Union agreed to in exchange for the West's recognition of its sphere of influence in Eastern Europe. (Even the arch-realist Henry Kissinger hailed this human rights breakthrough.)[4] Similarly, in the late 1970s and 1980s, sanctions imposed on governments in Central and South America that usually had little impact on the behavior of the target governments were crucial elements in altering international expectations and giving new force to the norms of the Universal Declaration and other international instruments. Some of the most striking differences between Cold War and post-Cold War international human rights politics owe as much to these normative changes as to changes in the global balance of power.

In addition, actions directed by Country A against Country B may have an impact on Country C. Knowing that one is likely to be subject to international pressure, because pressure has been applied elsewhere in a comparable case, may have a deterrent effect. This is especially true when the violations are not seen as crucial to the survival or prosperity of the regime—that is, when they are more of a convenience, against which the inconvenience of international pressure needs to be weighed; when a practice is preferred, all other things being equal, but international pressure makes other things no longer equal.

Actions with no direct effect on the target country may also alter the direction of foreign policy in the sending state. For example, the initial decision of the Carter administration to suspend aid to Guatemala in 1977 established a precedent that influenced policy in a number of later cases in the Americas and elsewhere.

International and bilateral human rights policies may also be undertaken primarily to satisfy domestic constituencies. American policy toward Cuba—with the exception of the Obama (and, to a lesser extent, Biden) administrations—is among the most obvious is a striking example. There certainly is something troubling in the notion of a "successful" policy that satisfies national political constituencies while having no effect on the target country. But if that is what it is designed to do then that reality ought be acknowledged. For example, periodic changes in American support to the UN Fund for Population Activities are driven almost entirely by domestic political debates about abortion.

We can also note that international and bilateral human rights policies may have punitive effects even when they have no remedial effect. Making the lives of human rights violators less pleasant is a good thing, even if it does not improve the lives of their present or future victims.

Even where there is no discernible impact—immediately or in the future, remedial or punitive, in the direct target or in other countries engaging in similar violations—there may be a diffuse impact. International human rights policies reinforce and help to further disseminate international human rights norms. Over time, the cumulative effect of policies that reinforce both the substance and the binding nature of international human rights norms may subtly but significantly change the context of national or international action. In the most optimistic scenario, new generations of leaders and citizens may, as a result of regular and aggressive international human rights policies, internalize human rights norms to a greater extent than their predecessors have.

Finally, whatever the impact of our policies, they may be appropriately undertaken simply because they are right. Our values demand that we act on them. Taking a stand is something that we owe ourselves (and those who share our values).

4 Drawbacks, Problems, and Criticisms

4.1 Foreign Policy Priorities and Trade-Offs

The foreign policies of most states can, in a highly stylized fashion, be said to include security, economic, and "other" goals. Most states tend to rank these classes of goals in roughly this order. But there are also gradations within each category. High-order security interests usually take priority over all other objectives of foreign policy, including human rights. And there is nothing wrong with that *as a matter of national foreign policy*. Low-level security interests, however, often are, appropriately, sacrificed to major economic or other concerns, including human rights. And this too is entirely appropriate.

Issues of trade-offs are regularly raised in discussions of international human rights policies. Some human rights advocates are uncomfortable with—even critical of—the idea that human rights are balanced against competing foreign policy objectives. Such criticisms, however, fail to take seriously the idea that human rights are but one of many interests pursued in foreign policy. Human rights interests *should* be balanced against other national interests *in national foreign policies*. And sometimes other national interests appropriately take priority.

Moralists may see the demands of human rights as categorical. Foreign policy decision-makers, though, are not independent moral actors. Their job is not to realize personal, national, or global moral values but to pursue the national interest of their country. They are officeholders, with professional and ethical obligations to discharge the duties of their office.

There certainly are moral and legal constraints on the pursuit of the national interest. But the principal aim of national foreign policy is to serve the national interest—which includes many objectives that regularly conflict and thus must be balanced against one another.

Most democratic countries today include fostering the broad goal of the international realization of human rights in their definition of the national interest. But the national interest, and thus the goals of foreign policy, are not reducible to human rights. The issue then is not whether human rights are appropriately balanced against other objectives of foreign policy—there is no viable alternative to such balancing—but the weights assigned to the values being balanced.

Setting priorities among various interests is an essential part of the process of defining the national interest. States, however, have great latitude in setting the weight that they attach to human rights objectives in their foreign policy. There is no requirement that they include international human rights goals. But if they do include international human rights objectives, states are free to use the full range of foreign policy instruments, short of force, on their behalf.

For those states that have included international human rights in their foreign policies, however, we can reasonably demand that human rights actually enter into calculations balancing competing interests, with a weight that roughly matches their stated place in the hierarchy of national interests. Two tests are particularly appropriate and revealing. If human rights objectives are pursued with friends as well as enemies, or if particular human rights policies cause problems in other areas of ongoing relations, then there is at least prima facie evidence that human rights really are being taken seriously in a country's foreign policy.

People may reasonably disagree over whether a state has appropriately ranked its international human rights objectives or is doing enough on their behalf. At minimum, though, we should insist that pursuing human rights objectives should sometimes be inconvenient, even costly (as is the pursuit of security and economic objectives regularly). Otherwise, human rights are not really a part of foreign policy but a moral add-on after the "real" foreign policy decisions have been made—which was the typical situation before the transformation of foreign policies, noted above, that took place in the 1970s, 1980s, and 1990s.

There certainly is something morally disquieting about subordinating international human rights objectives to national security objectives, let alone economic objectives of foreign policy. But often this is the right thing to do, all things considered, *as a matter of serving the national interest*. Critics may reasonably argue for moving international human rights objectives higher on the list of national foreign policy priorities. In the foreseeable future, though, there is no prospect that they will reach the highest level, let alone occupy the pinnacle alone. The national interest and the "human interest" represented by universal human rights cannot be expected to coincide. We can, though, reasonably work to bring them closer together.

4.2 Inconsistencies in Human Rights Policy

Human rights advocates are also often critical of inconsistent policies that treat comparable human rights violations in different countries differently.

Issues of consistency do have a special force in moral reasoning. In fact, as the Golden Rule suggests, morality is in significant measure a matter of not making an exception for oneself (or those one is allied with). From a purely deontological (i.e., duty-based) moral point of view, comparable human rights violations require comparable responses. But even then an identical response to every comparable violation of any particular right is not required. For example, one's duty is not unconnected from one's capabilities, as suggested by the moral maxim "ought implies can."

Considered from a consequentialist moral standpoint, cost-benefit calculations are essential. Few would consider the United States to be morally bound, all things considered, to risk nuclear war in order to remedy human rights violations in China simply because we acted strongly to remedy similar violations in, say, Guatemala. Conversely, the fact that no state is willing to threaten the use of force to free Tibet from Chinese domination, and thus risk nuclear war, does not mean that considerations of moral consistency should have precluded the use of force in, say, East Timor. Balancing competing values *requires* taking account of *all* the values involved. And consistency requires treating like cases alike, *all things considered*, not just looking at human rights violations.

We should thus not bemoan trade-offs of human rights to other foreign policy interests any more than we bemoan the sacrifice of economic interests to human rights interests, *so long as these trade-offs properly reflect reasonable assessments of the value of the interests at stake.* And we should not criticize as inconsistent treating comparable human rights violations differently—any more than we bemoan pursuing comparable international economic interests more aggressively in some countries than in others—so long as the differences reflect a reasonable balancing of the full range of national interests at stake in the particular cases.

Hypocrisy, however, is a completely different matter. When the subordination of international human rights objectives cannot reasonably be justified in terms of previously established foreign policy priorities, we have an unjustifiable sacrifice of human rights interests rather than a defensible foreign policy trade-off. And if human rights almost always lose out in a contest with almost any other foreign policy objective, we have concrete evidence of a very low effective evaluation of the significance of a country's international human rights objectives. (The problem here, though, is not inconsistency. Rather, the complaint is that the state in question consistently gives inadequate weight or attention to international human rights objectives.)

We should also note that our discussion so far has drawn the distinction between morality and foreign policy overly sharply. In countries with international human rights policies, human rights are matters of both moral and national interest. Moral inconsistency thus does pose problems for foreign policy—although, here, hypocrisy seems more the problem than inconsistency. And such cases should not be confused with a policy that carefully balances human rights against other national interests. Such a policy is not likely to undermine seriously the moral value of human rights. In fact, by clearly identifying just what place human rights have in a nation's foreign policy, such reasoned trade-offs may provoke discussions that lead to increasing the relative place of human rights in a nation's foreign policy.

4.3 Blowback

A final concern is when states subject to international human rights pressures push back. This problem is not new. As we noted in Chapters 1 and 4, there has always been some reticence about the West using global norms to infringe upon the sovereignty of states in the Global South. As the relative power of these states has grown, though, their ability to more successfully push back against human rights pressures has also grown. For example, as China's power has risen, it has been willing, especially in sub-Saharan Africa, to enter into aid relationships without the human rights conditionalities that often come with Western aid.

The Philippines under Rodrigo Duterte from 2016 to 2022 offers an extreme example of blowback against international human rights pressure. Upon assuming the presidency, Duterte vowed to enact a series of radical policies to combat drug-related crime. And he delivered on this particular campaign promise. National and transnational journalists and human rights groups documented mass arrests and extrajudicial killings of drug users, petty criminals, and street children by government agents, paramilitaries, and individual vigilantes. Official Philippine police records indicate that by late 2021 the death toll from Duterte's "drug war" was more than 6,200; thousands more were victims of extrajudicial or vigilante-style killings. And many observers (including the United Nations) believe the actual death toll is much higher. The UN special rapporteur on summary executions reported that Duterte had given ordinary citizens a "license to kill."[5]

Duterte's threats to withdraw from the United Nations were certainly empty, but they were a striking example of his sense of impunity. Somewhat less incredible were his taunts and threats in response to pressure from the United States. "Prepare to leave the Philippines," he remarked in 2019, in reference to the military basing agreement between the two countries. In one particular anti-American tirade, Duterte taunted, "You know, tit for tat ... if you can do this, so (can) we. It ain't a one-way traffic. Bye-bye America," while praising China for its promise of a "grant" of $14 million in small arms to assist Duterte's antidrug efforts, as well as a $500 million long-term "soft loan" guarantee for other equipment. "So what do I need America for?"[6]

Duterte's successor, Bongbong Marcos, repeated this sentiment, vowing to strengthen ties with China during his presidential campaign. Since coming into office, though, the geopolitical realities of Southeast Asia—especially China's aggression against Philippine ships in the South China Sea—have led to warmer relations between the Philippines and the United States. Marcos has even withdrawn from China's "Belt and Road" development initiative.

While perhaps an extreme example, it is not even close to unique. And it vividly illustrates the limits of standard international human rights pressures. The recalcitrant government of even a not particularly wealthy or powerful country with a reasonably good human rights record, which would ordinarily be a sign of at least some openness to international human rights pressures, may not only successfully resist but actively flout international policies that challenge its human rights violations—especially if that government has considerable popular support for its human rights violations (as in the Philippines or in the persecution, ethnic cleansing, and genocide of Muslim Rohingya in Myanmar) let alone if the government can effectively repress popular resistance (as in North Korea and many states in Central Asia). Most human rights violators are able to ignore most international human rights pressures most of the time at only modest cost. And some who thumb their noses at those pressures may even gain some degree of local respect for standing up against challenges to national sovereignty.

5 Political Rhetoric Versus Political Will

For many countries, it is quite easy to say, "We value human rights in our foreign policy." The important questions, though, are *how much* are human rights valued, both intrinsically and relative to other national interests and how seriously are those values in fact taken in the practice of foreign policy.

Many states have made substantial progress toward a more serious incorporation of human rights into their foreign policies. Most, if not all, though, could pretty easily do more. Compared to forty years ago, most democratic states today have more aggressive and more effective international human rights policies. That, however, is nowhere near enough. The moral demands of human rights continue to push for a deeper penetration of human rights into national foreign policy and a greater willingness to take full advantage of the space available for the pursuit of international human rights objectives.

As we have noted, successful resistance by recalcitrant governments is the norm. But even moderately more aggressive international human rights policies might significantly increase the costs of such recalcitrance (or even modestly reduce the likelihood of success). And in target countries with a certain degree of openness to international human rights pressures, whether out of a desire to improve or because of limited incentives or capabilities to resist, even relatively modest improvements in the strength, persistence, or consistency of bilateral human rights policies could have a significant impact.

Such modest improvements are well within the reach of almost all countries with active bilateral international human rights policies—if they decide to make the effort. No state is anywhere near to pushing the limits of what inalterable national and international political constraints on their international human rights diplomacy allow. Any state that really wants to do more can—if it really wants to. In all but the most difficult cases, limited desire is at least as serious a constraint on the success of bilateral international human rights policies as limited capabilities.

Discussion Questions

1. What do you think of the distinction drawn in this chapter between *human rights policy* consistency and *foreign policy* consistency? Is it really appropriate to treat similar human rights situations differently because of other foreign policy interests? How does your answer to this question change if you adopt the perspectives of, say, a foreign policy decision-maker, a human rights advocate, a concerned citizen of your own country, or someone who sees herself as a citizen of the world?
2. How can one justify trading off human rights? Are human rights really the kind of thing that is appropriately balanced against, say, the economic interests of corporations? What are your criteria for judging whether a trade-off is justified?
3. How do your answers to the preceding question vary when the human rights in question are those of your fellow citizens versus those of foreign citizens?
4. Can a viable international human rights policy be constructed by responding to violations according to the principles of severity, trends, responsibility, and efficacy? Are all of these criteria of equal weight? Are there other principles that are no less important?
5. If sanctions are not a particularly effective means of addressing human rights concerns (and sometimes lead to worse outcomes) then why do policymakers continue to rely on them? Do they just sound like "a good idea," because doing nothing would seem like the worst option? What's the best way to determine whether or how sanctions should be used (and evaluated)?
6. What is the mix between limited desire and limited opportunities in explaining the relatively modest achievements of most human rights foreign policies? Is the assessment

at the end of this chapter too optimistic in suggesting that there is considerable space available for stronger and more effective policies?

7. Think about your own country's human rights diplomacy. Has it gotten the balance right between human rights and other national interests in general? In specific prominent recent cases?

Suggested Readings

The bulk of the literature on human rights in foreign policy in general was published decades ago, when countries first began to address human rights more seriously. Very little has been written recently on the general question of human rights and foreign policy—although many of the suggested readings in the following chapter address the issue. Two pamphlets from the late 1970s remain well worth reading, even though the examples are dated. (1) Evan Luard, *Human Rights and Foreign Policy* (Pergamon Press, 1981), provides a good short introductory discussion, with an especially thorough presentation of the means available for use on behalf of human rights. (2) Hans Morgenthau's *Human Rights and Foreign Policy* (Council on Religion and International Affairs, 1979) offers a classic statement of the realist perspective. A newer survey by István Lakatos, *Comparative Human Rights Diplomacy* (Palgrave Macmillan, 2022) provides a comprehensive picture of human rights diplomacy of countries in Sub-Saharan Africa, Asia, Latin America and the Caribbean, Asia, Muslim states, and the European Union.

Notes

1 See www.state.gov/j/drl/rls/hrrpt/.

2 A recent study has attempted to understand these causal mechanisms empirically. See Ryan Liou Yu-Lin, Amanda Murdie, and Dursun Peksen, "Revisiting the Causal Links between Economic Sanctions and Human Rights Violations," *Political Research Quarterly* 74, no. 4 (December 2021): 808–921. Another recent study examined similar outcomes as the result of UN sanctions (rather than bilateral sanctions) on North Korea and Haiti: Katharina L. Meissner and Patrick A. Mello, "The Unintended Consequences of UN Sanctions: A Qualitative Comparative Analysis," *Contemporary Security Policy* 43, no. 2 (2022): 243–273.

3 Moshin Habib et al. 2018. *Forced Migration of Rohingya: The Untold Story*. Ontario International Development Agency. Online at https://catalogue.nla.gov.au/catalog/78574805

4 Henry Kissinger, *Diplomacy* (Simon & Schuster, 1994), 759–761.

5 See https://www.thenationalnews.com/world/asia/philippines-can-survive-without-america-says-president-1.216602

6 See https://www.thenationalnews.com/world/asia/philippines-can-survive-without-america-says-president-1.216602

Human Rights in U.S. Foreign Policy

8

Building on the general discussion of human rights and foreign policy in Chapter 7, this chapter looks in some detail at human rights in US foreign policy. We do so both because the United States has enjoyed a position of leadership in the contemporary world and because of the long American tradition of framing its foreign policy in terms of supporting humane values and practices. Furthermore, since the mid-1970s, commitment to upholding human rights has been a central feature of the stated foreign policy of the United States—although the first and especially the second Trump presidencies represent significant departures. We also look at US foreign policy because we are Americans and because we believe in the importance of scrutinizing the policies and practices of one's own country.

Following a brief historical overview of US international human rights policy, we will explore in some detail the (first) Trump, Biden, and (second) Trump presidencies, followed by an examination of American "exceptionalism" as a perspective for understanding American international human rights policies and practices. We then consider two Cold War-era case studies (Central America and South Africa) and a contemporary case study (Israeli settlements in the West Bank). We then compare US policy to other Western middle powers. The Problem that concludes this chapter looks at another side of American exceptionalism, namely, the reluctance of the United States to ratify international human rights treaties.

1 Historical Overview

As we saw in Chapter 1, concern for the protection of human rights was integral to American postwar policy, especially in the creation of the United Nations. President Harry S. Truman was a strong supporter of human rights at the United Nations and in 1946 named Eleanor Roosevelt as the American representative to the newly formed Commission on Human Rights. The Commission unanimously elected Roosevelt as chair and she guided it

DOI: 10.4324/9781003373520-10

through its first significant agenda item: the drafting of an international bill of rights, which became the Universal Declaration and the two Covenants (see Chapter 1, Sections 2 and 3).

In the late 1940s and early 1950s, however, significant opposition to international human rights treaties emerged from conservative lawyers (represented by the American Bar Association) and lawmakers. Fear of "backdoor communism" (through the inclusion of economic and social rights in the Declaration and the draft Covenant), fear of compromising American sovereignty (along with congressional concerns about an overly active and independent presidency), as well as fear of additional pressure for dismantling systematic racial discrimination, led to substantial support for a constitutional amendment proposed by Ohio Republican senator John W. Bricker. Under Article II, Section 2 of the US Constitution, treaties are negotiated and signed by the president and then must be ratified by a two-thirds vote of the Senate to become law. Among other things, the Bricker Amendment would have required the president to secure congressional approval prior to entering into any treaty-making negotiations and would have also extended the requirement of Senate approval to executive agreements. Both requirements would have pushed the United States back toward isolationism and seriously undermined the further development of the institutional architecture of postwar international society.

When General Dwight D. Eisenhower, a Republican, assumed office as president in 1953, he announced that the United States would neither continue to participate in negotiating the Covenants nor sign any multilateral human rights treaties. After further discussions, the Bricker Amendment was withdrawn. Mary Lord—a granddaughter of Charles Alfred Pillsbury, the founder of the Pillsbury Company—replaced Eleanor Roosevelt as the American delegate to the Commission on Human Rights and the official American human rights policy at the United Nations moved to emphasize advisory services rather than treaties.

This turn away from the immediate postwar enthusiasm for human rights reflected a fundamental change in the priorities of the United States as the Cold War developed between the West (with the United States as its anchor) and the Communist world (the USSR, its Eastern European satellites, and then, after 1949/1950, China and North Korea). American policy came to be oriented around **containment**: halting the expansion of Soviet power and influence.

This was seen as requiring that human rights concerns be subordinated to strategic and ideological rivalry with the Soviet Union—leading the self-proclaimed "leader of the free world" to support, repeatedly and enthusiastically, policies and regimes that violently suppressed democracy and human rights in the name of "freedom" (understood as anticommunism). For example, the United States supported coups d'état in Iran (1953), Guatemala (1954), and Chile (1973) to prevent allegedly communist takeovers and backed a veritable rogues' gallery of right-wing authoritarian governments, including Ferdinand Marcos in the Philippines, the Somoza family in Nicaragua, the Pahlavi dynasty in Iran, Fulgencio Batista in Cuba, and the avowedly fascist Francisco Franco in Spain. As Franklin Roosevelt supposedly said of Nicaragua's Anastasio Somoza García, "[He] may be a son of a bitch, but he's our son of a bitch."

At the United Nations, the United States continued to keep a low human rights profile during the 1960s and early 1970s. Although the United States supported the Convention on the Elimination of All Forms of Racial Discrimination in 1965 (which followed on the heels of the passage of the Civil Rights Act of 1964 and the Voting Rights Act of 1965) and voted for the adoption of both International Covenants in December 1966, American involvement at the 1968 International Conference on Human Rights in Tehran was mostly concerned with keeping in check more strident Third World demands regarding anticolonialism.

By the mid-1970s, a relaxation of Cold War tensions—the policy of **détente** with the Soviet Union—began to open policy space for human rights to return to a more prominent place in US foreign policy. The path to this end, though, was rather unusual.

The leading American architect of détente was the **realist** Henry Kissinger, who was President Richard Nixon's national security adviser (and later served as secretary of state under President Gerald Ford). Kissinger saw détente as a way for the United States to back down from many of its more ideologically motivated stances toward the Soviet Union in favor of a more stable and less immediately hostile relationship. This, however, angered many in Congress, both for ideological and principled reasons. And human rights emerged as a way to assert a central moral dimension in American foreign policy.

Soviet violations of fundamental human rights and, in particular, the refusal of the USSR to allow Soviet Jews to emigrate became the focal point of controversy—precisely when the Nixon administration was attempting to open up not only diplomatic but also trade relations between the United States and the Soviet bloc. One result was the 1974 Trade Act, which included a provision introduced by Senator Henry M. "Scoop" Jackson and Representative Charles Vanik that denied special trade preferences to nonmarket (command) economies that restricted freedom of emigration and other human rights.

Furthermore, the détente-inspired 1975 Conference on Security and Cooperation in Europe (the Helsinki Conference), which finally accepted the geo-political realities of the post-World War II East–West divide, included, as a result of Western European pressures, a limited range of human rights issues. Basket III of the Helsinki Accords stipulated that all parties, including the Soviet-bloc countries, respect certain fundamental human rights principles, including freedom of speech, conscience, and religion or belief. In the following years, this provided unprecedented, if limited, international support for Soviet-bloc human rights advocates and dissidents such as Václav Havel in Czechoslovakia, Lech Wałęsa in Poland, and Andrei Sakharov in the Soviet Union, as well as Karol Wojtyła, a Polish cardinal who in 1978 became Pope John Paul II. Basket III, reflecting the American pressure on discrimination against Soviet Jews, also included important provisions on freedom of emigration and family reunification.

By the time Jimmy Carter entered the White House in January 1977, the international and internal moral excesses of anticommunism—most immediately, the war in Vietnam and the domestic lawlessness of the Watergate scandal—had, along with the emergence of détente, created space for a renewed commitment to human rights in American foreign policy. In 1976, the Ford administration had created the post of Assistant Secretary of State for Human Rights and Humanitarian Affairs. The Carter administration drafted Presidential Review Memorandum 28 (PRM-28), which outlined reinvigorated American support for human rights and created the Bureau of Democracy, Human Rights, and Labor within the State Department. That same year, Carter also signed the American Convention on Human Rights and both International Human Rights Covenants.

These changes, however, were largely symbolic. And other international events came to preoccupy the Carter administration, most notably the Iranian revolution in April 1979 and the seizure of fifty-two American hostages in November; the socialist Sandinista victory in the Nicaraguan revolution in July 1980; and the Soviet invasion of Afghanistan in December 1980. And, with the Cold War heating up again, the Senate refused to ratify the American Convention and the two International Covenants (not to mention SALT II—the second US-Soviet nuclear arms limitations treaty).

When Ronald Reagan became president in 1981, US foreign policy shifted strongly and explicitly toward a confrontational stance toward communism in general and the Soviet Union in particular. Although the Reagan administration did not entirely shed the new human rights apparatus that Carter had established, it dramatically downgraded attention to human rights and ostentatiously dropped all attention to economic and social rights (other than the right to private property). And the Reagan administration's ambassador to the United Nations, Jeane Kirkpatrick, argued that support for anticommunist dictators *was* support for human rights, because the greatest threat to human rights was communism.

"Democracy"—which in practice was interpreted to mean the election of pro-American governments—became the centerpiece of Reagan's "human rights" policy. In a speech to the British House of Commons in 1982, Reagan argued that, by fostering the "infrastructure of democracy," the United States would leave "Marxism-Leninism on the ash-heap of history." In 1983, the United States created the National Endowment for Democracy, a bipartisan nonprofit organization that receives annual appropriations from Congress. The Endowment fosters the growth of democratic institutions and civil society overseas, including political parties, trade unions, and an independent media.[1]

Although these efforts were central rhetorical elements of Reagan's approach to winning the ideological conflict with the Soviet Union, especially in communist Eastern Europe, American foreign policy in other parts of the world, especially in Central America, undermined much of his lofty rhetoric (see Section 8.4.1 below).

There was a modest softening of the Reagan administration's anticommunist stance in its second term. Of perhaps greatest symbolic importance, in 1988 the United States signed the Torture Convention and, after forty years, finally ratified the Genocide Convention. And throughout the 1980s, an active American international human rights policy was driven largely by a bipartisan coalition in Congress that refused to sacrifice international human rights to ideological and geopolitical struggles against communism.

As we emphasized in Chapter 1, the end of the Cold War opened up new policy opportunities for the administration of Bill Clinton, who took office in January 1993. (The presidency of George H. W. Bush [1989–1993] was a transitional era, both in the world and in American foreign and human rights policy.) Clinton's State Department was reorganized to place development, democracy promotion, and human rights, as well as reinvigorated engagement with the United Nations, at the heart of US foreign policy. With significant support from civil society organizations, the United States actively lobbied for strengthening UN human rights mechanisms at the 1993 World Conference on Human Rights. Most notably, it pressed for a UN High Commissioner for Human Rights, a position that the United States had long supported in words but now was willing to exercise political resources to help create. The United States also lobbied successfully to ensure that the 1994

Conference on Population and Development (held in Cairo, Egypt) reaffirmed women's reproductive health as a human right. And Hillary Clinton's speech at the 1995 World Conference on Women, held in Beijing, popularized the slogan "women's rights are human rights."

Early in Clinton's first term, the Senate finally ratified the Covenant on Civil and Political Rights—but only with a reservation that claimed that ratification would have no effect in American law. (It did not, however, ratify the Covenant on Economic, Social, and Cultural Rights.) The following year, the Senate ratified the Convention on Racial Discrimination and the Torture Convention. But although Clinton signed the Convention on the Rights of the Child (CRC) in 1994, the Senate has (for petty partisan political reasons) refused to ratify it, leaving the United States today the *only* country in the world that is not a party. Before leaving office in January 2001, President Clinton signed the Statute of the International Criminal Court (the Rome Statute), but he declined to submit it to the Senate, where bipartisan fears over "the loss of American sovereignty" would have precluded even a serious discussion of ratification.

The administration of George W. Bush was initially hostile to international multilateral institutions—for example, "unsigning" the Rome Statute and withdrawing US support for the Kyoto Protocol to the UN Framework Convention on Climate Change. And the terrorist attacks of September 11, 2001 dramatically reoriented American foreign policy. In particular, counter-terrorism regularly trumped human rights in American foreign policy.

Particularly remarkable was the decision of the G.W. Bush administration not to seek a seat (which would have been effectively automatic) on the newly established Human Rights Council, which replaced the Commission on Human Rights in 2006. And the following year, citing what it viewed as the Council's continuing "harassment" of Israel (and its failure to condemn human rights violations in Iran, Cuba, and North Korea, targets of American ire), the US Senate voted to cut off American funding to the Council. Nonetheless, the Bush administration continued to pursue a limited international human rights policy focused on a narrow range of rights, especially freedom of religion, the right to private property, and combating modern slavery.

During his two terms in office (2009–2017), Barack Obama moved the United States back to an international human rights posture closer to that under the Clinton administration. In 2009, the United States joined the Human Rights Council, redeployed resources within the State Department largely as they had been during the Clinton years, and generally returned to a broad conception of human rights (although giving special attention to the human rights of women and girls and strongly supporting the Council's efforts to address discrimination based on sexual orientation and gender identity).

In 2011, Obama signed a Presidential Study Directive (PSD-10) that declared the prevention of mass atrocities and genocide to be a "core national security interest and core moral responsibility" of the United States and established the Atrocities Prevention Board within the State Department's Bureau of Conflict and Stabilization Operations. Although there continued to be no political possibility of the United States becoming a party to the Rome Statute, Obama's first National Security Strategy document included engagement with the International Criminal Court (ICC) as an observer to its annual meeting of the Assembly of States-Parties. Furthermore, the Obama State Department (under Secretaries of State

Hillary Clinton and John Kerry and UN ambassadors Susan Rice and Samantha Power) strongly supported the work of the Court, especially with respect to sharing information needed to indict suspected humanitarian criminals.

2 U.S. Human Rights Policy since 2017

In the last (2020) edition of this book, we wrote extensively about the departures from the post-Cold War, largely bipartisan consensus on American leadership in the area of human rights that typified the policies of the Trump administration (2017–2021). Immediately after its publication, matters got much worse as the COVID pandemic set in and Trump began to reject the consensus of public health experts on mitigating the spread of the virus, with the administration and its supporters seeing policies surrounding closures of schools and businesses, masking and social distancing, and vaccine mandates as ominous evidence of efforts by "the deep state" to control the lives of Americans. In the summer of 2020, the murder of George Floyd by a Minneapolis police officer was the catalyst for nationwide protests against police violence. These were met in Washington DC by a bizarre show of force: police, using tear gas and wielding batons, cleared Lafayette Square across from the White House of protestors so that Trump and some of his advisors (including the then-Chair of the Joint Chiefs of Staff, General Mark Milley, who was dressed in battle fatigues) could march across the square to St. John's Episcopal Church and stage a photo-op, with Trump holding a bible (upside-down).

Trump lost the 2020 election to Joe Biden but refused to accept the results. He and many of his advisors engaged in a number of efforts to (often illegally) challenge that outcome, including an attempt to exploit a loophole in the 1876 Electoral Count Act to contest the counting of ballots during a joint session of Congress. Egged on by a fiery speech on the morning of January 6, 2021, armed "patriot" groups led an insurrection on the US Capitol. While it ultimately failed, what happened that day has left an enduring scar on the American political psyche as well as shocking many around the world. How could this have happened in the most powerful country in the world, whose very existence is predicated on the principles of democracy and the rule of law?

January 6th was the denouement of four years that were marked by significant departures from the post-Cold War American human rights policies of both Republican (Bush and Bush) and Democratic (Clinton and Obama, and later Biden) administrations.

2.1 The First Trump Administration (2017–2021)

The Trump administration's rhetoric about human rights generally reflected Trump's rejection of the multilateral institutions and partnerships that the United States forged in the decades following World War II—what many refer to as the "rules-based post-war international order"—in favor of an aggressive and often personalistic unilateralism. Trump dismissed the United Nations and other international organizations and processes (e.g., the Paris climate accord), denigrated NATO and other long-established security relationships, and emphasized bilateral "deal-making" (e.g., in a trade war with China and in security relations with North Korea and Iran). And these unilateral initiatives were advanced in the name of American interests defined very narrowly (and often rather peculiarly) as "America First."

The Trump administration regularly prioritized security and economic interests over human rights. As Trump's first Secretary of State, Rex Tillerson, put it in May 2017 (announcing that the United States would de-emphasize human rights in its foreign policy), "if we condition too heavily that others must adopt this value that we've come to over a long history of our own, it really creates obstacles to our ability to advance our national security interests, our economic interests."[2]

Trump also regularly and admiringly embraced authoritarian leaders, such as the thuggish Jair Bolsonaro of Brazil and Rodrigo Duterte of the Philippines, who boasted of his government's practices of disappearances and extrajudicial executions. Trump even spoke of the "love letters" he exchanged with Kim Jong-un of North Korea. And he repeatedly professed admiration for Vladimir Putin, going so far as to take Putin's word that Russia did not attempt to interfere in the 2016 election, contradicting the findings of the American intelligence community.

The American commitment to human rights was further undermined by the selective, partisan deployment of the language of human rights. For example, when dealing with Iran, the United States regularly highlighted human rights violations that are far less severe than violations of the same rights in Saudi Arabia (about which the Trump administration usually remained conspicuously silent). And while the human rights of Israelis were regularly invoked, the rights of Palestinians or Egyptians were ignored. Human rights became, at best, an instrument to attack perceived enemies.

Considerable elements of an American international human rights policy continued to be implemented on a day-to-day basis, in accord with established laws (e.g., on human rights reporting) and everyday bureaucratic practice. Trump's foreign policy, however, reflected such a profound disinterest in international human rights that it would have been only a slight exaggeration to say that the United States had no international human rights policy during the first Trump presidency.

Beyond these shifts in American rhetoric, there were a number of high-profile American actions that were deeply troubling from a human rights perspective. For example, in June 2018, the United States abruptly announced—in the middle of the three-year term to which it had been elected in 2016—that it would withdraw from the UN Human Rights Council. (Iceland was elected to fill the vacancy.) The reason, ostensibly, was that the Council focused too much attention on criticizing Israeli policies in Palestine, giving other countries with poor human rights records a "pass." Of course, leaving the Council just meant the loss of a strong voice to address such concerns. And the announcement three months later that the United States would end cooperation with the ICC suggested a deeper motivation, namely, a reassertion of unilateralism and the reversal of the human rights initiatives of the Obama administration.

Another example of the Trump administration's abandonment of long-established American human rights policies and goals came in July 2019, when Trump's second secretary of state, Mike Pompeo, announced the creation of a new "Commission on Unalienable Rights,"[3] the goal of which was to advise the State Department and provide "fresh thinking about human rights discourse where such discourse has departed from our nation's founding principles of natural law and natural rights."[4] This was widely read (rightly in our view) as code for de-emphasizing women's and LGBTQ+ rights and economic and social rights (other than the right to property)—a reading largely confirmed by the predominance of religious and social conservatives among the Commission's members.

Even more ominously, in announcing the Commission, Pompeo said, "I hope that the commission will revisit the most basic of questions: What does it mean to say or claim that something is, in fact, a human right? How do we know or how do we determine whether that claim that this or that is a human right, is it true, and therefore, ought it to be honored?"—apparently rejecting the fact that there is an authoritative body of international human rights law. And he went on to ask, "How can there be human rights, rights we possess not as privileges we were granted or even earn, but simply by virtue of our humanity belong to us?"[5]

U.S. foreign policy, however, including human rights policy, is not exclusively the preserve of the executive branch. When Congress pushed back, Trump usually acquiesced, producing an oscillation between narrower and more expansive visions of American human rights objectives. For example, in the face of intensifying repression of ethnic Uighurs (Uyghurs), who make up a significant minority especially in China's Xinjiang province—more than 1 million Uighurs have been relocated to "re-education camps"[6]—Trump's State Department responded with formulaic protests over these policies, reflecting a low level of concern with an issue that had no discernible connection to Trump's "America First" foreign policy. Congress therefore drafted and passed the 2020 Uyghur Human Rights Policy Act,[7] which was adopted in the House of Representatives by a vote of 413-1 and duly signed into law by President Trump. And even then, the fact that America's rival, China, was being targeted seemed an essential element in this bipartisan consensus.

Congress has long been interested in human rights, going back to the Nixon and Ford administrations. It has a tradition of independent legislative advocacy for human rights, even in the face of active presidential resistance (as was the case during the first term of the Reagan administration). Although the president is the principal architect of American foreign policy, on particular issues Congress can play an active independent role. And it has recurrently done so in the case of international human rights, usually on a bipartisan basis.

The Trump administration's general reorientation away from human rights internationally was accompanied by a number of high-profile *domestic* initiatives that were contrary to or in tension with international human rights norms. For example, in early 2017 Trump halted the entire American refugee admissions program for 120 days and placed on hold all travel to the United States of persons from seven Muslim-majority countries, pending further review of admissions procedures. And future refugee admission from those countries, it was announced, would give priority to persons belonging to "minority religions" (read: Christians)—which probably violates the US Constitution (and international law). Although initially blocked by the courts, more modest versions of such policies were designed and implemented.

The administration's policies along the border with Mexico also raised serious human rights concerns. For example, migrants (mostly from Central America) seeking asylum from violence were forced to stay in Mexico, in increasingly dangerous circumstances, pending the outcome of asylum hearings in the United States. And contrary to long-standing refugee and asylum policy, as well as ordinary notions of decency, children were separated from their parents—explicitly to deter migration.

Consider also Trump's decision to pardon three American servicemen who had been convicted of violations of the Uniform Code of Military Justice for what amounted to war crimes. In a fourth case, that of Eddie Gallagher, a Navy SEAL officer who had been acquitted of several charges but demoted for posing in a photograph with a detainee's corpse, Trump reversed the demotion, arguing that international humanitarian law inappropriately ties the hands of commanders and soldiers who are just trying to "do their job" overseas.

Civil rights enforcement was downgraded in the Trump Department of Justice, which also cut back on efforts to reform systematic rights violations by local police departments. The administration did little to encourage the reauthorization of the 1994 Violence Against Women Act, which was caught in legislative limbo (a victim of unrelated partisan bickering and the 2018 government shutdown) until it was finally reauthorized under Joe Biden's administration. Some transgender people were prevented from enlisting in the military. Migrants were regularly demonized. Trump publicly called for the deportation of four members of the House of Representatives (who were, of course, American citizens, three by birth). And like dictators throughout the world, Trump regularly challenged the patriotism of his political opponents and repeatedly branded the press "the enemy of the people."

2.2 The Biden Administration (2021–2025)

When Joe Biden assumed the presidency in January 2021, he moved quickly to repair some of the damage resulting from Trump's foreign (and domestic) policies, including in the area of human rights. Biden's seasoned and highly experienced foreign policy team reaffirmed vital alliance relationships and tried to reestablish American leadership at the United Nations. The administration confirmed its commitment to human rights and international law, rejoining both the Paris Climate Agreement in 2021 and securing a seat on the UN Human Rights Council in 2022. Acknowledging the contemporary context of a global competition between democracies and autocracies in the contemporary world, the opening paragraphs of Biden's 2022 National Security Strategy confirmed the centrality of human rights principles among those his administration sought to promote:

> No nation is better positioned to succeed in this competition than the United States, as long as we work in common cause with those who share our vision of a world that is free, open, secure, and prosperous. This means that the foundational principles of self-determination, territorial integrity, and political independence must be respected, international institutions must be strengthened, countries must be free to determine their own foreign policy choices, information must be allowed to flow freely, universal human rights must be upheld, and the global economy must operate on a level playing field and provide opportunity for all.[8]

The Biden administration, however, did not simply reaffirm past policies and priorities of earlier administrations. It went well beyond the Obama administration's support of global

LGBTQ+ rights. There was a new emphasis as well on protecting and supporting human rights defenders.[9] In 2021, the administration hosted the first virtual "summit for democracy" (subsequent summits were held in 2023 and 2024), whose themes included defending against authoritarianism, fighting corruption, and promoting respect for human rights.

There is much, though, to criticize in the Biden record. For example, one observer noted that the Biden administration's guest list to the first democracy summit was a "cynically drawn up, bureaucratically crafted, agency-structured invitation list that includes states that by any measure are falling way down the democracy rankings or aren't democracies at all,"[10] including leaders from authoritarian (but pro-American) regimes in Angola, the Democratic Republic of the Congo, and Iraq.

Contrary to Biden's pronouncements during the campaign, the administration largely stayed the course with respect to bolstering problematic bilateral relationships with unsavory regimes. Saudi Arabia is a particularly striking example. Although Biden promised to make the Saudi leader Mohammed bin Salman ("MBS") "a pariah" for his role in assassinating and dismembering dissident Saudi journalist Jamal Khashoggi in Istanbul in 2018, in 2022 Biden "fist-bumped" bin Salman after a state visit where the two states issued the "Jeddah Communique," bolstering their strategic ties (without a single word in the document about the dismal human rights situation in Saudi Arabia). Biden also maintained strong ties to other dictatorial regimes, for example, with Egyptian strongman Abdel Fattah Al-Sisi, congratulating him for hosting the 2022 annual climate summit, COP27, while his police arrested peaceful protesters.[11]

Finally, American military support to Israel in the Gaza War (see also Chapter 11, Section 7.2) overshadowed the administration's attempts to return to a more traditional human rights foreign policy. The administration tried desperately—and unsuccessfully—to strike an impossible balance between, on the one hand, political and military support for a key strategic, political, and cultural ally that had suffered a brutal assault by Hamas militants and, on the other, criticizing Israel for the conduct of a brutal campaign that has led to the deaths of tens of thousands of Palestinian civilians, the near total destruction of all civilian infrastructure, and a severe food emergency.

The situation was so untenable that the administration ultimately declined to seek to renew its term on the Human Rights Council, which would have begun in 2025. Iceland, Switzerland, and Spain had already announced their bids for the three vacancies for the Western Group. In the shadow of the Gaza war, the administration had lost the political capital it would have needed to persuade one of them to withdraw their candidacy to avoid having four countries competing for three seats. The UN General Assembly elects Council members, and Biden saw the writing on the wall. The Gaza war made the risk of the United States losing an election to the Council highly likely.

2.3 The Second Trump Administration (2025–)

In his first year in office, Trump has taken radical steps to jettison long-standing institutions and practices. With a compliant Congress (both houses are controlled by slim but so-far-fairly-disciplined Republican majorities), Trump has radically wielded unprecedented executive authority that challenges, in many respects, the constitutional guardrails that are designed to keep executive power in check. Dozens of lawsuits challenging Trump's actions are slowly making their way through the courts. Trump's choices for key cabinet-level positions—all approved by the Senate—have begun to radically restructure and reorient the work of government. Loyalty to Trump, rather than knowledge, understanding, or experience in defense, diplomacy, health, education, or law enforcement has resulted in, for example, a Fox News personality becoming Secretary of Defense (Pete Hegseth), an anti-vaxxer becoming Secretary of Health & Human Services (Robert Kennedy, Jr.), a professional wrestling promoter becoming Secretary of Education (Linda McMahon), and a conspiracy theorist becoming Director of the FBI (Kash Patel).

The manner in which Trump has wielded his authority belies a deep authoritarian ethos. In June 2025, *New York Times* columnist Jamelle Bouie put it succinctly: "Most everyone other than apologists and professional contrarians would agree at this point that President Trump aims to make the United States a personalist autocracy, where his whims are policy and his will is law."[12]

In late April 2025, Amnesty International issued a report on the first hundred days of Trump's second presidency.

> President Trump has led with cruelty and chaos, creating a human rights emergency that has affected millions of people by suppressing dissent, undermining the rule of law, and eroding norms and institutions essential to the protection of human rights.…When we look at the cumulative effect of the Trump administration's actions, it amounts to a sweeping attack on human rights and the systems that uphold them. From this perspective, the damage and devastation of the first 100 days are undeniably clear.[13]

The report highlighted ten "compounding assaults" on human rights. Within the United States, these include attacks against migrants and asylum seekers (lack of due process; rescinding protective visa programs; ending birthright citizenship; mass deportations to countries with atrocious prison conditions); undermining the rule of law (including ignoring judicial rulings); targeting free speech and lawful protest; attacks on freedom of the press (targeting journalists; suing media outlets; restricting access of journalists to the White House—while also granting press pool privileges to "media" outfits that engage in disinformation and conspiracy theories); and discrimination against minority groups (especially the LGBTQ+ community).

Since the release of the Amnesty report, the human rights situation has become even more dire. Arrests and detentions at the hands of Immigration and Customs Enforcement agents have increased dramatically (although actual deportations have not kept pace), often targeting immigrants at workplaces and courtrooms (the latter is especially cruel because most of these are asylum seekers who are required to report to the court). After protests against these immigration enforcement practices began in Los Angeles and included minor instances of vandalism, Trump nationalized the California National Guard, deploying 4,000 troops to the city, later adding 400 active-duty Marines. Democratic officeholders have been arrested or detained, one—California Senator Alex Padilla—for asking a question of Homeland Security Secretary Kristi Noem during a press conference.

Turning to Trump's human rights-related foreign policy, on his inauguration day, January 20, 2025, Trump established the "Department of Government Efficiency" (DOGE) and put billionaire Elon Musk in charge of the new entity. The mission of the Department ostensibly was to eliminate "waste, fraud and abuse" throughout the federal government (Musk originally claimed he could eliminate $2 trillion in federal spending). Among Musk's first targets was the US Agency for International Development and its nearly $22 billion budget (representing 0.3 percent of the total federal budget). Musk gleefully posted on X (formerly Twitter) that he was going to "feed USAID into the woodchipper." The dismantling of the agency and its operations—including PEPFAR, the global HIV/AIDS prevention and treatment program[14]—was swift and ruthless. There was almost no pushback from Republicans in Congress. The United States, which has always been the largest single contributor (in absolute terms) to global health, food relief, governance (e.g., the UN system), and human rights programs, has literally abdicated its humanitarian responsibilities—in just a few months.

Similar fates have been visited upon a whole host of smaller programs that support America's "soft power," including shuttering or significantly curtailing the congressionally-established United States Institute of Peace—which Trump bizarrely (and almost certainly illegally) renamed for himself in December 2025—the Woodrow Wilson Center, and the Fulbright Student and Scholars programs (all members of the Fulbright board that approves Scholar grants recently resigned in protest as the State Department had begun to rescind certain awards to scholars pursuing "prohibited" gender- and DEI-related research). The Peace Corps is also bracing for significant cuts. When we originally drafted this chapter in December 2024, we were hopeful that the near-unanimous confirmation of Marco Rubio signaled some kind of foreign policy moderation—perhaps a return to the policies of the first Trump administration, but hopefully not much worse. Clearly we were wrong.

In April 2025, Secretary Rubio announced his proposal for a dramatic reorganization of the State Department that will gut long-standing policies and programs supported by the Office of Democracy, Labor, and Human Rights (DLR). It will eliminate all regional human rights offices as well as the Office of Multilateral and Global Affairs and the Office of Global Programming (the two largest offices in the Bureau). It will create a new "Office of Natural Rights," rename the current Office of International Labor Affairs the "Office of Free Markets and Fair Labor." There will be a new Deputy Assistant Secretary for "Democracy and Western Values." These changes would result in an estimated overall reduction in DLR staff of 80 percent.

The reorganization points to a continuation and deepening of some of the moves we saw in the first Trump administration. The State Department will now focus solely on a few cherry-picked issues: religious freedom (also a priority in the G.W. Bush administration), antisemitism, trafficking in persons, and "Western values," which will be a huge gift to the Chinese, Russians, and others from the Global South in their ongoing human rights "normfare" (see Chapter 5, Section 1.4.1). It is unclear what will happen to the statutorily mandated responsibility to prevent atrocities under the Elie Wiesel Genocide and Atrocities Prevention Act of 2019.[15]

In addition, Rubio immediately suspended the completion of the congressionally-mandated State Department's 2025 human rights country reports, which were compiled during the Biden administration, to remove critiques about government corruption, restrictions on political participation and freedom of movement, or retaining political prisoners without due process. Other topics to be eliminated from the reports are gender-related violence and targeting of people with disabilities. The report on El Salvador—where the United States has deported more than 200 migrants to a notorious prison—CECOT—some without due process—has redlined any references to dangerous prison conditions there.[16] The reports are usually released annually in March or April; they were finally released in August 2025 but, because of the corruption of the process of their publication, will be of little use to anyone.

Trump has received some pushback from the courts—although that system is stressed under the significant weight of literally hundreds of lawsuits, many of which will take years to be resolved. But unlike during the first Trump administration, there has been almost no push-back from Congress. And it is too early to tell what the public reaction will be after the impact of the cuts to domestic services and programs comes to be appreciated.

It is clear, though, that significant numbers of Americans are alarmed by what they are witnessing, especially in the United States. Weeks after the Los Angeles protests prompted the (perhaps illegal) deployment of the National Guard and Marines to that city, over 2,100 "No Kings" rallies around the United States coincided with a military parade in Washington D.C., to celebrate the 250th anniversary of the US Army's establishment (on Trump's 79th birthday). A second set of rallies occurred in October. Taken together, "No Kings" were the largest political demonstrations in American history. According to the American Civil Liberties Union (one of the demonstrations' organizers), more than 5 million people attended the nationwide marches in June, and 7 million in October. And the level of civic engagement in 2025 has far outpaced what we saw in the first Trump administration. The Crowd Counting Consortium at Harvard University estimates that the cumulative number of political protests, rallies, and demonstrations from inauguration day 2025 to mid-June totals nearly 15,400, compared to a little over 5,000 at the same point in 2017.

3 Human Rights and American Exceptionalism

American foreign policy since World War II has always advocated freedom, democracy, and human rights. There are many ways, though, to achieve these goals—which, as we have seen, often compete not only with other foreign policy objectives but also with one another. As the world's most powerful state, the United States has both a considerable interest in and broad responsibilities toward a stable international society and the protection and provision of "global common goods," including human rights. But, as the historical overview in the preceding sections has suggested, there have been considerable (and recently quite dramatic) fluctuations in the American commitment to international human rights.

These fluctuations partly reflect ideological and policy differences between administrations of the two major political parties. They also, though, reflect the fact that the United States has always "done human rights" its own way. This is usually discussed as a matter of **American exceptionalism**, the belief that the United States is different from (and generally superior to) most other countries, in large part because of its domestic commitment to individual rights, democracy, and the rule of law.

The isolationist variant of American exceptionalism, expressed with particular clarity in George Washington's Farewell Address, portrays the United States as a beacon of hope for an oppressed world—but only an example, not an active participant in the struggle for freedom overseas. No less powerful, however, has been interventionist exceptionalism, which stresses an active American mission to spread its values through direct foreign policy action, sometimes even using military force.

This interventionist strand, however, has often callously equated the strategic, political, and economic interests of the United States with democracy and human rights. Furthermore, there has been a strong tendency to emphasize civil and political rights and the right to private property, sometimes to the exclusion of (other) economic and social rights. This has contributed to an American tendency to react suspiciously to regimes, opposition groups, and "revolutionaries" that prioritized economic redistribution. Although this was most striking during the Cold War, Trump and his allies have revived the tactic of labeling social and economic reformers as Marxists, socialists, and communists—and thus anti-American.

A combination of anticommunism and crude self-interest has also been at the heart of a striking American inconsistency toward elections. During the Cold War, the United States regularly, and rightly, criticized one-party elections in communist countries. But the mere existence of elections in anticommunist countries was usually accepted as evidence of the ruling regime's democratic character. Elections that brought (alleged) communists to power were bad and had to be overturned. When force or fraud brought anticommunists to power, that was an acceptable price to pay to keep communists out of power and on the run. And even today, electoral democracy is not something the United States is willing to even hint at as desirable in places such as Saudi Arabia.

Other strands or elements of American exceptionalism are less controversial but still important to consider—what some observers call "exemptionalism": the idea that American domestic institutions and indeed the US Constitution itself necessitate exemptions from the human rights rules that other countries must follow. Human rights are seen as for "them" but not for "us," because we already have constitutional rights, and, in any case, we really "invented" human rights. In addition, American power has for a good century now given the United States the "right" to define for itself and its foreign policy what human rights are and how they ought to be pursued. (This is perhaps the most charitable way to interpret the Commission on Unalienable Rights—which ostentatiously uses the infrequent variant of "inalienable" that Jefferson adopted in the Declaration of Independence—and the use of the language of natural rights.)

Such exemptionalism has unfortunate international *and* domestic implications. For example, the United States regularly arrogates to itself the power to refuse to participate in global mechanisms (like the ICC), to bend the rules—or worse, to be exempt from rules altogether. For example, the United States declared that combatants captured in Afghanistan after the November 2001 invasion (which was authorized by the UN Security Council) were not proper combatants and therefore could be legally denied the protections of the Fourth **Geneva Convention**—and then moved many of them to the American military base in Guantánamo Bay, Cuba (held under the terms of a disputed lease with Cuba), where the United States has maintained that neither international law nor most US law applies. More generally, the United States strongly supports prosecuting others in the International Criminal Court but has aggressively negotiated exemptions for Americans from states that have accepted the jurisdiction of the ICC (and thus might be called on to turn over indicted Americans to the Court).

Domestically, exemptionalism is evident in the continuing American refusal to provide basic economic and social rights such as universal access to health care, housing, and parental leave and by the refusal to be legally bound by most of the international human rights treaties that it has ratified (an issue to which we will return at the end of this chapter).

4 Case Studies

This section looks at three cases studies, two historical (Central America and South Africa) and one contemporary (the Israeli-occupied West Bank). We think that they provide both useful detail and perspective. But you should feel free to skip any that are not of interest to you – or jump to Section 5, where we compare American international human rights policy to that of other Western countries.

4.1 US Policy in Central America (Historical)

Central America, the geographical area that lies between North America (Canada, the United States, and Mexico) and South America, became a major international human rights concern in the 1980s, largely because of US support for the right-wing government of El Salvador and parallel US efforts to overthrow the elected leftist government of Nicaragua. These countries will be our focus here.

4.1.1 Human Rights in El Salvador

Salvadoran independence from Spain in the 1820s was in many ways less significant than the economic reforms in the second half of the nineteenth century that transferred one-third of the country's land to a small coffee oligarchy. For the following half-century, protests by dispossessed peasants were ruthlessly suppressed, culminating in the systematic killing of at least 10,000 people and as many as 30,000 in the *matanza* (massacre) of 1932.

Elections were held regularly, but the official military-backed party used patronage, threats, and, when necessary, blatant fraud to ensure victory for its candidates. And the ruling oligarchy regularly used force against those seeking a more egalitarian society. In the mid-1970s, more than two-thirds of children under age five suffered from malnutrition.

The government of General Carlos Humberto Romero, installed after the fraudulent elections of 1977, imposed total press censorship, outlawed not only strikes but also public meetings of all sorts, and suspended judicial due process. Death squads, which worked closely with the Salvadoran security forces, became a regular part of the Romero regime's repressive apparatus. A succession of military juntas between 1979 and 1983 supervised an effective reign of terror that in response provoked an armed civil war. Americas Watch, a human rights NGO, estimated that out of a total population of fewer than 5 million, there were more than 30,000 government-sponsored murders in 1980–1983 alone (roughly equivalent, at the time, to killing one and a quarter million Americans).

The election of José Napoleón Duarte as president in 1984 (largely as a result of US pressure) helped to reduce the level of violence. The human rights situation, however, remained dismal. The government estimated that death squads were killing "only" about thirty people a month in 1985, although most independent observers put the number substantially higher. Torture continued. The number of political prisoners even increased, apparently because of the decline in political murders.

A UN-mediated end to the civil war was finally agreed to at the end of 1991. The arrival of UN monitors in 1992 stopped the fighting and initiated efforts at structural political reform (especially greater civilian control over the armed forces). And, by 1997, in the annual Freedom House ratings of political rights and civil liberties, El Salvador had returned to the level it held in the early 1970s (just barely "free" in the human rights NGOs' categorization). (In recent years, though, its rating has declined to "partly free" because although elections are largely free and credible, widespread corruption, a concentration of powers in the executive, and a militarized response to gang violence are eroding the rule of law.)

4.1.2 Human Rights in Nicaragua

Nicaragua's early political history was not much different from that of El Salvador. In 1936, however, Anastasio Somoza García seized power and initiated what would be more than forty years of authoritarian family rule. When Somoza was assassinated in 1956, power passed first to his son Luis Somoza Debayle and then to his younger son, Anastasio Somoza Debayle, who ruled until overthrown in 1979.

Although the Somozas retained the forms of democracy, elections were rigged, and civil and political rights were regularly violated. (Large-scale systematic killings, though, were not part of their repertoire.) Economic and social rights were also systematically infringed, both through the predatory accumulation of immense personal wealth by the Somozas and their cronies and through disregard of social services. For example, in the early 1970s, the Nicaraguan government spent three times as much on defense as on health care.

Massive corruption in the cleanup and recovery effort following the 1972 earthquake in the capital city of Managua, which left perhaps 10,000 dead and hundreds of thousands homeless, exacerbated and highlighted the endemic problems of inequality. Two years later, Somoza was reelected in a contest that even by Nicaraguan standards was farcical. In January 1978, the pace of disaffection accelerated after the assassination of Pedro Joaquín Chamorro, the leader of the moderate opposition. Even the business community turned against Somoza, under whom it had profited, organizing a general strike to protest Chamorro's death. Eighteen months later, Somoza was forced into exile.

Somoza was swept from power by a mass popular revolt incorporating many different social and political groups. Although its military forces were led by the Sandinista National

Liberation Front (FSLN), established in 1961 as a radical breakaway from the Soviet-oriented Nicaraguan Socialist Party, during his final two years in power Somoza was opposed even by Nicaragua's conservative Catholic Church and by the United States, the Somozas' traditional patron.

The revolution, although widely supported, had immense human and economic costs. About one-fifth of Nicaragua's population of roughly 2.5 million became refugees. Casualties included 40,000–50,000 people killed, 150,000 wounded, and perhaps 40,000 orphaned. The war also disrupted agricultural production and most other sectors of the economy. The nation's gross domestic product (GDP) fell by one-fourth in 1979 and by another one-fifth in 1980. Direct economic losses from the revolution were about $2 billion, or roughly Nicaragua's entire annual GDP.

Human rights conditions generally improved in revolutionary Nicaragua. The Sandinista government increased spending on social programs, especially health care, and redirected spending for education toward mass literacy. Personal and legal rights were fairly widely respected. Internationally recognized civil liberties were extensively implemented for the first time in Nicaraguan history. Mass political participation was actively fostered. And the 1984 election was generally considered by outside observers to have been relatively open and fairly run.

Nevertheless, the government itself admitted serious human rights violations during the forced relocation of indigenous populations on the Atlantic Coast. Restrictions on freedom of the press, freedom of association, and due process were imposed. Sandinista-controlled "mass popular organizations" (civil society organizations organized by the party) and the government-controlled media received preferential treatment. Political opponents, however, operated under fewer constraints, and with far less fear of retaliation, than Somoza's opponents had. And human rights NGOs such as Americas Watch consistently judged human rights conditions to be significantly better in Nicaragua than in neighboring El Salvador and Guatemala.

This record, although acceptable only in relative terms, was noteworthy because the Sandinista government was under intense attack from US-financed "contras" (a shortened form of the Spanish word for counterrevolutionaries). Contra strategy emphasized terrorism, including kidnappings, assassinations, and attacks on farms, schools, health clinics, and civilian economic targets – the kinds of terrorist attacks that, ironically, US-supported governments in neighboring Guatemala and El Salvador argued required repressive policies in response.

With the winding down of the Contra War in 1988 and 1989, respect for civil and political rights again improved. In national elections in February 1990, the Sandinistas were voted out of power, initiating two decades of lively contestation between the Left and Right. And although this historical case study strictly ends here, it should be noted that in November 2016, in elections that the head of the Organization of American States observer mission described as "worrying," Ortega was reelected to a third term, after the Sandinista-dominated Supreme Court overturned term limits and excluded the leader of the opposition from the contest. In 2018, the rule of law effectively collapsed as the regime and its allies violently repressed organized opposition. The 2021 elections looked much like the fraudulent polls of Somoza. Today, most civil liberties are severely curtailed and freedom of association, except for some FSLN-aligned trade unions, is systematically denied. Freedom House in 2025 ranked Nicaragua not free, with a ranking of 14 (out of 100), which placed it below countries including Ethiopia, Egypt, Cambodia, and Vietnam.

4.1.3 US Policy in Central America

In the early twentieth century, US policy in Central America was directed toward establishing military, economic, and political **hegemony**. Central America was strategically significant for its proximity to the United States, the Panama Canal, and Caribbean sea lanes. US pressure and intervention were also regularly used to further the interests of US banks and corporations. By the 1920s, Central America had become a special US sphere of influence; "our backyard," as it was still often put in the 1980s.

After World War II, however, anticommunism became an increasingly important motivating force. By the 1980s, when Central America reemerged as a focal issue in US foreign policy, economic interests were largely irrelevant. For example, US exports to Nicaragua averaged just under $200 million per year from 1976 to 1978 and total US direct foreign investment was a meager $60 million. US policy was driven principally by the fear that domestic instability might increase support for local communists and their Soviet (and Cuban) backers. US policy thus usually supported the military and traditional civilian elites, to the detriment of the rights of most Central Americans. Bruce Jentleson[17] calls this the "ABC" policy—Anything But Communism—regardless of the human rights implications.

Consider Nicaragua. In 1912, US troops prevented a liberal political revolution and then remained until 1933, except for eighteen months in the mid-1920s. Furthermore, the United States was the leading force behind the creation of the National Guard, the principal base of Somoza power. Economic interests and strategic concerns over a potential second canal through Nicaragua explain the initial US involvement. But, after World War II, the Somozas' support of US Cold War policies became their major asset. In Guatemala and El Salvador, US policy was similar.

The postwar US record on economic and social rights in Central America was a bit more mixed—or at least not entirely negative. The Alliance for Progress, a major foreign aid initiative for Latin America launched in 1961, brought substantial increases in US aid to Central America. This seems to have contributed to economic growth in the 1960s and early 1970s. US aid also helped to improve life expectancy and literacy. The benefits of growth, however, were distributed so unequally that the gap between rich and poor actually widened in the 1960s and 1970s. And in El Salvador, Guatemala, and Nicaragua alike, US-backed governments regularly used their power against political parties, trade unions, peasant organizations, and most other groups that tried to foster more rapid reforms or structural changes in society or the economy.

The Carter administration entered office in 1977 intent on giving human rights at least an equal place in its policy. In Central America, the administration took both concrete and symbolic action. Most dramatically, Carter, with congressional support, cut aid to Guatemala. But although new military aid was cancelled, already committed (pipeline) aid was continued. And Carter never seriously pressed for major structural reforms.

When Nicaragua emerged as a major concern of US foreign policy in the fall of 1978, internal turmoil rather than human rights was the major American concern. Carter's goal was to remove Somoza without yielding power to the Sandinistas, who were seen as too closely tied to Cuba and the Soviet Union. The desire to avoid "another Cuba" dominated policy.

United States efforts to strengthen Nicaragua's political center, however, suffered under political and financial retaliation by Somoza. And the assassination of Chamorro had deprived it of its most respected and effective leader.

After four frustrating months of US mediation, Somoza simply refused to leave. Carter responded by terminating military and economic aid, withdrawing the Peace Corps, and halving the size of the US Embassy in Managua. But when these sanctions failed to convince Somoza to step down, there was little that could be done short of the use of force—which Carter refused to consider, for reasons of principle and policy alike.

In June 1979, when the Sandinistas (FSLN) launched their "final offensive," the United States again tried to promote a centrist "third force." The pace of events, however, combined with the moderate opposition's lack of organization and foresight, proved fatal. When Somoza left in July, power passed to a provisional coalition government dominated by its most astute and best-organized faction, the FSLN.

The Carter administration attempted to set aside its suspicions. Food and medical supplies were sent almost immediately. When Carter left office in January 1981, eighteen months after Somoza's fall, the United States had provided $118 million in aid to Nicaragua—more than the United States gave to any other Central American country in the same period.

In El Salvador, however, the United States continued to describe the repressive military governments as reformist, despite massive and mounting violations of civil and political rights and a lack of progress on land reform and economic and social rights. Furthermore, the Carter administration also included skeptics among its high officials, most prominently the national security adviser, Zbigniew Brzezinski. As security concerns increasingly came to dominate policymaking, the Carter administration began moving the United States toward what would become President Ronald Reagan's new approach.

Central America (along with Afghanistan) became a test case for the Reagan administration's new global political strategy. By summer 1981, the Central Intelligence Agency (CIA) was working with the military opposition in Nicaragua. On March 14, 1982, the Contra War began when two bridges were destroyed by former members of the National Guard who had been trained by the CIA.

The rationale for this new approach had already been laid down by Jeane J. Kirkpatrick, a professor of government (and lifelong Democrat) who had become disillusioned with Carter's approach toward noncommunist authoritarianism in the Americas. In an influential article[18] that helped to earn her the position of US ambassador to the United Nations in the Reagan administration, Kirkpatrick argued that Carter had failed to understand that the most serious threats to human rights were posed not by authoritarian dictatorships but by totalitarian communists. For the Reagan administration, the global strategic rivalry with the Soviet Union *was* a struggle for human rights, regardless of the actual human rights practices of the governments in question.

The American-backed campaign of military and economic aggression against Nicaragua had devastating consequences—created, in an appalling irony, by terrorist tactics supported by an American administration that came into office promising to replace the Carter administration's "misplaced" emphasis on human rights with a global campaign against terrorism. As many as 40,000 people were killed and at least a quarter million were displaced. Food production declined by at least one-quarter. Advances in health care and social services were reversed by terrorist attacks on clinics, schools, and social service offices. By 1988, Nicaragua's economy had been destroyed, with hyperinflation raging at 31,000 percent per year.

The strong and sustained US support for terroristic opposition to the freely elected government of Nicaragua contrasted sharply with the strong US support for the government of El Salvador. The human rights situation in El Salvador was far worse than that in Nicaragua under the Sandinistas (or Somoza). And, in addition to the tens of thousands of Salvadorans killed, Americans were also victims. In December 1980, four American churchwomen were abducted, raped, and murdered. In March 1981, two officials of the American Institute for Free Labor Development were assassinated in the San Salvador Sheraton Hotel. Yet massive aid continued—about $500 million a year in 1984 and 1985 (compared to less than $100 million in 1979 and 1980 combined), totaling almost $4 billion for the decade.

As Americas Watch put it, "So consistent is this [American] double standard that it can be fairly said [that] the Reagan administration has no true human rights policy."[19] Criticisms of the human rights practices of leftist regimes and the defense of the human rights practices of friendly governments were simply a continuation of the struggle with the Soviet Union by other means.

Rhetoric, however, exaggerates the differences in American policy under Carter and Reagan. Carter spoke of human rights as the heart of US foreign policy, but in practice, they were only a secondary goal. And Reagan's attempts to relegate human rights to the bottom of the list of US foreign policy objectives were at least partially defeated by Congress. Carter did significantly elevate the place of human rights in US policy toward Central America. But they never reached the top. Reagan did force human rights back down the list. But they never reached the bottom.

The first Bush administration's Central America policy, both in word and in deed, lay between those of its predecessors. Bush generally supported the Salvadoran and Guatemalan governments, despite their lack of control over the military. He did, however, act to prevent further deterioration. And, in Nicaragua, he pursued a somewhat less belligerent strategy of opposition to the Sandinistas.

The end of the Cold War led to a decline in Central America's geopolitical significance—and thus US attention. But human rights concerns remained an important, and largely nonpartisan, part of US foreign policy in the region. And improvements in national human rights practices across the region meant that US initiatives often were met with somewhat less resistance, although with continued concern for national sovereignty and fear of US regional hegemony.

In recent years, Central America has returned to American headlines primarily in the context of immigration. Hundreds of thousands of Guatemalans, Salvadorans, Hondurans, and Nicaraguans have fled lawlessness, corruption, and gang and political violence, seeking refuge and economic opportunity in the United States. By contrast, very few illegal migrants come from Costa Rica or Belize, where human rights conditions are by some measures better than in the United States.

4.2 US Policy toward South Africa (Historical)

For nearly a half-century, South Africa was synonymous with **apartheid**, a distinctive style of unusually deep and wide-ranging systematic legalized racial domination. Officially abolished in 1992, apartheid was a major international human rights issue for thirty years.

4.2.1 A System of Racial Domination

Racial discrimination in South Africa goes back to the initial Dutch colonization in 1652. Indigenous hunter-gatherers (San, or "Bushmen") were largely killed off or pushed out, and local herding peoples (Khoikhoi, or "Hottentots") were forced off their lands. Slaves began to be imported in 1658. Blacks, discriminated against in voting from the very beginning, were legally excluded from many jobs after 1911 and lost the formal right to vote in 1936.

With the electoral victory of the conservative Nationalist Party in 1948, race became the basis for regulating all aspects of life in South Africa. The Nationalist government created a totalitarian bureaucracy to enforce racism throughout South African society.

The Population Registration Act of 1950, the cornerstone of apartheid, required racial registration of each person at birth. The Group Areas Act of 1950 (amended in 1957) consolidated and extended earlier laws designating land by race. The 1954 Natives Resettlement Act provided for forced removals of black people from white-designated land. These racial designations, however, had little connection to previously existing facts. More than 3.5 million black people were removed from white areas and another million were forced to relocate within designated black areas, often great distances away from their actual homes.

Controls on the movement of nonwhites resulted in a series of "pass laws" and regulations that made it illegal for most black people to be in urban areas for more than seventy-two hours without special permission. The result was the creation of black townships, with inferior housing, education, and social services, on the outskirts of (white) cities, often two hours away from where township residents worked. Because of the absurdities of the system of restrictions on movement, the ordinary nonwhite person was subject to the constant threat of prosecution. More than one-fifth of the nonwhite population could expect to be prosecuted for pass-law violations within a ten-year period, a staggering level of legal intrusion on the basis of just one set of rules. And because prosecutions often led to expulsion from the area and the loss of a person's only source of income, the pass laws were an extraordinarily powerful instrument of social control.

Increasingly repressive internal security laws were passed to repress the inevitable political opposition. By 1967, few legal safeguards remained for those accused of political offenses. Over the next decade, at least a hundred people died while being detained by the police or security forces, usually after having been tortured. The best-known victim was

Black-Consciousness activist Steve Biko, who was killed while in police custody in 1977. And many who were not formally detained were brought in by the authorities for questioning, often as a not-so-subtle warning.

As a result, most nonparliamentary opposition was forced underground. This does not mean, though, that there was no resistance. The African National Congress (ANC), the leading political group in contemporary South Africa, was founded in 1912. The 1952–1953 pass-law demonstrations marked the beginning of organized resistance to apartheid. Resistance took new forms, however, after the police fired on a group of peaceful demonstrators on March 21, 1960, killing sixty-nine people and wounding about 200 others in what quickly came to be known as the Sharpeville Massacre.

When the ANC and several other groups were banned, a number of leading activists of the 1950s, including Nelson Mandela, having concluded that peaceful protest alone could not be successful, launched a (quite ineffective) sabotage campaign. When Mandela and several other leaders were convicted in 1964 and sentenced to life imprisonment, the ANC was forced into exile. And, as opposition increased, the white government weathered mass protests and riots in 1976 and 1977, through a combination of force, new restrictions, and minor concessions.

Peaceful opposition also continued, despite government efforts to make it illegal. South African churches became particularly important because almost all overtly political opposition organizations were banned. The award of the Nobel Peace Prize in 1984 to Bishop Desmond Tutu symbolized this struggle. Black trade-union activity also increased and became politically important in the mid-1980s.

New and unusually violent uprisings in the townships broke out in the fall of 1984 and lasted for nearly two years. Torture and abuse of those detained increased dramatically. Official violence against those not detained also increased. Symbolic of the new level of overt brutality was the widely seen footage of armed security-force personnel popping up from their hiding place inside a passing vehicle and opening fire on unarmed children. Even more ominous was the dramatic increase in violence by police-sponsored vigilante groups.

Direct repression was accompanied by no less severe social and economic exploitation and degradation. For example, the average white person under apartheid had an income more than twelve times that of the average black person. A black child was almost ten times more likely to die before the age of one than a white child. Other standard statistical measures revealed a similar picture.

4.2.2 US Policy on Apartheid

Before the Sharpeville Massacre in 1960, the United States treated apartheid as an internal South African matter. The turmoil following Sharpeville, however, raised the specter of revolution and mobilized American fear of communism. The United States thus began to treat apartheid as a matter of international concern. The Eisenhower administration even agreed to put apartheid permanently on the agenda of the UN Security Council. And the Kennedy administration imposed a selective arms embargo even before the Security Council called for a voluntary embargo at the end of 1963.

As the immediate crisis receded, however, so too did US attention. Sanctions remained in effect. They were, however, minor and had no discernible impact.

The Nixon administration changed course, arguing that a closer association with South Africa would put the United States in a better position to press for reform. This approach, however, had no more impact than the Kennedy–Johnson strategy of dissociation. Part of the problem was weak and inconsistent implementation, with US concessions being tied to no particular demands on South Africa. In other words, there was no real policy on South Africa.

There were also major conceptual flaws in both the punitive and engaging American approaches. The South African government, although willing to ease some elements of "petty apartheid" (for example, by desegregating some public facilities in large cities), was unwilling to end—or even discuss the ending of—racial separation (and thus discrimination, given the unavoidable inequality of coercively imposed policies of separate treatment for different groups). The sanctions and inducements that the United States (and other countries) were willing to use fell far short of what would have been necessary to make the white government consider changing its policies.

The other conceptual error in US policy was an excessive reliance on economic change and private enterprise. Liberals and conservatives alike believed that South Africa's atavistic racial policies would inevitably be eroded by the modernization that accompanied economic development. In practice, however, South Africa's immense bureaucracy, which intervened with totalitarian thoroughness in all aspects of life, largely prevented changes in the fundamental character of apartheid.

After the Portuguese coup in April 1974 led to the rapid decolonization of Angola and Mozambique, even these modest US efforts against apartheid were largely abandoned in favor of a focus on regional security—that is, containing expanding Soviet influence. South Africa now appeared as a pro-Western regional power.

The riots in Soweto in 1976, which reflected mass popular opposition to racial rule, returned apartheid to the center of international attention. Jimmy Carter did change US rhetoric. But actions, such as US support in the Security Council for a mandatory arms embargo, were largely symbolic. Furthermore, Zbigniew Brzezinski, Carter's national security adviser, favored a policy that, like Henry Kissinger's earlier in the decade, emphasized regional security. As Brzezinski's influence grew in the second half of Carter's term, US policy took on an increasingly Cold War tone, stressing the Cuban presence in Angola and the Soviet naval threat in the South Atlantic and Indian Oceans. Even more than in Central America, the end of the Carter administration is best seen as preparing the way for Reagan's policies.

Reagan's policy of "constructive engagement" returned to the Nixon-era strategy of pursuing closer relations, supposedly to increase US leverage. But there was no serious effort to use that leverage. Despite international calls for new sanctions, the United States eased restrictions on the sale of aircraft, computers, and nuclear-related equipment with dual military and civilian uses. The United States became South Africa's largest trading partner and a major investor. But the United States did not insist on any concrete human rights improvements in return for closer relations.

Events in South Africa, however, again forced a reevaluation of US policy. Violence erupted in August 1984 (in protest over elections held under the new constitution of 1983, which completely excluded black people from direct political participation). When repression once more tightened, constructive engagement lost any remaining credibility. As late as July 1986, Reagan still argued, in reference to South Africa, that "we and our allies cannot dictate to the government of a sovereign nation—nor should we try"—despite supporting a terrorist war against the freely elected government of Nicaragua and the decades-old policy of comprehensive sanctions against Cuba.

Change in US policy came from a bipartisan congressional coalition that in 1986 overrode a presidential veto of a new sanctions bill. This reflected the culmination of the mobilization of antiapartheid NGOs over many decades.

Activity in South Africa by US NGOs goes back to at least 1912, when the National Association for the Advancement of Colored People was involved in the initial formation of South Africa's ANC. In the late 1970s and 1980s, groups like TransAfrica focused their efforts on apartheid. Other NGOs, such as the American Friends Service Committee, the Interfaith Council on Corporate Responsibility, and the Lawyers' Committee for Civil Rights Under Law, made South Africa a major priority. In addition, churches, state and local governments, colleges and universities, student organizations, unions, and black organizations divested assets in corporations that did business in South Africa. Many of these actions were coordinated with divestment campaigns in other countries, with international antiapartheid groups such as the International Defense and Aid Fund and with other international NGOs such as the World Council of Churches and the Lutheran World Fund. They were also facilitated by Bishop Desmond Tutu's Nobel Peace Prize and his well-publicized visit to the United States at the end of 1984.

It is important not to overestimate US efforts. American sanctions were limited and quite incomplete. Nonetheless, South Africa was losing access to international capital (although in the short run more from lender fear caused by the 1984–1986 township riots than from sanctions). And the loss of US support, even if the Reagan administration never actively opposed the white government, created concern among many of South Africa's less conservative leaders and citizens, particularly in light of the growing internal crisis.

Apartheid ultimately collapsed because of the inability of the white government to keep opposition repressed. Nonetheless, changes in US policy, particularly in the context of the global antiapartheid campaign, made a small contribution to the final demise of apartheid. And even though American sanctions were largely symbolic, it was a very different sort of symbolism than had been typical of US policy in the preceding years.

4.3 Israeli Settlements in West Bank Palestine

Perhaps no other American foreign policy relationship is at once as central and as contentious as its very special relationship with Israel. Since being one of the first countries to recognize Israeli independence in 1948, the United States has remained a stalwart political, economic, and military ally. However, cognizant of its broader geopolitical interests, the United States has always sought friendly relations with Arab states as well. It has also seen itself (although has not always been seen by others) as an "honest broker" for peace in the region.

We look here narrowly at Israeli settlement policy in the occupied West Bank. (Israel unilaterally evacuated and dismantled its settlements in the Gaza Strip in 2005—although new settlements in Gaza appear likely as we write this at the end of 2025.) This not only provides an excellent example of the complexities of US–Israeli international human rights relations but also allows us to look at American policy toward an ally that in many areas has an excellent human rights record but that in other ways is a gross and persistent systematic violator of international human rights and humanitarian law. In addition, by focusing on settlement policy—rather than Israeli violations of human rights such as arbitrary arrest and detention, torture, denials of freedom of movement, the use of collective punishments, and a general practice of **impunity** (see under **amnesty**) for security forces—this case also illustrates the increasingly important interaction of human rights law with the law of armed conflict, to which we will return in some detail in Chapter 11.

During the Six-Day War in June 1967, Israel captured and occupied the West Bank of the Jordan River (which had been under the administration of Jordan), the Golan Heights (part of Syria), and Egypt's Gaza Strip and Sinai Peninsula. To this day, the West Bank, which is our focus here, has not been recognized internationally as Israel's. In fact, Israel itself agrees that most of this land is Israeli-occupied territory, not part of the state of Israel, and it has accepted the Palestinian Authority as a legitimate administrative authority in the West Bank.

As a matter of both international and Israeli law, the West Bank remains a territory under the military occupation of Israel. Therefore, the laws of war govern Israel's actions there.

An occupying authority, according to the **Geneva Conventions**, is prohibited from taking measures that might lead to a de facto annexation of the territory, such as forcibly altering the demographic structure of the territory (for example, through population transfers). This, however, is precisely what successive Israeli governments have done through their settlement-building policies in the West Bank. Not only has this displaced Palestinians and brought nearly half a million Israelis to live, ostensibly permanently, on Palestinian territory, but these settlements have also been crafted into a coherent network secured by the Israeli Defense Forces. (In this case study, we do not address the more than 200,000 Israeli settlers in East Jerusalem, whom Israel—with almost no international support—claims have a different legal status than do the settlers in the West Bank. Neither do we consider some 30,000 settlers in the Golan Heights.)

Settlement policy has often been controversial in Israel's multiparty democracy, leading to recurrent freezes on new settlements and occasionally even minor withdrawals from particular settlements. Since the early 2000s, however, Israeli governments—and particularly governments headed by Benjamin Netanyahu—have been at least steadfast, and often enthusiastic, in their support of not merely maintaining but expanding Israeli settlements in Palestinian territory.

This has created immense problems for American policy, the primary stated goal of which has long been a final settlement to the Israeli–Palestinian conflict in the form of a "two-state solution." Even setting aside the political problems caused by its flagrant illegality, Israeli settlement policy, by changing facts on the ground, has made it more difficult to imagine a final territorial settlement acceptable to both Israel and Palestine. Every American presidential administration since 1967 thus has, with varying degrees of intensity and sincerity, condemned Israeli settlements.

Despite the fact that settlement activity has expanded under every American president since Lyndon Johnson, American action has been weak and inconsistent. For example, US law requires that aid to Israel (which has usually been in the range of 3–4 billion dollars a year) be reduced dollar for dollar by what Israel spends on settlement activity. The last such reduction, however, was in 2005.

Upon assuming office, Barack Obama urged Israeli leaders to freeze settlement activity in the West Bank. In his 2009 Cairo speech, Obama forcefully repeated the long-established policy that the United States "does not accept the legitimacy of continued Israeli settlements. This construction violates previous agreements and undermines efforts to achieve peace. It is time for these settlements to stop." But after a ten-month settlement freeze, new settlements resumed—and the prospects for peace remained dismal. The United States not only failed to institute diplomatic sanctions; in 2011, it even vetoed a draft resolution in the Security Council condemning the Israeli settlements as illegal—despite continued American insistence that the settlements are illegitimate and undermine peace efforts. And not only does the United States continue to refuse to link military aid to settlement drawdowns, but a ten-year, $38 billion dollar arms deal confirmed in September 2016 was the largest ever American aid package of its kind. In 2022, US military aid was about 5 billion dollars. The Gaza War ballooned that amount to over $20 billion in 2024.

This policy of largely verbal opposition reflects the priority given to a long-standing special relationship, the central place of Israel in America's established geopolitical orientation to the region, the historical memory of the Holocaust, and American domestic politics—involving not only ethnic electoral mobilization in large and politically important states such as New York and Florida but also an extremely active and effective pro-Israel lobby that extends far beyond Jewish groups and their supporters. These factors, plus a general inclination in post-9/11 American foreign policy to tolerate human rights violations by friends undertaken in the name of antiterrorism, have made supporting Israel quite popular with both the American public and American legislators. Israel's human rights violations and flouting of international humanitarian law in the Occupied Territories thus have been kept on the back burner, even by a president such as Obama, who seemed inclined to want to do more.

The first Trump administration, however, abandoned any pretense of even-handedness. The United States largely eliminated even formulaic protests against new (and old) Israeli settlements and, in a gesture of immense symbolic significance, moved its embassy from Tel Aviv to Jerusalem. And what passed for the Trump administration's peace plan largely involved pandering to right-wing (American and Israeli) visions of a triumphant Israel and a crippled Palestine. As with much of the rest of Trump's foreign policy, the Trump approach to peace in the Middle East in general and Israeli settlements in West Bank Palestine in particular has been a flagrant, and often flamboyant, disregard of international law and a warm embrace of the rights-abusive policies and practices of an American "friend."

The Biden administration returned to long-standing American policy, condemning (but not acting concretely against) settlements and reaffirming support for a two-state situation.

But following the brutal massacre of some 1,200 Israelis by Hamas on October 7, 2023 (and the kidnapping of 250 more) and while international attention was focused on Israel's retaliatory war against Gaza, settler lawlessness and violence increased substantially in the West Bank. About 1,000 Palestinians were killed by the Israeli military or settlers in the West Bank in the two years following October 7. But although many of the perpetrators are known to the Israeli authorities, almost none have been brought to justice.

The Biden administration did speak out, repeatedly, against settler violence. It even imposed sanctions on some individuals. But those actions were swamped by US support for Israel's brutal war in Gaza, which has killed more than 70,000 Gazans—by comparison, Ukraine, which has a population seventeen times that of Gaza, has lost about 15,000 civilians and 50–60,000 soldiers since 2022 in its war with Russia—and has damaged more than three-quarters of all the buildings, roads, and orchards in the territory. And where the Biden administration at least regularly complained about "excesses" in the Israeli response to October 7, the second Trump administration has backed away from even verbal criticism—which only bodes increased violence by Israeli settlers in the West Bank and may even embolden the Israeli government to make moves toward annexing some Palestinian land. In May 2025, the Israeli government announced twenty-two new settlements; an additional nineteen settlements were approved in December 2025—the largest expansions in decades.

5 Other Western Approaches to International Human Rights

Although the United States led the way in the 1970s in introducing human rights into bilateral diplomacy, many other countries have also incorporated human rights into their foreign policies. Particularly notable have been the efforts of the so-called *like-minded countries*, a dozen or so smaller (and largely Western) countries that since the mid-1970s have attempted to act together in international diplomacy as intermediaries between the larger Western countries, with which they are formally or informally aligned, and the countries of the Global South, for whose aspirations they have considerable sympathy. Norway and the Netherlands, in particular, have emphasized human rights in their foreign policies, signaled by white papers on the subject in 1977 and 1979.

Even more than in US policy, foreign aid has been a central instrument in the international human rights policies of the like-minded countries. Development assistance tends to be not only an important element of their foreign policies but also a matter of consensus among the major political parties. In the Netherlands, there is even a separate minister for development cooperation within the foreign ministry. By contrast, in the United States, foreign aid is a relatively peripheral part of foreign policy yet, especially during the 1970s and 1980s, a subject of considerable partisan political controversy.

Furthermore, the United States tends to base initial foreign aid decisions on political and humanitarian factors, occasionally modifying allocations at a later stage in light of human rights concerns. The like-minded countries, which lack the resources to engage in a massive, global foreign aid program, target their development assistance at a small set of countries—variously called "core," "program," or "priority" countries—with which they seek to develop relatively intensive, long-term aid relations. The Dutch and Norwegians, in particular, have emphasized both civil and political rights and economic, social, and cultural rights in selecting program countries. In Norway, selection criteria since 1972 have included a strong preference for countries in which "the authorities of the country concerned [are] following a development-oriented and socially just policy in the best interests of all sections of the community," reflecting the fact that social justice is given roughly equal priority to civil and political rights largely across the Norwegian political spectrum. And, as early as 1973, the Dutch officially emphasized a "close relationship between peace, a just distribution of wealth, international legal order and respect for human rights."[20]

Even more striking than the selection of priority countries has been the relatively rapid response of the like-minded countries to changes in human rights conditions. For example, Norway broke its aid relationship with Uganda in 1972, the year that Idi Amin overthrew the government of Milton Obote and embarked on a dictatorial career that made him one of the most notorious human rights violators of the decade. The Netherlands dropped Uganda from its list of program countries in 1974. The United States, by contrast, was Uganda's largest trading partner until October 1978, less than a year before Amin was overthrown.

Sweden stopped all assistance to Chile shortly after Pinochet's coup and was a significant international supporter of the work of the Vicaría, a Catholic human rights organization in Chile. Canada was also a vocal critic of military rule in the Southern Cone. In the 1980s, as ethnic violence escalated in Sri Lanka, a country with which Norway had developed close ties in the 1970s, the Norwegians dramatically downgraded their relationship. Canada, the Netherlands, and the Nordic countries all increased their aid to Nicaragua in the 1980s, reflecting a radically different understanding of human rights than that held by the Reagan administration.

The Dutch response to the deteriorating human rights situation in its former colony of Suriname is especially revealing. It strongly condemned the 1980 military coup. Following the execution of fifteen opposition figures in 1982, the Netherlands not only suspended all aid but also refused to provide new aid for the remainder of the decade. The Dutch also led the effort to apply international pressure on Suriname. The contrast to US behavior toward its clients in Guatemala and El Salvador, who were guilty of much more severe human rights violations, is striking. The Dutch even carried human rights into relations with Indonesia, a country of far greater importance, and accepted some real economic and political costs as a result.

The like-minded countries also adopted an approach to South Africa in the 1970s and 1980s very different from that of the United States. Starting in 1969, Sweden and Norway provided both political support and development assistance funds to the ANC during its exile from South Africa. The Dutch adopted a similar policy in 1973. And in the 1980s, these efforts were expanded into broad, high-priority programs for the whole region of Southern Africa and a leading role in the international movement for sanctions against South Africa.

Since the end of the Cold War, these countries have continued to pursue their human rights policies in such distinctive ways. And they have been joined by countries from the Global South such as Costa Rica and South Africa, which have also put human rights at the forefront of their foreign policies.

We should be careful not to romanticize the policies of the like-minded countries. Considerations other than human rights are central, sometimes even overriding, in their foreign policies. For example, Dutch aid sanctions against Indonesia did not extend to trade or other economic relations. Canada also pursued close relations with Indonesia for commercial reasons. Economic interests in South Africa seriously delayed Canada's decision to adopt sanctions and led Norway to exclude shipping from its initial sanctions. Nonetheless, the overall international human rights record of the like-minded countries is clearly superior to that of the United States, both in avoiding associations with severe violators and in responding to abuses in countries with which they have special relations. The like-minded countries have also given human rights a much higher priority in their multilateral foreign policies. And these differences have been particularly pronounced since the first Trump presidency.

6 Explaining Differences in Human Rights Policies

In a cogent analysis that has stood the test of time, Jan Egeland, in comparing Norwegian and US international human rights policies in the 1980s, argued that "small and big nations are differently disposed to undertaking coherent rights-oriented foreign policies." In fact, Egeland asserted that the relatively meager international human rights accomplishments of the United States are "because of, rather than in spite of, her superpower status."[21]

Small countries, in this analysis, are not so much better as they are less constrained than large states. "The frequency and intensity of the conflict between self-interest and [international human rights] norms seems, in short, proportional to a nation's economic and military power, as well as to its foreign policy ambitions."[22] Large states have multiple interests and responsibilities that preclude the consistent pursuit of human rights objectives. Small states rarely have to choose between human rights and other foreign policy goals. (Of course, some small states are not interested in human rights, either at home or abroad. We are concerned here only with the different constraints large and small states that have chosen to pursue international human rights policies.)

This explanation focuses on the structure of the international system. Large states are also more likely to pursue bilateral policies because they are more likely to have the power to achieve their aims without multilateral support (this is especially true of the United States). Small states, by contrast, tend to prefer international organizations because multilateral processes increase their opportunities for influence. Such structural explanations would also seem to be supported by the fact that larger powers, such as Britain, France, Japan, and, to a lesser extent, Germany, have international human rights policies closer to those of the United States than to those of Norway or the Netherlands.

Size alone, however, cannot explain even the differences that are influenced by relative power. For example, despite declining American power, the United States remains reluctant to operate through multilateral channels (unless it can control the organization). As Germany's power grows, it continues to rely heavily on multilateral organizations. Britain has tended to pursue a much more unilateral foreign policy than have France, Germany, or Japan. Among small states, traditionally Sweden, Austria, and especially Switzerland have emphasized a neutral foreign policy. (Russia's invasion of Ukraine in 2022, however, compelled both Sweden and Switzerland to align more closely with Europe.

Switzerland adopted sanctions against Russia. Sweden ended two centuries of neutrality by joining NATO in 2024.) Size or power at most inclines states in certain directions.

Furthermore, numerous factors unconnected with size are also important. Why did the United States emphasize international human rights in the 1970s while other large powers did not, and Japan still does not? Why did Britain intervene in its sphere of influence so much less frequently than did the United States (or France)? Why are human rights as a foreign policy issue so much more controversial in the United States than in most other Western countries? Why does Belgium have a much less active international human rights policy than does the Netherlands, its larger neighbor? Such questions can be answered only if we take history, political culture, and institutions into account.

Throughout the Cold War era, the United States viewed the world in East–West terms. But the Cold War was not simply a bipolar political rivalry between hegemonic states; it involved a heavy emphasis on ideology. As a result, Americans generally assumed that radical reformers and their programs were Soviet-backed, inspired, or influenced. And without the ideological element, many actual or attempted political changes in the Third World would not have been deemed such a threat to the United States.

Ideology, however, has nothing to do with size. Many small states, especially in Latin America, were at least as anticommunist as the United States. Conversely, it is historically rare for a large state to define its interests in ideological terms.

Consider also the tendency of the like-minded states to view international conflicts more in North–South than East–West terms. During the Cold War, these countries saw the principal lines of international cleavage as dividing rich and poor, not capitalist (or liberal–democratic) and communist. For example, in 1982, Mark MacGuigan, the Canadian secretary of state for external affairs, argued, "Instability in Central America ... is not a product of East-West rivalry. It is a product of poverty, the unfair distribution of wealth, and social injustice. Instability feeds poverty and injustice. East-West rivalries flow in its wake."[23] The Dutch and the Nordic countries shared this view.

Some part of this might be related to size. For example, it is not surprising that a country like Canada, which fears being overwhelmed by the United States, or the Netherlands, which borders on powerful Germany and is not far from France and Britain, is more sympathetic to a perspective that sees differences in power as no less important than differences in ideology. But size alone cannot explain the difference in ideological perspective.

We can see this even in Egeland's own analysis. In explaining the "strong moral impact" on Norwegian policy, he stressed four factors: (1) no legacy of imperialism and intervention, (2) a good domestic human rights record, (3) a high level of foreign aid and support for changes in the world economy to favor Third World countries, and (4) consistent support for decolonization and national liberation movements.[24] The first of these factors is perhaps related to size—although Belgium, Portugal, and the Netherlands had significant colonial holdings, German, Austrian, Russian, and American colonial holdings were small, and the Netherlands rapidly overcame its imperial legacy. The other three factors, however, have little or nothing to do with size.

Size explains almost nothing about internal human rights records, as a comparison of pairs of similarly sized countries such as the United States and the Soviet Union, China and

India, Japan and Indonesia, and Costa Rica and Guatemala vividly illustrate. Nor does size have much to do with levels of foreign aid. The United States chooses to be niggardly, whereas Norway and the Netherlands (and Japan) choose to be relatively generous.[25] And the United States had a better record on supporting decolonization than small states such as Portugal and Spain or second-tier powers such as Britain and France.

Much the same can be said of the role of consensus in Norwegian international human rights and foreign policy, another factor Egeland emphasized. Foreign policy consensus is hardly characteristic of small states, as the varying policies of dozens of Third World countries indicate. In the Nordic countries, foreign policy consensus is a function of both a parliamentary system that combines the lack of a sharp division between executive and legislative branches with a strong reliance on a professional foreign and civil service (in contrast to the extensive use of political appointees in the US bureaucracy) and a political tradition that ensures direct representation and special consideration for all major social groups.

Size does not explain why Norway and the Netherlands in the 1970s embarked on unusually active international human rights policies but Austria, Belgium, and Greece did not. Likewise, size cannot explain either the active (if inconsistent) international human rights policy of the United States or the lack of an active international human rights policy by China.

How a country defines its interests certainly is constrained, and often shaped, by its power and its position in the international system. But power and position do not come even close to determining interests. Most impediments to strong international human rights policies lie in the relatively free decisions of states to give greater weight to other foreign policy objectives. Most of the factors that contribute to aggressive efforts to pursue international human rights in a country's foreign policy have much more to do with its national political culture and contingent political facts (for example, the election of Jimmy Carter) than with its international political position. For example, Dutch membership in Amnesty International, on a per-capita basis, exceeds American membership in the National Rifle Association, until recently one of the most powerful interest groups in the United States.

National political culture is especially important in explaining the striking differences between the attitudes of the United States and the like-minded countries toward economic and social rights. American foreign aid has been used almost exclusively in the pursuit of civil and political rights objectives. Humanitarian objectives such as nutrition, literacy, and health care have not been perceived in the United States in terms of human rights. Foreign aid and human rights are seen as two fundamentally separate issues that are only tactically linked. The like-minded countries, by contrast, see development assistance as central to their international human rights policies. They also emphasize the intrinsic importance of economic, social, and cultural rights and their interdependence with civil and political rights.

Differences between the United States and the like-minded countries are largely matters of choice. Norway and the Netherlands place a relatively high value on international human rights not because they are small and weak but because of how their citizens understand themselves, their place in the world, and the obligations associated with their identity.

Problem 8.1 US Ratification of Human Rights Treaties

The Problem

The United States is a leading global advocate of human rights and regularly makes use of the body of international human rights law and procedures to criticize other states. But the United States, although a party to the Covenant on Civil and Political Rights, the Convention on Racial Discrimination, and the Torture Convention, has refused to ratify the Covenant on Economic, Social, and Cultural Rights, the Women's Rights Convention, the Convention on the Rights of the Child (the only state in the world that has failed to ratify), and the Convention on the Rights of Persons with Disabilities (which it played an outsized role in drafting). It also does not permit individual communications under the treaties to which it is a party. And the United States is not a party to the regional American Convention.

This is widely seen by other countries as hypocrisy (which is mirrored in its embrace of prosecution in the ICC and the tribunals for the former Yugoslavia and Rwanda but its refusal to submit itself to the ICC's jurisdiction). This hypocrisy not only hinders American international action but threatens to undermine what we have argued is the most important contribution of the global human rights regime, namely, an agreed-upon set of comprehensive global standards.

A Solution

The obvious solution is for the United States to ratify these treaties. But this is almost certainly not going to happen in the foreseeable future. In other words, there is no practical solution. The best we can do is understand what is behind this problem and why it persists.

Opposition to human rights treaties in the US Senate has historically been concentrated among (although by no means exclusive to) Republicans, going back to the Bricker Amendment controversy (see Section 8.1 above). As the Republican Party has moved further and further toward unilateralism and an exclusionary nationalism, its objections have ostensibly been based on fear of infringements on American sovereignty and challenges to the supremacy of American courts. But there is simply no rational legal basis to such fears—although they have considerable emotional appeal to a growing and increasingly fearful and willfully ignorant segment of the American electorate.

There is a limited basis for concerns that some treaties may be inconsistent with the US Constitution. Such concerns, however, can easily be handled by attaching reservations, understandings, or declarations to American ratification, which would effectively exempt the United States from those provisions. In fact, this is precisely what the United States did with perhaps the most blatant conflict between international human rights law and American constitutional law, namely, the provision of Article 4 of the Racial Discrimination Convention that requires legally prohibiting "all dissemination of ideas based on racial superiority or hatred." This clear conflict with deeply embedded American constitutional law that protects "fighting words" and "hate speech" was easily handled by a declaration that rejected any infringement of free speech that does not incite violence. In ratifying a treaty, one may (within certain broad limits) pick and choose among the obligations a state undertakes, especially when the reservations include only a few particular provisions of a treaty.

It has also been claimed that some international human rights treaties threaten "American values." This has been at the heart of opposition to the CRC. In fact, however, such arguments have little or nothing to do with the substance of the CRC. They simply give vent to a highly politicized vision of "family values," a minority view that is as inconsistent with existing American law as it is with the CRC. (It is absurd to claim that Americans have a different conception of families and the place of children than every other country in the world, all of which have ratified the treaty.) And if there are any real problems, reservations, again, provide a ready and effective remedy.

American values, law, and sovereignty have been in no way harmed or infringed upon by the human rights treaties that the United States has ratified. Nor would they be harmed by ratification of the other treaties. What we see here is a particularly striking example of American exceptionalism and exemptionalism. Any legitimate worries about ratification largely involve a desire to continue to sweep under the rug parts of American law and practice that fall short of international human rights norms.

This situation can only be expected to continue. No president has been willing to even try to expend the amount of political capital that would be needed to overcome Senate opposition. (One-third of the Senate can block ratification.) Only a small segment of the American population attaches positive significance to US ratification of international human rights treaties. And almost no one would vote on that basis. But an important part of the Republican electorate can be mobilized against ratification—and the charge of sacrificing American sovereignty has considerable resonance in the political center. The electoral calculus is thus clear: nothing is to be gained from supporting ratification but something may be lost. Therefore, international human rights treaties continue to sit on the shelf—even though the Conventions on Discrimination Against Women and the Rights of the Child actually have considerable substantive attraction to most Americans, probably even including most who oppose ratification.

Further Problems

International scrutiny is a mechanism to help states hold themselves to the highest standards. It also provides citizens of participating states with supplemental mechanisms that in some cases can help them to achieve effective enjoyment of their rights. This is particularly true in countries with relatively good human rights records and active civil societies—that is, countries such as the United States. The United States is thus depriving its citizens of a limited but not insignificant mechanism to guarantee their rights.

Americans are also becoming increasingly isolated from the rest of the Western world, where the language of human rights has largely been incorporated into national law and politics. This too is likely to lead to slower human rights improvements, both absolutely and relatively, in the United States.

If this continues, America's leadership role may be challenged. People across the globe have for two centuries looked to the United States as a human rights inspiration. The refusal of the United States to participate fully in the body of international human rights law and practice may ultimately lead to that leadership passing to Europe—or, even more tragically, the global movement for human rights having no politically important leader.

The absence of the neutral point of reference provided by international human rights law may also contribute to the ongoing erosion of respect for civil liberties and political rights in the United States. Consider the annual ratings of Freedom House, an American NGO that in the 1980s was widely, and not entirely unfairly, criticized for a pro-American bias and a denigration of economic and social rights. Consistent with its mission, however, Freedom House continues to consider only civil and political rights in its Global Freedom scores. And it certainly has no axe to grind with the United States. In other words, it is perhaps the most sympathetic to the United States of all serious evaluators of comparative human rights performance.

In 2021, 2022, 2023, and 2024, the United States received a Global Freedom score of 83 (out of 100), down from 89 in 2017 (when Freedom House adopted its current methodology) and 86 in 2018–2020 (it ticked up a point to 84 in 2025). Freedom House notes American shortcomings in presidential elections, the impartiality of electoral laws, minority political rights and electoral opportunities, control of elected officials over policy, safeguards against official corruption, government transparency, media freedom, academic freedom, trade union freedoms, judicial independence, due process in criminal and civil proceedings, protection from violence, personal social freedoms, and equality of opportunity. And the United States received a score of only 2 (out of 4) on the question, "Do laws, policies, and practices guarantee equal treatment of various segments of the population?"

Where does this score place the United States? With Croatia, Panama, Romania, and South Korea. In 2025, more than twenty European countries had higher scores. And outside of Europe, another twenty-four countries—among them Argentina (85), Australia (95), the Bahamas (90), Barbados (94), Belize (88), Cabo Verde (92), Canada (97), Chile (95), Costa Rica (91), Japan (96), Mauritius (86), New Zealand (99), Taiwan (94), and Uruguay (96)—outscored the United States. Just slightly below the United States were Romania (82) and Poland (82).[26] And, to repeat, Freedom House addresses only civil and political rights, where the US record is better than on economic and social rights.

We expect that in the 2026 report, the US Freedom in the World Score will drop further as a result of the slew of assaults on human rights under the second Trump administration. Most Americans are blithely unaware of the considerable shortcomings of American domestic human rights practice when measured by neutral international standards. The failure to take objective international standards seriously, as reflected in American refusal to ratify international human rights treaties, helps to support this unfortunate ignorance—and underscores the unjustified arrogance of American exceptionalism and exemptionalism, which the Trump administration seems committed to celebrating and exacerbating.

Discussion Questions

1. Was the domination of post-World War II US foreign policy by anticommunism a poor policy decision? Should anticommunism have been assigned a less overriding priority? Or was the problem that anticommunism was pursued with unreasonable zeal? Is there an important lesson here about an ideological (or moralistic) foreign policy that leads to such excess? If so, should we reconsider the arguments of the realists?
2. Should the United States be able to define for itself which internationally recognized human rights it wishes to recognize or pursue? If so, why? How can we sustain and enforce an international human rights policy if states can pick and choose the parts they want to comply with? Conversely, though, why should the United States (or any other sovereign state) have to comply with international human rights norms, no matter how widely accepted they are?
3. Grant the description above of American foreign policy under Trump as, at best, disinterested in human rights. What exactly is wrong with that? Why shouldn't the United States choose, through its duly elected president, that it no longer has a central and abiding foreign policy interest in international human rights? Why isn't "America First" a perfectly sound and sensible basis *for American foreign policy*?
4. The United States has had a relatively active and aggressive bilateral international human rights policy but has been reluctant to participate in most multilateral international human rights regimes. Isn't this a double standard? Can it be justified? Why should other countries take US international human rights policy seriously when the United States is so reluctant to open itself to international human rights scrutiny?
5. In reviewing the evidence of US policy toward Central America, South Africa, and Israel (and Myanmar in Chapter 7)—and any other cases that you are familiar with—what strikes you more: the continuities or the changes between different US administrations? Were the differences largely symbolic? If they were, how serious a criticism is that? How large a role does symbolic rhetoric play in foreign policy? In international human rights policy?
6. Looking at these cases, which is more striking to you: the weight given to human rights or the weight given to other concerns? Is it fair to say that the United States

strongly supports international human rights only when the costs to the United States of doing so are low? Assume that the answer to that question is yes. Is that inappropriate? *Should* human rights have a lower priority than security and economic interests? Is there a general answer to that question? Should it be a matter of case-by-case balancing? If so, in which of these cases do you think the United States has gotten the balance right? Where has it gotten it wrong?

7. The same question might be asked about the differences between the international human rights policies of the United States and the policies of the like-minded countries. When it comes to making difficult choices and sacrificing their own interests, just how different are Canada, Norway, and the Netherlands from the United States? Compare, for example, the Netherlands' policy toward Indonesia and its policy toward Suriname. Is the difference a matter of kind or merely a matter of degree?
8. Consider the emphasis of the like-minded countries on economic, social, and cultural rights. Is their approach better than or just different from that of the United States? Why? Does your answer change if you look at the issue from the perspectives of foreign policy, foreign aid policy, and international human rights policy?
9. Why do you think that international human rights policies were a matter of intense partisan controversy in the United States in the 1970s and 1980s but not in Norway and the Netherlands? What explains the fact that, since the early 1990s, a nonpartisan consensus on the importance of international human rights policies emerged in the United States as well? And why has it eroded over the past decade?

Suggested Readings

Claire Apodaca, *Human Rights and U.S. Foreign Policy* (Routledge, 2019) is among the most recent assessments of American human rights policies since the Nixon administration. Apodoca argues that each presidential administration has prevaricated about the "meanings" of human rights, as shaped by ideology, bureaucratic politics, lobbying and competition among American stakeholders.

Harold Hongju Koh, "A United States Human Rights Policy for the 21st Century," *Saint Louis University Law Journal* 46 (Spring 2002): 293–344, is a powerful programmatic statement by Clinton's former assistant secretary of state. In our view, there is no single piece that does a better job of provoking serious thought about the appropriate contours of American international human rights policy.

Three books from the early 2000s are somewhat dated but still of great use. Debra Liang-Fenton, ed., *Implementing U.S. Human Rights Policy* (U.S. Institute of Peace Press, 2004) provides more than a dozen superb case studies of U.S. human rights policy toward a wide range of prominent countries, focusing on the immediate post-Cold War era. Kathryn Sikkink, *Mixed Signals: U.S. Human Rights Policy and Latin America* (Cornell University Press, 2005), provides a comprehensive overview of U.S. human rights policy toward Latin America, covering the entire post-World War II era. Michael Ignatieff, ed., *American Exceptionalism and Human Rights* (Princeton University Press, 2005), is an excellent collection of essays covering a wide range of both domestic and international human rights issues. Harold

Koh, "America's Jekyll-and-Hyde Exceptionalism," 111–144, and John Ruggie, "American, Exceptionalism, Exemptionalism, and Global Governance," 304–338, are particularly good and especially relevant to the issues covered in this chapter. For a more recent discussion of exceptionalism, see David P. Forsythe and Patrice C. McMahon, *American Exceptionalism Reconsidered: U.S. Foreign Policy, Human Rights, and World Order* (Routledge, 2017).

Stewart Patrick's *Sovereignty Wars* (Brookings Institution, 2018) takes a broader view of recent debates about American sovereignty with several chapters that address international law and human rights in particular. For more critical assessments, see Julie Mertus, *Bait and Switch? Human Rights and U.S. Foreign Policy*, 2nd ed. (Routledge, 2008) and Ilia Xypolia, *Human Rights, Imperialism, and Corruption in US Foreign Policy* (Palgrave Macmillan, 2022).

There are also two excellent recent books on the Reagan era: Rasmus Sinding Søndergaard, *Reagan, Congress, and Human Rights: Contesting Morality in US Foreign Policy* (Cambridge University Press, 2020) and William Michael Schmidli, *Freedom on the Offensive: Human Rights, Democracy Promotion, and US Interventionism in the Late Cold War* (Cornell University Press, 2022).

For good illustrations of competing views on human rights and American foreign policy in the late 1970s and early 1980s, see (on the liberal side) Arthur Schlesinger Jr., "Human Rights and the American Tradition," *Foreign Affairs* 57, no. 3 (1979): 503–526 and Stanley Hoffmann, "Reaching for the Most Difficult: Human Rights as a Foreign Policy Goal," *Daedalus* 112 (Fall 1983): 19–49; and (on the conservative side) Jeane J. Kirkpatrick, "Dictatorships and Double Standards," *Commentary* 68 (November 1979): 34–45 and Henry A. Kissinger, "Continuity and Change in American Foreign Policy," in Abdul Aziz Said, ed, *Human Rights and World Order* (Praeger, 1978), 154–167. See also Joe Renouard, *Human Rights in American Foreign Policy: From the 1960s to the Soviet Collapse* (University of Pennsylvania Press, 2016).

On human rights in the foreign policies of other countries, Alison Brysk, *Global Good Samaritans: Human Rights as Foreign Policy* (Oxford University Press, 2009), is the place to begin. (Brysk looks at Sweden, Canada, Costa Rica, Japan, and South Africa.) Older but still useful is David P. Forsythe, ed., *Human Rights and Comparative Foreign Policy* (United Nations University Press, 2000).

Notes

1 www.ned.org/about/.
2 www.reuters.com/article/us-usa-diplomacy-tillerson-idUSKBN17Z2BJ.
3 https://2017–2021.state.gov/commission-on-unalienable-rights/.
4 www.federalregister.gov/documents/2019/05/30/2019-11300/department-of-state-commission-on-unalienable-rights.
5 www.washingtonpost.com/opinions/2019/07/12/do-these-human-rights-spark-joy/.
6 Austin Ramzy and Chris Buckley, "The Xinjiang Papers," *New York Times* (November 16, 2019), at www.nytimes.com/interactive/2019/11/16/world/asia/china-xinjiang-documents.html.
7 www.congress.gov/bill/116th-congress/senate-bill/178.
8 https://www.whitehouse.gov/wp-content/uploads/2022/10/Biden-Harris-Administrations-National-Security-Strategy-10.2022.pdf.

9 https://www.whitehouse.gov/briefing-room/statements-releases/2021/10/14/statement-by-president-joseph-r-biden-jr-on-the-united-states-election-to-the-human-rights-council-hrc/.
10 https://www.smh.com.au/world/north-america/congo-in-china-out-biden-s-democracy-summit-guest-list-raises-eyebrows-20211209-p59g7f.html.
11 https://thehill.com/opinion/3924376-double-standard-will-biden-truly-champion-human-rights/.
12 https://nytimes.com/2025/06/18/opinion/trump-miller-immigration-ice.html.
13 https://www.amnesty.org/en/latest/news/2025/04/president-trumps-first-100-days-attacks-on-human-rights/.
14 Some elements of PEPFAR funding—mostly for life-saving HIV/AIDS treatments—were spared from a rescission package Congress approved in July 2025. However, as many observers have noted, the public health infrastructure necessary for delivering HIV treatments had been largely eliminated by the DOGE cuts.
15 https://www.justsecurity.org/114200/state-department-reorganization-human-rights/.
16 https://www.npr.org/2025/04/18/nx-s1–5357511/state-department-human-rights-report-cuts.
17 Bruce Jentleson, *American Foreign Policy: The Dynamics of Choice in the 21st Century*, 5th ed. (W.W. Norton, 2013), 146–149.
18 Jeane J. Kirkpatrick, "Dictatorships and Double Standards," *Commentary Magazine* 68, no. 5 (November 1979): 34–45. Available online at www.commentarymagazine.com/articles/dictatorships-double-standards/.
19 Cynthia Brown, ed., *With Friends like These: The Americas Watch Report on Human Rights and U.S. Policy in Latin America* (Pantheon Books, 1985), 20. Compare with the Watch Committees and Lawyers' Committee for Human Rights, *The Reagan Administration's Record on Human Rights in 1986* (Watch Committees and Lawyers' Committee for Human Rights, 1987), 49, 92–99; and *The Reagan Administration's Record on Human Rights in 1987* (Watch Committees and Lawyers' Committee for Human Rights, 1988), 106. On the Reagan administration's systematic misrepresentation of the facts, see Americas Watch, *Managing the Facts: How the Administration Deals with Reports of Human Rights Abuses in El Salvador* (Americas Watch, 1985).
20 Quoted in Charles Cooper and Joan Verloren van Themaat, "Dutch Aid Determinants, 1973–85: Continuity and Change," in *Western Middle Powers and Global Poverty: The Determinants of the Aid Policies of Canada, Denmark, the Netherlands, Norway, and Sweden*, edited by Olav Stokke (Almquist and Wiksell International, 1989), 119.
21 Jan Egeland, *Impotent Superpower—Potent Small State: Potentialities and Limitations of Human Rights Objectives in the Foreign Policies of the United States and Norway* (Norwegian University Press, 1988), 3, 5.
22 Egeland, *Impotent Superpower*, 15.
23 *Statements and Speeches* 82/12 (Bureau of Information, Department of External Affairs), quoted in Rhoda E. Howard and Jack Donnelly, *Confronting Revolution in Nicaragua: U.S. and Canadian Responses* (Carnegie Council on Ethics and International Affairs, 1990).
24 Egeland, *Impotent Superpower*, 23.
25 Norway and the Netherlands are usually the world's two leading aid providers on a per capita basis; for most of the past thirty years, they contributed eight to ten times more per capita than the United States.
26 https://freedomhouse.org/explore-the-map?type=fiw&year=2024; Freedom House 2025 Countries and Territories Report, https://freedomhouse.org/country/scores.

9 Transnational Human Rights Advocacy

Having explored how states engage human rights in their relations with other states—globally, regionally, and in their foreign policies—we turn now to transnational actors, understood as "private" actors (that is, not states or multilateral organizations) that operate across state borders. We will be concerned primarily with **nongovernmental organizations** (NGOs), that is, private, *noncommercial* groups with an issue-specific mandate. (Chapter 10 will look at firms and business investment decisions.) More precisely, here we will focus on transnational or international nongovernmental organizations (INGOs)—NGOs that operate internationally. The Problem for this chapter will focus on the promises and pitfalls of mass-appeal human rights advocacy.

The term "NGO" is a catchall that describes a variety of groups and organizations that conduct many different types of activities. They are generally thought of as a species of civil society organization, understood as a group organized for a civic (noncommercial) purpose, which may or may not include a charitable element. In the United States, such groups are typically called "nonprofit" or "charitable" organizations. Internationally, the focus tends to be on the NG in NGO—that is, that they are independent of (and sometimes critical of) the state.

But not always. In particular, development-oriented NGOs, especially in poorer countries, may be engaged in service provision, outreach and education, and implementation of development programs, giving their activities a quasi-governmental character. More generally, NGOs that engage in policy advocacy, monitoring and evaluation, or research in support of programs regularly collaborate with, and sometimes actively support, governments and intergovernmental organizations. Nonetheless, NGOs thus understood should be distinguished from GONGOs: *government-organized* "nongovernmental" organizations.

In the world of human rights, the principal focus of NGO activity is the state itself. Most human rights NGOs conduct fact-finding about human rights violations, assist victims of violations, and advocate to change state policies and practices. This does not, though, always pit human rights NGOs against the state, especially in countries open to

DOI: 10.4324/9781003373520-11

improving their human rights practices. In fact, NGOs often play a vital role in ensuring the democratic accountability of governments. Many governments thus have come to accept, and sometimes even appreciate, the work of national and international human rights NGOs in monitoring and improving compliance with national and international human rights law. (See also Section 5.1 on the role of NGOs in the Universal Periodic Review process.)

About 300 INGOs define themselves as human rights organizations. These will be our principal focus here. There are also, however, thousands of INGOs that define themselves in other terms but engage centrally in human rights programming and advocacy. For example, most of the large development-assistance and disaster-relief organizations today explicitly use the language of human rights to describe key aspects of their missions. In addition, tens of thousands of national NGOs deal centrally with human rights.

There are two principal types of self-identified human rights INGOs. Some, like Amnesty International, Human Rights Watch, Human Rights First (formerly the Lawyers Committee for Human Rights), and the International Federation for Human Rights, address human rights generally (although, as a practical matter, they tend to have specific areas of special concern). Others focus explicitly on a subset of internationally recognized human rights or even a single right. Prominent examples include Minority Rights Group, Anti-Slavery International (the world's oldest human rights NGO, founded in 1839), and Article 19 (which addresses freedom of expression, taking its name from that provision in the Universal Declaration).

Rather than discuss transnational human rights advocacy generally, though, the first half of this chapter presents two brief case studies of Amnesty International and Human Rights Watch. This focus on two particularly influential organizations arises in part from the great diversity of transnational human rights NGOs, which makes it difficult to talk about transnational action in general and almost impossible to provide anything even close to a comprehensive survey. The sections following the case studies, however, discuss the expansion of NGO activities on human rights in general, as a reflection of growing civil society involvement in and engagement with a system that remains largely driven by states.

1 Amnesty International

Amnesty International (AI) is one of the most important actors in the global human rights regime—and in many ways the emblematic transnational human rights NGO. To many people, especially in the West, human rights advocacy means the kinds of things that Amnesty does: research on human rights abuses and violations and direct-appeal campaigns through letters, petitions, and protests directed at governments, corporations, and other leaders and decision-makers to stop abuses and act to remediate human rights violations. It is important to recognize, though, that Amnesty, like all NGOs, is guided by a mission that includes a limited range of actionable goals. It does not address anything close to all human rights, despite considerable efforts in recent years to expand its mandate.

AI was founded in 1961 by British lawyer Peter Benenson to draw attention to the plight of prisoners of conscience—individuals detained because of their political, religious, or other beliefs—across the globe. Individual prisoners were identified and verified by the organization, which both publicized their plight centrally and organized local chapters to "adopt" them—typically in clusters of three, one each from the capitalist, socialist, and non-aligned worlds—and advocate on their behalf, usually through letter-writing campaigns addressed to officials of the government holding the prisoner.

In the 1970s, under the leadership of Nigel Rodley, who led its Legal and International Organisations office, Amnesty refined its strategy of aggressive but nonpartisan public advocacy with effective behind-the-scenes lobbying, both nationally and internationally. In 1973, it began its campaign of Urgent Action appeals. Torture (and later abolition of the death penalty) became a special focus. AI played a major role in securing the adoption of the 1975 Declaration on the Protection of All Persons from Being Subjected to Torture and Other Cruel, Inhuman, or Degrading Treatment or Punishment, a decisive step on the way to the 1984 Convention Against Torture. In 1977, it was awarded the Nobel Peace Prize (following the award in 1974 to Seán MacBride, the chair of AI's International Executive Committee from 1961 to 1975, for his lifetime of work on behalf of human rights), and, in 1978, the organization was awarded the United Nations Prize in the Field of Human Rights. By 1979, Amnesty International had a global membership of 200,000—up from 15,000 a decade earlier.

In the 1980s, Amnesty continued to grow and to penetrate the public consciousness. Emblematic were the series of high-profile fund-raising events that took their title from the 1979 Secret Policeman's Ball. Begun by Monty Python member John Cleese and involving major stars such as Sting and Eric Clapton, the events generated publicity for human rights advocacy among individuals who previously might not have had much interest in the topic. (Bono, the current king of celebrity campaigning for social justice, was in the audience at an early show, which he has identified as a major formative influence.)

The 1986 Conspiracy of Hope tour included five shows in the United States. It was hugely successful in raising awareness of AI among young Americans and increasing their membership. The 1988 Human Rights Now! International tour featured famous artists such as Bruce Springsteen and the E Street Band, Peter Gabriel, Sting, and others. The tour was incredibly complicated to organize, as it traveled to a number of countries, such as Hungary, Costa Rica, Zimbabwe, and India, countries that rarely saw such large-scale shows.

With the end of the Cold War, Amnesty continued to grow, evolving into an organization with a broader focus. Today, in addition to the older work on prisoners of conscience, torture, and the death penalty, the organization works on the rights of disadvantaged groups, especially women, children, minorities, indigenous peoples, and refugees, and on eradicating poverty. AI has also devoted considerable attention and resources to expanding membership outside the Western world, symbolized by the fact that, between 1992 and 2021, its secretary-general, the chief executive officer of the organization, has been from the Global South: Pierre Sané of Senegal (1992–2001); Irene Khan of Bangladesh (2001–2010); Salil Shetty of India (2010–2018); and Kumi Naidoo of South Africa (2018–2019). Naidoo stepped down for health reasons and Julie Verhaar took over as acting secretary-general. Agnès Callamard of France became AI's secretary-general in 2021. (She continues to hold the post in 2025.)

In addition, AI has shifted from a large London base to opening offices in Africa, the Asia-Pacific, Central and Eastern Europe, Latin America, and the Middle East. The purpose is to allow AI to respond more quickly to human rights abuses and important events around the globe. AI has even developed a mobile app that works like a panic button for activists who are at risk of being arrested or detained. These examples show that Amnesty International is attempting to aid activists and dissenters across the globe in relevant and meaningful ways.

Today AI comprises around 2 million members and 5 million supporting activists worldwide, organized into more than fifty country "sections" and a number of "structures" (which are essentially aspiring sections). The highest authority of the organization is the International Council, which meets every two years. Its equivalent of a board of directors is the International Executive Committee, which meets twice a year. An International Secretariat of more than 500 professionals carries out work in several areas, focused on research, campaigning, communications, and international law and organization. In 2023, AI spent approximately €383 million on its various activities.

In 2024, Amnesty was in the midst of campaigns such as Protect the Protest (a global campaign to highlight crackdowns on nonviolent actions); In the Shadow of Industries in Congo (focusing on the detrimental health effects of extractive industries); and Human Rights Defenders (advocating for human rights activists around the world). Its annual global letter-writing campaign, Write for Rights, calls upon individual supporters to appeal to state leaders and elected officials to support and demand justice for individuals defending human rights and facing abuses and detention.

In 2022–2023, AI issued appeals for urgent action on behalf of individuals in over fifty countries in every region of the world. These urgent appeals often lead to results: in 2021, for example, Zahra Sedighi-Hamadani was arrested by Iranian authorities for speaking out in support of LGBTQ+ rights on social media and in a BBC documentary. She was sentenced to death in September 2022. AI issued an urgent appeal and an Iranian court overturned her sentence. She was released on bail in 2023 (the case was sent back to a lower court for retrial).

2 Human Rights Watch

Human Rights Watch (HRW) is more than a decade younger than Amnesty International and is not a mass-membership organization. Based in New York, its roots are in Helsinki Watch, a group formed in the United States in 1978 to monitor compliance with the 1975 Helsinki Final Act (see Chapter 8, Section 1), which included human rights commitments by the countries of Europe on both sides of the Iron Curtain (plus the United States and Canada). Helsinki Watch pioneered the "naming and shaming" tactic of publicly shaming abusive governments' practices through reports, media coverage, and direct exchange with policymakers, which contributed to the dramatic democratic transformations in the late 1980s. The Helsinki model was replicated in other regional watch groups—Americas Watch, founded in 1981; Asia Watch, 1985; Africa Watch, 1988; and Middle East Watch, 1989—which were united under the umbrella of HRW in 1988.

HRW monitors human rights conditions in more than ninety countries and publishes reports on violations of international human rights norms set out by the Universal Declaration and human rights treaties. HRW works both by talking with people who were abused or have witnessed abuses and by reaching out to journalists, human rights advocates, country experts, and government officials. They publish their findings in approximately hundred official reports and hundreds of news releases each year, as well as the widely read annual *World Report*. HRW also engages in public campaigning and political lobbying.

HRW has always had a broader focus than Amnesty International—although initially with much greater attention to civil and political rights than economic, social, and cultural rights. This began to change in the 2000s. HRW reports that it now places a much greater emphasis on economic and social rights than do other human rights organizations. However, HRW will address human rights abuses only where there is credible, reliable evidence of violations and where a perpetrator of violations can be clearly identified. (These are requirements of successful naming and shaming.) Nearly all of its work involving economic and social rights thus addresses officially sanctioned or condoned discrimination (especially discrimination and violence against women) or direct violations of economic and social rights by the state (for example, a forced eviction policy).

In the 1990s, HRW also significantly expanded its scope to include violations of the laws of war and individual criminal responsibility for war crimes and genocide. (In 1997, it shared the Nobel Peace Prize as a founding member of the Campaign to Ban Landmines.) Over the past two decades, it has also focused considerable attention on human rights violations associated with antiterrorism policies and practices, and it has begun to supplement its traditional on-the-ground fact-finding with statistical research, legislative analysis and monitoring, satellite photography, bomb-data analysis, and other new methods and technologies.

In 2024, HRW had revenue of $102 million, $83 million of which was raised from contributions and special events. (In order to maintain an unbiased approach to research and advocacy, HRW does not accept money from governments, either directly or indirectly.) In financial terms, its ten principal programs focus on Africa ($8.5 million), Asia ($10.9 million), the Americas ($3.8 million), Europe and Central Asia ($8.1 million), the Middle East and North Africa ($8.3 million), the United States ($5.5 million), Women's Rights ($5.4 million), Children's Rights ($4.9 million), LGBTQ+ Rights ($2.6 million), and Disability Rights ($3.9 million). Expenditures on other programs totaled $21.6 million.[1]

HRW's research and advocacy reporting output is formidable. In 2023, HRW issued forty separate reports in addition to its annual report, covering a range of topics as diverse as the Ugandan government's crackdown against environmental defenders, the abuse of women prisoners in Japan, government-mandated internet blackouts in India, mass killings of Ethiopian migrants at the Saudi/Yemeni border, inadequate housing and social support for asylum seekers in the United Kingdom, the lack of electricity in Lebanon, the post-coup crackdown on lawyers in Myanmar, and several reports on violence and targeting of LGBTQ+ people and their allies.[2]

As this list suggests, HRW understands human rights rather broadly, including not only the established body of international human rights law but also additional rights (particularly protection against discrimination on the basis of sexual orientation or gender identity), the linkages between human rights and environmental crises and climate change, and violations of the laws of war and other harm to civilians in armed conflicts. HRW is effective because governments and human rights activists have confidence in the high quality of the sourcing and fact-checking that goes into its research. These foundations are critically necessary for putting pressure on governments to change their behaviors and establishing the legal and moral groundwork for meaningful change.

3 Nonpartisan Action

HRW is unusually independent and aggressive in its actions. It thus provides a focus for a broader discussion of bias and legitimacy in the actions of human rights NGOs.

Like other transnational human rights NGOs, the work of HRW depends on its ability to obtain reliable information about violations. Its reporting and advocacy thus are shaped not simply by the severity of violations in a country but by its ability to work in that country (or to obtain reliable information from individuals with recent firsthand local knowledge). In addition, as an advocacy organization, it has a special interest in addressing situations where its work may bring concrete results—not to the exclusion of countries where short-term changes are unlikely or even inconceivable but with special attention to countries that are open or vulnerable to the pressures of publicity. And HRW, like all human rights NGOs, has issues of special organizational concern.

As a result of these political realities, HRW, like all other advocacy groups, has been accused of bias. But rather than factual errors in its reports—which, of course, do occur occasionally (but very rarely)—such complaints typically involve claims, usually by the targeted governments and their partisans, that other countries with equally bad or worse records are not comparably targeted or that the violations identified are somehow justified in the case in question.

During the Cold War, such complaints were the staple of Communist Party state dictatorships and military dictatorships of both the Right and the Left. Today, when leaders such as Teodoro Obiang Nguema Mbasogo in Equatorial Guinea, Alexander Lukashenko in Belarus, or Vladimir Putin in Russia make such complaints, they are largely ignored. But particularly in the United States, HRW has in recent years been a special target of defenders of Israel's antiterrorism policies and its policies in the Occupied Palestinian Territories (see Chapter 8, Section 4.3). The ensuing debates provide a useful lens on the nature of nonpartisan human rights advocacy.

Nonpartisan does not mean nonpolitical. In fact, human rights advocacy is and must be intensely political. It is principally about how a state treats its own nationals and others over whom it exercises jurisdiction. Demands to stop human rights violations are demands for changes in legal and political practices. When violations are severe and systematic, human rights advocacy in effect demands that a regime either fundamentally transform its character or put itself out of business.

The vital question, then, is whether (political) advocacy for human rights is carried out in a nonpartisan fashion; that is, in a way that is not based on or intended to promote any particular party, person, or cause (other than human rights). Human rights advocates might properly be called partisans for human rights. They claim, though, to pursue their activities in an otherwise nonpartisan fashion. And nonpartisan action is central to the legitimacy and the power of NGO advocates in particular, who have few resources on their side other than their single-minded commitment to human rights.

Let us grant, for the sake of argument, the accuracy of the principal complaints of the "friends of Israel" who condemn HRW: that many other regimes with human rights records comparable to and even much worse than Israel's—including most of Israel's enemies—have not been comparably criticized.[3] But although reasonable people may disagree about the reliability of particular sources, virtually every particular claim is sourced. And, despite extensive efforts to debunk HRW's reporting, only rare and isolated errors have ever been identified, most of which have been connected with difficulties imposed by the Israeli government and its military in gathering and verifying information.

A few governments engage in human rights violations that they do not seek to justify in any serious fashion. Most, though, claim a higher purpose that justifies unfortunate sacrifices being imposed on individuals and groups in their society. (Anti-terrorism is a popular (and easily abused) excuse.) But whether such arguments are persuasive is, ironically, a political question—and usually an inescapably partisan one. And most human rights advocates refuse to engage in such partisan political debates. Rather, they decry the violations, independent of any and all alleged justifications.

Human rights advocates do not—and should not—look at all sides of a partisan political conflict. Although "balanced" or "evenhanded" approaches may be appropriate for others, the job of human rights NGOs is to focus narrowly (perhaps even single-mindedly) on human rights. And that focus is essential to nonpartisan action. If there is a legitimate justification for a breach or violation, the government in question can present that to its people, its friends and allies, and the international community. The work of an organization like HRW, however, is documenting violations.

There is a danger, certainly, of selecting (otherwise legitimate) targets of criticism based on partisan criteria. In the case of HRW, however, there is no evidence of such partisanship. (Its 2025 World Report looks at human rights in almost a hundred countries.[4]) Its reach is truly global, as reflected not only in its annual report but also in the list of recent reports noted above. And its work on Israel falls well within its regional and substantive mandates. Furthermore, its extensive work on human rights in the United States, where it is based, shows an admirable willingness to look at human rights violations at home, not only abroad. (The US section of Amnesty International similarly targets American domestic human rights practices—much to the chagrin of many Americans.)

HRW's work on gay, lesbian, bisexual, and transgender rights actually raises more questions about partisanship (compare Problem 3 in Chapter 3). Such rights are not specifically part of established international human rights law. Therefore, targets may respond, with a certain degree of plausibility, that they are being held to standards that neither they in particular nor the international community in general have endorsed. This, for example, has been the response of Iran (when its president and other officials have not foolishly denied the existence of LGBTQ+ people in Iran).

This brings us back to the central contribution of the Universal Declaration to human rights advocates, namely, providing almost universally agreed-upon standards of international human rights. NGOs that stay within the substantive scope of the Universal Declaration are protected against charges of partisanship (on the grounds of the substance of their concerns). Those who go beyond settled international human rights law do risk (not necessarily (il)legitimate) charges of applying contested standards. But the common charge of attempting to impose its values is ludicrous, given that the only power being exercised is that of publicity. Nonetheless, advocacy on behalf of disputed values is very different from advocacy on behalf of settled principles of international human rights law.

4 NGO Legitimacy

This discussion raises the broad issue of the legitimacy of NGOs and of their advocacy. To put it bluntly, who authorized NGOs to be human rights watchdogs?

The simple answer is international human rights law. Human rights NGOs, in their typical work of reporting and advocacy, merely draw attention to practices that are, at least on their face, inconsistent with uncontroversial principles of international law. Furthermore, they are simply engaging in the collective exercise of their members' right to freedom of expression. Target governments may persecute, and even criminalize, such organizations and activities in their own territories. But that is simply an expression of the problem to which human rights NGOs are drawing attention.

The full picture, though, is not quite that simple. As noted above, human rights advocacy is intensely political. And when external actors criticize governments that have considerable local political legitimacy, the issue of NGO legitimacy may be more than just a smoke screen behind which vicious governments seek to hide.

Here, nonpartisanship becomes essential. International human rights law has considerable international, transnational, and national legitimacy in the contemporary world. So long as human rights INGOs operate in a nonpartisan fashion within the confines and on behalf of established international human rights principles, they partake of that legitimacy—particularly when, as is usually the case, their activity is focused on publicizing evidence of violations.

The legitimacy of external actors is further enhanced when their advocacy parallels or supports that of national actors. In democratic and other relatively open regimes, the existence of genuinely nonpartisan local human rights NGOs making parallel arguments enhances the legitimacy of international actors. And where levels of repression do not allow space for local human rights NGOs (or civil society actors in general), indirect evidence that international actors are supporting local advocates serves a similar role.

Human rights INGOs are important and legitimate actors in the global human rights regime. Article 71 of the UN Charter formally recognizes their contributions to global governance and creates space for them to interact substantively with states in nearly every organ of the organization. While they lack the legal and political authority of states and the international legal authority of multilateral actors, as advocates, however, they have the moral and legal authority of international human rights law behind them. And as long as they engage in truly nonpartisan action within their mandate, they are not merely legitimate but important members of the international community.

That said, it is important to bear in mind that not all human rights NGOs are truly "non-governmental." Many states, particularly in the Global South, have authorized "GONGOs"; government-organized NGOs. These actors are in many respects creatures of the state, receiving vital financial and other forms of support from their governments. Some organizations established through official channels or legislatures (e.g., the National Endowment for Democracy or the Corporation for Public Broadcasting in the United States) operate (almost completely) free of state interference or direction. This is in contrast to Chinese GONGOs in which Communist Party officials are represented in their leadership, and whose agenda and messaging are directed by the state. The largest such GONGO, the China Society for Human Rights Studies, although it publishes reports and studies, organizes workshops, and holds side-events for UN diplomats during sessions of the Human Rights Council and other organs at the United Nations, is little more than a propaganda arm of the Chinese Communist Party.

5 Transnational Actors and Institution Building

In addition to their monitoring work, NGOs can also be vital resources for building state capacity to respect and protect human rights. NGOs often work with and assist governments to draft, enforce, and advocate human rights policy and protections. Transnational human rights advocacy can be an effective tool for normalizing, protecting, and enforcing human rights. INGOs and other actors collect data and monitor progress on human rights protection and enforcement, aiding the states in which they operate and bridging gaps that will lead to rights-protective governance.

Given all of this, a question remains whether INGOs have worked to institutionalize this work. Many INGOs have increasingly found that their greatest impact is through expanding partnerships with local NGOs, civil society, and government. This strategy has helped INGOs most successfully provide technical support, funding, and oversight to further institutionalize human rights and protections. And a new generation of researchers has begun to focus on the interplay between the availability of financial and other resources and their overall effectiveness for achieving human rights outcomes.

One question has been the tensions that may exist between what donors want as opposed to what actually delivers results. INGOs are reliant on the continued support of donors and other sources of funding to carry out their operations. Some organizations may feel pressured to prioritize donors' wishes, which may come at the expense of utilizing the most effective strategies, methods, and plans for developing the capacity of local institutions. To discourage this partiality, some NGOs are adopting alternative means of funding their operations, in particular by expanding partnerships with local NGOs and businesses that understand local needs, can optimize funds, and focus on sustainable and effective work that protects human rights.[5]

This is related to a broader set of questions. In short: what works, and why? What factors lead to successful and sustainable capacity-building and institutionalization for human rights? While INGOs based in the Global North have access to ample resources both in terms of funding and technical expertise, those working in the Global South often lack connections to local institutions, local NGOs and civil society organizations, and community leaders who understand more deeply the communities in which they work. Because this is often the case, INGOs are increasingly collaborating with local NGOs, civil society organizations, and local governments to ensure the sustained success of development projects, programs, and monitoring of human rights policies.

In order to establish global guidelines, in 2005 member-states of the Organization for Economic Cooperation and Development, which includes most of the largest donor states from the Global North, adopted the Paris Declaration on Aid Effectiveness,[6] which was supplemented in 2008 by the Accra Agenda for Action. The Paris Declaration outlined—and the Accra Agenda further clarified and expanded—five core principles:

- Developing countries must have *ownership* over the assistance, meaning they must develop their own strategies for poverty reduction while also making a commitment to improve their institutions and tackle corruption. Countries must have more say over their development processes through wider participation in development policy formulation, stronger leadership on aid coordination, and more use of country systems for aid delivery.
- Donor countries must *align* their aid programs behind these objectives and commit to engaging local actors in the delivery of services. This includes *local capacity-building* to achieve sustainability.
- Donor countries must *harmonize*, coordinate, and simplify procedures and share information to avoid duplication. This means that all partners must ensure *inclusivity* of all relevant stakeholders.
- Developing countries and donors must shift their focus to achieving and measuring actual *outcomes and results*.
- Donors and recipients must be *mutually accountable* for achieving those results.

The 2011 Busan Partnership for Effective Development Cooperation further expanded on these focus areas, expressing a consensus that developing countries at the receiving end of NGO assistance should lead the development process, emphasizing greater cooperation between international and local actors to build capacity within existing institutions and systems to strengthen them.[7]

Despite this long-term focus on local capacity-building, the results continue to be mixed, leading INGOs, scholars, and even official state aid and development organizations to rethink strategies of assisting and contributing to institutional development in the Global South. For example, in 2013, the United States Agency for International Development (USAID) began to implement a new strategy to expand direct partnerships with local NGOs, civil service organizations, and government institutions directly, including shifting over control of projects and programs to local groups. By shifting control of initiatives to local groups early on in the partnership, institutions are strengthened by the people who will constitute them, run them, and benefit from them, increasing their self-reliance, supporting long-term sustainability, and decreasing dependence on aid and assistance from international NGOs or states.[8]

Unfortunately, the Trump administration in 2025 effectively shut down USAID and announced its intention to channel aid primarily, if not exclusively, through governments—an approach that virtually all who have studied it have concluded is at best inefficient and much more subject to corruption and abuse.

Problem 9.1 Mass Appeals in Human Rights Advocacy

The Problem

As we mentioned in the case of Amnesty International, celebrities have been important actors in raising the visibility of many transnational human rights advocacy efforts. Consider, for example, the powerful symbolism of American First Lady Michelle Obama holding up a sign with the Twitter hashtag #BringBackOurGirls in response to the 2014 kidnapping of 276 schoolgirls in Chibok in Borno State, Nigeria, by Boko Haram, an ISIS-affiliated extremist group operating in Western Africa. (About 80–90 of the Chibok girls—who are now women—are still missing.) The ubiquity of social media provides an easily accessible and wide-reaching platform for transnational human rights actors, organizations, and celebrities to share and publicize their current causes and advocacy. Social media websites like Twitter, Facebook, and Instagram have made sharing and publicizing firsthand information and journalism about humanitarian issues and human rights abuses instant and global in their reach.

As some observers have noted, however, there is a cynical—and perhaps darker—side to the involvement of celebrity figures in transnational human rights activism. For example, Lilie Chouliaraki argues that the success of celebrity-based humanitarianism depends on spectacle and that Western audiences in particular must be shocked into pity, as that is the only thing that will elicit an effective response.[9]

According to these critics, campaigns such as these are geared toward conveying a manipulated image of suffering that is tailor-made for audiences that cannot possibly understand the real suffering of faraway strangers nor really alleviate their suffering. They instead give the illusion that a small donation or other easy and convenient acts of acknowledgment and financial support to a worthy cause will be enough to solve the problem—a phenomenon we have come to know as "slacktivism." Celebrity sound bites presuppose that a problem has a quick fix. These simple, digestible appeals are engineered for rapid and far-reaching engagement through visiting a website, liking, sharing, or retweeting a post, or clicking on a link.

The dangers of misdirected effort and even abuse, however, are starkly illustrated by the *Kony 2012* campaign, organized by the nonprofit Invisible Children, Inc. In March 2012, it launched a thirty-minute "documentary" video entitled *Kony 2012* to galvanize public opinion to secure the capture of the Lord's Resistance Army's (LRA) cultish leader, Joseph Kony, who had been indicted in 2005 by the International Criminal Court for war crimes and crimes against humanity.

The video immediately went viral, with more than 100 million views within six days. The US Senate adopted a resolution condemning Kony and supporting the Obama administration's prior decision to send military advisers to support countries and communities that had been affected by the LRA. The video also called for a nationwide "Cover the Night" action, with Invisible Children supplying posters, buttons, T-shirts, bracelets, and stickers to community organizers, who ultimately failed to attract people to the events.

Kony 2012 was endorsed by numerous celebrities known for their humanitarian work, including George Clooney, Bill Gates, Angelina Jolie, and Oprah Winfrey. These positive assessments, however, were matched by critics who pointed out that the film's information was out of date; that its portrayal of victims was exploitative; and that its message, which was delivered by white, American-based activists without any significant immersion in the field, failed to address the complex and nuanced circumstances in the areas where the LRA had been active. Furthermore, the consciousness raising did little more than foster "clicktivism" which enriched Invisible Children but did nothing to actually solve the problem of child soldiering, assist in the rehabilitation or reintegration of child soldiers, or assist the communities victimized by the LRA. After hundreds of millions were briefly captivated and spent millions of dollars in donations and for media kits, nothing happened. Kony remains at large.[10]

The popularity of these campaigns shows the rise of populist forms of diplomatic activity. And even the deeply state-centric United Nations has endorsed and at times used these initiatives, with the establishment in recent years of celebrity goodwill ambassadors, showing that celebrity diplomacy can occupy public space and affect credible diplomatic interventions throughout the international community.

A Solution

Obviously, the Internet and social media are important tools for human rights advocacy groups to engage the public, put pressure on authority, and reach interested supporters. But lately, many organizations are prioritizing public support and awareness over effective strategies of activism.

In *The Mass Appeal of Human Rights*,[11] Joel Pruce argues that the increasingly antipolitical entertainment and consumer-product-driven awareness campaigns of transnational human rights advocacy organizations cheapen authentic and effective human rights activism into a spectacle. These campaigns have effectively shifted the focus of transnational advocacy groups away from intensive data collection, report writing, and fact-based advocacy toward one preoccupied with maintaining public attention. Instead of yielding effective activism, human rights mass campaigns are loud for a brief amount of time but do not lead to concrete, let alone lasting, action.

Pruce argues that human rights advocates should behave more like activists, thinking up creative and disruptive means of spreading information, attracting attention, and demanding political action to address human rights concerns. By breaking the repetitive, predictable, and apolitical formula of email lists, celebrity campaigns, and benefit concerts, and instead engaging in more personal and direct human rights advocacy that is rooted in an ideological and political perspective, Pruce believes the quality of the attention and support for human rights causes will outweigh the quantity of limited and cheap mass engagement.

But a solution that questions the benefit and effectiveness of the participation of the mass public, whose members possess less technical knowledge and political power, raises important questions for the future of human rights advocacy. Should it be reserved for radical activists, scholars, and politicians and not the public? Or is there value in the public's participation, however limited or ineffective? On the one hand, more people are more aware of more human rights violations, abuses, and deficiencies throughout the world. And these organizations and campaigns have made it easier for us to respond with the click of a smartphone. On the other hand, the groups and organizations running these campaigns have created a space for themselves as a kind of middleman: slick and enticing publicity machines, or worse, "merchants of suffering."

Discussion Questions

1. How should we evaluate the impact of traditional human rights advocacy (e.g., what Amnesty International and Human Rights Watch do) versus newer forms of social-media-based advocacy, like consumer campaigns?
2. Is it better that human rights advocacy efforts move from the complex research- and data-driven report to direct actions that are easy to access, understand, and respond to? Or should effective human rights advocacy require more work?
3. Consider the Kony 2012 case mentioned in Problem 9.1. What should be the role of a campaign such as this one (using social media, commodification, and consumerism to raise awareness about a human rights problem)? Is this legitimate advocacy, or does it manipulate people to engage in clicktivism? Is that worse than doing nothing or not knowing about human rights problems in other parts of the world?
4. Does the spectacle of human rights mass appeals and consumer campaigns take away from the serious work of human rights advocacy groups? What are the differences between advocacy and meaningful activism?
5. Is there a better way for NGOs to achieve international legitimacy? Is the issue of legitimacy a truly serious one or primarily a diversion raised by the targets of transnational advocacy?

6. Grant that human rights INGOs have a certain kind of legitimacy. So, though, do states. How should we deal with the resulting conflicts? Are there good general rules? Or does it depend on the particular NGO and the particular state?
7. The distinction between *political* and *partisan* that we have drawn may be clear in theory. Is it so clear in practice? How can action addressed against a government really be nonpartisan? Are there multiple senses of *nonpartisan* operating in such discussions?

Suggested Readings

Peter R. Baehr, *Non-governmental Human Rights Organizations in International Relations* (Palgrave Macmillan, 2009), provides a comprehensive analytical survey. Fiona McGaughey, *Non-Governmental Organisations and the United Nations Human Rights System* (Routledge, 2021) charts the historical development of NGOs' roles at the UN, emphasizing how reliant the organization has become on their work, especially in the area of fact-finding. Charity Butcher and Maia Carter Hallward, *NGOs and Human Rights: Comparing Faith-Based and Secular Approaches* (University of Georgia Press, 2021) engages an extensive dataset of more than 300 NGOs that work with the Human Rights Council, as well as dozens of in-depth interviews, to compare these differently oriented civil society actors' approaches to human rights. The essays collected in Bertrand Ramcharan, Rachel Brett, Ann Marie Clark, and Penny Parker, eds., *The Protection Roles of Human Rights NGOs: Essays in Honour of Adrien-Claude Zoller* (Brill, 2022) explore the protection roles played by NGOs historically as well as examining how they are responding to future challenges such as artificial intelligence and digital threats.

Kenneth Roth, the Executive Director of Human Rights Watch from 1993 to 2022, has recently published what can be described as an advocacy memoir, *Righting Wrongs: Three Decades on the Front Lines Battling Abusive Governments* (Knopf, 2025). It provides an engaging introduction into the details and dilemmas of advocacy work. (The chapter on Israel directly addresses the nonpartisan character of HRW's work and the care with which it is undertaken.)

Stephen Hopgood, *Keepers of the Flame: Understanding Amnesty International* (Cornell University Press, 2006), offers an excellent analysis of AI that, although deeply sympathetic to the work of the organization, is often critical of its practice. It remains the best work on the organization. Ann Marie Clark, *Diplomacy of Conscience: Amnesty International and Changing Human Rights Norms* (Princeton University Press, 2001) is also a valuable study of this iconic organization. Her more recent book, *Demands of Justice: The Creation of a Global Human Rights Practice* (Cambridge University Press, 2022) examines how global appeals led by organizations such as Amnesty International have fundamentally shaped the current global justice environment. Other recent works examining Amnesty's role in the global human rights movement include Miriam Ganzfried's *Amnesty International and Women's Rights: Feminist Strategies, Leadership Commitment and Internal Resistances* (Transcript Publishing, 2021), which is the first comprehensive look at AI's work on women's rights; Renata Meirelles, *State Violence, Torture, and Political Prisoners: On the Role Played by Amnesty*

International in Brazil During the Dictatorship (1964–1985) (Routledge, 2019); and Tom Buchanan, *Amnesty International and Human Rights Activism in Postwar Britain, 1945–1977* (Routledge, 2020).

Philip Alston, ed., *Non-state Actors and Human Rights* (Oxford University Press, 2005); and George Andreopoulos, Zehra F. Kabasakal Arat, and Peter Juviler, eds., *Non-state Actors in the Human Rights Universe* (Kumarian Press, 2006), are the best, although somewhat outdated, broad scholarly studies. *The Journal of Human Rights Practice*, published by Oxford University Press, in an excellent resource for current research in the field of human rights advocacy.

NGO activism, however, is not without its problems. David Kennedy, *The Dark Sides of Virtue: Reassessing International Humanitarianism* (Princeton University Press, 2004), is a brilliant analysis of the pitfalls of advocacy that matches its potent criticisms with a genuine sympathy and commitment to a more just and humane world. Michael Ignatieff's, *Human Rights as Politics and Idolatry* (Princeton University Press, 2001) offers a powerful warning about the dangers of excessive self-righteousness and rigidity, again from the perspective of a sympathetic scholar-activist.

Mahmood Monshipouri, ed., *Information Politics, Protests, and Human Rights in the Digital Age* (Cambridge University Press, 2016) and Tristan Anne Borer, ed., *Media, Mobilization, and Human Rights: Mediating Suffering* (Zed Books, 2012) canvass the promises and pitfalls of media-based advocacy. As featured in Problem 9.1 in this chapter, Joel Pruce's, *The Mass Appeal of Human Rights* (Palgrave Macmillan, 2018) argues that while social engagement strategies are effective in attracting masses of supporters, they also weaken the viability of human rights by commodifying its practices.

Finally, Mette Eilstrup-Sangiovanni and J. C. Sharman, *Vigilantes beyond Borders: NGOs as Enforcers of International Law* (Princeton University Press, 2022) explores the causes and consequences of a novel, provocative, and potentially problematic approach to global governance: NGO enforcement of international law. A briefer version of their argument can be found in Mette Eilstrup-Sangiovanni and J. C. Sharman, "Enforcers beyond Borders: Transnational NGOs and the Enforcement of International Law." *Perspectives on Politics* 19 (1) 2021: 131–147.

Notes

1 https://www.hrw.org/sites/default/files/media_2025/05/2024_HRW_Annual_Report.pdf.
2 For a complete list of HRW's extensive library of reports, see www.hrw.org/publications.
3 The Israel-based organization NGO Monitor, which describes itself as "Israel's most prominent watchdog of human rights groups" (www.ngo-monitor.org), is a leading source of such arguments. It is literally true—because no single organization could cover all of the many dozens of countries with comparable or worse records. But HRW has issued comparable criticisms of Myanmar, Russia, Iran, and the United States, as well as several reports on North Korea—a list that to us at least does not suggest partisan political bias.
4 https://www.hrw.org/world-report/2025.
5 See, for example, www.unaids.org/sites/default/files/media_asset/jc579-strategies_ngo_en_2.pdf.

6 See www.oecd.org/dac/effectiveness/parisdeclarationandaccraagendaforaction.htm.
7 www.oecd.org/dac/effectiveness/49650173.pdf.
8 https://www.americanprogress.org/wp-content/uploads/2013/11/ProcurementReform.pdf.
9 Lilie Chouliaraki, "The Theatricality of Humanitarianism: A Critique of Celebrity Advocacy," *Communication and Critical/Cultural Studies* 9, no. 1 (2012): 2.
10 In 2019, Invisible Children seemed to have gone defunct. But their website shows financials through 2021 and reports having helped reintegrate those captured by the LRA to their communities.
11 Joel Pruce, *The Mass Appeal of Human Rights* (Palgrave Macmillan, 2018).

10 Human Rights, Business Firms, and Rights-Conscious Investment

This chapter looks at another type of "private" actor in the global human rights regime: for-profit businesses and investors in such firms. As we have seen, obligations to protect and enforce internationally recognized human rights fall almost exclusively on states. Businesses, however, have significant roles in respecting and implementing internationally recognized human rights.

All persons—natural, legal, and social; national and international—have duties not to deprive anyone of the enjoyment of internationally recognized human rights. These obligations are particularly pressing on firms, which have special duties with respect to the rights of their workers and an often-outsized impact on their lives (and the lives of the communities in which they work and reside).

Firms may also be incorporated within national systems of human rights provision. For example, in most countries, employment is central to most people obtaining food and housing (through markets). In the United States, a majority of workers receive health insurance through their employers.

Firms and other private actors may also undertake voluntary supererogatory activities (i.e., actions that are desirable but not required) that improve the enjoyment of human rights. For example, providing childcare, schooling, or health care at a worksite rarely is a matter of obligation. Therefore, a firm that is financially able but chooses not to do so ordinarily would not be infringing human rights. Providing such services, however, does contribute to their more effective enjoyment.

In this chapter, we take the perspective of an investor or investment manager. An investment perspective allows us to address the role of businesses with an eye to one way in which ordinary individuals can participate in an important type of human rights activism. We begin by exploring basic principles and frameworks for rights-conscious investment decision-making.

DOI: 10.4324/9781003373520-12

1 Rights-Conscious Investing

Investors may have intrinsic or instrumental interests in the human rights performance of firms in which they invest.

Corporations and investors today often have explicit environmental, social, and governance (ESG) objectives and standards. Human rights cut across social and governance issues and spill into environmental concerns. Human rights also frame ESG goals in ways that have broad social and political resonance and permit linking socially conscious investing to widely endorsed international legal standards.

Box 10.1 UN Guiding Principles on Business and Human Rights

The *Guiding Principles on Business and Human Rights,* which seek to implement a "protect, respect, and remedy" framework for human rights, were endorsed by the United Nations Human Rights Council and the General Assembly in 2011. They have been widely adopted by states, firms, and human rights advocates across the globe and have changed the practices of many firms and some governments, especially in liberal democratic and social democratic countries.

Among the most important of the thirty-one enumerated principles are the following, which emphasize the mutual but differing obligations of states and business enterprises.

1. States must protect against human rights abuse within their territory and/or jurisdiction by third parties, including business enterprises. This requires taking appropriate steps to prevent, investigate, punish and redress such abuse through effective policies, legislation, regulations and adjudication.

11. Business enterprises should respect human rights. This means that they should avoid infringing on the human rights of others and should address adverse human rights impacts with which they are involved.

12. The responsibility of business enterprises to respect human rights refers to internationally recognized human rights – understood, at a minimum, as those expressed in the International Bill of Human Rights and the principles concerning fundamental rights set out in the International Labour Organization's Declaration on Fundamental Principles and Rights at Work.

13. The responsibility to respect human rights requires that business enterprises: (a) Avoid causing or contributing to adverse human rights impacts through their own activities, and address such impacts when they occur; (b) Seek to prevent or mitigate adverse human rights impacts that are directly linked to their operations, products or services by their business relationships, even if they have not contributed to those impacts.

17. In order to identify, prevent, mitigate and account for how they address their adverse human rights impacts, business enterprises should carry out human rights due diligence. The process should include assessing actual and potential human rights impacts, integrating and acting upon the findings, tracking responses, and communicating how impacts are addressed.

22. Where business enterprises identify that they have caused or contributed to adverse impacts, they should provide for or cooperate in their remediation through legitimate processes.

25. As part of their duty to protect against business-related human rights abuse, States must take appropriate steps to ensure, through judicial, administrative, legislative or other appropriate means, that when such abuses occur within their territory and/or jurisdiction those affected have access to effective remedy.

Protection is primarily the responsibility of states. Firms, however, have substantial obligations to respect the human rights not only of workers but of all people who are affected by their activities. And, although providing remedy for violations is largely a duty of states, firms often will be appropriately involved, and bear certain burdens, in efforts aimed at redress.

If one has an *intrinsic interest* in human rights, violations are considered a cost to be weighed against the financial benefits of the investment. Conversely, contributing to the more effective enjoyment of human rights is considered a nonfinancial benefit that increases the attractiveness of the investment.

The human rights practices of firms and the governments in countries where they operate may also affect financial returns, creating an *instrumental interest* in human rights. These impacts may be direct (e.g., systematic corruption, which tends to be especially prevalent in rights-abusive countries, imposes direct financial costs on firms), indirect (e.g., when rights abuses engender social disorder, businesses often suffer), or reputational (e.g., brands may be tarnished and shareholder value reduced by association with especially reprehensible labor practices or rights-abusive governments).

Investment managers may also have a *fiduciary interest* in human rights if their clients have either directly identified human rights concerns (e.g., no investment in firms that employ unfree labor) or have specified ESG objectives that might be appropriately implemented through a focus on particular human rights.

In other words, even investors with no intrinsic interest in human rights or broader ESG objectives may have compelling reasons for considering human rights in investment decisions.

The following sections attempt to identify the kinds of circumstances in which rights-conscious investors may be called to act and to explore some appropriate kinds of responses. For simplicity and clarity, we begin by assuming that an investor is considering a potential investment in a single firm operating in a single sector in a single country.

2 When Action Is Called For

Three features of the local human rights context are especially important in determining whether to invest.

- *The overall human rights record* in the country (or the area where the firm operates). A rough five-value scale will often provide a useful starting point: very good, good, mixed, poor, and very bad.[1]
- *The human rights impact* of the activities of the firm, including both direct impacts and externalities (unintended consequences). Here too a five-point scale is useful, ranking violations (or improvements in enjoyment) as very minor, minor, modest, major, and severe/extreme.
- *Association or complicity* with human rights violations perpetrated, sponsored, or tolerated by the state, its agents, or its allies.

2.1 General Human Rights Conditions and Particular Firm Impacts

Where the overall human rights situation is extremely bad (e.g., Venezuela, Myanmar, Eritrea, Afghanistan), the pervasiveness of repression makes it unlikely that a firm can plausibly dissociate itself from rights-abusive actors and practices. Investment therefore probably ought to be seen as prima facie prohibited for at least intrinsic and reputational reasons. Conversely, where the overall human rights situation is very good (e.g., Norway, Sweden, and Canada), there should be a general presumption of permissibility.

Most countries, however, have more or less mixed human rights records, which requires that assessments also consider the human rights impacts of the activities of the firm. In fact, the particular actions of a firm may even reverse an initial negative or positive assessment. For example, if Venezuela were to allow investment in food production for local consumption, the direct positive human rights impact might overcome the prima facie prohibition—especially if most of the food were distributed in ways that did not allow the government to reward its supporters or punish those seen as less loyal. Conversely, in Norway and Sweden, some petroleum, mining, logging, wind energy, and tourism projects in or adjacent to the traditional lands of the Sámi (an indigenous Finno-Ugric people) might not stand up to human rights scrutiny.

2.2 Red Lines and Red Flags

Identifying "red lines" and "red flags" can contribute greatly to clear and consistent investment decisions.

There are some lines that, at least prima facie, can never be legitimately crossed. Common examples include slavery (in both chattel and "modern" forms), genocide, systematic legal discrimination based on race, ethnicity, or religion, and the widespread use of extra judicial executions. A potential investment that grossly, systematically, or persistently crosses human rights red lines, either through the firm's own actions or through complicity with the perpetrator, almost never will pass muster.

In working through investment decisions, it is also useful to have identified red flags, which can be raised for many reasons: for example, because violations approach a red line (e.g., systematic but not legally sanctioned discrimination); because of a slippery slope toward more severe violations (e.g., restrictions of judicial independence and the banning of opposition political parties); because of spillovers into other domains (e.g., discrimination rarely is restricted to the enjoyment of one human right); or simply out of special interest (e.g., prioritizing freedom of religion because it is especially important to an investor).

Even modest human rights violations in the workplace probably ought to be considered red flags in most rights-conscious investment practices because of the direct responsibility of the firm. These would at minimum involve health and safety concerns (which in major or severe forms might reasonably be considered red lines). For many investors, workplace red flags will also include some terms and conditions of work (e.g., wages, hours, leave, and unionization), evaluated either by absolute standards or relative to local competitors and conditions.

The ILO Declaration on Fundamental Rights Principles and Rights at Work[2] identifies four rights of special concern:

> (a) freedom of association and the effective recognition of the right to collective bargaining; (b) the elimination of all forms of forced or compulsory labour; (c) the effective abolition of child labour; and (d) the elimination of discrimination in respect of employment and occupation.

Rights-conscious investors, we would argue, should treat violations of these rights as at least large red flags. Most rights-conscious investors probably will want to treat forced labor[3] and child labor[4] as red lines.

An investor might also want to think about the idea of yellow flags, understood as practices that alone might raise relatively minor concerns but that when combined are more problematic (or might be useful as warning signs of larger problems in the future). Because there is a huge range of possible yellow flags, it would be hard to specify a list beforehand outside of workplace violations. It is crucial, though, to remember that simply assuring that an investment does not cross red lines or raise red flags is only, at best, minimal human rights due diligence.

2.3 Direct Responsibility, Complicity, Association

Investment decisions ought to give special emphasis to the obligations of all actors not to deprive people of the enjoyment of their internationally recognized human rights. Actions or omissions by firms that harm workers, consumers, or broader communities in ways that limit or reduce their enjoyment of internationally recognized human rights should count heavily against investment. And we would argue that any major or severe violations directly attributable to the firm (for example, violent union busting) should be considered crossing a red line.

Even where a firm is not directly responsible, it may be sufficiently tied to human rights violations that rights-conscious investors might or should choose not to invest. Here we can usefully distinguish (indirect) *association* from (more direct) *complicity*, in the strong sense of "being an accomplice; partnership in an evil action."[5] We should also distinguish violations that do and do not directly benefit a particular firm (or the economic sector in which it operates).

For example, Singapore combines a generally very good record on most economic, social, and cultural rights (at least for citizens of Singapore) with a mixed record on civil and political rights. Freedom House rates Singapore as "partly free," noting strong barriers to opposition political parties and substantial limits on freedom of expression, assembly, and association.[6] But the police and security services are professional and not major instruments of repression, the rule of law is generally respected, the state bureaucracy is not corrupt, and (despite major restrictions on freedom of association) civil society activity is generally tolerated if it falls within generally well-known informal limits ("out of bounds markers").

Simply by operating in Singapore, firms do associate with a regime that systematically violates many human rights. Few firms, though, either derive any special benefit from those violations or are in any significant sense an accomplice in them. Therefore, most rights-conscious investors probably will reasonably decide to invest—so long as the investment is financially attractive and the particular activities of the firm have only minor negative human rights impacts.

In sharp contrast, petroleum operations in the Niger Delta of Nigeria often are both complicit in and benefit from severe systematic human rights violations. For example, a complex combination of private security contractors, military units, and police and soldiers seconded to or hired by the firm operate in an environment where insurgency, criminality, and vandalism are often serious problems.[7] The resulting (often severe) human rights violations are reasonably attributable (in part) to the firm, even if "all it was trying to do" was protect its assets and workers in a difficult environment.[8]

A different kind of complicity, which is also present in Nigeria, arises from state participation in commercial activities. In many countries, an arm of the state (e.g., the Army of Pakistan or the Revolutionary Guards in Iran) participates in commercial activities. In such cases, it is important to consider how closely a firm is associated with human rights violators and violations. And the worse the overall record of the investment partner, the more that even mere association—minimally, operating in a country—looks like complicity.

3 Making an Initial Assessment: Red, Green, and Yellow Baskets

Rights-conscious investment assessments might appropriately begin by sorting potential investments into "red," "green," and "yellow" baskets.

"Red" investments include those in countries with very bad overall (or local) human rights conditions, where red lines are regularly crossed, where the firm is actively complicit in or benefits from gross and systematic violations, or where the activities of the firm contribute directly to major or severe violations. (Any one of these shortcomings should make the investment prima facie unacceptable.) Some investors may also want to put investments in countries with poor (but not very bad) overall records and a number of red flags in this basket.

"Green" investments would be in countries with very good or good human rights records, where violations of the rights of workers or local communities attributable to the firms are very minor or minor, where no red lines are crossed and few red flags are raised, and where the firm neither is complicit in nor significantly benefits from gross or systematic violations by others. (All of these conditions must be met.)

"Yellow" investments include all the rest. Usually, this will be the biggest batch. And considerable further work usually will be required to determine if such not-necessarily-unacceptable options are, in the end, all things considered, acceptable.

4 Responding to Human Rights Conditions

After having determined whether to act on human rights concerns, investors must determine how to do so. Here, too, there are no simple rules (other than that we usually can just say no when red lines are crossed or when dealing with severely rights-abusive regimes). This makes it crucial to be clear about both what one is trying to achieve and the likelihood of success.

4.1 The Purposes of Action

How one responds to violations depends in significant measure on what one hopes to achieve. Four common aims can be identified.

- *Change*. Sometimes one aims to change policies or practices and alter outcomes to reduce violations or improve enjoyment of internationally recognized human rights. This is rarely directly possible for investors. But firms frequently find themselves positioned to contribute to improved enjoyment of work-related rights. And investors occasionally may be positioned to push firms to make such changes.
- *Punishment*. Rarely will investors have the resources to inflict significant material punishment on rights-abusive firms (let alone the governments of the countries where they operate). Even imposing reputational costs usually falls outside the power of investors. (The principal exceptions involve boycotts or sanctions in particularly egregious cases (e.g., Myanmar) or relatively isolated high-profile violations (e.g., soccer balls, baby formula, and cocoa).)
- *Protest*. When investors (and firms) often cannot reasonably hope to change human rights practices, especially when violations are produced or tolerated by the state,

action is fundamentally a protest; making a statement—perhaps with an aspiration to contribute to change in other or future cases or to impose some reputational cost. (Protests often are easier for investors than firms, which often have sunk costs or valuable relationships that investors do not.)

- *Witness*. Action may be largely internally driven. Our values, simply because they are our values, call on us to stand up for them, irrespective of our impact on the world.

When a firm is positioned to improve the enjoyment of internationally recognized human rights (e.g., by improving terms and conditions of labor or supporting free trade unions), the argument for action is particularly compelling (especially when improved practices are required by obligations not to deprive). But distancing oneself from violations over which one has no control may sometimes be sufficient reason to act. And providing symbolic or moral support to victims, advocates, or the idea of international human rights may also be an appropriate and convincing ground for action.

In other words, even though investors rarely can produce change or significantly punish bad actors, that does not make rights-conscious investing pointless. Protests may be important—to those protesting or those whose rights are being violated (who feel supported or vindicated by recognition of their suffering). And repeated and widespread protest may perhaps over time contribute to changing baseline expectations (and through them, altering practice). At minimum, even if rights-conscious investors cannot be part of the solution, they may reasonably aspire to keep from being part of the problem.

4.2 A Typology of Orientations

Building on the distinction between intrinsic and instrumental motives for rights-conscious investing, we can identify a range of broad orientations running from "merely instrumental" (i.e., concerned only with the damage of rights-abusive practices to a firm's reputation or bottom line) to "perfectionist" (in which an investor, for intrinsic reasons, refuses any participation in or complicity with all but the most minor human rights violations). We can also distinguish minimalists, who demand only that there be no compelling human rights reason not to invest, from maximalists, who require that investments make positive human rights contributions. Combining these two dimensions yields a simple typology (Figure 10.1).

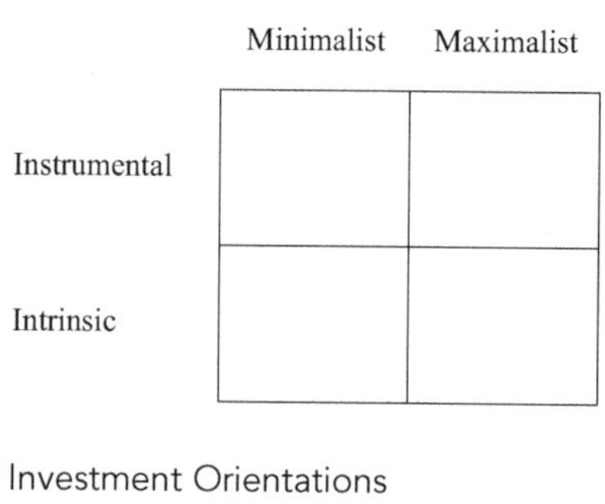

Figure 10.1 A Typology of Investment Orientations

We suspect that most investors (and firms) lie toward the top-left (instrumental-minimalist) corner of this space. (Their primary goal is to avoid reputational and financial costs.) But even such a narrow orientation toward rights-conscious investing, if it is clear and explicit, can be significant.

We should not, however, ignore the wide range of options that go beyond protecting brands and bottom lines. Nor should we only emphasize "negative" and reactive responses that focus on avoiding, reducing, or eliminating violations.

At least a few investors will want to look for opportunities to make a positive impact. For example, in addition to asking whether *x*, *y*, or *z* is required by local workplace safety regulations (or industry-wide best practices or company rules), one would seek out firms that work actively to improve workplace safety. Or, in addition to asking whether wages conform to local legal standards or how they compare with local competitors, an investor might ask whether the firm is doing all that it can to realize "the right to just and favorable remuneration ensuring for himself and his family an existence worthy of human dignity."[9]

"Positive" endeavors may even involve supererogatory—desirable but not required—actions in which the lines blur between respecting human rights and acting out of considerations of social justice or corporate social responsibility. This is especially true of initiatives that explicitly link the workplace with better enjoyment of other human rights (e.g., on-site health services) or with the communities within which it is embedded.

We stress more-than-minimal strategies because if firms and investors don't ask what they might do to improve the enjoyment of human rights by workers, their families, and communities—if we don't go beyond duties not to deprive—we may miss opportunities that might have been pursued had they been identified. And we suspect that at least occasionally firms or investors will be surprised by the opportunities that present themselves.

4.3 Selectivity and Tradeoffs

In discussing human rights and foreign policy, we addressed issues of selectivity and tradeoffs (see Chapter 7, Section 4). Similar considerations arise in the case of rights-conscious investment.

Private actors must make choices about which rights to address, where. (Even states cannot simultaneously address all aspects of all human rights everywhere.) Such selectivity, despite being unavoidable, trades off some rights and some places against others. Rights-conscious investors therefore should be able to state clearly which rights are (and are not) considered in their decisions—and why.

A very different kind of tradeoff arises from the fact that firms and investors have financial interests and obligations. In fact, financial considerations *ought* to be central for economic actors. Here too, handling tradeoffs in a responsible and principled way requires clarity about what is being balanced against what, according to what standards.

The resulting talk of tolerable levels of human rights violations—of how much one is (and is not) willing to pay to avoid participating in violating human rights—ought to be unsettling. Completely clean hands, however, often are not possible. For example, even firms that take workplace safety seriously are likely to have accidents in which firm policies and practices are partly to blame (e.g., the speed at which a production line operates). And, in many industries and workplaces, more might be done to provide greater protections than is legally required.

Investors need to be forthright but not apologetic about the real but limited role of human rights in their investment decisions. Investing usually can be rights-conscious. Sometimes it can be rights-respecting. Rarely, though, can it be rights-driven, let alone rights-determined—except when red-basketing a potential investment.

4.4 Consistency

Investors also face questions of consistency. Principled action typically aims to treat like cases alike—above all, not making an exception for yourself (or those to whom you are connected) and therefore treating "everyone" (i.e., all those with whom you interact) equally (or at least comparably).

All social action, however, is positioned. We are all "office holders"—for example, parents, children, siblings, classmates, employees, citizens, and members of private voluntary organizations—with "professional ethics" that often demand actions different from what an abstract moral agent would do after consulting the moral law, the principle of utility, the word of God, or some other context-free standard. For example, as we argued above, foreign policy decision-makers ought to give special consideration to nationals and the national interest—which judged by universalistic moral standards is an immoral form of collective egoism. Similarly, firms have special obligations to their workers and fiduciary responsibilities to their stockholders.

Therefore, investment decisions (and the human rights policies and practices of firms) often will, all things considered, treat "the same" human rights violations differently. Done properly, though, there is nothing wrong with this. Human rights principles operate within investment policies that include other objectives that sometimes take priority. Therefore, it may prove permissible, or even required, to prioritize financial considerations over minor or modest human rights concerns.

Investors should strive for coherent and reasonably consistent *investment* policies. There are no clear-cut rules. We can, however, aspire to rigorously assess particular cases according to a clear and explicit framework of evaluation. Investors can also reflect on past decisions, both individually and as a stream of practice, to help think about new cases and to assist in further developing an orienting framework.

4.5 Focal Rights

The necessity of selectivity also raises the issue of criteria for selecting priority or focal rights. We have already stressed focusing on rights on which a firm has a direct impact (or a clear if indirect impact). We also have noted priorities based on interest.

The interdependence of rights, and thus the possibility of spillovers, also suggests priorities. For example, health is related to the enjoyment of a great variety of human rights. Education is complexly interrelated to income and health. More broadly, nondiscrimination and freedom of association, which guarantee inclusion and participation, can be useful indicator rights, both because of their intrinsic importance and because of their interconnections with other rights.

Rights-conscious investors should, at minimum, be able to state clearly which rights they prioritize in what kinds of cases—and why.

5 A Checklist or Flowchart for Rights-Conscious Investors

Pulling together the discussion so far, imagine a three-step process in which an investor begins by clarifying objectives and gathering basic information, then identifies clearly unacceptable and clearly acceptable investments, and then moves on to consider potential investments that have human rights problems that might not be unsurmountable.

Initial Questions

1. What are your red lines?
2. What are your red flags?
3. Are your goals more instrumental and negative or more intrinsic and positive?
4. What is the overall level of human rights performance in the country (or locality)?
5. What are the (negative and positive) human rights impacts of the operations of the firm?
6. Does the firm benefit from systematic human rights violations committed by others?
7. Can the firm plausibly be considered complicit in gross violations by others?

First Screening

Red-lighted investments. Any of the following conditions is likely to render a proposed investment prima facie prohibited.

a) The host country has a very bad overall (or local) human rights record.
b) Red lines are regularly crossed.
c) The activities of the firm have major or severe negative effects on the human rights of workers or local communities.
d) The firm is complicit in or significantly benefits from gross and systematic human rights violations by the state, its agents, or its allies.

Green-lighted investments. When *all* of the following conditions are met, an investment usually will stand up to human rights scrutiny.

e) The country has a very good or good overall (and local) human rights record.
f) No red lines are crossed and few red flags are raised.
g) The violations of the human rights directly attributable to the firm are very minor or minor.
h) The firm neither is complicit in nor significantly benefits from gross violations by others.

Second Screening

For the remaining cases, the more conditions e), f), g), and h) that are met, the more likely the investment will be justifiable. In addition, the following conditions may count in favor of an investment.

i) Modest violations are at least no worse than typical of firms in that sector in that country.
j) Returns on investment are unusually high. (We are talking about rights-conscious investing, with investment as the noun.)
k) Few potential investments with better human rights records are available that meet all the other goals of the investor.
l) The firm's activities improve human rights conditions for workers or local communities.
m) The firm engages in appealing social or community activities.
n) The firm has a good environmental record.
o) The firm is a "good actor" in a problematic sector or country.

6 Addressing More Complex Cases

We have so far assumed that we are dealing with an initial investment in a single firm operating in a single sector in a single country. This section looks at differences between investing and divesting and the problems of aggregating different human rights impacts in multifaceted investments.

6.1 *Life-Cycle Issues*

Even when we are dealing with a single firm operating in a single sector in a single country, situations may change after an initial investment has been made. For example, there may be a dramatic decline in the overall human rights situation in the country or new immediately relevant violations (e.g., a violent crackdown on trade unions).

Can the firm reduce or contain violations to an acceptable level? Is this backsliding likely to be temporary (and thus something the firm might try to ride out)? If not, are the violations sufficiently severe that they demand major financial sacrifices (e.g., selling at a loss) or, in an extreme case such as the initiation of genocide, perhaps even writing off an investment?

There is a point at which complicity with human rights violators or violations becomes too problematic (especially in highly publicized cases with significant potential reputational costs). But the necessity of balancing fundamentally incommensurable values makes it extraordinarily difficult to give a principled answer to the question of how much one should be willing to pay to stop complicity—especially when that complicity arises after the fact of the investment.

Investors usually have the option of divestment. Selling the investment, however, typically just changes the owner of, rather than reduces, violations—often, a cynic would note, at low cost to the investor. But if this is indeed the most that financial considerations allow, and if one is clear that one's action is fundamentally a protest taken out of respect for human rights, then simply divesting may indeed be the best course of action, following the prudential maxim of choosing the least bad as the good.

6.2 Aggregating Projects and Firms

Aggregating products and firms add further complications. The problems become especially severe when a firm, product, or investment instrument combines projects of different sorts or in places with very different human rights records. And global supply chains increasingly present such problems even for a single firm producing a relatively small number of similar or related products.

Thinking abstractly, we might begin by making an inventory of the human rights contexts in each of the discrete units of production or investment. There is not likely to be a practical way to add up the separate assessments and mechanically determine whether some threshold has been crossed. But if nearly all the individual pieces pass the relevant human rights tests, that counts in favor of going ahead with a financially attractive investment. Conversely, the more negative marks on the ledger, the more difficult it will be to justify the investment.

The substance and severity of the problems, however, are also crucial considerations. As with individual projects or firms, factors that counsel against investing even where most parts of the investment stand up to human rights scrutiny include a bad overall national human rights record, considerable direct negative impact, significant complicity with violations, and human rights practices that cross red lines, raise red flags, or infringe on focal rights. And it will be important to be clear about how far toward the "perfectionist" or maximalist end of the spectrum one wants to land. (Does the investment need a positive justification? Or is it enough that it not receive a clear human rights veto?)

Occasionally the decision is relatively easy. For example, several minor (or perhaps even one or two modest) concerns often (usually?) will not tip the balance. Conversely, crossing redlines in one segment of a firm or one item in an investment package usually will demand rejecting the investment (for both intrinsic and instrumental reasons)—or at least require a very strong set of reasons to invest.

Most often, though, we will find ourselves back addressing, now at a higher level of aggregation, the unanswerable question of how much (of what) is too much. Our (understandable) desire for clear, principled decisions that leave our hands clean must give way to the necessity of casuistry; reasoning shaped by the particularities of the case, often in the context of competing obligations. Decisions usually come down to determining, in a rough and ready way, how much unacceptable behavior is tolerable in a particular rights-conscious investment, balancing, as best we can, the incommensurable human rights and financial factors that demand consideration.

That clearly is not an inspiring statement of the work of rights-conscious investing. But it does seem to us a clear statement of what can reasonably be hoped for. And we would argue that usually avoiding being a part of the problem, while sometimes being a force for improving the conditions of people's lives, is a worthwhile endeavor.

Hypothetical: Problems with Suppliers

The argument so far has been that much of rights-conscious investing depends heavily on the details of the case. We therefore close this chapter with a hypothetical and two case studies.[10]

If our research and due diligence lead us to believe that a company is doing all it can possibly do on human rights and is generally following international best practice, but at some point it is linked to human rights violations (e.g., via one of its suppliers), how should we think about our investment in the company?

Focusing on the suppliers in question and assuming that no better-performing alternatives are readily available (at an acceptable price), the approach outlined above suggests the following framework for assessment.

First, nothing useful can be said at the level of "human rights violations," which come in greatly varied forms of varied severity. The more severe and systematic the violations, the more likely one wants to stay away from the investment. Violations that cross a red line, raise red flags, or infringe on focal rights strongly suggest not investing. For minor and modest violations, local comparisons may be an important consideration.

Second, we must determine the nature of the suppliers' responsibilities. Are they directly causing violations? Do they benefit from violations committed by others? Are they in some other way complicit? And even if they are only minimally associated (by presence) with a repressive regime, is the general human rights situation sufficiently bad that it taints any firm operating there?

Third, we need to specify the aims of our action. Assuming that there is no possibility of changing the suppliers' behavior or punishing violators, are we satisfied with action that amounts to protest or witness? And how perfectionist do we want to be (for what reasons) about dissociating from violations?

Fourth, we need to identify the place in the supply chain. Relevant questions include the number of suppliers, the proportion of production costs or value added, and the proportion of the labor in the production process. The more minor and isolated the problematic parts, the less unattractive the investment.

Combining these considerations, we can identify four types of cases of interest.

- The supplier crosses a red line (e.g., employs child labor in unsafe conditions). Even if this is only a tiny part of a large supply chain, almost all rights-conscious investors should avoid this investment, for both reputational and intrinsic reasons.

- The suppliers' practices are of more than minor concern but do not come close to a red line. For example, they have a higher-than-average rate of workplace injuries or are partly owned by an arm of a state with a problematic human rights record. Here, the crucial considerations are likely to be the investor's tolerance for not-clearly-over-the-line violations and the place of the suppliers in the supply chain. Although different investors might reach different decisions, the paths [in the plural] to reasoned decisions are fairly clear.
- The supplier's practices are not particularly problematic but the overall human rights situation in the country (or the locality) is very bad. Here, it seems to us, reasonable investors may reasonably disagree. Some might argue that the firm (and through it the investor) is only related to a supplier that does not have any real responsibility for violations. Others might claim that the overall human rights situation is sufficiently bad that it is implausible to deny that the supplier is complicit.
- One or a few suppliers (out of many) (a) cross no red line but (b) raise a red flag and yet (c) have only modestly problematic workplace practices that are not worse than average in the locality. If in addition the overall human rights situation in the country is no worse than very mixed and the investor is willing to tolerate modest violations in small, isolated parts of the supply chain, then an investment probably can be justified (the more so the more that the problems are minor and isolated).

Case Study: Inditex (Zara)

Inditex, headquartered in Spain, is an apparel firm with over 7,000 stores in more than 200 markets and net sales in 2024 of about €38.6 billion (about 70 percent of which was generated by the Zara brand). It presents itself as placing a significant intrinsic value on sustainability and protecting workers' rights and other human rights in its supply chains. And its extensive ESG activities seem to provide significant reputational benefits, both in the market and internally.

The apparel sector, however, has a long history of notoriously bad labor conditions.[11] In addition to "ordinary" industrial accidents, the inherent nature of the work makes musculoskeletal problems difficult to avoid. Poor ventilation, inadequate cooling (and heating), noise, and dangerous exposure to particulates and chemicals are common in apparel factories, many of which are housed in dangerous, even deadly, buildings (as illustrated by a well-publicized fire at Tazreen Fashions in 2012 and the Rana Tower collapse in 2013 in Bangladesh, which killed over 1,100 workers).

Rights-conscious investors thus should approach the apparel industry with skepticism. But as a purported "good" firm in a traditionally "bad" industry, Inditex presents an interesting case. And considerably better than average human rights performance would mean that the firm is not merely avoiding inflicting harm but, in a small but real way, is helping to improve human rights conditions.

In 2021, Inditex purchased products from 1,790 suppliers with 8,756 declared factories operating primarily in Asia (55 percent of suppliers), the EU (21 percent), and non-EU Europe (12 percent).[12] But 97 percent of production took place in twelve countries, allowing us to attempt a general human rights assessment. Table 10.1 lists the Freedom House Global Freedom Score (1 is the lowest [Syria, Tibet, South Sudan] and 100 [Norway, Finland, Sweden] the highest[13]) and the 2021 Human Development Index (HDI) ranking (1 is highest [Switzerland] and 191 [South Sudan] is the lowest)[14] of these countries.

Table 10.1 Major Inditex Supplier Countries

Country	*Freedom House*	*HDI*
Argentina	84 (free)	47 (very high)
Bangladesh	39 (partly free)	129 (medium)
Brazil	73 (free)	87 (high)
Cambodia	24 (not free)	146 (medium)
China	9 (not free)	79 (high)
India	66 (partly free)	132 (medium)
Morocco	37 (partly free)	123 (medium)
Pakistan	37 (partly free)	161 (low)
Portugal	95 (free)	38 (very high)
Spain	90 (free)	27 (very high)
Turkey	32 (not free)	48 (very high)
Vietnam	19 (not free)	115 (high)

Clearly there are several countries of concern, especially China (which we briefly address in Box 10.2), Vietnam, and Cambodia, but also Turkey, Pakistan, and Morocco.[15] But probably only China falls in the red basket on an initial assessment, and that is largely because of systematic ethnic and religious repression in Xinjiang and Tibet. One might reasonably put China in the yellow basket because no factory that produces for Inditex operates in either Xinjiang or Tibet.

Can Inditex's record in regulating and monitoring human rights practices in its supply chain reasonably be seen to overcome the problematic nature of the industry and the general human rights conditions in some supplier countries? We are not sure. But a plausible case can be made for investment.

Inditex's 2014 Global Framework Agreement with the international union federation IndustriALL Global Union was the first ever to cover a retail supply chain.[16] Inditex has an admirable Code of Conduct for suppliers, including absolute prohibition of child labor and forced labor[17] and support for freedom of association and collective bargaining and occupational health and safety.[18] And Inditex seems to have a robust system of supply-chain monitoring. In 2021, 17,477 audits were conducted (an increase of about 40 percent over the average of the preceding three years), including 6,119 traceability audits without advanced notice and 5,840 social audits (out of a total of 8,756 factories). Twenty-five suppliers were rejected. Furthermore, in Asia nearly a quarter of applicants did not pass pre-assessment audits.[19]

Given the nature of the industry and the large number of production facilities, some abuses undoubtedly do occur.[20] Publicly available sources, though, suggest that there are no large systematic problems and that, while there is still considerable room for improvement, Inditex is reasonably diligent in its efforts and responsive to public expressions of concern.

For example, the 2019 and 2023 Corporate Human Rights Benchmark (CHRB) reports of the World Benchmarking Alliance[21] ranked more than fifty large apparel companies (Table 10.2).[22]

Inditex was ranked third in each year, suggesting that it is a (relatively) "good actor" in a problematic sector. But the quick drop-off as we move through the top ten sug-

Table 10.2 CHRB Ratings (Apparel)

2019								
Firm	*Rank*	*Score*	*Governance*	*Due Diligence*	*Remedies*	*Practices*	*Responses*	*Transparency*
Adidas	1	83	7.4/10	21.4/25	15/15	16.1/20	15/20	8.4/10
Inditex	3	65	7.8/10	14.3/25	4.6/15	15/20	17.5/20	6.4/10
Nike	10	44	2.7/10	11.6/25	2.9/15	12.8/20	10/20	4.8/10

2023							
Firm	*Rank*	*Score*	*Governance*	*Due Diligence*	*Remedies*	*Practices*	*Responses*
Puma	1	53	3.8/10	15.4/25	11.5/20	12.0/25	10.7/25
Inditex	3	42	5.3/10	16.2/25	7.0/20	10.4/20	3.3/25
Adidas	8	34	3.1/10	8.2/25	9.0/20	8.3/20	5.6/25

gests that such "good actors" are rather rare exceptions.[23] And consistent with the "bad sector" story, despite the fact that most of the rated firms are well-known brands (which we would expect to perform better than unbranded producers), the majority of firms scored below 20 (out of 100) in 2019 as did more than three-fifths in 2023 (although the apparent decline largely reflects a change in methodology and the application of more stringent standards).

Nonetheless, it appears that Inditex, except in rare and isolated instances, participates (through its suppliers) in only very minor or minor direct human rights violations and that it is not complicit in human rights violations of others. Its responsiveness suggests that reputational risks to investors are relatively low. And it offers industry-leading levels of respect for workers' rights (which may have both intrinsic and instrumental value to investors). Therefore, adding the stipulation that no red lines have been crossed either grossly or systematically, Inditex would seem to meet reasonable minimum standards for rights-conscious investment.

In addition, Inditex engages in modest supererogatory activities that benefit workers and their communities. In 2021, it invested €63.5 million in community corporate investment (CCI) projects, donated 5.9 million garments, devoted 206,000 hours to CCI projects by employees during working hours, and raised an additional €56 million from other sources.[24] Some rights-conscious investors might consider this a positive factor in their overall assessment (although others might sneer at the fact that Inditex's direct financial contribution was only about 2 percent of its profit for the year).

Inditex, however, has since 2019 been dogged by reports of suppliers using materials from Xinjiang, where cotton picking and yarn and textile manufacturing regularly use forced labor, underscoring the intrinsic and reputational dangers of investment in places with very bad human rights records. And, apparently in response to pressure from China, Inditex deleted a statement on its website expressing concern about forced labor in Xinjiang[25]—reflecting a troubling limit on the ability of the firm to dissociate itself from red-line human rights violations in a country where, in addition to its production activities, in early 2024 it operated over a hundred stores.[26]

Therefore, a decision not to invest in Inditex, for either intrinsic or instrumental/reputational reasons, would also be defensible.

Box 10.2 Rights-Conscious Investing in China

China presents a particularly challenging case for rights-conscious investment.

Political freedoms and civil liberties are almost completely denied. And, in recent years, the situation has deteriorated. But the enjoyment of economic and social rights has improved steadily and dramatically. (Over the past four decades, nearly 800 million

Chinese people have escaped extreme poverty!) Furthermore, it is often possible to produce goods in places like Shenzhen or Shanghai at arm's length from systematic human rights violations and with relatively minor direct negative human rights impacts.

In Xinjiang and Tibet, however, genocide, brutal political repression, and a frighteningly invasive totalitarian surveillance state[27] clearly cross what we think should be multiple red lines in any rights-conscious investment strategy. We thus want to say that rights-conscious investments in China should almost always be prohibited.

We presume, though, that many investors will be unwilling to conclude that nearly all investments in China should be avoided because of human rights violations thousands of miles away from (and otherwise largely unconnected with) those investments. And this is in many ways understandable, at least from the perspective of an investor—especially an investor with minimal and merely instrumental interests in human rights.

Nonetheless, it seems to us difficult, at best, to justify *rights-conscious* investments that are even indirectly associated with such severe systematic human rights violations—especially because we are confident that there would be less tolerance for comparable violations in a country less central to global supply chains. Investment in China seems more like selling out human rights than making reasonable, principled tradeoffs.

Therefore, even if one determines in the end that the practicalities of global supply chains "require" a China exception, rights-conscious investors should be, at best, deeply troubled. At minimum, investors and investment managers who invest in firms with significant Chinese operations should both explicitly acknowledge this apparent hypocrisy and strive to keep such exceptions infrequent and limited.

Such clarity and transparency may—*should*—open one to penetrating and troubling questions. Failure to confront those questions directly, though, risks undermining one's claim to rights-conscious investing.

Case Study: Rio Tinto

Rio Tinto is the world's second-largest metals and mining corporation. Based in London and Melbourne, it had consolidated revenues in 2024 of $53.7 billion (about 60 percent from iron ore). It lists "impeccable ESG credentials" on its website as one of its four core objectives.[28] And, on first impression, Rio Tinto too might seem to be a good actor in a bad sector. We argue, however, that it is difficult to defend a rights-conscious investment in Rio Tinto because of crucial differences between the apparel and mining sectors.

Table 10.3 lists the 2021 Freedom House and HDI scores for the fourteen countries in which Rio Tinto operates mines.

Table 10.3 Rio Tinto Operating Countries

Country	*Freedom House*	*HDI*
Argentina	84 (free)	47 (very high)
Australia	95 (free)	5 (very high)
Brazil	73 (free)	87 (high)
Canada	98 (free)	15 (very high)
Chile	94 (free)	42 (very high)
Guinea	34 (not free)	182 (low)
Iceland	94 (free)	3 (very high)
Madagascar	61 (partly free)	173 (low)
Mongolia	84 (free)	96 (high)
Mozambique	43 (partly free)	185 (low)
New Zealand	99 (free)	13 (very high)
Oman	24 (not free)	54 (very high)
South Africa	79 (free)	109 (high)
The United States	83 (free)	21 (very high)

None of these countries has a very bad general human rights record. Red flags are raised by the Freedom House ratings of Oman, Guinea, and Mozambique and by very low HDI ratings for Guinea, Madagascar, and Mozambique. The particulars of Rio Tinto's record and practices, however, seem to us decisive to a rights-conscious decision to invest (or not).

Table 10.4 places Rio Tinto relative to more than fifty extractive industry firms in the 2019–2023 Corporate Human Rights Benchmark Reports.

Table 10.4 CHRB Ratings (Extractives)

2019								
Firm	*Rank*	*Score*	*Governance*	*Diligence*	*Remedies*	*Practices*	*Responses*	*Transparency*
Rio Tinto	1	76	7.7/10	20.5/25	10.8/15	14.4/20	15.2/20	7.5/10
BP	10	53	5.4/10	13.8/25	9.2/15	8.8/20	10.8/20	6/10

(Continued)

Table 10.4 (Continued)

			2023				
Firm	*Rank*	*Score*	*Governance*	*Diligence*	*Remedies*	*Practices*	*Responses*
Repsol	1	66	4.7/10	17.8/25	11.5/20	14.4/25	18/20
Rio Tinto	5	44	5.8/10	14.7/25	11.5/15	15.3/20	3.8/20
BHP Group	10	40	4.4/10	11.1/25	8/15	11.8/20	4.6/20

Rio Tinto dropped from first in 2019 to fifth in 2023 as a result of a large decline in its responsiveness to reports of problems.[29] But it remains a "top performer" in its sector. And there are many good things that can be said about Rio Tinto's operations—perhaps most dramatically that for five straight years (2019–2023) the firm had no fatalities on any of the sites that it directly managed.[30]

Four features, however, make it risky, at best, for rights-conscious investors.

First, Rio Tinto in 2024 had only sixty-one sites (compared to Inditex's more than 8,000 factories and 7,000 stores). A serious problem at any one point amounts to a significant problem for the firm as a whole.

Second, when problems do occur, the size and character of mining operations often give them outsized negative impacts. Even the best-run operations in the most favorable circumstances usually cannot avoid severe negative externalities. For example, Rio Tinto is currently in a dispute with villagers in Madagascar about compensation claims.[31] And Human Rights Watch expressed considerable concern about an iron ore mine in Guinea that began production in late 2025.[32]

Third, mining involves large, concentrated investments and expenditures. This can cause serious problems in countries where respect for human rights is poor or where corruption is embedded. And especially where the operation makes a significant contribution to national or local economies or budgets, it may be difficult to distance the firm from systematic human rights violations perpetrated by the state or its allies or the corruption of local officials. Rio Tinto has been entangled in corruption charges in Guinea,[33] which led to a criminal investigation,[34] and Mozambique,[35] which has led to a civil fraud suit in the United States[36] and fines in the United Kingdom and Australia.[37]

Fourth, pretty much any mine, even in countries with strong safeguards and robust enforcement, raises more or less serious environmental concerns.

There thus is a high probability, whether through accident, incompetence, or corruption, of a well-publicized brand-damaging error—which in fact occurred to Rio Tinto in May 2020 when it destroyed rock shelters in Juukan Gorge in Western Australia that showed continued human habitation going back at least 46,000 years. The blasting was not technically illegal. Nonetheless, public outcry caused the CEO and two other executives to step down and has forced Rio Tinto to work hard to try to repair relations with indigenous communities.[38]

In extractive industries it is extraordinarily difficult to avoid causing both intrinsic and reputational harm. Intentions certainly are important. And Rio Tinto does seem to work diligently to correct its errors. But the firm, it seems to us, should be off-limits to rights-conscious investors.

Finally, in February 2022, Rio Tinto published a comprehensive external review of its workplace culture that reached "disturbing findings of bullying, sexual harassment, racism and other forms of discrimination throughout the company."[39] Rio Tinto immediately pledged to implement all recommendations. And the report itself is an indicator of good intentions. But shocking levels of sexual violence against women workers, and the dangerous nature of company camp and village facilities, would alone be a red line for many rights-conscious investors. And it is deeply troubling that this could occur in a firm with an apparently sincere commitment to human rights.

Problem 10.1 Mining of Critical Minerals for the Transition to Clean Energy

The Problem

The energy transition away from fossil fuels (in order to moderate human-caused climate change) requires massive quantities of many minerals[40] that are produced in ways that adversely affect the environment and human rights. Can we avoid imposing suffering on local communities in the pursuit of this global collective good?

Consider lithium, which is central to current battery technologies.[41] Demand is expected to more than double in the next five years and more than double again in the following five years. And most of that demand will need to be met by new mines. Extracting lithium from the brine underneath salt flats or in clay, however, uses unsustainably large quantities of water in arid regions and produces huge quantities of waste that can contaminate surrounding water and soil. Hardrock mining of lithium also produces dangerous waste. In countries with relatively good environmental regulations and enforcement, these "negative externalities" may be mitigated—but not entirely avoided. (Accidents are inevitable in even the best-run mining operations.) In countries with weaker regulation (e.g., Bolivia), local communities are already seeing environmental degradation and health impacts.[42]

Cobalt presents an even more dismal picture. The Democratic Republic of the Congo (DRC) produces about three-quarters of the world's cobalt—much of it in appalling conditions of unregulated "artisanal" mining. Even formal mining in the DRC involves dangerous working conditions and extensive environmental degradation.[43]

Although the situation is somewhat less dire in Indonesia, the world's second largest producer, there too workers and neighboring farmers, farms, and forests are being harmed.[44]

We truly *need* huge quantities of lithium and cobalt (and many other minerals). But we have almost no mechanisms to redress the harms caused to local individuals and communities in the pursuit of this global collective good.

Possible Solutions

Once more, we run up against the limitations of our system of national implementation of internationally recognized human rights. States bear not merely primary but in this case near-exclusive responsibility to protect the rights of those harmed by mining. Some states do a relatively good job. Others, though, perform less well. And still others lack the will or capacity to do much of anything.

Redressing the harms caused by mining demands protecting workers, preventing damage to local communities, remediating damage, and compensating the injured—which require sustained governmental commitment and capacity to enforce protective laws and policies against often powerful mining companies and those in the government and society who benefit from mining.

In the case of worker safety, a relatively small number of people are engaged in well-understood processes, in a limited area. This makes effective regulation *relatively* easy. (The risks associated with particular mining processes are well known and dangerous practices [and their consequences] can be relatively easily seen or discovered by trained monitors with access to worksites.) Firms have a relatively strong and direct interest in the health and safety of their workers—or at least some firms are susceptible to legal and political pressures to take their workers' rights seriously. And many improvements in workplace safety have modest costs, especially in relatively poor conditions.

Even here, though, national variation is extreme—and provides a striking illustration of the interdependence of civil and political rights and economic and social rights that we emphasized in Chapter 4.

In countries like Australia and Canada, with strong national and provincial workplace safety systems grounded in a deep commitment to protecting internationally recognized human rights, mining has been made *relatively* safe for miners. (In Australia, an average of about ten miners a year die in workplace accidents (out of a mining workforce of about 275,000). The average Australian has roughly the same chance of dying in an auto accident as an Australian miner has of dying in a workplace accident. Mining is about as safe/dangerous as driving to work.) Regulations are strong, enforcement is generally good, and workers, the press, and civil society organizations provide powerful external oversight.

Further Problems

In countries like China and Russia, though, even where regulations on paper seem sound, enforcement is problematic as a result of the largely unchecked power of national and local elites, corruption, the systematic suppression of workers' rights, a muzzled press, and the repression of autonomous civil society organizations. In countries like the DRC, workers are simply left to suffer—although firms often could act on their own to improve workplace safety if they wanted (or were pressured) to do so.

Perhaps the best locales for effective advocacy are countries like Bolivia and Indonesia, which have mixed records on civil and political rights that provide some openings for political, legal, and civil society action against the inadequate enforcement and corruption that plague their mining sectors. In such countries, if multinational mining firms are also subject to investor and government pressure "at home," there may even be possibilities for an alliance of local and transnational actors pressuring both firms and governments to improve the conditions in which miners work.

Preventing damage to local communities is a more difficult task. Threats come in at least three forms: daily exposure (usually by air), cumulative exposure to or buildup of contaminants that may be only modestly harmful at low levels but are seriously dangerous at higher doses, and accidents (especially the release of contaminated water from holding pits or ponds).

Mitigating daily exposure may in some cases be relatively easy or inexpensive. (For example, dust can often be reduced by pre-wetting soil or rock and even modest buffer zones around a site can sometimes dramatically reduce exposure.) But in contrast to workplace safety, the costs of containing dangerous byproducts often are relatively high. Furthermore, the relatively diffuse nature of the harm, and the fact that it often appears to be relatively modest in nature, makes mobilizing remedial action more difficult, especially when (as is often the case) those exposed are economically, socially, or politically disadvantaged, marginalized, or even despised.

The problems are even more severe with buildups and exposures over time. And because preventing accidents requires persistent and often expensive efforts over extended periods, efforts often fall victim not only to complacency, inattention, or just plain bad luck but also to misguided cost-cutting measures, weak governmental oversight, and corruption. Even relatively high-performing countries have less than perfect records in protecting neighboring communities and ecosystems. Most major mining countries have relatively (and often absolutely) poor records.

Remediation and compensation usually are expensive even for wealthy countries. And even where required by law, they are usually difficult to implement. A common pattern is protracted legal disputes over responsibility between firms and governments, leaving harmed communities to wait years or more for what prove to be poorly designed or inadequately resourced remediation or compensation schemes.

So far, we have not mentioned international mechanisms—because there are none. No multilateral mechanism exists to tax production or use in order to redistribute the proceeds to those harmed. And, as far as we are aware, no individual countries or groups of countries are seriously considering bilateral compensation schemes—which, even if they were implemented, probably would have only a modest impact.

International legal norms on workplace health and safety, developed principally through the International Labor Organization, only work when embodied in detailed national (and local) laws, regulations, and enforcement practices—bringing us back to the problems of national implementation.

Industry-specific "best practices" may be of some use. The case study of Rio Tinto, however, suggests that even the best-meaning mining firms will end up harming local communities. The more typical case is that workers, local communities, and local ecosystems suffer (more or less severe) harm from mining.

Individual firms can do relatively better or worse at mitigating their damages. Individual countries also can do relatively better or worse at protecting individuals, communities, and ecosystems. But given national and international politics as they are, it seems inescapable that the rights of many local communities will be sacrificed to the global public good of the energy transition—which may be more "green" than oil and gas but is hardly clean.

This conclusion may be depressing. But that sometimes just is how the world is. And it reminds us that human rights do not always by themselves tell us what we ought to do; that human rights provide an incomplete account of social justice.

Should we forgo lithium mining because the rights of some people will be violated, sometimes severely? Certainly not. This is clearly a case in which the utilitarian standard of the greatest good for the greatest number—here, a net average increase in utility for literally billions of people—takes precedence. (The trumps are themselves trumped; the *prima facie* priority of human rights gives way, all things considered, to a great global increase in average utility.) As political realists remark, prudence is a matter of choosing the lesser evil as the good.

Considerations of utility, however, do not eliminate the demands of human rights. Individuals, firms, and governments continue to have human rights obligations to workers and local communities that have been harmed by mining. Even where the policies and practices that cause suffering are justifiable by utilitarian public policy standards, rights-holders can and should insist on the no less real harms and injustices imposed on them. And they retain their claims to protection and remedy. They also can make the additional argument that those who are benefiting from their suffering owe them special obligations.

A human rights perspective also reminds us that the "negative externalities" of public policies that benefit great numbers often are concentrated in relatively small communities that suffer severely. And, in this case, the suffering is especially troubling because people are victimized largely based on where they have the (mis)fortune to live. Although not exactly the same as discrimination on the basis of race or religion, it is analogous. Suffering is imposed on a group defined by a morally irrelevant criterion.

Furthermore, these infringements of human rights, although in some sense "unintentional," are *knowing* and the result of public policy *choices*.

Human rights do not always provide the final answer to public policy questions. They must, however, be a central part of any reasoned policy debate. And, in this case, (and many others) human rights remind us that even defensible public policies may *also* be unjust; that they deprive people of the enjoyment of their internationally recognized human rights—and that these persisting deprivations demand remedy, even when our legal and political systems are unable to provide it. Human rights keeps the issue open and the pressure on.

Discussion Questions

1. How would you assess the mix of "business" and "human rights" concerns in the human rights policies and practices of firms? In general? In a particular country? In a particular industry or sector? In a particular firm that you know something about?
2. Are businesses more an underexploited resource in the struggle for human rights or a peripheral part of a global human rights regime dominated by states, NGOs, and multilateral institutions?
3. Is rights-conscious investing by individuals of more than symbolic importance? Is symbolic significance nonetheless significant?
4. If firms respond to human rights pressures largely to protect the values of brands, as often appears to be the case, what does that tell us about the kinds of pressures that are likely to have an effect—and the kinds of effects they are likely to be able (and unable) to achieve?
5. Human rights activism is largely about shaming and blaming. Which kinds of firms are more (or less) susceptible to shaming? What kinds of shaming strategies are which kinds of firms most susceptible to? How is shaming firms similar to and different from shaming states? Which types of firms? Which types of states?
6. Recently in the United States, some state legislatures have sought to discourage firms and investment managers from pursuing ESG policies and practices. Is there a rational policy basis for such measures? Should governments be in the business of telling businesses that they should not support human rights? Flipping the script, would it be acceptable (or advisable) for governments to *require* firms to have ESG goals and policies?
7. Should undergraduate and graduate business programs at colleges and universities require coursework on rights-conscious investing? How could this kind of requirement be "normalized" within such programs?

Suggested Readings

The Guiding Principles on Business and Human Rights (https://www.ohchr.org/documents/publications/guidingprinciplesbusinesshr_en.pdf), noted in Box 10.1, provide a good place to begin looking in more detail at the place of businesses in the global human rights regime. John Ruggie, who was a leading force in the development of the Guiding Principles, has written two useful articles on their development and impact: John Gerard Ruggie, "The Social Construction of the UN Guiding Principles on Business and Human Rights," in Surya Deva and David Birchall and Ruggie, John Gerard, Caroline Rees, and Rachel Davis, eds., *Research Handbook on Human Rights and Business* (2020). "Ten Years After: From UN Guiding Principles to Multi-Fiduciary Obligations," *Business and Human Rights Journal* 6, no. 2 (2021):179–197. Choudhury, Barnali. *The UN Guiding Principles on Business and Human Rights: A Commentary* (Edward Elgar Publishing, 2023) provides a detailed point-by-point commentary. See also Brigitte Hamm, "The Struggle for Legitimacy in Business and Human Rights Regulation: A Consideration of the Processes Leading to the UN Guiding Principles and an International Treaty," *Human Rights Review* 23, no. 1 (2022): 103–125.

Florian Wettstein, *Business and Human Rights: Ethical, Legal, and Managerial Perspectives* (Cambridge University Press, 2022) is a useful textbook on the subject. See also Ilias Bantekas and Michael Ashley Stein, *The Cambridge Companion to Business and Human Rights Law* (Cambridge University Press, 2021) and Peter T. Muchlinski, *Advanced Introduction to Business and Human Rights* (Edward Elgar Publishing Limited, 2022). Three large edited volumes provide comprehensive overviews of the field: Surya Deva and David Birchall, eds., *Research Handbook on Human Rights and Business* (Edward Elgar Publishing, 2020); Ilias Bantekas and Michael Ashley Stein, *The Cambridge Companion to Business and Human Rights Law* (Cambridge University Press, 2021); and Jan Wouters, eds., *Research Handbook on Global Governance, Business and Human Rights* (Edward Elgar Publishing, 2022). Robert McCorquodale, *Business and Human Rights* (Oxford University Press, 2024) is a recent overview focused on international law.

Herman Aguinis and Ante Glavas, "What We Know and Don't Know about Corporate Social Responsibility," *Journal of Management* 38 (2012): 932–968 is a classic work on corporate social responsibility. Among more recent works, Fatima, Tahniyath and Said Elbanna. "Corporate Social Responsibility (CSR) Implementation: A Review and a Research Agenda Towards an Integrative Framework," *Journal of Business Ethics* 183 (2022): 105–121 and Carol Newman, et al., "Corporate Social Responsibility in a Competitive Business Environment," *The Journal of Development Studies* 56 (2020): 1455–1472 provide useful introductory overviews. See also McPhail et al., "Reimagining Business and Management as a Force for Good," *British Journal of Management* 35, no. 3 (2024): 1099–1112 and Edith Ebele Agu, Toluwalase Vanessa Iyelolu, Courage Idemudia, and Tochukwu Ignatius Ijomah, "Exploring the Relationship between Sustainable Business Practices and Increased Brand Loyalty," *International Journal of Management & Entrepreneurship Research* 6, no. 8 (2024): 2463–2475.

Good recent work on ESG policies and their impacts include Hadiqa Ahmad, Muhammad Yaqub, and Seung Hwan Lee, "Environmental-, Social-, and Governance-Related Factors for Business Investment and Sustainability: A Scientometric Review of Global Trends," *Environment, Development and Sustainability* (2023): 1–23; Delgado-Ceballos, et al., "Connecting the Sustainable Development Goals to Firm-Level Sustainability and ESG Factors: The Need for Double Materiality," *Business Research Quarterly* 26 (2022): 2; and Almut Schilling-Vacaflor and Maria-Therese Gustafsson, "Towards More Sustainable Global Supply Chains? Company Compliance with New Human Rights and Environmental

Due Diligence Laws," *Environmental Politics* 33, no. 3 (2024): 422–443. On the 2024 EU Directive on Corporate Sustainability, see Nicolas Bueno et al., "The EU Directive on Corporate Sustainability Due Diligence (CSDD): The Final Political Compromise," *Business and Human Rights Journal* 9, no. 2 (2024): 294–300.

Notes

1 Freedom House's Global Freedom score provides a rough and ready way to operationalize this for civil and political rights, with "Free" corresponding to what we are calling very good (90+) and good (70–89) records, "Partly Free" (40–69) to what we call mixed records, and "Not Free" to poor (16–39) and very bad (0–15) overall records. https://freedomhouse.org/countries/freedom-world/scores?sort=asc&order=Country. Unfortunately, there is no readily available single measure for economic and social rights. Below we use the HDI as a very rough proxy that in its bottom range (low development) usually accurately identifies poor and very bad conditions. See https://hdr.undp.org/sites/default/files/2021-22_HDR/HDR21-22_Statistical_Annex_HDI_Table.xlsx.

2 www.ilo.org/resource/ilo-1998-declaration-fundamental-principles-and-rights-work-and-its-follow.

3 www.ilo.org/global/topics/forced-labour/lang--en/index.htm provides a useful introduction to the topic.

4 www.ilo.org/global/topics/child-labour/lang--en/index.htm is a useful introduction.

5 *Oxford English Dictionary*. There is also a weaker sense of "complicit" as "involved knowingly or with passive compliance." This falls between our categories of (indirect) association and (direct) complicity.

6 https://freedomhouse.org/country/singapore.

7 Although many of the details have changed, the analysis in Rita Abrahamsen and Michael C. Williams, *The Globalisation of Private Security. Country Report: Nigeria* (Aberystwyth: Department of International Politics, University of Wales, 2005) remains insightful. https://gsdrc.org/document-library/the-globalisation-of-private-security-country-report-nigeria/.

8 This responsibility may even be legal. For example, Shell has been subject to suits in various jurisdictions for its activities in Nigeria over nearly two decades. See, for example, (www.business-humanrights.org/en/latest-news/shell-settles-human-rights-suit-for-155m/), https://cja.org/what-we-do/litigation/amicus-briefs/kiobel-v-shell/, https://www.reuters.com/world/africa/nigerias-top-court-says-shells-appeal-should-be-heard-after-oil-spill-claim-2024-01-05/#:~:text=The%20case%2C%20one%20of%20several,that%20damaged%20waterways%20and%20farms, and https://corpaccountabilitylab.org/calblog/2024/1/3/shell-to-face-constitutional-claims-for-violating-the-right-to-a-clean-environment.

9 Universal Declaration of Human Rights, Article 23(3).

10 The first three cases were actually posed to one of us (Donnelly) when he was consulting for a medium-sized investment management firm trying to incorporate human rights considerations more fully and more deeply into their investment practices.

11 https://cleanclothes.org/unsafe-workplaces provides a useful brief introduction. In a bit more depth, focusing on Asia, see https://www.ilo.org/wcmsp5/groups/public/---ed_protect/---protrav/---travail/documents/projectdocumentation/wcms_681644.pdf.

12 These (and all other otherwise unattributed) figures are from the company's 2021 Annual Report. https://static.inditex.com/annual_report_2021/en.html.

13 https://freedomhouse.org/countries/freedom-world/scores?sort=asc&order=Country, last accessed December 14, 2022.

14 https://hdr.undp.org/sites/default/files/2021–22_HDR/HDR21–22_Statistical_Annex_HDI_Table.xlsx.

15 Similar to China, Turkey's overall score is pulled down considerably by its very bad record in the Kurdish region. And the other four countries have significantly better ratings on civil liberties than political rights (which would be significant if one argued that civil liberties, in general, are of greater day-to-day significance for the activities of businesses and employees). In 2021, Inditex had 451 suppliers in China, 194 in Turkey, 173 in Morocco, 48 in Pakistan, and less than 10 in both Vietnam and Cambodia. https://www.statista.com/statistics/1099842/number-of-product-suppliers-of-inditex-group-by-region/

16 https://www.industriall-union.org/inditex.

17 It has a better-than-average benchmark ranking from Know the Chain, which monitors practices to prevent forced labor. https://knowthechain.org/benchmark/?ranking_year=2020&ranking_sector=apparel-footwear. See also https://static.zara.net/static/pdfs/UK/act-on-modern-slavery/act-on-modern-slavery-en_UK-20220729.pdf.

18 The Code can be accessed through a link on https://www.inditex.com/itxcomweb/en/group/our-ethical-commitment. https://static.inditex.com/annual_report_2021/en/documents/human-rights-2021.pdf provides an overview of the firm's human rights practices and assessment methodologies.

19 https://static.inditex.com/annual_report_2021/en/documents/statement-of-non-financial-information-2021.pdf. Section 6 addresses the firm's reporting principles and indicators.

20 The Business and Human Rights Center has asked for and received responses from Inditex on twenty-one reports of abuses, which we think presents a useful sampling of the kinds of issues that arise. See https://www.business-humanrights.org/en/companies/inditex/#associated_responses.

21 See https://www.worldbenchmarkingalliance.org/corporate-rights-human-benchmark-2017–2019/ and https://www.worldbenchmarkingalliance.org/publication/chrb/rankings/segment/apparel/.

22 For definitions and a full description of the methodology, see https://assets.worldbenchmarkingalliance.org/app/uploads/2021/04/CHRB2019MethodologyAGAPEX.pdf and https://www.worldbenchmarkingalliance.org/publication/chrb/methodology/.

23 For a skeptical view of the impact of human rights monitoring in the textile sector, see Justine Nolan, "Regulating Human Rights in the Textile Sector: Smoke and Mirrors," in *Research Handbook on Global Governance, Business and Human Rights*, edited by Jan Wouters et al. (Edward Elgar Publishing, 2022).

24 https://static.inditex.com/annual_report_2021/en/positive-impact/community-investment.html.

25 https://qz.com/1988896/under-pressure-in-china-zara-deleted-a-statement-about-xinjiang, https://www.globaltimes.cn/page/202103/1219411.shtml.

26 This is down from nearly six hundred in 2019, although the decline seems to have been entirely for retail business reasons, including a company-wide emphasis on online sales (which increased by 16 percent in China in 2023). https://www.statista.com/statistics/674653/number-of-zara-stores-by-country/#:~:text=Zara%20is%20the%20Spanish%20clothing,as%20shown%20in%20this%20statistic, https://www.reuters.com/business/retail-consumer/zara-owner-inditex-slashes-china-stores-digital-focus-2024-03-14/.

27 See, for example, https://www.ohchr.org/en/documents/country-reports/ohchr-assessment-human-rights-concerns-xinjiang-uyghur-autonomous-region, https://www.hrw.org/report/2021/04/19/break-their-lineage-break-their-roots/chinas-crimes-against-humanity-targeting, https://www.hrw.org/world-report/2022/country-chapters/china-and-tibet.

28 www.riotinto.com/en (last accessed December 15, 2022). See also www.riotinto.com/en/invest/reports/annual-report.

29 Direct comparisons across time are not possible because of changes in the methodology and what appears to be a tightening of standards. These figures are useful only for comparisons across the sector in a given year.

30 www.riotinto.com/en/sustainability/health-safety-wellbeing.

31 https://theecologist.org/2022/dec/02/villagers-demand-rio-tinto-compensation. There are also broader ongoing disputes about waste from the mine. https://www.pwyp.org/wp-content/

uploads/2015/03/2021-INVESTOR-BRIEFING-ON-QMM-MADAGASCAR.pdf, https://news.mongabay.com/2019/12/concerns-about-radioactive-contamination-dog-rio-tintos-madagascar-mine/.

32 www.bbc.com/news/world-europe-55748674.

33 In 2016, Rio Tinto fired two top executives for possibly illegal payments (https://www.reuters.com/article/us-rio-tinto-guinea-terminates/rio-tinto-fires-two-top-executives-over-guinea-payments-idUSKBN13B2Y4),

34 A bribery investigation was opened in the UK (https://www.theguardian.com/business/2017/jul/24/rio-tinto-sfo-investigation-guinea-suspected-corruption), which apparently continued at least into 2020 (https://www.ft.com/content/66aeb1b9-7f7a-4713–866c-c756d82bf3c5), but seems not to have led to either prosecution or a deferred prosecution agreement.

35 https://www.reuters.com/article/rio-tinto-plc-fraud-timeline/timeline-rio-tinto-faces-fraud-charges-over-mozambique-coal-investment-idUKL4N1MT21Y.

36 https://www.sec.gov/news/press-release/2017–196, https://www.reuters.com/article/uk-rio-tinto-mozambique-probe/u-s-judge-rejects-sec-bid-to-expand-rio-tinto-fraud-lawsuit-on-mozambique-coal-business-idUSKCN2AW0NL.

37 www.thetimes.co.uk/article/record-fine-leaves-rio-tinto-in-a-hole-ftpzsgld7, https://globalinvestigationsreview.com/article/rio-tinto-fined-in-australia.

38 https://assets.worldbenchmarkingalliance.org/app/uploads/2023/04/Special_process_for_assessing_RioTinto_2023CHRB.pdf provides a brief summary and an assessment of Rio Tinto's response.

39 www.riotinto.com/en/news/releases/2022/rio-tinto-releases-external-review-of-workplace-culture.

40 International Energy Agency, *The Role of Critical Minerals in Clean Energy Transitions* (Paris, 2021, https://www.iea.org/reports/the-role-of-critical-minerals-in-clean-energy-transitions/mineral-requirements-for-clean-energy-transitions); IEA, *Global Critical Minerals Outlook 2024* (www.iea.org/reports/global-critical-minerals-outlook-2024).

41 *The Lithium Market* (https://lithiumharvest.com/knowledge/lithium/the-lithium-mining-market/), although produced by a firm (Lithium Harvest) involved in alternative forms of production, provides a solid overview.

42 Aylwin, José, et al. *Lithium and Human Rights in the High Andean Salt Flats of Argentina, Bolivia and Chile.* International Research Development Centre of Canada (2025) (https://observatorio.cl/wp-content/uploads/2025/08/lithium_and_human_rights_in_the_high_andean_salt_flats_of_argentina_bolivia_and_chile.pdf).

43 Baumann-Pauly, Dorothée. *Cobalt Mining in the Democratic Republic of the Congo: Addressing Root Causes of Human Rights Abuses.* NYU Stern Center for Business and Human (2023).

44 Nasution, Miftahul Jannah, et al., "The Impact of Increasing Nickel Production on Forest and Environment in Indonesia: A Review," *Jurnal Sylva Lestari* 12, no. 3 (2024): 549–579. (https://sylvalestari.fp.unila.ac.id/index.php/JHT/article/download/847/650). (Cobalt is a secondary product of nickel mining in Indonesia.)

Part III

Contemporary Issues

11 Humanitarian Intervention and the Responsibility to Protect

A primary organizing principle of a system of sovereign states is the norm of **nonintervention**. International human rights law conforms to that principle. Participating in human rights regimes does not entail a loss of sovereignty. Quite the contrary, states exercise their sovereignty when they choose to be bound by international human rights obligations and agree to be scrutinized by international human rights institutions (see Chapter 5). But, as we have seen, this is a system of mild monitoring that only the overly sensitive (or guilty) would call "interference." Nothing in the array of human rights law and institutions authorizes intervention, let alone coercive punishment, for noncompliance with human rights norms.

The principal exceptions are systematic, massive, and flagrant violations of certain key rights that lead to significant loss of life and destruction of livelihoods. Such violations may rise to the level of international crimes. And, under certain circumstances, the international community may be empowered to intervene coercively. This chapter looks at the issue of humanitarian intervention and the responsibility to protect against genocide and other humanitarian crimes.

This chapter is a long one. It is written, though, so that it can be read in parts. Sections 2.1–2.3, dealing with Bosnia, Rwanda, and Kosovo, can be read separately (or skipped as time or interest dictates). The same is true of the case studies in Sections 5.1 (East Timor), 5.2 (Libya), and 5.3 (Sudan). Similarly, Sections 3, 4, and 6, which address the authority to intervene, the dimensions of the right to humanitarian intervention, and issues of justifiability, can also be read a la carte. Our advice, if you are not planning to read the whole chapter, is, after reading the next section, which defines genocide and humanitarian crimes, to look first at a couple of the case studies, as your interests dictate, and then pay careful attention to Section 4, which sketches the meaning and the parameters of the right to humanitarian intervention (and the responsibility to protect) in contemporary international law and politics. We also think that most readers will find the general assessment and conclusion about the future of humanitarian intervention and the responsibility to protect in Sections 6 and 7 of interest.

DOI: 10.4324/9781003373520-14

1 Genocide and Crimes against Humanity

The Convention on the Prevention and Punishment of the Crime of Genocide was adopted by the UN General Assembly on December 9, 1948, the day before the Universal Declaration. This reflected the central role of the Holocaust in crystallizing international concern with human rights. The Genocide Convention defines genocide as a crime and creates a separate set of obligations for addressing it. Genocide, however, is not mentioned in either the Universal Declaration of Human Rights or the International Human Rights Covenants. There are separate bodies of genocide law and international human rights law— although in practice they regularly intersect.

The Convention defined a new crime in international law: genocide, "the intent to destroy, in whole or in part, a national, ethnical, racial, or religious group," whether committed in time of peace or of war. Genocidal acts include killing members of the group; causing serious mental or physical harm to members of the group; deliberately inflicting conditions on the group "calculated to bring about its destruction"; imposing measures intended to prevent births within the group; forcibly transferring children of the group to another group; and conspiracy to commit genocide, direct and public incitement to commit genocide, and complicity in genocide.

The Convention establishes several obligations of states with respect to *preventing* genocide and *punishing the perpetrators*. Article VIII also allows signatories to call upon competent organs of the United Nations to prevent or suppress acts of genocide. It does not, however, establish any specific parameters for doing so. And, by implication, it does not empower states to take action outside the framework of the UN Charter.

In the 1990s, however, genocide and other humanitarian atrocities in Europe, Africa, and Asia led to the development of a *practice* of armed **humanitarian intervention**. This in part reflected a new geopolitical environment, in which rivalry between the superpowers no longer prevented humanitarian action. It also, though, was a response to the unusually brutal character of these conflicts, which were wars within, rather than between, states that largely ignored the traditional distinction between civilians and soldiers, often intentionally targeting the civilian population of the other side—even defining those civilians as "the enemy."

Unlike genocide, which is a crime whose characteristics are clearly defined by a legal convention to which states have agreed, there is no similar convention on **crimes against humanity**.[1] Rather, these crimes are defined in a variety of international legal instruments that make up the corpus of **international humanitarian law** (sometimes called the law of armed conflict, although crimes against humanity may be carried out during times of war or peace). Emerging out of customary international law, international humanitarian law has been codified in the Hague and Geneva Conventions, the practice of the Nuremberg and Tokyo war crimes tribunals and the ad hoc tribunals for the former Yugoslavia and Rwanda, the Statute and practice of the International Criminal Court, and the actions of various other bodies (e.g., UN Security Council Resolution 1820 of 2008, which established that rape could be a war crime and a crime against humanity).

This chapter begins by looking at cases from the 1990s that led to the emergence of a new set of norms on humanitarian intervention. In addition to the former Yugoslavia, particularly Bosnia-Herzegovina and Kosovo (which introduced **ethnic cleansing** to the world's vocabulary), we also discuss the dramatically contrasting examples of Rwanda and East Timor. Together, they document the acceptance, in barely a decade, of a right to armed humanitarian intervention. After examining the codification of these changes in the language of the responsibility to protect (R2P) (Section 3), we turn to a discussion of the complexities of these emerging norms and practices in two more recent cases, Sudan and Libya. Then, after addressing some of the complexities in justifying humanitarian intervention, this chapter concludes with a discussion of the civil war in Syria (2011–2024) and the ongoing war in Gaza.

2 Case Studies from the 1990s

2.1 *Bosnia*

Yugoslavia was created at the end of World War I, an assemblage of the previously independent states of Serbia and Montenegro; the former Austro-Hungarian territories of Slovenia, Istria, Dalmatia, Croatia-Slavonia, Vojvodina, and Bosnia-Herzegovina; and Macedonia, taken from the Ottoman Empire's last European holdings. Although the dominant Serbs actively discriminated against other ethnic groups, different groups lived together more or less harmoniously (except under Nazi occupation during World War II, when Serbs were targets of genocide by the Ustasha, a local fascist group operating a puppet regime in Croatia).

After World War II, the communists, the strongest force in the resistance to Nazi rule, reorganized Yugoslavia under the leadership of Josip Broz Tito. In a country in which every ethnic group was a minority (roughly two-fifths were Serbs and a fifth Croats), a federal political system granted substantial power to six republics (Serbia, Croatia, Slovenia, Bosnia-Herzegovina, Macedonia, and Montenegro) and two autonomous regions within Serbia (Kosovo and Vojvodina).

For three decades, the system worked tolerably well. (The principal exception was the treatment of ethnic Albanians in the Kosovo region of Serbia.) Tito's death in 1980, however, removed the final arbiter from a system with immense potential for squabbling and deadlock. The accumulated inefficiencies of decades of control by nine separate communist bureaucracies (six republics, two autonomous regions, and the federal government) ended the economic growth that had greased the system. By the mid-1980s, Yugoslavia faced a political and economic crisis well beyond the capabilities of its ruling communist functionaries.

2.1.1 The Breakup of Yugoslavia

In 1987, Slobodan Milošević seized on Serbian nationalism to consolidate his rapid rise to power in the Serbian Republic. Milošević skillfully manipulated memories of Ustasha brutality, fostering hatred of Croats. He also invoked the quasi-mythic grandeur of Serbia's fourteenth-century Nemanjić dynasty. He aimed to paint Muslims, who made up about one-sixth of the country's population, as enemies, successors of the Turks who had defeated medieval Serbia.

Using tactics made famous by Hitler, Milošević and his front group, the Committee for the Protection of Kosovo Serbs and Montenegrins, organized more than hundred mass protest demonstrations with average turnouts of more than 50,000 people. By February 1989, the last vestiges of regional autonomy in Vojvodina and Kosovo were eliminated. In addition, Milošević's allies had been installed in Montenegro, leaving him in firm control of half the country. Kosovo, whose population was 90 percent ethnic Albanian, was particularly severely repressed.

The other republics, especially Slovenia and Croatia, had the legal and political power to block this protofascist Serbian imperialism. But this only led Milošević to rely increasingly on extralegal means. For example, arms shipments for the Yugoslav National Army "inexplicably" began appearing in Knin, Croatia's principal ethnically Serbian city, in the fall of 1990. After negotiations to maintain a loose federal system failed, Slovenia and Croatia, fearing the worst, declared independence on June 25, 1991.

Slovenia was ethnically homogeneous and prosperous and did not share a border with Serbia. Within weeks, it established its effective independence with the support of the European Community (the predecessor to the current European Union). In the last four months of 1991, however, Serbs and Croats fought a brutal war that targeted opposition civilians no less than opposing armies. When the fifteenth ceasefire—reached on January 2, 1992, and supported by 14,000 peacekeepers of the United Nations Protection Force (UNPROFOR) in the former Yugoslavia—held, international attention shifted to the even more brutal conflict in Bosnia-Herzegovina (hereafter referred to as Bosnia).

Bosnia was in many ways a microcosm of Yugoslavia, itself a republic of minorities. In the 1991 census, 44 percent of the population identified themselves as Muslims, 32 percent as Serbs, 17 percent as Croats, and 7 percent as Yugoslavs or other. In fact, Bosnia was the only Yugoslav republic without an ethnic majority.

Although Bosnia had been a place of considerable ethnic tolerance, especially in the capital of Sarajevo, when war did come, it hit with unprecedented ferocity. And Bosnia's Muslims were particularly vulnerable because they lacked the support of neighboring co-nationals.

Separatist Serbs gained control of two-thirds of the territory of Bosnia. They perfected and popularized the strategy of ethnic cleansing, introduced by Croatian Serbs the preceding year, which aimed to rid "Serbian" territory of Muslim (and Croat) residents through systematic terror and sporadic murder. Relief supplies were blocked. Villages and cities were shelled from a distance when they could not be shot up and burned at close range. Captured men were routinely tortured or murdered, often en masse. Women, children, and the elderly were sometimes shot, often physically abused, but more typically "merely" forced to flee. And Serbian soldiers systematically, on orders from superiors, raped young Muslim women to degrade them and shame their families.

2.1.2 Responding to the Bosnian Genocide

The international community was often, and in many ways justly, criticized for doing too little, too late. However, it did not sit by and idly watch the genocide, as it had during the Cold War in places like Uganda and Cambodia.

The UN Security Council imposed an arms embargo on all parties and placed Serbia under a comprehensive economic embargo. A special war crimes tribunal was created. Peacekeepers were sent to protect civilians and facilitate the delivery of humanitarian assistance. And much of the international community exerted considerable diplomatic and political pressure on Serbia and its Bosnian allies. When a peace agreement was finally signed at Dayton in December 1995, there were 50,000 UN peacekeepers in the former Yugoslavia, at an annual cost of about $2 billion (about $4 billion in current prices); 3,000 humanitarian workers were in the field; and the Office of the United Nations High Commissioner for Refugees alone was spending $500 million a year on humanitarian assistance.

Initial responses, however, were timid and largely reflected geopolitical concerns, especially a desire to keep Yugoslavia intact. The international community was willing to allow immense suffering in order to prevent Yugoslavia from becoming a precedent for an even more catastrophic breakup of the Soviet Union—which, it must be remembered, had not yet dissolved. (There was no way of knowing then that its breakup would be anywhere near as peaceful as it ultimately proved to be.) By the time the war entered its Bosnian phase, however, the Soviet Union had already broken up, and the European Community had recognized the independence of Croatia and Slovenia. Although geopolitical concerns continued to intrude, for the remainder of the conflict, the United States, Europe, the United Nations, and even Russia maintained sustained efforts in humanitarian assistance, peacekeeping, and diplomacy that were without parallel during the Cold War.

2.1.2.1 Multilateral Human Rights Agencies

In August 1992, at the first special session in its history, the UN Commission on Human Rights appointed Tadeusz Mazowiecki, former prime minister of Poland, as special rapporteur. Never before had the Commission responded with anything even close to such speed. And the vigor of its response was equally striking. The Security Council also acted (relatively) rapidly and with resolve. An arms embargo and trade sanctions were followed by the creation, in February 1993, of the International Criminal Tribunal for the former Yugoslavia, which by 1996 was actively prosecuting war criminals.

These initiatives, however, responded to, rather than tried to stop, the genocide—because there was no appetite among any of the great powers to use force. And, barring armed intervention, there was no way to stop Croatia, Serbia, or Bosnia's Serbs from seeking to realize their objectives through violence.

2.1.2.2 Humanitarian Assistance

Humanitarian assistance aims to cope with some of the most pressing human consequences of war (and other political and natural disasters). Humanitarian workers seek not to prevent or punish violence but to ease the burden on civilian victims. Even these limited tasks, though, undercut the Serbian strategies of pursuing ethnic cleansing in the countryside and strangling Sarajevo. The Bosnian Serbs therefore saw humanitarian assistance as intensely political—which it was, given their strategy—and consistently used all means in their power, including force, to stop international relief from reaching its targets. (Muslim and Croat forces much more irregularly prevented aid deliveries.)

The international humanitarian response in Bosnia was swift, sustained, and relatively effective. The United Nations used strong diplomatic pressure and limited force to deliver aid to more than 2 million people. Nonetheless, the suffering in Bosnia was horrible. More than one-third of Bosnia's people were forced to flee their homes. Most of the Bosnian Muslims who did not flee were forced to endure extended Serbian sieges. The more than 200,000 deaths in Croatia and Bosnia were proportionally equivalent to the deaths of about 5 million Americans.

Nevertheless, to have dramatically reduced this suffering, those providing assistance would have had to issue a credible military threat to enter the conflict on the side of Bosnia's Muslims. Leading states simply were not willing to endorse such an option, preferring instead to rely on diplomacy, humanitarian assistance, and sanctions short of the use of force.

2.1.2.3 Peacekeeping

The soldiers that the United Nations sent in under the banner of UNPROFOR were peacekeepers. **Peacekeeping** involves interposing neutral forces *with the permission of the belligerents* in order to monitor or maintain a truce or settlement agreement. Peacekeepers are lightly armed and are authorized to use force only for self-defense. The aim of peacekeeping is not to repulse or punish an aggressor. That is a job for collective security enforcement, as in the Gulf War of 1991.

UNPROFOR's mandate was restricted to limiting the extent and severity of the fighting. The international community condemned ethnic cleansing. It was willing to prosecute those responsible once the fighting ended. But it would not take the military steps necessary to end the conflict.

UNPROFOR aimed less to prevent war (soldiers shooting soldiers) than war crimes (soldiers massacring civilians). To the Serbs, however, this represented a hostile external world frustrating their objectives—which they were well on their way to achieving when the United Nations intervened. They thus focused their efforts on subverting UNPROFOR and completing the ethnic cleansing of "their" country. This was a near-certain recipe for disaster.

The mission of UNPROFOR came to rely heavily on the institution of United Nations Protected Areas, or "safe areas." First established in 1992 in Croatia, they were extended to Bosnia in 1993. In July 1995, however, the "protected area" of Srebrenica was overrun, as an appalled and ashamed UN contingent found itself able only to stand by and watch. Adult men were separated from the rest of the refugees, who were sent fleeing. Of the "protected" population of about 40,000, more than 7,000 were slaughtered and buried in mass graves.

With people now dying as an unintended but very real consequence of the "best efforts" of the international community, the West, and particularly the United States, finally intervened. The North Atlantic Treaty Organization's (NATO) intensified air strikes, coupled with the Croatian victories in Krajina and renewed pressure applied to Milošević, forced the Bosnian Serbs to the negotiating table. A marathon three-week session at Wright-Patterson Air Force Base in Dayton, Ohio, backed by immense US pressure, produced a peace agreement on December 14, 1995.

2.1.2.4 Assessing the Bosnian Intervention

Viewed in isolation, Bosnia appears as largely a failure of international action. Nonetheless, Bosnia and its people were, quite literally, kept alive. More than 2 million people received humanitarian assistance. International action helped to keep Sarajevo from falling, thus averting an even greater disaster. The arms embargo prevented an even larger bloodbath (especially if one attributes part of the relatively good record of the Bosnian Muslims to their lack of opportunities to exact revenge). And UN peacekeepers sent to the border of Macedonia in December 1992 stopped the fighting from moving East and South.

Taking a comparative perspective, this suggests that Bosnia was not merely a success but a major breakthrough. *Relatively* strong international action came *relatively* rapidly. In the end, armed force was brought to bear. And international action was decisive in ending the conflict. Bosnia marked a crucial step in transforming international responses to genocide.

Precedents, however, are made by later actions that treat them as constraining. They do not automatically cause comparable action in the future. Furthermore, their meaning changes as they become embedded in streams of action. The meaning of Bosnia emerged only as the international community confronted new genocides in Rwanda, Kosovo, and East Timor.

2.2 Rwanda

If Bosnia is the success story of the early 1990s, Rwanda was the great, and horribly tragic, failure.

Ethnic conflict in Rwanda was in large measure the creation of Belgian colonial rule. After receiving control over Rwanda (and Burundi) from Germany after World War I, the Belgians exacerbated the tensions between the two main groups in the territory, the majority Hutu and the minority Tutsi. After having purged Hutus from the largely Tutsi elite, the Belgians used the Tutsi as an instrument of colonial domination, provoking understandable resentment from the Hutu majority.

In 1959, as independence was approaching, the Belgians decided to switch their support from the Tutsi to the Hutu, whose resentment turned into the violent assertion of political dominance once they took over the state. Some 20,000 Tutsis were massacred, and another 200,000 were forced to flee. In the ensuing years, sporadic ethnic violence, with short bursts of genocidal killing (particularly in 1964 and 1974), marked politics in Rwanda (and Burundi). The staggering scope of the violence that occurred in 1994, however, was unprecedented.

The prelude to genocide began in October 1990 when the Rwandan Patriotic Front (RPF), made up primarily of Tutsis living in refugee camps in Uganda, invaded Rwanda. The Hutu-dominated military government of Juvénal Habyarimana portrayed this as an attempt to (re)impose Tutsi domination and responded with increased repression. A cease-fire to this inconclusive conflict was negotiated in the summer of 1992, followed in August 1993 by a fragile peace agreement signed in Arusha, Tanzania (the Arusha Accords).

Meanwhile, the Habyarimana government and its radical Hutu supporters established a network of Hutu militias (Interahamwe), which by the spring of 1994 numbered about 30,000 fighters. Radio stations, especially the government-controlled Radio Mille Collines, spread increasingly virulent anti-Tutsi propaganda. From the national cabinet down to local mayors, preparations were laid for a massive, organized campaign of violence against Tutsis and political opponents of the regime. The killings began on the night of April 6, 1994, after the plane carrying the presidents of both Rwanda and Burundi was shot down on its final approach to Kigali International Airport. (Responsibility remains a matter of considerable controversy, but forensic evidence points to radical elements within the Rwandan Armed Forces.)

Individual contingents of the United Nations Assistance Mission in Rwanda (UNAMIR), a peacekeeping force observing implementation of the Arusha Accords, tried to shelter some civilians. The formal mandate of UNAMIR, however, restricted the troops to monitoring. In any case, UN peacekeepers themselves quickly became targets. Ten Belgian soldiers were captured on April 7, tortured, and murdered.

Two weeks later, the Security Council unanimously agreed to cut the UNAMIR force from 2,500 to 270, despite estimates that more than 100,000 civilians had already been massacred. Not until April 30, when hundreds of thousands had been killed, did the Security Council even condemn the violence. Even then, it pointedly refused to call it a genocide, admitting only that "acts of genocide" had been committed. The United States, as late as June, also continued to refer only to "acts of genocide," wary of the international legal obligation under the Genocide Convention to respond.

The world stood by and watched while more than 750,000 Rwandans out of a prewar population of about 6,750,000 (proportionally the equivalent of roughly 30 million deaths in the United States) were butchered in a little more than three months. And butchered is a brutally accurate term: the machete was the weapon of choice of many of the génocidaires. Another 2 million Rwandans fled to Zaire (now the Democratic Republic of the Congo).

All of this was particularly troubling because information was available—in the media, at the United Nations, and in the major governments involved (France, the United States, and Belgium)—that genocide was imminent. In January 1994, the commander of the UN force, General Roméo Dallaire, asked for, but was denied, permission to confiscate the weapons of the Interahamwe. Throughout February and March, General Dallaire pleaded, with increasing desperation, for reinforcements and a more robust mandate—but the Security Council refused.

As we have noted, the United Nations is an intergovernmental organization, made up of and controlled by its member-states. The Security Council is dominated by its five permanent members (China, France, Russia, the United States, and the United Kingdom), each of whom can veto Security Council action. In the case of Rwanda, four of the permanent powers actively opposed UN action—especially France. The United States had recently been forced to make a humiliating withdrawal from Somalia and was unwilling to consider involvement in another small, fractious African country. France, which considered itself to have special geopolitical interests in Central Africa, had particularly strong relations with the Habyarimana government and had substantially increased its military support to the Rwandan government in response to the RPF invasion in 1990. Britain appeared willing to consider stronger action but had no desire to lead on the issue of Rwanda. Russia and China had "principled" objections, insisting that the conflict was an internal Rwanda. All these political forces conspired against UN intervention. And, in a particularly cruel irony, Rwanda happened to occupy one of the ten rotating seats on the Security Council and used this position to try to minimize the scope and severity of the problem.

Most of the killing occurred in the first six weeks. By the time the Security Council did finally act, in late June 1994, most of the killing had ended. Furthermore, the French-led intervention—Operation Turquoise—authorized by the Security Council ostensibly to protect civilians from further genocidal acts and from RPF countermeasures, established a "safe zone" in the Southwest of the country that allowed tens of thousands of perpetrators to escape into neighboring Zaire (now the Democratic Republic of the Congo), under the protection of French military forces.

Because of the low-tech nature of the genocide, even as few as several thousand troops could have stopped much, perhaps even most, of the killing. However, those states with the knowledge and power to do something chose inaction. In their defense, few expected anything like the scope of violence that occurred—although a willingness to tolerate tens of thousands of deaths is still shameful. As the tragedy unfolded, though, and appreciation grew of the opportunity for humanitarian action that had been forfeited, a deep sense of shame spread through the international community.

2.3 Kosovo

When the next major humanitarian crisis arose, in Kosovo in 1998 and 1999, the contrasting lessons of Bosnia and Rwanda weighed heavily on the minds of decision-makers and public opinion. Key international actors, led by the administration of President Bill Clinton in the United States and the government of Prime Minister Tony Blair in Britain, seem to have learned from Bosnia and Rwanda that successful humanitarian intervention was both (politically and logistically) possible and (morally, perhaps even politically) necessary.

Kosovo was an autonomous region of Serbia, not a republic of Yugoslavia. This was crucial, because when Yugoslavia (and then the Soviet Union) broke up, it did so according to the old internal boundaries. Thus, federal republics (such as Serbia, Bosnia, and Slovenia and, in the USSR, Russia, Kazakhstan, and Georgia) easily received local and international recognition of their independence. Other internal units, such as Kosovo in Serbia (Yugoslavia) and Chechnya in Russia (USSR), did not.

As discussed above, this left Kosovo's ethnically Albanian population under the increasingly brutal domination of Serbia. Throughout the mid-1990s, the Kosovo Liberation Army carried out sporadic, quite ineffective guerrilla operations that had little popular support.

The Serbian government, however, responded with increasingly brutal repression, including attacks on civilians. The Serb massacre of fifty-eight people in Prekaz in February 1998 initiated a spiral of escalation. In the following twelve months, about 1,000 people, mostly ethnically Albanian Kosovar civilians, were killed. Perhaps even more ominously, more than 400,000 were forced to flee their homes.

Some debate remains about the intent of the Milošević government. The prevailing opinion in much of the West by early 1999 was that ethnic cleansing had begun in earnest. Efforts to get the Security Council to act, however, were blocked, primarily by Russia.

The Clinton administration, though, continued to argue, forcefully, that the lessons of Bosnia and Rwanda proved that early action was necessary. Britain and some other European states agreed. The problem was determining who would act, on what rationale, in the absence of Security Council authorization. Rather than act unilaterally or create an ad hoc coalition, they decided to use NATO, the Cold War alliance against the Soviet Union that had been trying to reinvent itself as a new kind of regional security organization.

A land invasion was ruled out, as the costs, in terms of troops mobilized and lives lost, were anticipated to be more than Western publics would accept. This left only airpower. From March 24 to June 19, 1999, NATO forces carried out an increasingly punishing campaign of aerial bombardments, including repeated attacks on the Serbian capital of Belgrade.

The Serbian authorities took advantage of the attacks to put into action a well-coordinated campaign of ethnic cleansing. About 10,000 people were killed, and nearly 1.5 million people were forced to flee their homes. The speed and efficiency of the Serbian actions clearly indicated Milošević's rather elaborate plan, which he had been waiting for the right moment to implement.

Three features of the Kosovo intervention deserve special mention.

First, it was undertaken as genocide began, or perhaps even before. In Bosnia, intervention occurred only when genocide was well under way.

Second, the intervention was undertaken despite the fact that the number of deaths was relatively low. The Serbian strategy of ethnic cleansing, which used exemplary violence to coerce people into fleeing the territory to be "cleansed," seems to have been, in part, a calculated attempt to stay under a perceived killing threshold for an international response. That tactic, however, proved unsuccessful.

Third, regional powers acted on humanitarian grounds, in the absence of Security Council authorization or any other particularly powerful legal justification. In effect, the negative precedent of Rwanda—something had to be done—took priority over the usual requirements of authorization and legality.

3 The Authority to Intervene

Who is entitled to intervene on behalf of (potential) victims of genocide? We can distinguish interveners by (a) their mode of action (unilateral or multilateral) and (b) the scope of the community within or for which they act (global or regional).

The authority of multilateral interveners arises from legal, political, or moral recognition by the political communities that the organization or its members represent. Multilateral intervention necessitates the building of political coalitions across states, which, even if it does not entirely eliminate the influence of national selfishness, substantially increases the likelihood of genuinely humanitarian motivation. At the very least, it makes the political self-interests involved somewhat less narrow. When the multilateral forum is the Security Council—which can act only with both a majority of its membership and the consent of the five permanent members—any use of force that is authorized is likely to have a very central humanitarian dimension to it.

"Unilateral" (that is, not formally authorized multilateral) actors—which include ad hoc coalitions—may or may not have comparable recognition by broader political communities. It is an empirical question whether a great power acting unilaterally intervenes with authority or merely as a result of its superior power. But great powers have engaged in far more *anti*-humanitarian than humanitarian interventions. Multilateral intervention thus is the preferred alternative, for practical as well as theoretical reasons.

Unilateral action by a great power with highly mixed motives nonetheless may save lives that would be lost while waiting for a more pure multilateral intervention that never comes. (Classic Cold War examples include the conflict between India and East Pakistan (Bangladesh) and Vietnam's invasion of Cambodia.) Furthermore, unilateral actors, being politically autonomous, may be able to intervene when multilateral action is blocked. And when unilateral actors intervene as de facto representatives of both victims and broader regional or international political communities, their actions may acquire considerable informal legitimacy.

The second distinction, between regional and global interveners, concerns the appropriate level for action within the international system. Regional and global actors may have different capacities and authorities. For example, regional multilateral action may be easier because of greater common interests within the region. Regional actors may also have the advantage of superior knowledge or authority because they are closer to the problem. But if a regional organization is dominated by a regional hegemon (for example, Nigeria in the Economic Community of West African States), it may be (perceived as) a captive of that state, undermining its legitimacy.

Let us apply this typology to Kosovo.

Global multilateral action was effectively blocked. China and Russia had a deep and relatively principled opposition to multilateral intervention. In addition, Russia had much more selfish political interests in its long-term relationship with Serbia.

The Organization for Security and Co-operation in Europe, the most obvious regional actor, lacked the unified political will needed to act in this particular case—let alone the legal authority to use force. A similar political situation also precluded action through either the European Union or the Council of Europe. Furthermore, unilateral action by the United States was definitely unacceptable to most, if not all, of the states of the European Union, as well as most states outside of Europe.

Nonetheless, the states of the European Union were unwilling—at least after a lot of political lobbying—to stand by and allow genocide to occur in Kosovo. NATO provided a convenient organizational forum for needed action that could not be otherwise authorized. Faced with a genuine dilemma, the members of NATO decided that intervention was the lesser of two evils.

Assuming that preemptive humanitarian intervention usually will be blocked at the global level, concerned states seem to be left with the uncomfortable alternatives of inaction, unilateral action, or regional multilateral action. This is a recipe for uneven and selective responses to humanitarian crises. There are large parts of the world where there is neither a viable regional actor nor a unilateral actor that has the necessary power, legitimacy, and commitment. Selectivity is further increased by the effective exemption of the permanent members of the Security Council from UN action and a comparable regional exemption of leading local powers such as Nigeria and India (and their allies).

Kosovo also raises the specter of what might be called coercive regionalism, in which the target of action is not a member of the intervening regional community. The opposite problem is suggested by the 2005 intervention of the African Union (AU) in Sudan: relying on (ineffective) regional intervention may be a way for global actors to avoid taking difficult or costly action.

Nevertheless, as long as we retain an international system structured around sovereign states—that is, for the foreseeable future—we are not likely to be able to evade these problems of authority and inequality. We are beginning to grapple with them, though, with a certain degree of success. And the UN-authorized intervention in East Timor later in 1999 largely removed doubts that a right to humanitarian intervention was being established as a matter of positive international law.

4 The Right to Humanitarian Intervention and the R2P

At the beginning of the 1990s, positive international law clearly prohibited armed humanitarian intervention, even in response to massive genocide. Not a single intervention against genocide had been widely endorsed as legal. And although the Security Council had the authority to determine that genocide represented a threat to international peace and security, in practice it had never exercised that authority.

The standard pattern, right through the end of the Cold War, was for the international community to wring its hands in anguish as genocide played itself out in places like East Pakistan (where in 1971 several hundred thousand were killed and some 10 million people put to flight in calculated ethnic violence), Cambodia (where more than 1.5 million people—about one-fifth of the total population of the country—died at the hands of the Khmer Rouge between 1975 and 1979), and Uganda (where more than a quarter-million people died during the rule of Idi Amin in the 1970s). Neighboring states, usually with powerful geopolitical interests, sometimes intervened. None of these interventions, however, was accepted as legal. And most were not even presented as primarily humanitarian by the interveners.

By the end of the millennium, however, the Security Council had authorized not only humanitarian interventions in Bosnia and East Timor but also peacekeeping operations in Sierra Leone, Liberia, the Central African Republic, and the Democratic Republic of the Congo that had a central humanitarian component. And, in the first decade of the twenty-first century, additional operations were conducted in Liberia, Côte d'Ivoire, Sudan, Burundi, Afghanistan, and Haiti. Today, we have both a well-established norm and a surprisingly clear pattern of practice of Security Council-authorized humanitarian intervention against genocide. And the example of Kosovo suggests considerable international toleration for genuinely humanitarian interventions taken in response to Security Council's inaction.

NATO's Kosovo intervention provoked the Canadian government to convene an independent commission to explore the changing nature of humanitarian law and humanitarian intervention in light of state sovereignty. The International Commission on Intervention and State Sovereignty (ICISS) was cochaired by Gareth Evans (an Australian lawyer and politician) and Mohamed Sahnoun (an Algerian diplomat) and included independent diplomats and lawyers from several countries, including Russia, Germany, the Philippines, Guatemala, India, and the United States. The ICISS completed its landmark report, *The Responsibility to Protect*, in December 2001.[2]

The ICISS posed a central question: If state sovereignty is a shield that protects states from intervention, as a matter of law, what are the limits (if any) of the duty of nonintervention? Does international law protect states that are very clearly engaged in massive and flagrant violations of human rights, especially including genocide and crimes against humanity?

The Commission began by noting changes since World War II in the makeup of the international system, especially the proliferation of sovereign yet weak states that are vulnerable to internal strife and violence. It also noted that the normative environment of international relations had changed in recent decades. In particular, the concept of state security had been supplemented by human security, and the ambit of human rights and humanitarian law had grown dramatically in extent and importance. These changes, the Commission argued, demanded a reconceptualization of sovereignty, especially in relation to human security.

The main conceptual problem, the Commission wrote, was one of framing the question, which begins with nonintervention as the default condition. The norm of nonintervention is enshrined in Article 2.7 of the UN Charter, which essentially prohibits any interference by the United Nations (or states) in matters "essentially within the domestic jurisdiction" of member-states. However, that prohibition does not apply to actions taken by the Security Council under its Chapter VII powers to authorize both nonmilitary and military action against states found to be a threat to international or regional peace and security.

The ICISS thus suggested that the right of noninterference was conditional, rather than absolute. If states are unwilling or unable to undertake their primary responsibility to protect their populations from grave harm, then the duty of protection shifts to the international community, which is then empowered to act. A doctrine of "the responsibility to protect" (R2P) suggests not merely a *right to intervene* but that, in situations of grave breaches of human rights and humanitarian law, there is *a duty (responsibility)* of the international community to intervene to protect basic rights.

The ICISS outlined several criteria, rooted in traditional "just war" theory, that would trigger the R2P.

1. The intervention had to be primarily for a *just cause*: to halt, avert, or prevent large-scale loss of life from, for example, ethnic cleansing, genocide, or other crimes against humanity. The violations must be gross and systematic and documented by clear evidence from credible sources.

2. States or other actors that intervene must do so with the *right intention*; that is, the just cause must be the principal motive for action. This does not mean that the interveners need to have purely humanitarian motives. Any *other* motives, however, must be clearly secondary to the humanitarian motive (and are inherently suspect).
3. The intervention must be a *last resort*. Other actions must have already been tried and have failed.
4. Under R2P, any armed intervention must be *proportionate* and have *reasonable prospects for success*. This is one of the biggest hurdles that any state or group of states that is considering an armed humanitarian intervention must take into account. Discussions about duties versus consequences often get hung up on this point, as there is always a danger that an intervention in a complex humanitarian emergency or crisis, if not done right, could easily spin out of control and lead to even worse humanitarian outcomes than would have been the case with not intervening.
5. Finally, the interveners must have *legitimate authority* to act. Authorization by the UN Security Council unquestionably provides such authority. The Commission, however, saw the NATO intervention in Kosovo as "illegal yet legitimate," a very interesting gray area.

In the case of Kosovo, there was widespread agreement in the Security Council that the threshold criteria for action were in evidence. Four Security Council resolutions had been adopted, demanding an end to the violence by the Serbian regime and Serbia had been shown to be a consistent violator not only of human rights and humanitarian law but also of Security Council resolutions. In the eyes of NATO, the action was genuinely a last resort, because it was clear that Russia and China were not willing to move to a military action under Chapter VII. Furthermore, the vote taken by NATO to intervene was unanimous among its eighteen member-states, which were widely considered to be "good citizens" of the United Nations. Finally, after the intervention achieved its goals, NATO returned as quickly as possible to working within the UN Charter framework to establish a ceasefire and begin the difficult work of post-conflict rebuilding (in UN Security Council Resolution 1244).

The R2P doctrine—with caveats—was accepted unanimously by the international community at the 2005 World Summit, a major policy summit coinciding with the sixtieth anniversary of the adoption of the UN Charter. The 2005 summit endorsed the basic principle that sovereignty cannot act as a shield to protect states from scrutiny with respect to the gravest of human rights and humanitarian crimes—although it did not endorse the notion that the international community always had an unquestioned responsibility to intervene.[3]

Quite the contrary, very few states accept the notion that outside actors have a *duty* to intervene. A *responsibility* to protect is, at best, an aspiration that few if any states with the capabilities to participate in protective actions acknowledge as a real obligation (responsibility). And there is no body of practice to support the idea of a duty to protect. States and the international community have only the right to humanitarian intervention. And they may choose not to exercise that right. They are authorized, but not required, to intervene in cases of genocide and crimes against humanity.

Furthermore, the right to humanitarian intervention applies only to genocide and crimes against humanity. There has been no spill over into other human rights violations, even in the cases of torture and slavery, where national courts are increasingly applying international human rights norms.

This poses a moral paradox. We seem willing to respond to certain kinds of graphic and concentrated suffering but to tolerate comparable or even greater suffering so long as it remains more diffuse. This paradox is by no means restricted to genocide. Consider, for example, the contrast between the relatively strong international reaction to the 1989 Tiananmen Square massacre in China, where hundreds of people died in a relatively telegenic way, and the weak reactions to the systematic and severe daily violations of the human rights of hundreds of millions of Chinese citizens. Even more striking is the substantial international willingness to respond to famines but a parallel unwillingness to deal with the far more severe problem of malnutrition.

On the one hand, if we take seriously the unity of all human rights and the idea that human rights are about a life of dignity, not mere life, then the restriction of humanitarian intervention to genocide and other humanitarian crimes is highly problematic. On the other hand, though, there are powerful practical, and even ethical, reasons to restrict humanitarian intervention to the most severe atrocities.

The restriction acknowledges the realities of mobilizing an international response adequate to bearing the considerable costs associated with military intervention, especially if that intervention is restricted to high-altitude bombing. Furthermore, a narrow humanitarian exception reflects an international system that gives priority to local and national communities. It remains rare—but no longer unheard of—for states and citizens to be willing to bear the costs of rescuing foreigners from the depredations of their own governments. An active sense of cosmopolitan moral community remains very, very thin.

The international community may have a *moral* obligation to prevent and respond to the most serious breaches of humanitarian law. It might even be argued that such a duty is implied by the very structure of the global human rights regime. National implementation of internationally recognized human rights, if it is more than a political compromise with the reality of state power, must assume that states are capable and not unwilling to protect the human rights of their citizens. This, however, is patently absurd in the case of genocidal regimes. To continue to act on the pretense of national protection appears as a cruel hoax. In such cases, as the ICISS suggested, residual responsibility reverts to the international community.

Nonetheless, international law recognizes only a right to humanitarian intervention. As with any right, the Security Council may choose not to exercise it; the Council is free to intervene, or not, as it sees fit. And the grounds for both acting and not acting may legitimately appeal to a variety of nonmoral considerations, to which we will turn at the end of this chapter.

5 Case Studies from the 2000s–2010s

This relatively optimistic reading was confirmed by the last case of humanitarian intervention in the 1990s, East Timor. But two cases from the new millennium, Libya and Sudan, paint a more problematic picture.

5.1 East Timor

The island of Timor was divided during the colonial era into East Timor and West Timor, held respectively by Portugal and the Netherlands. When Indonesia achieved independence, it received (only) the Dutch holdings in the East Indies (including West Timor, but not East Timor). Neither then nor in 1960, when the United Nations reorganized its decolonization machinery and classified East Timor as a Portuguese colony, did Indonesia claim East Timor.

In 1974, a coup removed the military government in Portugal, the only Western state still holding a substantial colonial empire (most notably Angola and Mozambique). Taking advantage of the situation, East Timor declared independence.

Indonesia, however, had other ideas. It invaded East Timor on October 16, 1975.

Indonesian rule was both viewed as illegal by most countries and rejected by most of the local population. Nonetheless, the government in Jakarta attempted to consolidate its rule through often brutal repression, sporadically supplementing such "sticks" with the "carrots" of special regional development assistance.

Particularly striking was the Dili Massacre of November 12, 1991. Indonesian troops opened fire on peaceful pro-independence demonstrators, killing at least 271 and wounding at least another 275. In addition, more than 250 people disappeared. Besides being unusually brutal, the Dili Massacre was widely publicized, galvanizing international attention in many countries previously uninterested in East Timor's plight (analogous to the impact of the Sharpeville Massacre on international responses to South Africa).

Eventually, international pressure induced Indonesia to permit a UN-sponsored referendum on independence. In the election held on August 30, 1999, more than three-quarters of the votes favored independence. Indonesia, however, balked. Local militias, which were already operating with the acquiescence, and often the assistance, of Indonesian military authorities, went on a sustained rampage that increasingly appeared to have genocidal aspirations. One-fifth to one-quarter of the population was forced to flee their homes, with thousands tracked down and killed in churches, schools, and public buildings where they sought refuge.

On September 15, 1999, the Security Council unanimously created the International Force for East Timor, led by Australia. In combination with intensive international political pressure and diplomatic activity, it restored order and produced Indonesian acquiescence to Timorese independence. On October 25, 1999, the Security Council established the United Nations Transitional Administration in East Timor. A week later, the last Indonesian troops left East Timor. On May 20, 2002, East Timor achieved full independence.

The technical illegality of Indonesia's occupation of East Timor facilitated such a strong response. Many countries that would have otherwise been reluctant to accept a UN military operation were able to view this as a decolonization issue more than a humanitarian intervention. Leading international actors, however, had Kosovo (and Rwanda) very much in mind. East Timor was widely understood as a turning point, completing the transformation of Bosnia from an isolated exception to a precedent in a continuing stream of customary law formation that in some complex way also included Kosovo.

The power of the emerging norm of humanitarian intervention against genocide is illustrated by the fact that almost all the conventional political and material considerations counseled inaction. Indonesia is a large, strategically located country (the world's largest majority-Muslim country) with considerable oil resources and a strong record of support for, and by, the West. In addition, there were well-founded fears, both within and outside Indonesia, about the susceptibility of the country to secessionist movements, some of which had been carrying on armed struggles for decades. East Timor, by contrast, is small, poor—whatever its oil resources, they are dwarfed by those of Indonesia—and of little material interest to anyone except its own people. Nonetheless, in the end, and with surprisingly little controversy, the major Western powers and the rest of the Security Council agreed to send soldiers to protect the Timorese people and enforce their decision to attain independence—in part because they had an international legal right to independence and the cost of action was relatively low, but in large measure because the international community was unwilling to allow their forced incorporation to be maintained through genocide.

5.2 Libya

Linked to the "Arab Spring" uprisings in Tunisia, Yemen, Egypt, Syria, and Morocco, mass protests broke out in Libya on February 17, 2011, against the government of Muammar Gaddafi. The largest was in Benghazi, a city in the west of the country. The crackdown by the regime was swift and ruthless. Gaddafi proclaimed that those rebelling against his rule would be "hunted down street by street, house by house, and wardrobe by wardrobe." By February 22, several NGOs were reporting systematic atrocities against civilian protesters, including mass killings. The UN Security Council acknowledged that "possible" crimes against humanity were occurring in Libya. That same day, the League of Arab States, which traditionally has been immensely respectful of the sovereignty of systematic human rights violators, voted to suspend Libya's membership.

On February 25, the UN Human Rights Council adopted a resolution to establish a commission of inquiry to explore the situation in Libya and recommended that the UN General Assembly consider suspending Libya's seat on the Human Rights Council (to which it had just been elected). The following day, the Security Council unanimously adopted a resolution that, among other things, imposed an arms embargo on Libya and travel bans and asset freezes on senior officials of the Gaddafi regime. The Security Council also referred the situation in Libya to the prosecutor of the International Criminal Court—an action it very rarely takes.

Such rapid and wide-ranging action was as impressive as it was unusual. Only a minority of voices from the West (mostly the United States, United Kingdom, and France), however, argued for more proactive measures. A majority of the Security Council and other regional actors urged restraint.

On March 12, the League of Arab States stated that the Gaddafi government had "lost its sovereignty" and urged establishing a no-fly zone as a way to protect civilians while also maintaining the principles of sovereignty and territorial integrity. The United States, on

March 15, agreed to cosponsor (with France, Lebanon, and the United Kingdom) a Security Council resolution authorizing the protection of civilians using "all necessary measures," including the establishment of a no-fly zone and NATO enforcement of the arms embargo. This resolution (1973) was adopted on a vote of 10–0, with Brazil, China, Germany, India, and Russia abstaining.

This action fell short of the demands of a robust R2P—despite the fact that it seemed to be a textbook case of the obligation as outlined by the ICISS. There was just cause, a sense of imminent danger, and the intervention seemed to be a last resort. Intervention also would have met the criteria for proportionality and prospects for success (and had the authorization of the Security Council).

The criterion of right intention, however, was contentious. As the practicalities of enforcing a no-fly zone became clearer—in particular as the diversion of government resources threatened to shift the balance of power—China and Russia began to suspect that the real intention was regime change: removing rather than restraining Gaddafi. And this view today continues to compete with a more benign reading of NATO enforcement actions.

The more serious problem, though, has been the ultimate failure to fulfill—some would argue even a lack of effort concerning—the third pillar of R2P, the "responsibility to rebuild." Gaddafi and his family are gone. Libya today is a failed state, fragmented and practically ungovernable. Since 2022, two "governments" claim legitimacy: the internationally recognized Government of National Unity (based in Tripoli) and the Government of National Stability, supported by the parliament in Benghazi. Small-scale conflicts and widespread if disorganized human rights abuses continue on a daily basis. The country has become a major transit point for migrants trying to reach Southern Europe (mostly Italy) by boat—an ongoing humanitarian crisis in itself.

One might speculate that China and Russia permitted the Libyan intervention (by abstaining rather than vetoing action) in order to expose R2P for what, in their view, it really is: a violation of national sovereignty and of international law, under the cloak of humanitarianism. One only needs to look at the situation in Syria to draw this conclusion (see Section 7.1 below).

In any case, Libya has made it clear that protection through limited armed intervention is far more difficult than Kosovo and East Timor may have initially suggested. And, like Iraq, Libya tragically demonstrates that establishing even basic political order, let alone a rights-protective regime, is extraordinarily difficult in a country that has suffered under a brutal personalist military dictatorship for decades. When politics has been that badly broken, neither national nor international actors are likely to have the knowledge, resources, or commitment to fix much.

This is not an argument for allowing brutal dictators to continue to abuse their people. It does, however, suggest that sometimes—and probably more often than we would like to admit—the best that can reasonably be hoped for from humanitarian intervention is a moderately civilized form of post-conflict politics that limits rather than seeks to remove gross and systematic human rights violations and that leaves space, and perhaps provides some foundations, for future progress. In other words, humanitarian intervention may often be only the lesser of two evils. And, if it is not done well, it is maybe not even that, especially in the short and medium run. (Some argue that Libya has been such a case, although it is impossible to compare to what was ostensibly prevented: a mass atrocity event that Gaddafi made clear he intended to carry out.)

We thus must give greater attention than has often been the case to the fact that those with a R2P are responsible for the consequences of their protective actions. When a relatively easy and quick fix, such as was carried out in East Timor, is not possible, the character of humanitarian intervention changes fundamentally. And when local actors are in no position to rebuild their society for themselves, and when foreign peoples and their governments are not willing to undertake the serious long-term commitment of effort and resources that it requires, intervention may replace one disaster with another.

5.3 Sudan

The roots of Sudan's long-running series of humanitarian crises go back to its colonial creation, which combined a largely Arab and Muslim North with a largely Black and Christian and animist South. When the country attained formal independence on January 1, 1956, Sudan was already in the midst of a civil war between North and South that continued until 1972—only to break out again in 1983, continuing, more on than off, until 2005. About half a million people died in the first phase of the civil war (out of a population of about 10 million at independence). Perhaps another 2 million died in the second phase. Although there was considerable brutality on both sides, most of the suffering was caused by military action by the (Northern-dominated) government that targeted civilians and used the denial of food, even in times of famine, as a standard tactic.

This particular humanitarian disaster was finally brought to an end in 2011. In January, the people of southern Sudan overwhelmingly voted for independence. In July 2011, the new country of South Sudan peacefully seceded—although peace between the two Sudans is hardly secure. And internal conflict between factions in South Sudan has been almost as deadly as the old North–South conflict, killing perhaps as many as 400,000 people (of a population of about 10 million at independence). A 2018 peace agreement greatly moderated the violence. The unity government called for in the agreement was finally formed in early 2020, and a new parliament was chosen the following year. Nevertheless, violence between armed militias continues to plague the country, resulting in ongoing humanitarian crises such as displacements, civilian deaths and casualties, and food insecurity.

The "solution" of South Sudanese independence was facilitated by the emergence of a humanitarian crisis in 2003 in Darfur, the western region of Sudan, which like the South is primarily non-Arab and non-Muslim (although with a much more substantial Arabized minority). Rebels in Darfur initially handily outmaneuvered the government army, which was stretched thin to begin with by the conflict in the South and another in the East. The government, however, quickly switched to a counter-insurgency strategy based on *Janjaweed* militias, composed of local mounted herders armed by the government, supported by government helicopters. Many thousands were killed, and more than 100,000 refugees were put to flight by the time the conflict moved to the forefront of international attention in 2004.

The violence directed at the non-Arab population was reminiscent of Serbian ethnic cleansing in Bosnia and Kosovo. A conscious effort seems to have been made both to limit the killing, which was aimed primarily at causing targeted populations to flee, and to engage diplomatically with critics in order to forestall an effective, full-scale multilateral intervention. But even this "restrained" violence forced more than 2.5 million people—40 percent of the prewar population—to flee and killed perhaps a third of a million people (three-quarters of those deaths being from disease among refugees).

The international response was, in many ways, rapid and robust. In April 2004, Chad brokered a ceasefire. In August 2004, the AU sent 150 Rwandan troops to monitor the ceasefire. They were soon joined by 150 Nigerians. The following month, the Security Council condemned the government for its actions in Darfur. In 2005, the AU peacekeeping force was expanded, first to more than 3,000 troops and then to almost 7,000. A peace agreement between the government and some rebels was signed at Abuja, Nigeria, in May 2006. At the end of August 2006, the Security Council authorized a force of more than 17,000 peacekeepers. Numerous efforts at ceasefires and final resolution were undertaken by both bilateral and multilateral actors, both inside and outside of the region, including prominently the United States. A major NGO response mobilized substantial pressure both on Sudan and especially on Western governments. Charges were even brought in the International Criminal Court against leaders of the violence, including the sitting president of Sudan, Omar al-Bashir. And a new, more promising peace agreement was signed by all the major parties in Doha, Qatar, in July 2011.

Compared to Kosovo and East Timor, though, these responses were somewhat timid and noticeably unsuccessful. The United States, already bogged down in wars in Afghanistan and Iraq, was unwilling to lead a more robust response. Without a substantial American commitment, a significantly larger force could not be raised. And even if it had been committed, no other power or group of powers had the logistical capabilities to support it in the field.

Darfur is a huge area (more than 190,000 square miles, roughly the size of Spain) with primitive infrastructure. The substantial majority of the population lives in widely scattered villages in a flat, semiarid terrain. A large and difficult ground operation thus would have been required to provide protection. (A small, lightly armed force, such as would have made a huge difference in Rwanda, could not provide protection against mobile militias backed by air support.)

The international politics were further complicated by China and Russia being even more reluctant than usual to permit armed intervention. China had major economic interests in the region, especially oil. And Russia was both locked in its own brutal separatist war in Chechnya and happy to take the opportunity to sell arms to Sudan's government, despite the UN embargo.

The regional environment also undercut stronger action. The AU was more than willing to intervene. But it lacked any substantial moral authority in Sudan, and it lacked the resources to do an effective job. Furthermore, its efforts were undermined by the indirect support that Sudan received from the Arab League.

The government in Khartoum was an astute and effective opponent. It appears to have carefully studied previous interventions. And it had a clear appreciation of the strengths of its position. Khartoum thus calibrated its actions, both internally and externally, to allow it to continue the ethnic cleansing of Darfur.

This again suggests that Kosovo and East Timor may have been *relatively* easy cases that created unrealistic expectations for future humanitarian interventions. Being forced out of East Timor was deeply embarrassing for the Indonesian government. But it had little material cost, especially because it has not in fact strengthened secessionist movements elsewhere in the country. Indonesia, in other words, was relatively open to international pressure and in the end not willing to fight further to keep a territory to which it had a questionable claim in the first place—especially given the internal political changes that were taking place within Indonesia, leading toward its effective democratization over the following several years. Furthermore, the Australian intervention in East Timor was successful, with a force about a quarter smaller than the clearly inadequate force the Security Council authorized for Darfur.

As for Kosovo, the NATO bombing campaign was not foreordained to succeed. In fact, almost up to the moment that it finally succeeded, it appeared to be failing. The loss of Kosovo, although a much more severe blow to Serbia than the loss of East Timor was to Indonesia, was not decisive, given its broader range of objectives, especially closer integration into Europe and the material (and psychological) benefits that would provide. And there was an internal opposition within Serbia that pressed the government to alter its policy.

The government in Khartoum, by contrast, had demonstrated itself willing to carry out decades-long massacres of people that, although technically fellow citizens, it viewed as culturally, ethnically, and racially inferior. It had the oil resources to support such policies, both internally and externally. It brooked no opposition to its rule, which even in the North of the country was highly repressive (although much less violent). It did not care much what the rest of the world thought of its actions. It needed nothing from outside (other than to sell its oil, which proved no problem). And it pursued its policies with considerable skill.

In other words, Sudan shows that a relatively effective and committed government can largely flout the international community, so long as it is willing to inflict sufficient suffering on its people. North Korea, Burma, and Zimbabwe present different variants of this pattern—which has no connection at all with genocides in "failed" states such as Somalia and Congo. Politically possible actions were simply inadequate to stop the killing.

But, even in Darfur, the international response had a (limited) positive impact. The death toll, horrible as it was, almost certainly would have been much higher had the international community not been watching carefully.

New violence, however, erupted in 2014, with many villages destroyed, men arrested, people beaten, and women systematically raped. In the fall of 2016, chemical weapons appeared to have been used against civilians. In December 2016, the chair of the South Sudanese Commission on Human Rights, Yasmin Sooka, addressed the twenty-sixth special session of the UN Human Rights Council, recounting mass atrocities that are being committed—the early warning signs of an impending genocide.

A coup led by the Sudanese military in April 2019, which ousted longtime dictator Omar al-Bashir, did not initially stop the violence in Darfur. In fact, the new military government even requested that it be given control over peacekeeping camps jointly operated by the AU and the United Nations. In late 2019, however, the military and pro-democracy advocates reached an agreement for a transitional government that many hoped would bring some degree of peace to Sudan.

Still another coup (the nineteenth in the country's history) occurred in October 2021, led by the Sudanese Armed Forces, leading to the outbreak of a new civil war in April 2023 between the Sudanese Armed Forces (SAF) and the ousted government's Rapid Support Forces (RSF) with the allied support of Janjaweed units. Most of the fighting has been in and around Khartoum. Observers estimate that more than 61,000 have been killed in Khartoum State alone, over 8.8 million have been internally displaced (more than half of them children) and another 3.5 million have left the country as refugees. The RSF has also engaged in a series of massacres of Masalit civilians in West Darfur, which the Biden administration and others have classified as genocidal. The group Genocide Watch cites UN estimates that anywhere between 10 and 15,000 civilians were massacred in 2023 alone. In 2025 Genocide Watch raised the "threat level" for genocide in Sudan to 9, "extermination," noting that the RSF's targeted massacres in Darfur mirror the genocidal intent of the 2003 genocide.

Even more significantly, the civil war has also precipitated a famine in Sudan. The Preparatory Committee of the Sudanese Doctors Union estimates that, since the start of the war, over 522,000 infants have died of malnutrition. In 2024, the United Nations estimated that over 750,000 Sudanese were at risk of starvation. Millions more are facing extreme food insecurity. For a time, international action in Sudan and South Sudan had been able to limit but not eliminate targeted political violence against civilians and produced little if any broader human rights progress. Now, however, the international community struggles to respond to these compounded crises with anything other than limited humanitarian responses. UN Security Council ceasefire resolutions (two were adopted in 2024) and arms embargoes have been largely ignored. Amnesty International reported in 2024 that large numbers of weapons continue to flow into the country, supplied by China, Russia, Turkey, Yemen, the United Arab Emirates, and Serbia.

6 Justifying Humanitarian Intervention

As the above cases illustrate, justifying humanitarian intervention in contemporary international politics involves a complex interaction of morality, law, and politics. The moral case for humanitarian intervention against genocide is relatively unproblematic. In Section 3.3, we used John Rawls's notion of overlapping consensus to circumvent disputes over foundational theories of human rights. In much the same way, we can see today an overlapping consensus on the use of armed force against genocide. Whatever their differences, most contemporary moral and religious doctrines agree that genocide is the kind of international crime that, at least in principle, justifies armed humanitarian intervention. Across a very wide range of moral theories and principles, *this* kind of suffering cannot be permitted.

Yet states and international organizations are not unencumbered moral agents. They are also subjects of international law and deeply political actors. And international law and politics impose their own standards of justification.

Throughout the Cold War, international law, emphasizing sovereignty and nonintervention, prohibited humanitarian intervention. Today, law and morality largely converge. But, as Rwanda and Kosovo illustrate, states still face a problem when the substantive standard of protecting victims of genocidal conflicts with the international legal requirement of UN Security Council authorization.

Justification becomes even more complicated when we recognize that states are also political actors. National leaders are *supposed* to take into account the political standard of the national interest. In addition to acting in accordance with the demands of law, morality, and humanity, they should consult the interests of their own state (and perhaps also the interests of international society).

Not only may political interests justify inaction that is morally demanded and legally warranted, but it also is essential that potential interveners consider the material and political costs, to themselves and others, of undertaking a morally and legally justifiable intervention. No less important, political interests—or at least the absence of competing political interests—may be a crucial final element in reaching a decision to act on moral and legal justifications.

How we balance these competing standards is, of course, a matter of intense controversy, both in general and in any specific case. But justifying humanitarian intervention requires that we take into account the full range of relevant moral, legal, and political principles—making justification a remarkably complex matter in many cases.

This is particularly true because most interventions arise from mixed motives. Humanitarian interventions typically are costly, both financially and in the risks to which they expose soldiers. States may occasionally accept such risks for purely humanitarian reasons. A number of states are even coming to see preventing or stopping systematic gross human rights violations as part of their national interest. But purely moral motives have been, and are likely to remain, rare.

Nonhumanitarian motives, however, do not necessarily reduce the justifiability of an intervention. Some political motives do not conflict with either humanitarian norms or international law. And, even when they do, we need to *balance* the competing considerations. So long as there are significant humanitarian motivations, interventions undertaken with mixed motives are likely to be perceived by at least some disinterested observers as justifiable, or at least excusable.

Issues of justification are also connected with questions of (in)consistency (see also Chapter 7, Section 4.2). Critics often present the impure as trumping the pure: because A did not intervene in x, which is in all essential ways similar to y, intervening in y is somehow unjustified, or at least suspect. Such an argument, however, reflects an absurd perfectionism that would paralyze states not just in cases of humanitarian intervention but in almost all areas of endeavor. (It would also probably prohibit most personal moral action.)

Inconsistency arguments do have real force when they point to partisanship: for example, supporting a practice among friends but intervening when an enemy does the same thing. Consistency, per se certainly is desirable, for all kinds of political, psychological, and perhaps even moral reasons. But as Peter Baehr nicely put it, "One act of commission is not invalidated by many acts of omission."[4] Inconsistent need not mean unjustified.

7 Conclusions: The Syrian Civil War, the War in Gaza, and the Future of Humanitarian Intervention and R2P

Throughout this chapter, we have explored the morality, ethics, law, and politics surrounding humanitarian intervention over the past nearly forty years. It seems that the Libyan case signaled a turning point. We now look at two failed cases—the Syrian Civil War (which has thankfully come to an end, but not as the result of any meaningful multilateral or unilateral intervention by the major powers in the region) and the ongoing humanitarian catastrophe in Gaza. Each in its own way illustrates the difficulty of responding effectively to severe humanitarian crises precipitated by armed conflict. Together, they may suggest that the hopes inspired by Kosovo and East Timor were, at best, exaggerated. As we suggested in Chapter 1, these cases of failure indicate that even in the clearest cases, the discordant goals of major powers auger a significant challenge to the global human rights project.

7.1 The Syrian Civil War

From 2011 to 2024, the war in Syria devolved into one of the most protracted and grave humanitarian crises since the Second Congo War (1998–2003). According to the Syrian Observatory for Human Rights, more than 656,000 people were killed, with roughly half of those deaths belonging to citizens. Additionally, 6 million refugees – out of a total prewar population of about 22 million—fled the country, most going to camps in Turkey, Lebanon, Jordan, and Egypt.

As in other countries in the region, protests against the government of Bashar al-Assad began in March 2011 (the "Arab Spring"). Government security forces responded brutally, resulting in tens of thousands of deaths and detentions. Resistance militias formed quickly and the situation had developed into a full-scale civil war by 2012.

Even during its most intense phases in 2014–2015, the war in Syria did not elicit any credible claims of genocide. (People were targeted primarily for political, not ethnic, racial, or religious reasons.) The violence, however, was brutal and lawless. Although rebel groups unquestionably committed war crimes, the government of Bashar al-Assad was responsible for the vast majority of the vicious inhumanity that characterized the conflict. It systematically resorted to mass arbitrary arrests, torture, and extrajudicial killing; the targeting of civilian sites, including schools and hospitals, even using chemical weapons; and the systematic denial in some areas of access to food and water.

In November 2016, the United Nations estimated that nearly 1 million Syrian civilians were living under siege. The most tragic case of these was the siege of Eastern Aleppo, which began in July 2016, trapping more than 275,000 civilians. In late December 2016, the al-Assad government reclaimed the last rebel-held areas of the city.

With the exception of Russian military intervention in support of al-Assad, the international community was effectively paralyzed throughout the conflict. R2P was often mentioned. But neither the Security Council nor any ad hoc coalition of powers was willing to authorize or provide the kind of massive armed intervention that would have been necessary to stop the atrocities. Why not? What would have had to change in order to bring these atrocities to an end?

Up until 2018, the war in Syria was really four different conflicts occurring in the same place. The core conflict was between the Assad regime and Syrian rebels trying to oust him. A second conflict was between al-Assad and Syria's ethnic Kurdish minority, whose goal is to declare an independent Kurdish state in Northern and Eastern Syria (which was a long-standing goal of some Kurds in Turkey as well). A third conflict involved the Islamic State (ISIS, or ISIL, or Daesh), which in 2014 captured significant territory in Syria and Iraq. ISIS had no allies and was essentially at war with all other factions involved in the conflict. American-backed interventions by Kurdish forces in Syria and Iraq eliminated this element of the conflict.

Finally, the entire situation in Syria (which, because of ISIS, crossed into Iraq) was complicated by numerous outside actors, all of which were supporting one or another of the various local actors engaged in the conflict. Al-Assad's government was supported by Iran, Russia, and the Lebanese militant group Hezbollah. Various rebel groups (and there were dozens of them, some working together, others opposed to each other) were supported by the United States (working with what it called "the moderate opposition") and Saudi Arabia (which was intensely concerned about Iran's influence in Syria). Other Arab states—Jordan, Qatar, and the United Arab Emirates—also supported some rebels.

Security Council (in)action was largely rooted in the involvement of Russia and the United States in the conflict. The Council was able to unanimously adopt resolutions in 2013–2014 calling for the removal of chemical weapons from Syria and demanding al-Assad grant access for the delivery of humanitarian aid. All mention of sanctions, however, was stripped from these resolutions to secure Russia's vote. And afterwards, the Russian military significantly stepped up its support of the Assad regime in the form of direct military engagement (mostly by its air forces), under the guise of combating ISIS and terrorism. Things became even more complicated when, in late 2019, the Trump administration abruptly ended its support of Kurdish forces in Northern Syria, paving the way for Turkish units to effectively invade Syria's northeastern border area to push the Kurds out.

In October 2016, both UN Secretary-General Ban Ki-moon and US Secretary of State John Kerry alleged Russian complicity in war crimes, insofar as its air campaign deliberately targeted schools, hospitals, and other civilian targets. The Russians had vetoed a 2014 draft resolution that would have referred the situation in Syria to the International Criminal Court (ICC) prosecutor, based on a call by the Human Rights Council's Independent International Commission of Inquiry that all alleged violations of international human rights law be investigated. Russia (often with the support of China) vetoed a number of other Security Council resolutions that would have demanded a halt to Syrian troop movements and prohibited the use of heavy weaponry in heavily populated areas, and overflights of cities such as Eastern Aleppo, and levied sanctions on the al-Assad government for noncompliance. In each case, the Russians called these resolutions "one sided" and blatant attempts to predetermine a political outcome—namely, the removal of the Assad regime from power. After the October 2016 veto, the UN emergency relief coordinator, Stephen O'Brien, told the

Security Council, "I am more or less at my wits end as a human being.... [S]hame on all of us for not acting to stop the annihilation of Eastern Aleppo and its people and much of the rest of Syria."

After the fall of Aleppo in 2016, the dynamics of the conflict shifted toward the containment and defeat of ISIS, which found itself besieged on several fronts by US-backed Kurdish forces, rebels backed by Turkey, and Assad's own forces backed by Russia. But Syrian government forces also continued to gain ground against the last remaining rebel strongholds in the country, again using chemical weapons in Khan Shaykhun in 2017 and in Douma in 2018. In both cases, the United States retaliated with airstrikes and missile attacks against the regime's military assets and chemical weapons facilities (with British and French backing in the case of Douma). The regime's efforts to defeat rebels in Idlib Province included targeted bombings of schools and hospitals. The Russian Federation vetoed a UN Security Council resolution drafted in response to the Douma attack. Both China and Russia vetoed a resolution (in September 2019) in response to the situation in Idlib (the Russians argued it would only protect "international terrorists from their final defeat in Idlib").

In the early 2020s, the conflict settled into a "low-intensity" pattern—until the outbreak of the Gaza war between Israel and Hamas in October 2023, which was joined by Hezbollah militants who have effectively controlled southern Lebanon for decades. Hezbollah benefited from the Syrian civil war insofar as territories held by the al-Assad regime allowed supplies from Iran (Hezbollah's main state-sponsor) to transit into Lebanon, which the militant group used to engage Israel after the outbreak of the Gaza war. However, after decimating Hamas' positions in Gaza—at an unfathomable cost in civilian lives and infrastructure—Israel moved to decapitate Hezbollah in Lebanon, ostensibly in order to secure northern Israel, whose towns and villages had largely been emptied after hostilities erupted in the wake of Hamas' attack on Israel.

Beginning in early November 2024, and largely backed by Turkey, a rebel coalition led by Hay'at Tahrir al-Sham (HTS) quickly began to move against government forces in Aleppo. To the surprise of almost everyone, they quickly took the city as al-Assad's army forces basically abandoned their post. Within days, HTS and several other groups had moved into Hama and Homs and seized Damascus in early December 2024. Al-Assad fled to Moscow, bringing the long-simmering conflict to a bittersweet end.

Under the leadership of Ahmed Hussein al-Sharaa (aka Abu Mohammad al-Julani), the various rebel factions came together to begin to form a transition government. Among the most dramatic developments has been the uncovering of the horrific legacy of enforced disappearances, torture, and execution of untold thousands of Syrian civilians by the al-Assad dictatorship.

As we go to press, there are a number of reasons to be cautiously optimistic about Syria's near-future. In March 2025, a provisional government was formed with al-Sharaa as president. South Korea, France, the United Kingdom, and—after a push by the Saudi government—Donald Trump have met with al-Sharaa and have begun to lift sanctions on the new government. Thousands of Syrian refugees, including many living in Europe—have returned home eager to engage in the country's transition and rebuilding. In September 2025, al-Sharaa stood at the rostrum of the UN General Assembly—the first Syrian head-of-state to address the

United Nations in nearly sixty years—and expressed a vision of hope for the future of Syria and the region.

The Syrian civil war confronts us with a very harsh reality: sometimes the international community simply is not in a position to respond effectively to even the worst of human tragedies. The Syrian conflict was a perfect storm in many respects: it was in a highly unstable region, involving not only many regional actors (especially Turkey, Iran, and Saudi Arabia) but also two of the most powerful states in the world—the United States and Russia. The ghosts of Cold War-era politics walk in Syria.

The problem in Syria was not legal; it was political. The United States acted timidly throughout the early years of the crisis, only threatening to intervene as a coercive measure to compel the Assad regime to dismantle its chemical weapons stockpiles. This so-called "red line" response, however, received lukewarm domestic support in the United States and (perhaps thankfully) was taken off the table when Russia intervened diplomatically and convinced al-Assad to agree to join the Chemical Weapons Convention and allow Syria's stockpiles to be removed from the country. And Russia appeared quite satisfied with the result.

This example thus reminds us not to confuse international action with action by international organizations. Those organizations, which indeed usually are the most effective mechanisms for carrying out humanitarian interventions, can act only when the leading powers allow them to. And when it comes to the use of military force, great power backing—or at least the willingness of great powers not to veto acting—is essential. The problem of humanitarian inaction is essentially a problem of states not being willing to accept the costs necessary to solve the problem—or, as in the case of Russia in Syria, preferring to intervene in a conflict for geopolitical rather than humanitarian reasons.

Finally, we should consider the possibility that Syria represents a process of successful learning from the debacles of intervention in Iraq and Libya. Debate will continue to rage over whether more aggressive action early in the civil war could have produced, if not a desirable outcome, a result better than what actually occurred. But there is no evidence that the United States or other Western states were willing to shoulder the immense long-term burden of rebuilding a Syria that quite likely would have been wrecked by regime change. Quite the contrary, there is overwhelming evidence of unwillingness. And if international actors are unable or unwilling to really fix—not just meddle in—a problem, is nonintervention the better (less bad) course of action?

Syria thus may be a reminder that sometimes *all* the politically viable options are unacceptable. This appears to have been the Obama administration's justification of its inaction. Politics, both national and international, is, at best, the art of the possible. When the desirable is not realistically possible, the only question may be which tragedy will we participate in, through which combination of (ultimately unjustifiable) action and inaction.

One might even argue that having not participated during the civil war, the international community may actually be better positioned to aid in post-conflict reconciliation and rebuilding. And assistance may be easier to mobilize, especially if, as in Syria, there is some hope of moving forward along a more promising path.

7.2 The War in Gaza

On October 7, 2023, Hamas militants launched a massive terrorist assault on numerous Israeli communities bordering Gaza and launched hundreds of rockets against Israeli cities. This was the deadliest attack against the Jewish people since the Holocaust. 1,129 Israelis and foreign nationals, including 815 civilians were murdered and Hamas took 251 hostages. Hamas militants also raped, mutilated, and tortured dozens of others.

In response, the Israeli Defense Forces (IDF) launched a massive invasion of Gaza. The war has unfolded in phases with brief pauses in the fighting to allow Gazans to move to "safer" places and allow some humanitarian aid to enter the country—followed by dramatic escalations in IDF military operations in new parts of the territory.

The humanitarian situation in Gaza has eclipsed the scale of destruction in Europe during World War II. Nearly the entire population of 2.3 million Gazans has been displaced, many multiple times. By the end of 2025, about 70,000 Gazans are confirmed dead (half of whom are women and children), with another 14,000 missing or presumed dead. About three quarters of all civilian infrastructure (housing, hospitals, schools, and roads) has been destroyed.

In October 2025, the Trump administration, supported by Gulf Arab state diplomacy, effectively imposed a twenty-point "peace plan" that has stopped most of the fighting. ("Only" two or three Gazans a day are being killed—down from ten times that number before the current "cessation" of hostilities.) This, however, came only after two years of international inaction. (The UN Security Council, largely because of US support for Israel, was unable to act, except for arranging a brief ceasefire in early 2025. And the Emergency Special Session of the United Nations General Assembly in October 2023 could only adopt several nonbinding resolutions.) And serious peace negotiations seem far off—as does even the beginnings of reconstruction in Gaza. (Even the famine that the United Nations declared in the summer has not been alleviated.)

There have, however, been important international legal efforts to address both Hamas's crimes that began the war and Israel's responsibility for war crimes, crimes against humanity, and genocide.

In January 2024, South Africa filed an application under the Genocide Convention with the International Court of Justice (ICJ), accusing Israel of committing genocide in Gaza.[5] The Court, having determined that the claims are plausible and agreeing to take on the case, ordered Israel to immediately comply with several provisional measures, including halting any activities that constitute acts of genocide, desisting in inciting genocide, enabling the provision of humanitarian assistance, and preserving evidence (it declined, however, to order Israel to suspend military operations, as South Africa had requested). Israel has refuted these claims, calling them "an obscene exploitation" of the Genocide Convention, and has ignored the provisional measures.

In addition, the Prosecutor of International Criminal Court (ICC) in May 2024 asked for arrest warrants for Hamas leaders Mohammed Deif, Ismail Haniyeh, and Yahya Sinwar—which have been rendered moot by their deaths. And in November 2024 the ICC issued arrest warrants for Israeli Prime Minister Binjamin Netanyahu and former Defense Minister Yoav Gallant.

A UN Commission of Inquiry, established by the Human Rights Council and led by former High Commissioner for Human Rights Navi Pillay, has issued three reports examining Israeli violations of international humanitarian law.[6] The third, issued in September 2025,

> ...concludes on reasonable grounds that the Israeli authorities and Israeli security forces have committed and are continuing to commit the following *actus reus* [action or conduct which is a constituent element of a crime] of genocide against the Palestinians in the Gaza Strip, namely (i) killing members of the group; (ii) causing serious bodily or mental harm to members of the group; (iii) deliberately inflicting on the group conditions of life calculated to bring about its physical destruction in whole or in part; and (iv) imposing measures intended to prevent births within the group.[7]

The Commission of Inquiry also found that Israeli President Isaac Herzog, as well as Netanyahu and Gallant, are responsible for incitement to commit genocide and that their actions are evidence of the necessary *mens rea*—intent—to commit genocide. The Commission also had several recommendations for all other members of the international community: to take all reasonable measures to prevent the further commission of genocide in Gaza; to halt all arms transfers to Israel where there is reason to suspect they may be used in the commission of genocide; to facilitate investigations and take actions—such as applying sanctions—against the State of Israel; and to cooperate with the investigations of the Prosecutor of the ICC on its investigations.

It will take years, though, before the ICJ makes a final determination in the South Africa case. And although its decisions are legally binding, the Court has no way to enforce its rulings. Furthermore, there is little likelihood that the ICC will be able to bring Israeli officials to justice.

As with Syria, the particular political context and circumstances of the Gaza War have conspired to thwart the application of the R2P in any meaningful way. Israel has enjoyed the support of the United States and its allies since its founding in 1948 (notwithstanding often sharply pointed criticisms of Israeli foreign policy). It possesses nuclear weapons and has one of the best-trained armed forces in the world. The idea of an armed intervention to stop the atrocities in Gaza was simply not plausible. And the United States, the only country with the capability to intervene, has instead strongly supported the Israeli war effort, not only diplomatically but with tens of billions of dollars in military aid.

Syria and Gaza make it clear that the immediate post-Cold War "era" of humanitarian intervention and R2P is at an end. Born of the atrocities of the 1990s and nurtured in a renewed and reinvigorated commitment to human rights and humanitarian law, the successes of that period were due not only to solid normative and strengthening institutional foundations but also to the political will and commitment to back up its tenets with political will and material capacity—most importantly by the United States, supported by its European allies.

The erosion of the political and material elements of a robust commitment to humanitarian law did not happen overnight. The United States lost enormous soft power resources fighting the "war on terror" (especially in Iraq and Afghanistan). This was followed by the retreat of the United States in the wake of the Libya intervention, which contributed to the paralysis over Syria. And, as America retreated, headwinds from powers such as China, Russia, and India were blowing ever stronger.

A real responsibility to protect requires political will and the use of power to be effective. And that just has not existed for the past two decades.

This does not necessarily mean a retreat to power politics or a return to a world in which genocide is recognized as an (unfortunate but unquestionable) exercise of state sovereignty. Nonetheless, the hope that humanitarian intervention against genocide was becoming a firmly established practice of international society now appears to have been in vain.

Discussion Questions

1. How do you interpret the rapid switch from ethnic tolerance to violent ethnic mobilization in the former Yugoslavia? Clearly, we are not dealing with primordial animosities, especially in the case of Serbs and Croats, who had no significant political contact with one another until the twentieth century. But what do you imagine the relative mix was between deep but repressed animosities and the opportunistic manipulation of differences that led to social and political discrimination? Which explanation is more frightening?
2. Is there any moral or theoretical significance in the sharp discrepancy in responses to genocide and responses to other kinds of human rights violations? What *dangers* are posed to international human rights policies when we respond forcefully only to unusually photogenic suffering? In thinking about this issue, consider the analogy of relatively strong international responses to famine but much more modest responses to the more serious problem of malnutrition.
3. In recent years, there has been much talk of a clash of civilizations and the development of anti-Islamic attitudes in the West, especially in the United States. How does Bosnia fit into such arguments? Some have charged that the West did not do more because the Bosnians were Muslims. Others have pointed to the responses in Bosnia and in Kosovo to show how the West was able to distinguish between politicized Islamists and ordinary adherents of one of the world's great religions. Which reading seems more correct?
4. The former Yugoslavia has been used in arguments about the place of race in contemporary Western foreign policies. Here, the comparison is with Rwanda. Did the West do more to stop genocide in Croatia and Bosnia, because the victims were White, than in Rwanda, where the victims were Black? What other explanations might there be? Is it as simple as the fact that the killing in Rwanda was over quickly? Remember the length of time it took to get the West seriously involved in Bosnia.
5. Bosnia and Rwanda illustrate a willingness to respond to genocide *after* it has occurred. Why is there no comparable international willingness to respond to *prevent* genocide? Is Kosovo the exception that proves the rule?

6. The war crimes tribunal for the former Yugoslavia, the parallel process for war crimes in Rwanda, and the creation of the International Criminal Court have finally introduced an element of personal international legal responsibility to human rights violations, at least in the case of genocidal warfare. This is obviously of great symbolic significance. But what is its practical value? In the particular cases? In the future? In answering these questions, try to recall the earlier discussions of the role of normative transformation and the relative strengths and weaknesses of individual petition procedures.
7. What *are* the lessons of Libya, Sudan, and Syria? To what extent do these cases undercut—or reveal the limits of—the progress of the 1990s? Is this a question that can be answered confidently before we know what comes next?
8. Would the world be a better place if there were a true R2P for victims of genocide? How could this be achieved? And what would its *costs* be?
9. What about a true international R2P for victims of (other) gross and systemic violations of human rights? Again, consider mechanisms, benefits, and costs.
10. Is justification for humanitarian intervention really as complex as suggested in this chapter? Or is it more a simple case of choosing between the obvious moral obligation to act against genocide and crimes against humanity and the unwillingness to pay the costs of discharging that obligation?

Suggested Readings

Two of the best introductory book-length discussions are Thomas G. Weiss, *Humanitarian Intervention*, 3rd ed. (Polity Press, 2016) and Aidan Hehir, *Humanitarian Intervention: An Introduction*, 2nd ed. (Palgrave Macmillan, 2013).

Nick Wheeler's *Saving Strangers: Humanitarian Intervention in International Society* (Oxford University Press, 2000) is perhaps the best single book on the topic considered as an issue in international relations, focusing on Cold War-era practice and its transformation in the 1990s. Samantha Power, *"A Problem from Hell": America and the Age of Genocide* (Basic Books, 2002), is a well-written, thoughtful, and engaging, even gripping, account that includes extended case studies of Bosnia, Rwanda, and Kosovo. Recent good books include Piotr Pietrzak, *On the Idea of Humanitarian Intervention* (Columbia University Press, 2021); Jonathan Perry, *The Ethics of Humanitarian Intervention: An Introduction* (Routledge, 2024); and Michael J. Butler, *Reconstructing the Responsibility to Protect: From Humanitarian Intervention to Human Security* (Routledge, 2024). Cian Moran, *The Evolution of Humanitarian Intervention in International Law: From the Ottoman Empire to the Russia-Ukraine War* (Brill/Nijhoff, 2025) and Fabian Klose, ed., *The Emergence of Humanitarian Intervention: Ideas and Practices from the Nineteenth Century to the Present* (Cambridge University Press, 2018) provide historical context.

The essential starting point for thinking ethically about humanitarian intervention is Michael Walzer, *Just and Unjust Wars* (Basic Books, 1977), 53–63, 101–108. This classic book lays out a strong ethical–legal defense of sovereignty (as a reflection of the rights of individual and communal self-determination) and then argues no less powerfully for a limited right to humanitarian intervention in cases of enslavement or massacre that shock the moral conscience of mankind. Terry Nardin, "The Moral Basis of Humanitarian Intervention," *Ethics and International Affairs* 16 (2002): 57–70 contrast statist defenses such as Walzer's with an alternative tradition that appeals directly to substantive principles of natural law and justice. See also Terry Nardin and Melissa S. Williams, eds., *Humanitarian Intervention* (New York University Press, 2006); John K. Roth, ed., *Genocide and Human Rights: A Philosophical Guide* (Palgrave Macmillan, 2005); and Larry May, *Genocide: A Normative Account* (Cambridge University Press, 2010).

William A. Schabas, *Genocide in International Law: The Crime of Crimes*, 2nd ed. (Cambridge University Press, 2009), is the authoritative international legal account. David Luban, Julie R. O'Sullivan, David P. Stewart, and Neha Jain, *International and Transnational Criminal Law,* 4th ed. (Aspen, 2023), tackles the issue from the perspective of international criminal law more broadly.

Although this chapter focuses its attention narrowly on international responses to genocide, readers are likely to be interested in further sources on the broader issue. Adam Jones, *Genocide: A Comprehensive Introduction*, 4th ed. (Routledge, 2023), is a good starting point. Dale C. Tatum, *Genocide at the Dawn of the Twenty-First Century: Rwanda, Bosnia, Kosovo, and Darfur* (Palgrave Macmillan, 2010), covers most of the cases considered in this chapter. Much recent debate has been structured around *The Responsibility to Protect*, the report of the International Commission on Intervention and State Sovereignty (available online at https://www.globalr2p.org/resources/the-responsibility-to-protect-report-of-the-international-commission-on-intervention-and-state-sovereignty-2001/), which can be read as an effort both to codify the normative progress of the 1990s and to begin a conversation over a more robust doctrine of armed humanitarian intervention. Alex J. Bellamy & Tim Dunne, eds., *The Oxford Handbook of the Responsibility to Protect*, (Oxford University Press, 2016) is an excellent wide-ranging overview. The academic journal *Global Responsibility to Protect* (published by Brill/Nijhoff) is a good source for recent developments in and applications of the idea.

On the broader UN role in armed humanitarianism, see Edward Newman, Roland Paris, and Oliver P. Richmond, eds., *New Perspectives on Liberal Peacebuilding* (United Nations University Press, 2009); William J. Durch, ed., *Twenty-First-Century Peace Operations* (U.S. Institute of Peace and the Henry L. Stimson Center, 2006); and Mats Berdal and Spyros Economides, eds., *United Nations Interventionism, 1991–2004* (Cambridge University Press, 2007).

Among more critical perspectives, classic works include David Chandler's *From Kosovo to Kabul: Human Rights and International Intervention* (Pluto Press, 2002) and David Rieff's *At the Point of a Gun: Democratic Dreams and Armed Intervention* (Simon & Schuster, 2005) and *A Bed for the Night: Humanitarianism in Crisis* (Simon & Schuster, 2002). Noam Chomsky, *A New Generation Draws the Line: Humanitarian Intervention and the "Responsibility to Protect" Today* (Routledge, 2025) is up to date and engaging.

Notes

1 The UN's International Law Commission has completed draft articles for such a treaty and sent its recommendations to the General Assembly in 2019 (see UN Doc A/74/10). In December 2024, the UN General Assembly adopted resolution 79/122 which calls for a "Conference of Plenipotentiaries" to convene in 2028 and 2029 to finalize the drafting process.

2 https://www.globalr2p.org/resources/the-responsibility-to-protect-report-of-the-international-commission-on-intervention-and-state-sovereignty-2001/.

3 See paragraphs 138–140 of the 2005 World Summit Outcome at www.un.org/en/development/desa/population/migration/generalassembly/docs/globalcompact/A_RES_60_1.pdf.

4 Peter R. Baehr, "Controversies in the Current International Human Rights Debate," *Human Rights Review* 2, no. 1 (2000): 32n75.

5 As we go to press, twenty-nine UN member-states have joined South Africa in the case, as have the AU, the Organization of Islamic Cooperation, the Arab League, and the Non-Aligned Movement. Over 1,400 NGOs, political parties and movements, unions, and other civil society actors have signed on in support of South Africa. A much smaller group of states—Austria, the Czech Republic, France, Germany, Guatemala, Hungary, Italy, Paraguay, the United Kingdom, and the United States—has joined Israel.

6 See https://www.un.org/unispal/un-human-rights-council-and-the-question-of-palestine/.

7 UN Doc. A/HRC/60/CRP.3, para. 252.

Globalization, the State, and Human Rights

12

It is difficult to talk about international relations today for more than a few minutes without at least raising the issue of globalization. In addressing the implications of globalization for human rights we will focus on the web of interconnected processes that challenge the political, economic, and cultural primacy of the state—which, as we have seen, has principal responsibility for implementing human rights. In particular, we ask whether globalization is undermining the protection and promotion of human rights.

1 Globalization

Globalization is generally understood literally to mean the creation of structures and processes that span the entire globe. People, goods, money, and ideas increasingly move and interact across—even irrespective of—national territorial boundaries. Markets, politics, and culture are increasingly becoming transnational, even global, not (only) national.

Globalization is typically understood to be especially closely connected to the spread of capitalist markets and the growing transnational integration of systems of production and distribution. This process goes back at least to the maritime expansion of the West that began in the late fifteenth century but accelerated dramatically in the nineteenth century. "The need of a constantly expanding market for its products chases the bourgeoise over the whole surface of the globe. It must nestle everywhere, settle everywhere, establish connexions everywhere," Marx and Engels famously wrote in the *Communist Manifesto* in 1848.

Globalization, however, is not merely an economic phenomenon. And globalization's other dimensions also have more or less long histories. For example, today's information technology revolution, involving high-speed digital networks with ever-growing bandwidth, has a lineage that stretches back not just through television, radio, telephone, and telegraph but to steamships, railroads, and clipper ships. The globalizing spread of ideas and practices of electoral democracy and individual human rights builds on the centuries-old

DOI: 10.4324/9781003373520-15

spread of sovereign territorial states and the incorporation in the nineteenth century of the entire globe into what was originally the European states system.

Nonetheless, the pace of change has accelerated dramatically and important qualitative differences began to be widely noted at the end of the twentieth century. Today, social, political, economic, and cultural action above, below, outside, around, and even without much concern for the state is a practical reality for a much greater number of individuals and groups, in a much greater number of arenas and areas of concern, than it was for the preceding few centuries—which was the era of the territorial state.

Particularly striking is the interaction and growing interdependence of material, institutional, and ideational change. For example, the transnational consolidation of capitalist markets has been accompanied by the spread of market ideologies supported by a vast array of multilateral agencies (the most important being the World Bank, the International Monetary Fund, and the World Trade Organization) and multinational banks and corporations. Revolutions in telecommunications and transportation have even begun to alter how we conceive of ourselves and the communities in which our lives are embedded and how we relate to governmental power.

The modern state, in its nineteenth- and twentieth-century form, developed in large measure to harness, and later to tame and regulate, the exponential technological, economic, and commercial changes driven by industrialization. States created managed currencies, centralized systems of banking and credit, policies to incentivize global trade, commerce, and investment, and government programs to regulate commercial activity, provide social insurance, and assist the poor in order to spread the benefits of new developments in science, technology, and industrial organization.

All of that now is changing.

The forces of globalization are increasingly challenging the state from above. Ever larger and stronger business enterprises are adopting a truly global (not merely multinational or transnational) form and outlook, causing even powerful states to lose control over aspects of their economies and polities that they have long been accustomed to dominating. Regional and international regimes and organizations increasingly influence, and sometimes even make, decisions that once were unquestionably the province of states. Transnational nongovernmental organizations (NGOs) and activists now exert powerful and sophisticated pressures on states (and businesses) on issues such as human rights and the environment.

Globalization is also contributing to challenges from below to the state, which in many places increasingly seems too large and cumbersome to respond effectively to the diverse needs of ordinary people. Local and regional autonomy has become a common theme, especially (but not only) in Europe.

Spain has perhaps gone the furthest among non-federal states in devolving spending and decision-making powers to regional authorities, not just in the Basque and Catalan regions but throughout the country. But even these moves to satisfy local demands have not been enough, as Catalan leaders and the central government in Madrid engaged in a very tense constitutional crisis in 2016. Consider also the creation of the Scottish and Welsh Parliaments in the United Kingdom (and the nearly successful independence referendum in

Scotland in 2014), the emergence of the Northern League as a powerful political force in Italy, and the revival of regional languages such as Breton in France and Frisian in the Netherlands. In many countries of the Global South as well, demands for greater autonomy are often focused on an intrastate region rather than on creating a separate state (the Kurds, for example, have been able to secure greater autonomy within Iraq, and have called for the same in Syria once the war there is over). "Localization" has become another dimension of globalization.

In fact, the local and the global are increasingly linked *without the intermediation of the state*. Multinational businesses provide the most obvious example (see the case study later in this chapter and Chapter 10). But new information and transportation technologies also allow the disenfranchised to leap over their own (often hostile or indifferent) states. For example, twenty five years ago Alison Brysk showed how indigenous peoples in the Americas are able to interact "virtually," as we now call it, with their colleagues and allies across the globe, dramatically improving their bargaining position vis-à-vis their own state.[1] This is a striking example of what Margaret Keck and Kathryn Sikkink call the "boomerang" model of transnational advocacy: local actors direct information and appeals to transnational colleagues, foreign states, and regional and international organizations, who respond by mobilizing external pressure on resistant states (see also Chapter 9).[2]

Some of these new flows of structures, processes, and opportunities are empowering. The spread of human rights ideas, and their rise to global pre-eminence in the post-Cold War era, can be seen as an element of globalization. More prosaically, individuals and groups with shared interests increasingly are able to interact, in real time, over immense distances, without regard to the boundaries between (or the interests of) states. The Internet and modern transportation networks have allowed a growing number of communities in the Global South to exploit the benefits of agricultural and craft cooperatives, fair-trade products, and alternative crops such as miniature vegetables for high-profit markets in developed countries. Mobile phones allow even small entrepreneurs in poor countries to make connections with customers and suppliers that open up previously unimagined possibilities for business and a better life for themselves and their families. Even anti-globalization protests have been significantly facilitated by global communications and transportation technologies.

However, other global flows that circumvent the state have a much darker side. Consider, for example, burgeoning transnational criminal enterprises, transnational human trafficking, sex tourism, the use of social media to recruit people to join terrorist groups, the global epidemic of dis/misinformation, the spread of illiberal democracy, and the growing market in private security services. There is also an ominous side to the ability of large global firms to accumulate wealth and power that increasingly escapes national regulation and is subject to, at most, only minimal international oversight.

No single chapter can even begin to approach the full range of human rights issues posed by globalization. Here, we focus on the challenge that the economic aspects of globalization pose to the effective operation of the liberal–democratic welfare state, which underpins the enjoyment of economic and social human rights in much of the world.

2 States and Human Rights

The state is both the principal violator and the principal protector of human rights. Much human rights advocacy—and much of the discussion in preceding chapters—has focused on state violations. Globalization, however, suggests focusing more on the essential role that states play in implementing and protecting human rights, especially (but not exclusively) economic and social rights. To repeat, we have a system of national (that is, state) implementation of international human rights.

As we have seen, most people enjoy their internationally recognized human rights, particularly when they require coercive enforcement, as a result of action taken by their own state. Even Europe's strong and effective regional human rights regime, as we saw in Section 6.1, is largely a supplement and spur to national action. In fact, the struggle of dispossessed groups has typically been a struggle for full legal and political recognition by the state, and, thus, inclusion among those whose rights it protects. Human rights advocacy is in many ways aimed at transforming the state from predator to protector of rights.

This is no less true of economic and social rights than it is of civil and political rights. Classical political economists across the political spectrum, from Adam Smith to Karl Marx, stressed that market systems of production and distribution, by freeing productive forces from political constraints, have immensely liberating potential. But Smith, no less than Marx, also recognized that these same productive forces (and those who control them) are typically indifferent to the fate of individuals unable to compete successfully in the predatory world of capitalist competition. Historically, the only mechanism that has been able to protect individual rights in market systems has been the state.

A human rights perspective on the state is neither pro- nor anti-state. Human rights advocates seek to promote a specific type of rights-protective state.

3 Markets and Liberal–Democratic Welfare States

The state envisioned by contemporary international human rights norms is liberal; that is, its legitimacy rests on protecting the human rights of its citizens. It is also democratic, in the sense that it is committed to universal political participation and, within the limits of the human rights of all, vests political power in the people. It is also a welfare state, with extensive economic and social obligations to protect and promote the well-being of all citizens. As we saw in Chapter 4, the state has a wide variety and range of obligations and duties with respect to economic and social rights, from creating and maintaining economic conditions that are conducive to sustained economic activity, to regulating markets, to serving as "provider of last resort" for those whose needs cannot be met through markets alone.

The experience of the Cold War and decolonization eras clearly showed that economic and social rights can be widely and sustainably provided only to the extent that markets are central to the national economy (which today is increasingly integrated into a global market-based economy). The inefficiencies of centrally planned or command economies almost always swamp any equity benefits, at least in the medium and long runs. For example, countries such as Cuba and Sri Lanka did achieve notable short- and medium-run economic success in the 1960s and 1970s. In the long run, however, neither growth nor equity has proved to be possible within a command economy. A considerable degree of economic efficiency, and thus reliance on markets, is necessary for *sustainable* progress in implementing economic and social rights.

States, therefore, play at least two vital economic roles. They must facilitate the operation of markets in order to foster economic growth. And they must (re)distribute opportunities and market-allocated resources to ensure that growth contributes to the enjoyment of economic and social rights by all.

Markets, by design, distribute the benefits of growth without regard for individual needs and rights (other than property rights). Markets seek economic efficiency in the aggregate—that is, maximizing the total quantity of goods and services produced with a given quantity of resources. Markets promise to produce more overall, not more for all (that is, everyone). And those who benefit from markets do not benefit equally.

Market distributions take into account only economic value added, which varies sharply across individuals and social groups. "Free" markets *necessarily* produce gross economic inequalities. The poor tend to be much "less efficient." Poor people, on average, have relatively few skills that are valued highly by markets. Their plight is then exacerbated when political disadvantage, whether formal (e.g., disenfranchisement) or informal (e.g., lack of effective access to decision-makers), contributes to a vicious rights-abusive cycle. Efficient markets improve the lot of some—ideally even most—at the cost of (relative and perhaps even absolute) deprivation of others. And that suffering is concentrated among society's most vulnerable members.

Advocates of markets readily admit that some are harmed, especially in the short run. Everyone, though, is supposed to benefit in the long run from the greater supply of goods and services.

"Everyone," however, does not mean each and every *individual*. Rather, economists refer to the *average* individual—an entirely abstract, "per capita" entity. And even the average person is assured of significant gain only at some point in the future. Here, now, and in the near future, many real flesh-and-blood individual human beings, families, and communities suffer. Even worse, because markets distribute the benefits of growth without regard to short-term deprivations, those who suffer "adjustment costs"—lost jobs, higher food prices, or inferior health care—acquire no market-based claim to a future share of the collective benefits.

Although markets rely on individual initiative, they ground a collectivist, utilitarian political theory. Markets are justified by arguments of collective good and aggregate benefit, not individual rights (other than the right to private property and economic accumulation). Free markets are an economic analogue to a political system of majority rule without minority rights.

The welfare state, from this perspective, is a device to ensure that a minority (or majority) that is disadvantaged within, or deprived by, markets is still treated with minimum economic concern and respect. Only when the pursuit of prosperity is tamed by economic and social rights—when markets are embedded in a welfare state—does a market-based economy merit our respect.

Without welfare states (or other comparable redistributive mechanisms), there is no necessary connection between market-led growth and development and the enjoyment of economic and social rights, *human* development, and welfare. And all existing liberal democracies use the welfare state to compensate (some of) those who fare less well in the market.

Individuals who are harmed by the operation of social institutions that benefit the whole (in this case, markets and private property rights) are entitled to a fair share of the social product that their participation has helped to produce. The collectivity that benefits in the aggregate has an obligation to look after individual members who are disadvantaged in or harmed by markets. The welfare state guarantees *all* individuals certain economic and social goods, services, and opportunities, irrespective of the market value of their labor.

In fact, one of the great human rights achievements of the past century has been the humanization of capitalist markets by welfare states. State regulation of hours, wages, and working conditions is widely accepted (in theory at least) in most countries throughout the world. Furthermore, citizens of most states—not simply those with developed market economies—consider their governments to be obliged to provide minimum levels of subsistence, housing, health care, and social services to those unable to acquire them through family or market mechanisms.

The welfare state, however, is under assault from economic globalization. As an international division of labor continues to deepen and expand, leading to a growing separation between locales of production and consumption, firms are increasingly free to move offshore, in whole or in part, to escape the higher costs imposed by welfare state guarantees of economic and social rights. States, by contrast, for all their power, remain largely tied to and limited by a particular territory. The resulting threats to economic and social rights are particularly evident in the developed market economies of the Global North, where benefits have already begun to erode.

This, of course, is only one side of the story of the rights consequences of globalization. In China, for example, integration into a global market has lifted literally hundreds of millions of people out of extreme poverty. And the capacities of many governments have been improved as a result of access to more tax revenue and the growing sophistication of national economies and societies. (See Problem 13.1 in Chapter 13.)

The impact of globalization on human rights thus typically has been mixed. In most countries, economic opportunities and living standards have been improved for many of those who have access to the global economy—at the same time that others are left behind and still others harmed (e.g., by the conversion of land used for subsistence farming into production of agricultural exports). Globalization has resulted in generally rising incomes. But inequalities of income and especially wealth have also risen, both within states and globally.

Globalization threatens "good" states as well as "bad" states. If liberal–democratic welfare states are undermined by globalization—and if we fail to create alternative mechanisms for implementing and enforcing human rights—then the substantial achievements of the human rights movement since the end of World War II will be at risk.

4 Democracy, Markets, and Human Rights

The idea of "market democracy," which became quite popular in certain circles in the United States and the United Kingdom in the early post-Cold War period, takes a somewhat different approach to the relation between markets, human rights, and politics. Following our tendency to distinguish human rights from related social practices, we argue that although well-functioning markets and democracies certainly are good things, especially when contrasted to command economies and authoritarian or totalitarian rule, they are not the same good things as human rights. Pursuing market economies and democratic polities, either separately or together, is a very different endeavor from (although not unrelated to) pursuing human rights—something that Americans in particular often forget. In fact, conflating "market democracy" with rights-respecting polities has contributed to the current wave of polarized populism we are witnessing globally, which poses serious threats to the realization of human rights.

4.1 Democracy, Democratization, and Human Rights

Democracy answers the question of *who* should rule. Democracy empowers the people and seeks to realize their collective good. Human rights, by contrast, address *how* governments should rule. Human rights empower autonomous individuals. They seek to ensure that personal and societal goals, including democratically defined goals, are pursued within the confines of guaranteeing every individual certain minimum goods, services, opportunities, and protections.

Human rights define the range within which democratic decision-making is allowed to operate. They are concerned with each rather than all, aiming to protect every person, against majorities no less than against minorities. Human rights ordinarily take precedence over the wishes of the people, no matter how intensely even the vast majority of society desires to abuse some individual or group. In fact, in well-functioning procedurally democratic states, where the majority is relatively well positioned to care for its own rights and interests, the *principal* function of human rights is to limit democratic decision-making that might negatively affect the rights of individuals and groups not in the majority.

In the decades following the end of the Cold War, the majority of people on this planet, for the only time in history, lived under more or less democratically elected governments. This momentous achievement is a source of legitimate satisfaction. We must not, however, overestimate its human rights significance—especially as the *quality* of democracy declines in many countries. And it is not inconceivable that in another decade most of the world's population will live in nondemocratic states.

In *electoral* democracies, leaders are chosen through procedurally fair elections. Candidates, however, may pursue narrow personal or sectional interest. Competition may be restricted (usually informally, but sometimes even formally). And the electorate may not have ready access to the information required to make an informed choice. As a result, not all electoral democracies are liberal. (They don't necessarily even aim to protect the rights of all.) And illiberal democracy readily slides over into electoral authoritarianism.

Furthermore, decreased tolerance for old forms of repressive rule or popular celebrations at the fall of a dictator do not necessarily indicate widespread support for democratic rule—let alone for broadly rights-protective regimes. In fact, one of the most disturbing lessons of contemporary democracy is that many people see voting as a device for acquiring personal or sectional advantage rather than a way to ensure widespread protection of human rights.

We can distinguish three levels of political progress toward respect for internationally recognized human rights.

Liberalization involves a decrease in human rights violations and an opening of political space for at least some previously excluded individuals or groups—roughly, progress in civil and political rights short of democratization. China has undergone periodic limited liberalizations. Poland liberalized in the 1980s, initially under the pressure of the Solidarity movement, before it democratized in 1990. South Korea liberalized in the 1980s before establishing electoral democracy in the 1990s.

By *democratization*, we mean the process of establishing electoral democracy. This involves a qualitative leap beyond liberalization. When "soft" authoritarian regimes allow truly fair and open elections—not just once or if they win—the political system is fundamentally transformed.

A *rights-protective regime* both makes the protection of internationally recognized human rights a central element of its mission and, through extensive, intense, and sustained effort, has achieved considerable success in realizing this aspiration. This is a *liberal* democracy. If one insists on using the language of democratization to describe transitions from electoral to liberal democracy, one might talk about the "deepening" of democratization—although it is respect for human rights, rather than for the will of the people, that deepens.

The term *democratization* is often used to cover all three kinds of change, on the assumption that they are phases of a single, largely linear process of development. Political development, however, is not naturally driven toward a single end. Resistance to authoritarian rule is often a reaction against injustice rather than a transition to democracy (or anything else).

Take Egypt for example. In the wake of the 2011 Arab Spring, which brought the downfall of longtime military strongman Hosni Mubarak, provides a perfect example. Mohamed Morsi of the Muslim Brotherhood became president in 2012 following Egypt's first free parliamentary elections in three decades. His implementation of Islamist policies generated a new round of protests (including the walkout of more moderate elements of the parliament). Conflict became more intense, and sometimes violent, after Morsi decreed his policies to be beyond the reach of parliament—until the military suspended the constitution, removed Morsi and the Brotherhood from power, and installed an interim government.

In 2014, a new constitution was adopted in a referendum that reportedly received 98 percent of the vote (but in which only 39 percent of the electorate participated). The head of the Egyptian Armed Forces, Abdel Fattah al-Sisi, resigned his commission and ran for president in May 2014, which he handily won. (He was re-elected in 2018 with 97 percent of the vote [there was no significant organized opposition and turnout was just above 40 percent].) Pro-Sisi parties, which dominated the legislature after the 2014 election, amended the constitution to increase presidential and military authority over the country and extended al-Sisi's term of office from four to six years and removed the two-term limit on a presidency—thus allowing him to be re-elected in 2023 (with, it was reported, 90 percent of the vote). In 2019, Human Rights Watch called the human rights situation under al-Sisi "abysmal,"[3] demonstrating that even democratic procedures such as constitutional referenda and elections may produce governments that violate human rights.

This emphasizes an important further distinction. Holding elections does not make a country democratic. When, as in Egypt (and many other countries), the government severely restricts who can run for office, systematically represses opposition parties and groups, and even restricts campaigning, there is nothing democratic about the resulting election. And the higher the margin of victory, the less credible the vote. (In North Korea, 99.91 percent of the vote in the November 2023 provincial elections went to the candidates, with a typical reported turnout of over 99 percent as well.[4])

Electoral democracy may be a necessary condition for a rights-protective regime. Free, fair, and open democratic elections may even foster *liberal* democracy by allowing human rights advocates political space and opportunities. But electorally democratic governments (and the people who support them) may use their power in ways that violate, threaten, or fail to defend internationally recognized human rights.

Especially in times of crisis or disillusionment, electoral democracy may even be prone to populist, protofascist demagoguery. In recent years, the proliferation of right-wing parties and populist politicians responding to terrorism, refugees and migration, and threats to "national identity" have managed to move voters in their direction in countries such as Brazil (Jair Bolsonaro), the Czech Republic (Andrej Babiš), India (Narendra Modi), Italy (Georgia Meloni), the Philippines (both Rodrigo Duterte and his successor Bongbong Marcos), the Netherlands (Geert Wilders), France (Marine Le Pen)—and, of course, the United States (Donald Trump, whose administration publicly claims that the fact that he won the election justifies attacking his enemies and ignoring laws that do not conform to the priorities of the administration). To these, we might add longer-serving leaders who have over time become more repressive while retaining majority electoral backing (e.g., Erdoğan in Turkey, Orban in Hungary, and Netanyahu in Israel).

Elections are only a device. They have very different meanings in different political contexts. All other things being equal, it is a good thing if leaders are freely chosen by and speak for the people. But even the most perfect democracy, we are arguing, is not an end but a means—to the protection of human rights. Only when supported by rights-protective political attitudes, policies, and institutions will elections lead toward deeply liberal–democratic regimes.

The danger, especially in US foreign policy, is that we will forget that democratization is, at best, a good start on realizing human rights—and that liberalization is only a prelude to such a start. Americans seem inclined to the convenient but dangerous illusion that, once elections have been held, the struggle for human rights—or at least America's part in the struggle—is largely over. Often, in fact, though, that is when the real struggle begins.

4.2 Markets and Economic Rights

As envisioned by the Universal Declaration and the Covenants, the enjoyment of most economic and social rights requires a robust (but sometimes delicate) relationship between markets and the state. The three core obligations of states for human rights—to respect, protect, and fulfill—provide some guidance.

Respecting economic and social rights requires states to make their realization a policy priority. That means ensuring that markets are incentivized to create opportunities for individuals to meet their own needs through market transactions—like finding employment, housing, and food. States do this through regulatory and fiscal policy. In the case of adequate, affordable housing, the state must see to it that developers and builders can operate and have incentives to build housing. Realizing the right to food might mean regulating markets in production and distribution to ensure people have access to affordable food.

Protecting economic and social rights requires states to adopt nondiscrimination legislation and policy in the fields of education, employment, housing, and access to health care as well as protective regulations for workplaces, housing, public health and safety, and the environment. And it requires enforcing rights-protective laws and policies and monitoring the success of rights-respecting activities.

The obligation to fulfill has many dimensions, but the most important are to be a provider of first resort for economic and social public goods that are not best secured through markets (like basic education and public health) and a provider of last resort for those individuals who cannot meet their own needs through normal market mechanisms (because markets are non-existent, impaired, or have failed). Examples would include unemployment insurance, health care, retirement income, and support for families and children.

All advanced industrialized democracies (i.e., the members of the Organization for Economic Co-operation and Development [OECD]) basically subscribe to this model of obligations, although there is a great deal of variation. Archetypical are the social democratic welfare states of Northern and Western Europe. The United States has also broadly accepted this model, although with a much heavier emphasis on markets than direct state involvement in provision. Despite all the gaps in its coverage, the United States is a huge welfare state. For example, workers and employers together are taxed one-seventh of an employee's income just to fund a single social welfare program: state-supported old-age pensions (Social Security). The protection of robust benefits through Medicare (health insurance for the elderly) is even more sacred. Even Americans, who are more individualistic and anti-statist than most Europeans, see their welfare state as an essential part of the American political ideal. Twentieth-century liberal democracies all pursued redistributive policies that protected individual rights and sought to achieve social justice.

The "backlash" against globalization, not just in the Global South and the former Soviet bloc but in the OECD countries as well, began in the 1990s, in reaction to the neo-liberal "Washington consensus," and continued throughout the 2000s. The global financial crisis of 2008 led to significant job losses. Subsequent "austerity" measures undertaken by governments in the OECD countries (the United Kingdom provides a striking example) led to further cuts in social spending. As global migration flows increased throughout the 2010s—spurred by the global economic crisis, wars and civil conflicts (Iraq, Afghanistan, the "Arab Spring" revolts in 2011), drug and gang-related violence in Central America, and climate change)—voters in Europe and the United States grew increasingly nervous about the further erosion of the welfare state, fearing that its benefits (job protections, health care, educational opportunities) would be "stolen" by outsiders. Advanced mobile technology and social media platforms, another product of globalization, were deployed to bring populist leaders who appealed to xenophobic, racist, and national tropes to secure votes and to save their "cultures" from destruction to power. The mid-2010s saw the rise of many reactionary, right-wing movements, and leaders we mentioned above.

The onset of the COVID-19 pandemic in early 2020 created further economic and political instabilities resulting from rising mortality and the precipitous decline in global economic activity. Many on the conservative right viewed public health efforts that were hastily deployed to control the pandemic—shutdowns of schools and businesses, travel restrictions, masking and social distancing, and campaigns to get people vaccinated—were often seen as dark intrusions on personal "freedom" by leftist "elites" who controlled the levers of state power for nefarious purposes.

The pandemic also left further economic instability in its wake. Global supply chains were significantly disrupted, driving up prices (and Russia's invasion of Ukraine further increased food prices). As the supply crunch began to ease in 2022, pent-up demand drove prices up further, prompting governments to raise interest rates to tame the resulting inflation. The previous decade's global financial crisis had left many poorer countries in debt, and the increase in interest rates have hit them especially hard, compelled them to slash public services, and/or increase taxes to pay off their international loans, leading to greater political unrest (as in Kenya) and further fueling the turn toward right-wing populist parties and leaders (as in Argentina). The 2023 elections for the European Parliament brought a greater number of rightist, illiberal parties into the governing structures of the European Union. And the 2024 election in the United States gave a central voice to an often explicitly illiberal populism and a politics of grievance rather than governance.

While there are some positive signs in some countries that these shifts to the right may be moderating, as evidenced by recent elections in Poland (before 2025), Czechia, and the United Kingdom, the confluence of negative economic, technological, and political forces and consequences that are increasingly exacerbated by globalization is bound to continue unabated. (For example, in the United Kingdom election in July 2024, although the Conservative Party suffered its worst losses in its 200-year history, the ultra-nationalist Reform UK Party under the leadership of Nigel Farage [who was the force behind Brexit] won a significant number of seats in Parliament. Turnout for the election was very low by historical standards, suggesting that a return to center-left politics in the United Kingdom may be short lived if Labour does not address the most pressing challenges facing the United Kingdom today, including the broken national health care system). The question becomes: what will this mean for human rights in the short and medium term?

5 An Alliance of States and Human Rights Advocates?

If the welfare state is increasingly unable to ensure economic and social rights for all, regional or global institutions might seem to present an obvious solution. The problem, of course, is that there is little evidence of the imminent emergence of global (or, outside of Europe, even regional) redistributive institutions. Virtually all states, including even well-to-do and committed liberal–democratic welfare states, remain extremely reluctant to transfer substantial authority or resources to supranational political institutions. And over the past two decades, there has been a sharp rise in the domestic political popularity of "economic nationalism."

Nonetheless, interstate mechanisms are not necessarily doomed to failure. For example, the harmonization of social policies in the European Union can be viewed as a collective regional effort to reduce the incentives of individual states to compete for jobs by dismantling the welfare state. Europe, however, looks very much like the exception that proves the rule. And even the Europeans seem uninterested in using the OECD, or some new institution, to spread cooperation on social policy across a wider range of developed market economies. The Eurozone crisis of 2011–2013 suggests a deep reluctance to bear substantial costs even on behalf of other EU members. And the 2016 decision by voters in the United Kingdom to leave the European Union (Brexit) demonstrated that economic globalization can provoke a democratic nationalist backlash—in this case, seeing workers from the rest of the Union as a threat to the economic security of Britain (and especially in England outside of relatively cosmopolitan London).

Transnational actors offer another potential mechanism for revitalizing economic and social rights. Even in these challenging times, human rights NGOs, trade unions, women's groups, environmentalists, indigenous peoples, and a host of other civil society organizations continue to share a common interest in (re)asserting welfare state control over global markets and multinational business. Civil society actors, however, are at an extreme disadvantage, both because of their relative lack of economic and political resources and because they face far greater problems in forming national and transnational alliances. In addition, although not as territorially bound as states, they are usually less mobile than the businesses against whom they are pitted.

The current international situation with respect to economic and social rights has parallels to conditions in Western Europe and the United States in the last half of the nineteenth century, where business had the upper hand and skillfully used its resources to protect its interests. Contemporary global firms also have the advantage of being able to play country against country—and in the United States, because of its federal system, state against state. Those seeking to strengthen the welfare state, by contrast, face the daunting task of (re) establishing control. Businesses need only evade regulation.

Advocates of economic and social rights, however, have resources of their own, including national electoral power and advanced communications technologies that increase their capabilities for national and transnational organization. Furthermore, unlike in the nineteenth century, they can draw on the moral force of authoritative international human rights norms and the accumulated experience of many decades of welfare state policies.

In addition, advocates of internationally recognized economic and social rights share a common interest with at least some government elites in controlling transnational business (in the United States, we can think of Elizabeth Warren or Bernie Sanders, both Democrats, who were seeking their party's nomination to become president in 2020). Especially in highly institutionalized liberal–democratic welfare states, human rights advocates and states share a deeply rooted desire to temper the efficiency of markets with rights-based concerns for at least minimally equitable distributions of social goods, services, and opportunities. Of course, state elites often seek control over business for their own selfish, even predatory, purposes. But even then, their shared desire to gain greater control over corporate practices and profits provides the basis for at least tactical political alliances with human rights advocates.

Once again, the issue is not the state per se but the type of state. Transnational businesses are using economic globalization to press for states that give greater emphasis to markets, the domain of social action where their power and skills to achieve their goals are greatest. On the other side, human rights advocates and allied elements of civil society are seeking to use their electoral, organizational, and moral power on behalf of welfare states. The fate of human rights thus is likely to depend, in the twenty-first century, as in the nineteenth and twentieth centuries, on who controls the state and how they use that control. In those countries where human rights advocates are maintaining or strengthening their position, an alliance with the state may prove the best way to reestablish the social control over markets necessary to ensure economic and social rights for all—although, as we noted above, the rise of populist nationalism in Europe and the United States has weakened the position of national as well as transnational human rights advocates.

The fundamental fact of globalization, however, is that no individual state acting alone is able to impose extensive new regulations or even hold onto its former ability to control its own firms—let alone its own economy. (The second Trump administration has quickly run up against this uncomfortable fact in its efforts to make America economically great again.) States and other international actors must cooperate, regionally and internationally, if they are to have a chance of humanizing global markets. And they must forge new alliances with national and transnational civil society actors. Whether this is practically possible, however, is by no means clear.

"My enemy's enemy is my friend," the old rule of realist international politics, applies today to states and human rights advocates. Whatever their past animosities, today they face a new common enemy. The future of human rights just might be determined by their ability to develop new forms of cooperation that protect the state as an essential mechanism for realizing human rights—at least until new mechanisms are created (which still seems, at best, very far off in a speculative future).

A central purpose of human rights advocacy has always been to empower people to force their state to treat them as they deserve to be treated—shaping states into instruments to protect, rather than ignore or even trample on, the human rights of their citizens. This has always required states and citizens to stand up to, and attempt to exert control over, national, transnational, and global actors and forces. That struggle continues. Human rights demand that it must continue. But we worry that some of the hard-won human rights progress of the twentieth century may be at significant risk—and that, in the near future at least, more of the work of human rights advocacy will be about holding the line rather than raising the bar.

Problem 12.1 Human Rights Obligations of Multinational Corporations

The Problem

Multinational corporations (MNCs) are immensely powerful actors that are becoming increasingly global in character (not simply multinational). Doesn't it make sense, then, to impose direct human rights obligations on MNCs? Why should their immense economic power not be matched with direct human rights responsibilities? Isn't this especially the case because globalization has restricted the ability of welfare states to provide economic and social rights for their citizens?

In 2011, Human Rights Council Resolution 17/4[5] endorsed a set of guiding principles regarding businesses and human rights[6] which affirm that states are obligated to prevent corporations from committing human rights abuses and that corporations are obligated to refrain from either committing human rights abuses or contributing indirectly to human rights abuses by other countries. Furthermore, they establish that states are obligated to provide remedies to individuals who have been harmed as a result of corporate human rights abuses. Resolution 17/4 also created the UN Working Group on Business and Human Rights to monitor progress in achieving these goals.[7]

These principles, which we addressed in Chapter 10, emphasize the fact that businesses, like all social actors, have a duty not to deprive people of the enjoyment of their human rights. And emphasizing that point is certainly appropriate given the immense economic (and often political) power of large corporations.

Here, however, we consider going further. Should states and regional and international organizations impose duties to protect or provide human rights directly on corporations? (On the distinction between duties to respect [i.e., not to deprive], to protect, and fulfill [i.e., provide], which is central to the following discussion, see Chapter 2, Section 7.)

A Solution

Imposing special direct human rights obligations on corporations to protect or provide human rights, we will argue, is not appropriate, either for business in general or multinational or foreign corporations in particular.

Businesses, like all other social actors, have obligations not to deprive people of the enjoyment of their rights. Large MNCs have unusually great opportunities to commit human rights abuses. But they are (and ought to be) neither more nor less bound not to deprive people of their rights than individuals, NGOs, or states—or, for that matter, smaller local businesses (which often have human rights impacts at least as extensive and as bad as their multinational colleagues).

This is not to argue against shareholders and citizens, in both home and host countries, pressing multinational firms to, for example, improve the working conditions of their employees, respect their rights to organize and bargain collectively, and not harm the health of those living near their factories or facilities. In fact, in this edition, we have added a new chapter (10) on businesses and human rights that emphasizes the roles of shareholders and citizens. Such activities, however, currently do not involve obligations to protect or provide human rights. And that, we will argue, is how it should be.

If a state wishes to, it may require firms of a certain size or value operating under their jurisdiction to provide their employees, or the communities within which they operate, with, for example, schools, clinics, or housing. (As we have already noted, employer provision is a central feature of the system of health care in the United States.) There is no good reason, though, why every state should do that—let alone that international human rights law should be revised to impose such obligations on some or all firms.

Why single out firms? Why not also wealthy individuals and families, churches, or charities?

More fundamentally, do we really want corporations to be responsible for protecting or providing our rights? As private, profit-making enterprises, they would seem to be particularly poorly suited to carrying out such duties. And in their areas of expertise and operation, self-regulation—that is, assigning firms duties to protect—is likely a recipe for disaster.

Many states might be misguided or inept in exercising their duties to protect and provide. But there is no reason to suspect that firms would systematically do a better job. The reliance of the United States on employer-provided health insurance is hardly a promising model. The Japanese system of firm-based provision, which worked well in the 1960s and 1970s, has come under considerable strain and plays a decreasingly small role in the overall system of provision. And there are few other examples of even limited success.

One might respond that the discussion so far "misses the point." The "real problem" is that corporations—especially large MNCs operating in poorer and even middle-income countries—regularly get away with rights-abusive practices.

This is, indeed, a problem. But it is a problem largely because governments fail to discharge their duties to protect. And usually that is not because they *cannot* control the activities of large firms. Rather they choose not to. Only rarely can firms hold governments hostage. Usually, governments do not want to bear the political costs—or members of the government and other supporters of the firm do not want to accept the personal, professional, or financial costs—of enforcing human rights protections against powerful violators.

Therefore, placing obligations to provide human rights on firms will rarely work. If the firm already is not respecting its duties not to deprive, why would we expect it to respect (usually much more burdensome) duties to provide? And if governments are not enforcing duties not to deprive, why would we imagine that they would better enforce duties to provide?

If the problem is a lack of local enforcement, though, what about multilateral enforcement? But do we really want global multilateral enforcement of even a limited range of human rights *in our own country*?

Corporations, both local and foreign, often do use their power in harmful ways, harming both workers and communities, both directly and through their influence over local and national governments. The solutions to such problems, however, are standard legal and political solutions, not new human rights duties. Not every wrong—not even every large systematic wrong—has (or ought to have) a human rights remedy.

Further Problems

Privatization of government functions has been a major area of discussion in the United States and some other countries for the past few decades. The record has been, at best, mixed. In some sectors, such as transportation and communications, private actors have often succeeded in providing services more efficiently (although usually less because they are private than because they are not monopolistic). But in others—consider health care in the United States—private provision has been disastrously inefficient (that is, much more expensive to provide a lower level of service). And here we are only talking about relatively simple issues efficiency; of cost for services.

Things become much more complicated when public authority and responsibilities are added to the mix. Consider private prisons in the United States and private security services and mercenary fighters ("private contractors") across the globe

Is there any reason to believe that profit-making businesses are better able to provide human rights than states? Which kinds of rights? What about nonprofit organizations?

Now ask the same questions about *protecting* human rights. Where might businesses have a comparative advantage? And even if we were to contract out service provision, ultimately responsibility would—or, we would argue, should—remain with the state.

None of this is intended to argue against mixed systems of provision. Nonetheless, it seems to us clear that the mix between state and nonstate provision is one of those areas where we should not merely expect but positively value international variations based on local culture, history, and politics. In some circumstances, it might be just as good, or even better, to shift some of the burden of provision to businesses. But there are likely to be few if any general rules about when that will work. And it certainly should not be internationally mandated, either for any particular right or class of rights or in any particular circumstance.

What, though, are the limits on designing a system of provision that makes unusually heavy use of private provision by corporations and not-for-profit providers? Consider this question in the context of the United States, which compared to other countries at a similar level of wealth and development relies unusually heavily on private provision of rights to, for example, health, housing, food, social security, and education. Does the American example overall cut more in favor of, or more against, arguments for nonstate provision? Are there significant differences between sectors? And even if one has a generally positive assessment of the American approach, does this suggest adopting it elsewhere? Or is the American approach justified primarily on grounds of historical tradition and appeals to other values (e.g., personal responsibility or "small government")?

Discussion Questions

1. When you use the term *globalization*, what exactly do you mean? Is it a recent phenomenon or a long-term process? What are its dimensions? Is the global spread of human rights itself a phenomenon of globalization?
2. Human rights advocates typically focus on states as a threat to human rights. This chapter suggests that globalization is forcing human rights advocates to emphasize the role of the state as protector. Has there really been a change? Hasn't the role of the state as protector always been central? If so, then why the increasing attention to that role now?
3. Is the welfare state really such a wonderful achievement? Is globalization making a positive contribution by freeing economic initiative from the shackles of excessive regulation? (*Which* regulations are "excessive" [on what grounds]?) Can't we see the shift produced by globalization in the balance of power away from states as basically a positive trend? Why do advocates of liberal–democratic welfare states want the state in our lives economically but out of our lives in other domains?
4. Why are Americans, who claim to be so individualistic, so attracted to democracy and markets, which are fundamentally collective systems of political justification? What kind of individualism is it that Americans really value?
5. The United States and several countries in Europe have recently turned toward more right-wing politicians. These political actors promise economic rights in terms of new jobs to be gained by reversing globalization. Is this the right way forward for economic recovery/growth? For human rights? Is it even possible? At what costs?
6. Will AI—here meaning artificial intelligence not Amnesty International—make things better or worse? How might AI empower defenders of human rights? How might it strengthen corporations and illiberal and authoritarian governments? What do you think the balance will be in the coming decade? In the following decades?

Suggested Readings

Perhaps the best discussion of human rights and globalization remains Rhoda E. Howard-Hassmann, *Can Globalization Promote Human Rights?* (Pennsylvania State University Press,

2010). Her answer to the title question is a strong but qualified yes—if the efficiencies of global markets can be harnessed to human development in ways comparable to those used by liberal and social democratic welfare states in the twentieth century. An article-length version of Howard-Hassmann's argument is also available: "The Second Great Transformation: Human Rights Leapfrogging in the Era of Globalization," *Human Rights Quarterly* 27 (February 2005): 1–40. A similar and in many ways complementary argument is developed in David Kinley, *Civilising Globalisation: Human Rights and the Global Economy* (Cambridge University Press, 2009). For a much more negative assessment, see Neve Gordon, ed., *From the Margins of Globalization: Critical Perspectives on Human Rights* (Lexington Books, 2004).

Jean-Marc Coicaud, Michael W. Doyle, and Anne-Marie Gardner, eds., *The Globalization of Human Rights* (United Nations University Press, 2003) and Alison Brysk, ed., *Globalization and Human Rights* (University of California Press, 2002) are classic early works still worth reading. Christopher Sabatini, (ed.), *Reclaiming Human Rights in a Changing World Order* (The Brookings Institution, 2023) is a useful recent collection. And although not addressed to human rights in particular, Christian Karner and Dirk Hofäcker, eds., *Research Handbook on the Sociology of Globalization* (Edward Elgar Publishing, 2023) is wide-ranging and up to date. Cambridge University Press's "Globalization and Human Rights" series (https://www.cambridge.org/core/series/globalization-and-human-rights/10C77D2100734BFE3D001026E77EB6AA) has published ten titles since 2017.

For interesting discussions that link democracy, globalization, and human rights, see Nicholas McMurry, *Participation and Democratic Innovation under International Human Rights Law* (Routledge, 2024); Deen K. Chatterjee, ed., *Democracy in a Global World: Human Rights and Political Participation in the 21st Century* (Rowman & Littlefield, 2008); and Nicolas Guilhot, *The Democracy Makers: Human Rights and International Order* (Columbia University Press, 2005).

On various forms of democracy, and their fate in the contemporary world, the V-Dem Institute *Democracy Report 2025* (https://www.v-dem.net/documents/60/V-dem-dr__2025_lowres.pdf) is an excellent place to begin.

Notes

1 Alison Brysk, *From Tribal Village to Global Village: Indian Rights and International Relations in Latin America* (Stanford University Press, 2000).
2 Margaret E. Keck and Kathryn Sikkink, *Activists Beyond Borders: Advocacy Networks in International Politics* (Cornell University Press, 1998).
3 www.hrw.org/world-report/2019/country-chapters/egypt.
4 https://www.reuters.com/world/asia-pacific/north-korea-cites-rare-dissent-elections-even-99-back-candidates-2023-11-28/.
5 Online at www.business-humanrights.org/sites/default/files/media/documents/un-human-rights-council-resolution-re-human-rights-transnational-corps-eng-6-jul-2011.pdf.
6 https://www.ohchr.org/sites/default/files/documents/publications/guidingprinciplesbusinesshr_en.pdf.
7 https://www.ohchr.org/en/special-procedures/wg-business.

Human Rights and Development

13

Development and human rights are not merely connected but interrelated. And the impacts flow in both directions. Most obviously, economic growth can provide the resources necessary to realize not only economic, social, and cultural rights but civil and political rights as well. Similarly, political development is essential to developing the state capacities required for the effective implementation, enforcement, and enjoyment of all human rights. No less importantly, though, the effective implementation of human rights can make a huge contribution to development. For example, workers who enjoy rights to health and education usually are more productive workers, rights to freedom of speech and the press foster the free flow of information that is essential for efficient markets, and democratic political rights can help to prevent the state from being captured by private interests.

This chapter examines the complex and varied ways that development and human rights have been related, both conceptually and institutionally, in post-World War II international relations.

1 "Development": A Conceptual History

Most approaches to development are rooted in ideas of progress, with special emphasis on economic growth, industrialization, and technological development (and other forms of economic "modernization") and the expansion of trade and finance. Other important dimensions of development, though, include social development (e.g., health and education), political development (changes in the structure of the state and its laws and policies), and the growth of a nonstate civil society sector.

In the Cold War era, two basic approaches to development predominated: a broadly "capitalist" or market-oriented approach (usually with a Keynesian twist) and a statist approach, which included both socialist and non-socialist (and even anticommunist)

DOI: 10.4324/9781003373520-16

variants. Market-oriented approaches, which were fostered internationally primarily by the West (and especially by the United States), emphasized the free flow of goods, services, and investment, arguing that the efficiencies of markets were most conducive to development. Statist approaches, inspired by the apparent success of Soviet and fascist economic responses to the Great Depression, argued that rapid industrialization and modernization required the state to marshal and direct resources.

Statist strategies argued for insulating policy from potentially destabilizing or disruptive political interference—including the restrictions imposed by human rights. Most countries that applied statist models also relied on nationalist or anticolonial ideologies to foster national unity in the pursuit of national development. In both variants, the claim was that often-severe restrictions in the short and medium term on the exercise and enjoyment of internationally recognized human rights was necessary to enhance the pace of development—on which human rights depended. "Development first," it was claimed, was the most efficient and most effective path to implementing human rights.

Market-oriented strategies, however, also tended to subordinate human rights to development, at least in the short and medium term. State intervention to better realize economic, social, and cultural rights was regularly rejected as slowing the pace of economic growth. Similarly, the exercise of civil and political rights, such as the freedoms of speech, press, assembly, and association, was frequently restricted (often systematically and sometimes violently) on the grounds that they created disunity, disruption, or a hostile climate for business and investment that impeded the overriding goal of development. American foreign policy, as we saw in Chapter 8, provided an extreme example in which "freedom" defined as anticommunism tended to displace civil and political rights and the right to property was treated as the essential and overriding economic and social right.

Both strategies had successes and failures in the three decades following World War II, which was an era of rapid expansion of the global economy. "The Golden Years," however, came to an end in the 1970s, which were marked by both a global downturn in the middle of the decade and the beginnings of what would come to be called globalization, which (as we saw in the preceding chapter) began to reshape both the global and national economies.

Furthermore, attention increasingly shifted to the fact that the gap between North and South was not narrowing. Many states in the developing world had achieved considerable economic growth in the 1950s and 1960s. State-led processes of economic development, however, had typically produced high levels of indebtedness and only modest levels of social and political development. Furthermore, few developing countries, whether socialist or capitalist, were able to achieve *continued and sustainable* development. Progress typically became "stuck"—or even worse.

In the 1970s and 1980s, this generated two principal kinds of responses. Supporters of statist development argued for a New International Economic Order (NIEO), involving massive transfers of resources from North to South and fundamental structural changes in global trade and finance to facilitate state-led development (see Section 4 below). The United States and United Kingdom, by contrast, pressed for an aggressive market-oriented program, which saw the problem, even in the West (where stagnation seemed to be replacing growth as the new economic norm), as too much state economic involvement.

Although many European states continued to support the postwar welfare state model (see Chapter 12, Section 3), they were increasingly marginalized by the "neo-liberal" minimal-state ideologies of Margaret Thatcher, prime minister of the United Kingdom from 1979–1990, and Ronald Reagan, president of the United States from 1981 to 1989.

This radical market-oriented strategy triumphed internationally in what came to be known as "the Washington Consensus." In the 1980s, international financial institutions, especially the World Bank and International Monetary Fund (which were dominated by Western powers and staffed largely by free market economists), began requiring that recipients of loans and aid adopt a set of policy prescriptions stressing tax cuts, deregulation, and reducing public sector spending. The resulting "structural adjustment" programs demanded not only greater openness to international markets and investment and the privatization of nationalized industries and public–private ("parastatal") agencies but also usually-quite-substantial cuts to social programs that aimed to better realize rights to food, health, housing, and education. Such "shock therapy" was presented as necessary to turn economies around and set them on the path to development (which would be in the long run interest of all).

In the 1990s, however, evidence began to mount that structural adjustment programs usually did not work as intended and that the Washington Consensus was based on a naively inappropriate "one-size-fits-all" model of development. Successes in some middle-income countries were swamped by failures, especially in sub-Saharan Africa, where declines in the enjoyment of economic and social rights were sometimes accompanied by *declines* in growth. And the distributional inequities of even "successful" structural adjustment programs became increasingly evident (see Problem 13.1).

As the new millennium began, the United Nations began to promote a new paradigm for development: sustainable human development, with a special emphasis on poverty alleviation. This approach, which continues to predominate today, balances an appreciation of the virtues of markets (and the vices of excessive state involvement in the economy) with a greater appreciation of their often-unfortunate human consequences. (Compare our earlier discussion in Chapter 12.) Development is understood to involve much more than economic growth. And the object, as well as the subject, of development is increasingly seen—in theory at least—as the human person (rather than economies or societies). This has opened new spaces for pursuing constructive interactions between human rights and development.

Today, we also have a more nuanced appreciation of the state's role in the economy than during the ideologically dominated Cold War era. In the West, with the partial exception of the United States, welfare state provision of economic and social rights remains both an ideal and a reality. And the success of state-led development in both "socialist" China and "capitalist" Japan and Korea has created a growing appreciation of the ways in which *effective* states can be vital agents of a kind of rapid development that brings people out of poverty and sets the economy on a path of sustainable further progress.

The issue is not *whether* the state should be involved but what kind of state is involved in what ways, for what purposes, and with what effects. Conversely, although market efficiencies are necessary for sustainable development, they alone are not sufficient—and even when they produce economic growth, they do not necessarily lead to human development.

We will return to these issues in Sections 6 and 7. First, though, we survey the ways in which human rights and development have been addressed in international law and international relations, with special attention to development assistance. (Those not interested in this history may reasonably choose to skim or skip Sections 2–5.)

2 Development and Human Rights—The Early Years

In the 1950s and 1960s, development became an increasingly important issue at the United Nations and in international relations more broadly. International law and practice, however, included little more than vague references to the importance of "international cooperation" for the achievement of both human rights and development. And development and human rights, although obviously intimately interrelated, were treated almost completely separately, especially at the UN, even in the 1970s.

The Commission on Human Rights, after it completed drafting the two Covenants and turned them over to the General Assembly in 1954, largely ignored economic and social rights, let alone development, focusing instead on civil and political rights, nondiscrimination, and the rights of minorities. Development issues were instead addressed elsewhere in the UN system: for example, in the Economic and Social Council's regional Economic Commissions for Europe, Latin America and the Caribbean, Africa, and Asia and the Pacific; the Commissions on Population and Development, the Status of Women, and Social Development; and specialized functional agencies such as the World Health Organization, the Food and Agricultural Organization, and the International Labor Organization (see Chapter 5, Section 4.3). And in these contexts, human rights were rarely addressed.

The UN's designation of the 1960s as a "development decade" led to both the creation of new institutions and arrangements and the beginnings of a broader view of development. The United Nations Conference on Trade and Development (UNCTAD) was launched in 1964; the United Nations Development Programme (UNDP) was established in 1965, and the World Bank reoriented its mission away from European postwar reconstruction to tackling "basic needs" in the Global South. Countries in the Global North began to establish development offices or agencies within their respective foreign ministries. For example, the U.S. Agency for International Development and the Peace Corps were launched during the Kennedy administration (1961–1963).

But no links were drawn between this growing international development regime and the global international human rights regime. Development and human rights were treated as entirely separate concerns.

3 Self-Determination, Decolonization, and Development

The growing number of formerly colonial states—the membership of the United Nations grew from eighty in 1956 to 122 in 1966—began to demand a greater voice in setting the global development agenda. The right to self-determination, which had been part of international human rights discussions since the early 1950s, became the core of an emerging vision of development and human rights.

The *principle* of self-determination appears in the UN Charter. It was not, however, articulated as a *right* in the Universal Declaration. In 1952, the UN General Assembly instructed the Commission on Human Rights to include the right to self-determination in the two Covenants in 1952.[1] But, as we saw above, they languished largely untouched for the next decade.

Many developing countries insisted that recognizing a right to self-determination was demanded not only as a matter of principle but also to establish governments committed to development and to facilitate further access to development resources. Furthermore, it was widely believed that ending colonialism and establishing national political independence would lay the foundation for ending exploitative imperial relations (for example, by nationalizing extractive industries such as petroleum and bauxite).

The right to self-determination is articulated identically in Article 1 of both Covenants, which were finally adopted by the General Assembly in December 1966:

1. All peoples have the right of self-determination. By virtue of that right, they freely determine their political status and freely pursue their economic, social, and cultural development.
2. All peoples may, for their own ends, freely dispose of their natural wealth and resources without prejudice to any obligations arising out of international economic cooperation, based upon the principle of mutual benefit, and international law. In no case may a people be deprived of its own means of subsistence.
3. The States Parties to the present Covenant, including those having responsibility for the administration of Non-Self-Governing and Trust Territories, shall promote the realization of the right of self-determination, and shall respect that right, in conformity with the provisions of the Charter of the United Nations.

These new ideas on self-determination interacted with new ideas on the nature of development that overlapped only partly with the state–market divide discussed at the outset of this chapter.

In the early 1960s, there was nearly universal agreement that the road to development was through "modernization" or "industrialization," driven centrally by trade. The relationship between trade (and investment) and development, however, was a matter of considerable controversy.

Economist W.W. Rostow's "take-off model" theorized that national economic development occurs in stages from pre-industrial "traditional" society toward high-consumption, fully industrialized modernization. The goal of developing countries therefore should be to move through those stages as quickly as possible. Many Third World states, though, drawing on dependency theorists such as Raul Prebisch (UNCTAD's Secretary-General from 1964 to 1969), argued that developing countries were effectively trapped in a subordinate position that blocked the path to industrialization.

Prebisch drew attention to the fact that the "terms of trade" (roughly, relative prices) of the primary products (i.e., agricultural and extractive [e.g., mineral] exports) that developing countries tended to specialize in (because of their market-based "comparative advantage") were declining over time, relative to the manufactured goods they purchased from the West or Communist East. (The amount of exported coffee or copper that could purchase an imported tractor in 1950 bought less than a full tractor by 1960—and would likely buy even less in 1970.) The steady long-term decline in the terms of trade effectively thwarted even "successful" developing countries from moving "up" to industrial production—or at the very least unfairly slowed their progress and increased the price of further development.

Following the first UNCTAD Conference in Geneva in 1964, the great majority of developing states formed the "Group of 77" (G-77), which began to call for a substantial reorientation of the global economy to put them on a firmer path toward industrialization and modernization (and thus development).

4 The (Original) Right to Development

Some members of the G-77 argued for negotiating with the developed world to try to improve terms of trade. Others, though, called for demanding development assistance *as a right*. For example, Doudou Thiam, a Senegalese diplomat, in a 1966 speech before the UN General Assembly,[2] argued that although "in theory, the old colonial pact was doubtlessly abolished …in practice it has been maintained … An actual pillage of the developing countries has been organized on a world-wide scale."[3] Therefore, Thiam argued,

> We must lay the foundations for a new world society; we must bring about a new revolution; we must tear down all the practices, institutions and rules on which international economic relations are based, in so far as these practices, institutions and rules sanction injustice and exploitation and maintain the unjustified domination of a minority over the majority of men. Not only must we reaffirm our right to development, but we must also take the steps which will enable this right to become a reality. We must build a new system, based not only on the theoretical affirmation of the sacred rights of peoples and nations but on the actual enjoyment of these rights.[4]

This new "right to development" was not framed in human rights terms. It was a right held not by individuals (or even by peoples) but by developing *states* (or the developing world as a whole) against developed states (or the international community as a whole). It was, however, linked, both conceptually and legally, to the general obligation (in the UN Charter) that countries pursue economic and social cooperation and development and to the right to self-determination specified in the Covenants.

Special attention was given to the right to permanent sovereignty over natural resources. The countries of the developing world were entitled to control over their own resources and to seek more favorable terms of global trade. The end of formal imperial rule was not enough; what was required was an end to persisting "neo-colonial" relations, rules, and practices, which remained embedded in markets and international economic regimes. And these demands increasingly came to be formulated in the language of a right to development.[5]

In the 1970s, however, efforts to codify a right to development were ultimately subordinated to broader calls for a "New International Economic Order"—most dramatically at the 1974 Special Session of the General Assembly. While the process resulted in the adoption of a Charter on the Economic Rights and Duties of States (CERDS), the term "right to development" had slipped away. And although the NIEO and CERDS did open a dialogue between the Global South and the Global North (especially Western Europe; the United States largely dismissed the effort) it did not herald the revolution Thiam had envisioned. Furthermore, and central for our purposes here, the push for the NIEO missed the opportunity to emphasize links between human rights and development, which remained almost completely unaddressed in UN discussions. In fact, most Third World states supported separating discussions of development, which were high on their list of priorities, from discussions of human rights, which they largely sought to avoid.

5 The (Human) Right to Development

A right to development, however, was far from dead. Following the 1968 International Conference on Human Rights (Tehran, Iran), which adopted a few resolutions on development, the Commission on Human Rights appointed Iranian diplomat Manouchehr Ganji to study the obstacles to realizing economic and social rights in developing countries. Following the publication in 1974 of his report "The Widening Gap," the Commission made a concerted effort to place more emphasis on economic and social rights—in sharp contrast to the broader United Nations focus on demands for the NIEO. And the Senegalese member of the Commission, Keba M'Baye, began to argue for understanding a "right to development" as a human right.

In 1977, the General Assembly adopted resolution 32/130, calling for "Alternative Approaches" to human rights. The goal was to reorient the Commission's work away from civil and political rights and toward economic and social rights, in order to promote the indivisibility of human rights. In 1981, the Commission established a working group to draft a Declaration on the Right to Development (DRtD), which the General Assembly adopted in 1986.

The Declaration defines development as

> a comprehensive economic, social, cultural and political process, which aims at the constant improvement of the well-being of the entire population and of all individuals on the basis of their active, free and meaningful participation in development and the fair distribution of benefits resulting therefrom.

Article 2 of the DRtD states that the human person is the central subject and beneficiary of the right to development. The Declaration, however, focuses principally on the collective aspects of development, the "unjust" nature of the global economic order, and the duties of individuals and communities for development—not the rights of human beings.

Furthermore, only a few selected human rights are addressed. And they are presented as largely instrumental. Consider Article 5:

> States shall take resolute steps to eliminate the massive and flagrant violations of the human rights of peoples and human beings affected by situations such as those resulting from apartheid, all forms of racism and racial discrimination, colonialism, foreign domination and occupation, aggression, foreign interference and threats against national sovereignty, national unity and territorial integrity, threats of war and refusal to recognize the fundamental right of peoples to self-determination.

In addition, the Declaration is largely devoid of specifics concerning the substance of the right to development. No attention is given to who is obliged to do what with respect to whom (other than seemingly substantial but obscure obligations of the Global North to the Global South). Neither is how the right to development might be the subject of rights claims ("justiciable") or how one would know if the component parts of the right to development are actually realized or violated.

Despite these shortcomings, the broad idea of a right to development has remained immensely attractive. And over the past four decades, the United Nations has continued to promote it as a mechanism to make conceptions and practices of development and human rights mutually reinforcing. From early 2020 through 2023, the UN's Intergovernmental Working Group on the Right to Development (WG-RtD) completed the drafting of the "International Covenant on the Right to Development," which the full Human Rights Council endorsed and agreed to submit to the UN General Assembly for formal adoption. Although the draft Covenant is considerably clearer in its content and implications, and even seeks to establish limited mechanisms of oversight and accountability, it appears that not only the United States but also several European states and Japan continue to have significant doubts about the viability of a legally binding instrument on the right to development. We will discuss the draft Covenant in some detail in the case study (Section 8) below.

6 A Human Rights-Based Approach to Development

The ICESCR entered into force in 1976. In 1986, a Committee on Economic, Social and Cultural Rights (CESCR) was created to monitor its implementation. This, along with the idea of a right to development and the beginnings of the debate over structural adjustment programs, set the stage for what has come to be known as a human rights-based approach (HRBA) to development.

The basic idea is that development policies and programs should not be separate from but coordinated with, and even driven by, human rights principles and practices. This in turn requires greater attention to the sometimes-competing priorities of human rights on the one hand and development assistance on the other. (For example, some development policies that aim to fulfill particular economic and social rights may be carried out in ways that infringe or even systematically violate some civil or political rights. And development assistance, as we saw in Chapter 8, often is granted for political or economic reasons, with little attention to human rights.)

In 1986, the Commission on Human Rights adopted the *Limburg Principles on the Implementation of the ICESCR*, which outlined the scope of obligations under the Covenant. The central insistence of the Limburg Principles was that the rights in the ICESCR, although subject to progressive implementation, were real legal obligations—and therefore implementation and reporting were not optional. The Limburg Principles even broached the topic of violations.

Over the next several years, the CESCR adopted a number of "General Comments" that addressed specific rights or categories of rights—their content, scope, and obligations. In 1997, the Commission adopted the *Maastricht Guidelines on Violations of Economic, Social and Cultural Rights*, which not only emphasized that the various rights in the Covenant include both broad and specific obligations but fully articulated the "respect, protect, promote, and fulfill" array of obligations (see Chapter 2, Section 7). This made it possible to try to establish human rights accountability in evaluating development policies and programs.

Previously, national and international development agencies had focused on broad social and economic indicators of "success," such as gross domestic product (GDP) per capita, infant mortality rates, and percentages of the population receiving different levels of schooling. Asking instead how "development" contributed (or did not contribute) to respecting, protecting, and fulfilling a wide range of specific human rights offered a new perspective of development—as well as a much more robust account of the scope of state obligations for economic and social rights.

For example, there are many ways in which the state might be held accountable for its obligation in Article 11 to "recognize the right of everyone to an adequate standard of living for himself and his family, including … housing."

- Respect (the duty not to deprive): the state may not actively prevent people from getting the housing they need.
- Protect (the duty to enforce): the state must ensure that people are protected from, e.g., discrimination in seeking out housing (for example, by repealing and prohibiting discriminatory laws or regulating the private market to ensure landlords are not discriminating).
- Promote: the state has an obligation to make public policy to ensure there is an adequate stock of housing. That might mean, for example, public spending programs to subsidize rent for those who cannot fully afford their housing.
- Fulfill (the duty to provide): the state itself may have to directly provide housing to those who cannot secure it on their own.

A human rights-based approach to development insists that already existing human rights law and practice provide a fruitful foundation for scrutinizing development policy and practice. Human rights, in other words, is a tool for evaluating the effectiveness of development policy (to provide the economic, social, and political environments that lead to human well-being and dignity) while also ensuring that development policies do not violate internationally recognized human rights.

7 Further Integration between Human Rights and Development

This new approach interacted constructively with a variety of other endeavors to reorient development thinking away from narrow macro-economic models and measures of development—especially growth in national income or GDP per capita—toward a focus on what is now usually called *sustainable human development*.

Under the direction of Pakistani economist Mahbub ul Haq, the UNDP introduced the human development index (HDI) and published its first Human Development Report in 1990. The index is a composite indicator of development that combines per-capita income with data on education and life expectancy (and, since 2010, income inequality).

The HDI greatly influenced Nobel Prize-winning economist Amartya Sen, whose landmark 1999 book *Development as Freedom* recast the concept of poverty not in terms of income alone, but as "capability deprivation." If people do not develop capabilities such as bodily health, practical reason, and affiliation, they usually can neither acquire more income nor transform the income that they do have into ways of life that adequately enhance human dignity.

Another important international milestone was the 2000 *Human Development Report*, timed to coincide with the UN Millennium Summit, which addressed the relationships between human rights and human development. It argued that the global human rights and development agendas, which had been separate from one another, were finally beginning to converge. It noted that the principles of justice and accountability that form the core of international human rights law were necessary for development policies to improve the lives of the poor—and (echoing Sen) that both the realization of human rights and of sustainable human development were necessary for promoting human freedom.

Other economists, such as Joseph Stiglitz (who was the World Bank's chief economist in the late 1990s, and critical of "shock therapy" policies associated with structural adjustment) and, later, Jeffrey Sachs of Columbia University, advocated for a paradigm shift in thinking about development that were reflected in the Millennium Development Goals (MDGs) adopted by the United Nations in 2000.

Core MDGs to eradicate extreme poverty and hunger, achieve universal primary education, promote gender equality, reduce child mortality and improve maternal health, and to combat epidemic and endemic diseases such as HIV/AIDS and malaria clearly overlap with the fulfillment of many internationally recognized economic and social rights. A human rights-based approach to achieving these goals adds that the ways in which they are achieved must also respect and promote key civil and political rights. And this dimension had an especially close connection to the eighth MDG, developing a global partnership for development.

Despite considerable progress on many of these goals (especially reducing absolute poverty), none of the MDG targets were met by the goal date of 2015. In response, in 2015, the United Nations adopted the 2030 Agenda for Sustainable Development, including seventeen Sustainable Development Goals (SDGs) to be achieved over the succeeding fifteen years. And unlike the MDGs, which were focused only on developing countries, the SDGs are global in scope. They also more clearly seek to combine traditional economic development goals (e.g., economic growth, industrial and infrastructure development, sustainable cities) with a focus on human development (zero poverty, zero hunger, clean water, health, education), reducing income and gender inequality and grappling with environmental challenges and climate change. Furthermore, each goal identifies specific targets—169 in total—and statistical measures of their achievement. (The Danish Institute of Human Rights has a very useful online tool [https://sdg.humanrights.dk] where a user can pick any of the SDGs or indicators and see how they are linked to specific human rights enumerated in core treaties and other documents. Our World in Data also has a visualizer that tracks the progress of achieving the SDGs, at https://ourworldindata.org/sdgs).

Finally, over the past two decades, many agencies within the UN system have explicitly adopted human rights-based approaches to *all* their development work. A pioneer in this respect was UNAIDS, a joint and co-sponsored program established in the mid-1990s to coordinate the HIV/AIDS-related work of several UN agencies. The UNDP also has adopted an HRBA. UNICEF considers itself to be the UN's institutional custodian of the Convention on the Rights of the Child.

Although this proliferation of rights-based approaches has been generally fruitful, the result sometimes has been inconsistent (and even competing) definitions. To address this, several UN agencies met in 2003 and adopted a statement (the "Common Understanding"[6]) addressing the guiding role of human rights in the UN's development policies and practices.

The first part of the Common Understanding states that all development-related programs must have as their goal the realization of human rights as established by the Universal Declaration and international human rights treaties. The third part stipulates that development policies and programs must contribute to the development of the capacities of duty-bearers to meet their obligations and of rights-holders to claim their rights. And the second part of the Common Understanding stipulates that human rights law must guide the entire development programming process, from planning to implementation, and identifies three guiding human rights principles.

- First, that all human rights are universal, inalienable, indivisible, and interrelated, and that the principle of nondiscrimination is fundamental to human rights.
- Second, that human rights law holds states in particular accountable as duty-bearers, and that accountability must apply the rule of law, so that rights-holders are enabled to claim their rights.
- Third, that all people, as agents and beneficiaries of development, must be able to fully participate in development policymaking and implementation.

These, we would note, are the "standard" understandings of human rights that have guided our discussion throughout this book. And they are now, in theory at least, fully embedded in the dominant understandings of development. As little as forty years ago, human rights and development were treated as fundamentally separable projects. Now, though, they are almost universally acknowledged to be not merely overlapping but, when done right, complementary and mutually reinforcing practices.

8 Case Study: The Draft Covenant on the Right to Development

This chapter has pointed to many North-South disagreements about the relationships between development and human rights. Many (but not all) Global North countries were reluctant to embrace the UN Declaration on the Right to Development (DRTD) in 1986. Today, though, with a few exceptions (most notably, the United States), most have come to accept the idea of promoting a right to development. But they have resisted attempts to turn norms into legal obligations.

Support for a legally binding instrument, however, remains strong within the Global South, which began calling for a treaty in the early 2010s. In 2018, the Human Rights Council endorsed drafting such an instrument.[7] This case study examines the process and substance of the draft International Covenant on the Right to Development, which the Human Rights Council sent in 2023 to the UN General Assembly (which by the end of 2025 still had not adopted it).[8]

8.1 The Drafting Process

Human Rights Council resolution 39/9 (2018) instructed Ambassador Zamir Akram of Pakistan, in his capacity as Chair-Rapporteur of Council's Intergovernmental WG-RtD, to "prepare a draft legally binding instrument…to serve as the basis for subsequent negotiations…." Akram appointed a five-person "Expert Drafting Group" (EDG) of international lawyers from Europe, Asia, America, and Africa to pull together a draft. The EDG published a "zero-draft" (rough, first pass version) in late 2019. Because of the COVID pandemic, though, the draft was not taken up formally by the Working Group until May 2021. Revised drafts were discussed extensively in 2022 and 2023.

Akram wanted the negotiating process to be open, transparent, and collaborative. (The WG-RtD is "open-ended"—any UN member-state, whether serving on the Council or not, as well as representatives from UN agencies, other international organizations, and accredited NGOs can participate in its deliberations.) In addition, the process was based on consensus. As with earlier international human rights treaties, there was no voting. Discussion continued until there was no active opposition to a provision or formulation.

With each draft, the EDG offered extensive legal commentary[9] on every article, sometimes down to very specific phrases, guided by the following principles.

1. The draft Convention contains *no new law*. Everything in it rearticulates already existing international law, norms, and international and regional agreements and arrangements.
2. Any textual modification must be in line with existing international law (treaties, customary law, and general principles of law) and UN resolutions.
3. Akram was tasked to guide this process in his capacity as Chair-Rapporteur of the Working Group. Therefore, the various drafts belonged to him (and through him the EDG) not the Council or any other group of state representatives.

The drafting sessions of the WG-RtD were mostly unsurprising.[10] Non-aligned states focused on the importance of cooperation and the domination of the global economy by the Global North. They also stressed national sovereignty. The European Union consistently objected to the draft treaty at the beginning and end of each session (only after the 2023 session did the EU suggest substantive textual modifications, some of which were incorporated into the final text). Most Latin American states were also skeptical of the purpose or necessity of a treaty. (The Russian Federation was opposed to just about everything that suggested the promotion of extraterritorial obligations.) Many largely technical modifications were made to facilitate consensus. The substance of core norms and institutions, however, remained largely unchanged.

As we noted above, Global South countries tend to stress the international obligations of states of the Global North to states of the Global South, emphasizing international cooperation, solidarity, and mutual respect, guided by respecting state sovereignty. They point especially to the legacies of European colonialism, the Global North's domination of markets and financial institutions, and the barriers Global South states face as a result of economic sanctions and other "unfair" trade and aid policies. (*Human* rights, as defined in the extensive body of international human rights law, are peripheral to this understanding of the right to development.)

Countries in the Global North tend to advocate a human rights-based approach to development (see Section 13.6 above), arguing that the imperative of economic development, although real and important, cannot excuse violating either civil and political or economic, social, and cultural human rights. In this understanding, sustainable development is predicated on rights-respecting practices and structural reforms at the state level, especially combating corruption, promoting democracy, and adhering to the rule of law, both domestically and internationally.

Given these opposing positions, one might have expected the WG-RtD discussions to have become deadlocked. In fact, however, the strong desire of the Global South for a treaty made it willing to accept a variety of modifications in order to achieve consensus. Thus, as we will see below, individuals and peoples are the objects of the right to development and a clear connection has been drawn between development and human rights.

In 2023, the Human Rights Council advanced the draft International Covenant on the Right to Development to the UN General Assembly for adoption. The term Covenant, rather than Convention, is symbolically important, following up on the 1997 decision of the UN General Assembly to incorporate the 1986 DRtD into the "International Bill of Human Rights," alongside the Universal Declaration and the two 1966 International Human Rights Covenants.

8.2 The Draft Covenant: Core Elements

8.2.1 Defining the Right to Development

The right to development is defined in Article 4.

1. Every individual and all peoples have the inalienable right to development by virtue of which they are entitled to participate in, contribute to, and enjoy civil, cultural,

economic, environmental, political, and social development that is indivisible from and interrelated and interdependent with all other human rights and fundamental freedoms.

2. Every individual and all peoples have the right to active, free, and meaningful participation in development and the fair distribution of benefits resulting therefrom.

At a broad theoretical level, disagreement persists about whether "peoples" (as a collective) can have human rights. Some argue that although groups may have rights, only individual human beings have *human* rights. Others argue that because human beings have individual and collective components to their identities, groups of human beings—most notably peoples or societies, but also ethnic or religious groups—may have human rights.

Nonetheless, there is fundamental agreement that the central agents and beneficiaries of an internationally recognized right to development are individuals and peoples—not states (let alone groups such as multinational corporations). Furthermore, "peoples" suggests that the right is a *democratic* right; that the state may only exercise the right to development if that privilege has been extended by the "peoples" involved. (The EDG was adamant about this point in the Commentaries they provided for each draft of the Covenant).[11]

This understanding of the right to development is reinforced by the fact that the draft Covenant, rather than defining development, describes it as having many dimensions (civil, cultural, economic, etc.). The EDG explained that this was not an oversight but a deliberate choice (much as the Disability Convention does not define "disability"). Individuals and peoples, as holders of the right to development, are empowered to define "development" for themselves. And, as we suggested in discussing the relativity of internationally recognized human rights (Chapter 3), they are entitled, through a democratic process of deliberation, to choose the priorities that drive state action—rather than the state determining for itself what individuals and its people need and desire.

The EDG's commentaries also stress that the right to development is *itself* a right. For many years after the adoption of the 1986 Declaration, it was often argued that the right to development was an "umbrella" right or a "vector" (a path and means to an end) through which other human rights could be realized. The draft Covenant rejects that understanding.[12] As the EDG explained:

> Some scholars have in the past contended that the formulation in the [Declaration on the Right to Development] is vague and theoretically problematic.[13] ... [In the draft Covenant, however, the] words "that is indivisible from and interdependent and interrelated with" highlight that right-holders are entitled to development that does not violate any of their human rights. The words "all *other* human rights and fundamental freedoms" reinforce that the right to development is not just about ensuring human rights in development, but more importantly, that development itself is a human right.[14]

Therefore, although the draft Covenant, unlike other human rights treaties, does not create new law—everything in it has already been expressed in treaty law, UN resolutions, and other agreements and mechanisms—by pulling together these previously separate strands into a newly recognized separate human right, the claim is, we get something that is more than the sum of the previously existing parts (although exactly how this occurs, and what the added substance is, remains obscure).

8.2.2 Core Duty: Cooperation

Among the obligations of states that the draft Covenant enumerates, the duty to cooperate (Article 13) is clearly the centerpiece. At 867 words, it is the longest single article in the Covenant, insofar as it incorporates articulations and details found in existing international law, agreements, and mechanisms. It is worth spelling out its contents.

In the first clause, states reaffirm and shall implement their duty to cooperate to:

- Solve problems (economic, social, political, humanitarian, environmental, etc.)
- End poverty
- Promote higher standards of living (full/productive employment; decent work; conditions of human dignity; economic, social, cultural, technological, environmental progress)
- Promote universal respect for human rights for all

The second clause stipulates that states have the *primary* responsibility for creating conditions necessary for realizing the right to development, including taking deliberate, concrete, and targeted steps, individually and jointly (with other states, international organizations, and civil society) in order to:

- Ensure that natural and legal persons do not impair the right to development
- Review existing legal instruments, policies, and practices to eliminate obstacles and to ensure that future instruments and arrangements do not include obstacles
- To mobilize economic, technical, technological, and financial resources to allow developing states to meet their obligations for realizing the right to development

Third, development financing, aid, and assistance (whether bilateral or multilateral) must adhere to internationally recognized effectiveness principles (see Section 13.7 above).

The final clause reflects an attempt to elaborate Article 28 of the Universal Declaration, which states that "[e]veryone is entitled to a social and international order in which the rights and freedoms set forth in this Declaration can be fully realized." In the context of Article 13, this includes

- Promoting a universal, rules-based, open, nondiscriminatory, equitable, transparent, and inclusive multilateral trading system
- Implementing the principle of special and differential treatment for least-developed countries
- Improving regulation and monitoring of global financial markets

- Enhancing representation and voice for developing countries in the decision-making processes of international financial institutions (such as the IMF and World Bank)
- Enhancing capacity-building for high-quality data in developing countries
- Encouraging the flow of development financing and assistance to states "where the need is greatest" (least-developed countries, land-locked and small island states, and African states)
- Enhancing North-South, South-South, and triangular forms of cooperation, particularly in science, technology, and innovation
- Enhancing mitigation actions and adaptive capacity, strengthening resilience and response, and reducing vulnerability to climate change and extreme weather events
- Eliminating illicit financial flows (e.g., tax evasion/avoidance; recovery of stolen assets)
- Eliminating illicit arms flows
- Assisting least-developed countries to reduce debt stress
- Facilitating safe, orderly, and regular migration and mobility of people

8.2.3 Other Duties

The draft Covenant enumerates a number of general and specific duties of states. These include duties to respect, protect, and fulfill all human rights and the right to development, to combat corruption, and to empower women and girls, and rural and indigenous peoples. They are also obligated to extend "specific and remedial measures" for realizing the right to development for both marginalized individuals and groups (domestically) as well as to the most vulnerable states (internationally).

The right and the duty to regulate are not confined to a specific article but are mentioned in several parts of the draft Covenant. For example, Article 11 (Obligation to Protect) includes the duty to regulate the business activities of "legal persons" both domestically and transnationally to ensure their activities do not violate the right to development.

Finally, Article 14 stipulates that "adopting, maintaining, or implementing" coercive measures "in order to obtain from [a state] the subordination of the exercise of its sovereign rights" constitutes a *violation* of the right to development. Codifying this prohibition has long been a goal of many countries in the Global South. However, the article is merely a rearticulation of a "soft law" obligation found in the "Declaration on Principles of International Law Concerning Friendly Relations" between states, adopted by the United Nations in 1970. The provision does not apply to sanctions that are endorsed by the UN Security Council, which is empowered by the Charter to adopt such measures.

8.3 Monitoring and Implementation

The draft Covenant seeks to establish a "Conference of States Parties" (CSP) and an "Implementation Mechanism" (IM) of experts. Unlike the other human rights regimes, there is no reporting requirement. States *may* choose to submit reports that the CSP may, within considerable limits, discuss. The CSP has a broad mandate to review the "effective implementation" of the Covenant and make policy decisions to strengthen the regime, such as the adoption of protocols or amendments and the promotion of "best practices." The CSP's members will be the states that have ratified the Covenant.

The IM, made up of independent experts, will report to the CSP. It will be empowered to review the (again, voluntarily submitted) reports of states-parties that are referred to it by the CSP, make recommendations, review obstacles to the implementation of the Covenant, and "comment" on reported failures of states to comply with the duty to cooperate.

We have argued that an important part of the power of multilateral human rights institutions stems from their ability to identify violations of a right, based on interpreting and elaborating the text of a treaty. How this might happen under the draft Covenant is unclear. While the IM will be comprised of experts acting in their personal professional capacity (as is the case for other TMBs), it would not have the same powers and responsibilities. Even where a state voluntarily reports on its practices, the IM may only "facilitate, coordinate, and assist, in a non-adversarial and non-punitive manner, the implementation and promotion of compliance with ... the Covenant." There will be no "naming and shaming." "Hearings and pleadings" are excluded.

It is possible that the IM will grow in stature and sophistication as, for example, the CESCR did. But we doubt that. (Its fate is more likely to be the effectively moribund Committee on the Elimination of Racial Discrimination, which largely engages in formulaic repetitions of vague platitudes and highly politicized discussions of a few particular cases.) Without any serious monitoring powers, the IM will not be able to exert even minimal pressure on states. And it is unlikely to have the buy-in from the wide range of states that would be necessary for it to contribute to the progressive development of jurisprudence on the right to development (for example, through General Comments; see Chapter 5, Section 3.2).

8.4 Prospects

Which states will join the treaty? There is little doubt that the lion's share of African and Asian states will ratify quickly. Many Latin American states, however, are skeptical: in the Council vote to send the draft to the General Assembly, five Latin American states abstained (three voted "yes"), mostly on the grounds that the text was not based on solid consensus and that many provisions lacked clarity. And nearly all the states in the Global North have expressed significant reservations: all thirteen Global North states on the Council voted against the resolution, citing the absence of consensus and prioritization of development imperatives over individual rights. Whether any of this will change will depend on the final process of adoption in the General Assembly. During the drafting process, Zamir Akram was clear that the role of the WG-RtD (and the Council) was simply to come up with a draft sufficiently grounded in existing law and practice to be worthy of negotiations among the entire UN membership—and that it was the Assembly's responsibility to grapple with the details. As Chair-Rapporteur of the Working Group, he fulfilled his mandate in a relatively timely manner (roughly three years). And the full Council did not change a word of the draft. (The draft Covenant was written by lawyers with a mandate to ensure that everything in it was supported by existing law and other agreements (such as Agenda 2030—the SDGs). The hundreds of changes made over the course of three years were carefully vetted before being incorporated.)

Once the UN General Assembly takes up the draft (presumably the General Assembly will call for a "drafting conference" lasting a week or two in 2026 or 2027), a more political process will allow member-states to propose changes. Although anything could happen, we suspect that the desire of the Global South to get a treaty, which as a practical matter requires consensus, will take priority over the desire for a stronger treaty. Something like the draft Covenant seems the only politically viable option now.

8.5 Conclusion: A Compromise?

For countries in the Global North that have been fundamentally opposed to a legally binding instrument on the right to development, there is not much to be worried about here. The draft Covenant is a far cry from Doudou Thiam's 1966 call for a "revolution" to "tear down all the practices, institutions and rules" of international economic relations. It is therefore not clear what the Global South has won—beyond the existence of a document they have desired for nearly half a century. Or if that assessment is too harsh, the contribution of the Covenant is not likely to lie in its technically legal character but rather in its broad normative aspirations and its codification of a significant, if thin, theoretical consensus on the inseparability of human rights and development.

The HRBA to development, which the draft Covenant references as reinforcing the overarching ambit of the concept of the right to development, is certainly not a centerpiece of the treaty. However, mechanisms for operationalizing that approach will carry on under the other treaty regimes, most importantly the Covenant on Economic, Social and Cultural Rights. How that mechanism will interface with the new RtD regime as envisioned in the draft Covenant will remain unclear for some time. But some level of convergence is plausible, in the longer term.

In our view—one that is shared among its supporters—the draft Covenant is a progressive attempt to rearticulate some of the economic dimensions of the promise of Article 28 of the Universal Declaration—that everyone is entitled to an international order within which human rights can be realized. It also not only rearticulates but usefully combines, within an ostensibly legally binding instrument, literally dozens of agreements and arrangements to achieve sustainable human development. And by creating an institutional frame for examining development policies—domestic and international—it might complement existing mechanisms for bridging the worlds of human rights and development.

Problem 13.1 The Global North, the Global South, and Market Redistributions

The Problem

As we discussed in Chapter 12, globalization has begun to erode the capacity of welfare states in the Global North to provide economic and social rights at the levels to which their populations had become accustomed. Other factors, including demographic changes and politically motivated overcommitments to beneficiaries, are also part of the explanation. But the new global division of labor has undoubtedly reduced the number of well-paid, low- and moderately skilled jobs available in developed market economies—which both creates new demands for benefits and restricts the ability of states to fund those benefits by taxing increasingly peripatetic firms.

But aren't the same global market forces dramatically *raising* incomes in numerous countries in the Global South? In fact, given the much greater marginal utility of improvements for poor people in the Global South compared to the losses likely to be suffered by middle-class beneficiaries in the Global North, isn't the net human rights impact of economic globalization positive?

A Solution

The extension of market efficiencies to regions previously suffering under closed or command economies creates new goods, services, and opportunities that can be mobilized to better provide economic and social rights for a much greater segment of the population (and perhaps also improve their capacities to demand and enjoy civil and political rights as well). But there is no automatic mechanism that ensures that the losses of relatively privileged workers in the Global North will be transformed into improved economic and social rights for large numbers of people in the Global South.

A transfer of resources from North to South should not be confused with improvements in the enjoyment of economic and social rights in the South. The crucial question is how those transferred resources are distributed in Southern countries. Were most of the benefits to go to a small elite—which in at least a few countries heavily dependent on natural resources is a plausible possibility—the net effect might even be negative. And the gains from industrial production, in different countries, different industries, and sometimes even different firms within an industry, can be divided in very different ways between labor, capital, and government. In addition, some portion of the resources lost by workers in the Global North goes not to workers in the Global South but to Northern capitalists.

Much depends on wage rates and working conditions in the new countries of production and the tax and spending policies of their governments. And those are a function of both local conditions, which may be more or less human-rights-friendly, and the possibility of firms increasing their share of the gains by threatening to move production to more "business-friendly" environments.

On balance, the living conditions of workers in many countries in the Global South have indeed improved, in some countries dramatically, as a result of the new global division of labor. Most notably, in China, *more than 800 million people(!)* have escaped extreme poverty since 1980, largely due to economic globalization, reducing the percentage of the Chinese population forced to endure a life of extreme poverty from more than 80 percent to barely 10 percent. And reductions in extreme poverty are occurring in other regions as well. For example, in seven of the ten years of the 2010s, and for the decade as a whole, sub-Saharan Africa grew more rapidly than the world's global average. (In a few of those years, Africa was the world's fastest-growing continent.) And even when governments have not been particularly concerned with redistribution or directly providing economic and social rights, in numerous countries, many people are enjoying better food, better housing, better health care, and better protection against economic fluctuations. (Remember that private provision is central, even the norm, for many economic and social rights, even in the Global North.)

This has been dependent on the fact that, so far at least, globalization has been a highly positive-sum game; that is, it has increased the total pie, not just redistributed it. For example, real global GDP, measured in 2017 dollars, increased from about $62 trillion in 1990 to more than $140 trillion in 2022. Some significant part of this growth can be attributed to the efficiencies of the increasing globalization of production. And this growth has made available resources to support widespread improvements in the enjoyment of economic and social rights.

Any deterioration in the enjoyment of any human rights by anyone anywhere is a legitimate matter of concern. Nonetheless, the particular losses to Northern workers—which, especially in Europe, have so far been extremely modest—would seem, on balance, to be a relatively minor worry in a broad, global human rights assessment. (We would note, though, that populist rhetoric concerning the effects of globalization on domestic labor markets has led to victories at the ballot box for more inward-focused, nationalistic, and xenophobic candidates who promise to challenge these trends—as in the United States with President Donald J. Trump's assertion that he will "make America great again.")

Further Problems

We should not, however, confuse averages, or even the norm, with every case. Where integration into global markets does not improve local productivity and efficiency, the benefits of growth rarely spread very far. Consider Nigeria, where a tiny kleptocratic elite has largely engrossed the proceeds of exploiting its immense oil wealth.

Economic globalization can be, but need not be, a boon to human rights. This is another way of saying that markets are a necessary but not sufficient condition for sustained improvements in economic and social rights.

Furthermore, it is not obvious that sacrifices by Northern workers are *necessary* for the improvement of economic and social rights in the Global South. Fair trade rather than free trade *might* allow for improving human rights for all.

Finally, the prospect of global firms being able to redirect a growing percentage of the benefits of national and international markets to themselves needs to remain a major concern of human rights advocates. In the long run, mechanisms comparable to national welfare states will be necessary to ensure that capitalism does not revert to the gross inequalities and inequities that led *all* developed market economies to establish highly redistributive welfare states.

Discussion Questions

1. The right to self-determination is included in both Covenants. But unlike all other internationally recognized human rights, it is a collective right of "peoples" (rather than an individual right of individual human beings). What difference does that make? Is it, as a result, any less (or more) important?
2. We know what individual rights are; who has them, how they can be exercised, what enforcement looks like. Can we say the same about rights of peoples? How can "peoples" exercise and claim rights? How can we specify what counts as respect for and violation of such rights?
3. What do you make of the right to "permanent sovereignty over natural resources"? Why prioritize this right in particular?
4. If you think that global economic justice is a matter of human rights, who (or what) holds the right? And who/what are the duty-bearers?
5. Countries in the Global South that were colonized by European states do not have an internationally recognized right to reparations. Should they? Why or why not? What would be the legal basis of that claim? Is there a *human* right to such reparations? What about those colonized by Japan (especially Korea)? Or by the United States (especially the Philippines)?
6. Do developing countries have a right to development assistance? If so, what would be the legal basis of that right? Is it a right of states? A *human* right? Both? Neither?
7. Do you think that a human rights-based approach to development policies and programs adds something important to those programs? What? Why do you think it might be important to think of people in developing countries as agents and beneficiaries of development, rather than as passive recipients?
8. Imagine that because I feel that I ought to help you out financially (but I have no legal, contractual, or other duty to do so) I give you $10 a day for two months. Then I stop.

Do you have a right to continue to receive $10 a day from me? Why? Even if not, do I have a duty to continue to help you? (Would it make a difference if I had done it every day for ten years and then stopped?)

9. "Fair trade" seeks to assure that resources move not just from North to South but from Northern consumers to Southern workers. What are the barriers to moving from free trade to fair trade?
10. Although we did not mention it in this chapter, the global climate crisis is already having an impact on development—and the UN is predicting even more dire consequences in the decades ahead. How can we claim rights for development when the causes of underdevelopment are global, rather than national? Does the climate crisis necessitate a truly global duty-bearer?

Suggested Readings

Peris S. Jones, *Human Rights and Development* (Routledge, 2024) is a good recent overview. Stephen P. Marks and Balakrishnan Rajagopal, eds., *Critical Issues in Human Rights and Development* (Edward Elgar, 2021) is also useful. Although a bit dated, Peter Uvin's, *Human Rights and Development* (Kumarian Press, 2004) is still an excellent primer on the topic of development and human rights generally. (Uvin's *mea culpa* on Rwanda, *Aiding Violence: The Development Enterprise in Rwanda* (Kumarian Press, 1999) is an excellent critique of the tragic consequences of thinking of development in narrow technical or economistic terms.)

For those looking for general background on the development of the global economy since the late nineteenth century, Jeffry Frieden's *Global Capitalism: Its Fall and Rise in the Twentieth Century, and its Stumbles in the Twenty-First* (W. W. Norton, 2020) offers a comprehensive and very accessible account. On the ethical dimensions of the topics raised in this chapter, good places to start are Thomas Pogge, ed., *Freedom from Poverty as a Human Right: Who Owes What to the Very Poor?* (Oxford University Press, 2007) and Daniel E. Lee and Elizabeth J. Lee, *Human Rights and the Ethics of Globalization* (Cambridge University Press, 2010). Among the more interesting sustained explorations we would single out David Miller, *National Responsibility and Global Justice* (Oxford University Press, 2007) and Thomas Pogge, *World Poverty and Human Rights: Cosmopolitan Responsibilities and Reforms* (Polity Press, 2008). Samuel Moyn's *Not Enough: Human Rights in an Unequal World* (Belknap/Harvard, 2018) argues that neoliberalism effectively quashed whatever promise human rights had for achieving economic justice.

Among the earliest compendiums exploring both the right to development and rights-based approaches was Bård A. Andreassen and Stephen P. Marks, eds., *Development as a Human Right: Legal, Political, and Economic Dimensions* (Harvard University Press, 2006). On human rights-based approaches in general, two key edited volumes are Margot E. Salomon, Arne Tostensen, and Wouter Vandenhole, eds., *Casting the Net Wider: Human Rights, Development, and New Duty Bearers* (Intersentia, 2007) and Sam Hickey and Diana Mitlin, eds., *Rights-Based Approaches to Development: Exploring the Potential and Pitfalls* (Lynne Rienner Publishers, 2009). Markus Kaltenborn, Markus Krajewski, and Heike Kuhn, eds., *Sustainable*

Development Goals and Human Rights (Springer Open, 2019) looks at the SDGs through a human rights lens.

A legal/judicial approach to development-related rights at the national level can be found in Varun Gauri and Daniel Brinks, eds., *Courting Social Justice: Judicial Enforcement of Social and Economic Rights in the Developing World* (Cambridge University Press, 2008). Katharine Young, *Constituting Economic and Social Rights* (Oxford University Press, 2012) is a cross-national study of how economic and social rights are instituted as law at the national level and their impact on constitutional law generally. For another excellent cross-national study focused on the context of dignity in constitutional law, see Erin Daly, *Dignity Rights: Courts, Constitutions, and the Worth of the Human Person* (University of Pennsylvania Press, 2012).

For a review of how UN development agencies integrated human rights into their work in the crucial years around the turn of the millennium, see Joel Ostreich, *Power and Principle: Human Rights Programming in International Organizations* (Georgetown University Press, 2007).

A number of titles have examined the development of specific indicators for measuring progress toward the achievement of economic and social rights, including Shareen Hertel and Lanse Minkler, *Economic Rights: Conceptual, Measurement, and Policy Issues* (Cambridge University Press, 2007) and Lanse Minkler, *The State of Economic and Social Human Rights: A Global Overview* (Cambridge University Press, 2013). A groundbreaking approach that has been adopted by the Human Rights Measurement Initiative (HRMI, which we discuss in Chapter 14) is Sakiko Fukuda-Parr, Terra Lawson-Remer, and Susan Randolph, eds., *Fulfilling Social and Economic Rights* (Oxford University Press, 2015).

Notes

1 UN General Assembly resolution 545 (V), February 2, 1952.

2 UN General Assembly, *Official Records*, Twenty-first Session, 1414th Plenary Meeting, September 23, 1966.

3 United Nations General Assembly, *Official Records*, paragraph 223.

4 United Nations General Assembly, *Official Records*, paragraph 228.

5 For example, in 1967, Thiam claimed the right to development had taken on a legal dimension: "Development and aid must no longer be regarded as moral issues or matters of charity; they constituted a juridical obligation." (see: G-77 Doc. MM.77/I/SR.14, October 25, 1967, in Odette Jankowitsch and Karl Sauvant, *The Third World without the Superpowers: The Collected Documents of the Non-Aligned Countries, Volume I* (Oceana Publications, 1978), pp. 311–312. And in 1968, at the second UNCTAD summit in New Delhi, India, Thiam urged member-states to adopt a "universal declaration of the rights of the developing countries"—a complement to the Universal Declaration of Human Rights. (see UNCTAD, *Proceedings of the United Nations Conference on Trade and Development, Second Session*, pp. 133–184).

6 https://unsdg.un.org/resources/human-rights-based-approach-development-cooperation-towards-common-understanding-among-un.

7 Human Rights Council Resolution A/HRC/RES/39/9 (2018).

8 Human Rights Council Resolution A/HRC/RES/54/18.

9 There were effectively four official drafts of the Convention/Covenant. For each draft, the EDG issued an annotated version with extensive legal commentaries on each preambular clause and article: first draft (UN Doc. A/HRC/WG.2/21/2/Add.1); first revised draft (UN Doc. A/HRC/WG.2/23/2/Add.1); second revised draft (UN Doc. A/HRC/WG.2/24/2/Add.1); and the final draft adopted by the Human Rights Council (UN Doc. A/HRC/54/50/Add.1).

10 One of us (Daniel) attended the WG-RtD sessions in 2022 and 2023 and had extensive conversations with secretariat staff and the lead drafter within the EDG.

11 See note 4 above.

12 The formulation in the Declaration led to this understanding that the entitlements of the right to development are those "in which all human rights and fundamental freedoms can be realized."

13 The Commentary cites Jack's notorious "In Search of the Unicorn: The Jurisprudence and Politics of the Right to Development," *California Western International Law Journal* 15, no. 3 (1985): 473–509.

14 UN Doc. A/HRC/54/50/Add.1., pp. 39–40.

14 What Has Been Achieved? And What Is Left to Be Done?

In the 2010s, some prominent human rights scholars challenged the continuing effectiveness of the global human rights project.[1] Whatever its achievements, do its deficiencies merely remind us how much more needs to be done? And how will the significant disruptions within the post-Cold War global order that we have witnessed in the 2020s shape both the human rights regime and its outcomes?

Critics often draw particular attention to problems of weak global and regional institutions, symbolized by a monitoring process that states themselves effectively control (self-reporting); pervasive double standards in the application of human rights policies and criticisms; and the regular subordination of human rights to other foreign policy goals. Despite the proliferation of treaties, monitoring mechanisms, and advocacy groups, gross and persistent systematic violations continue in literally dozens of countries and the idea of all human rights for all remains a distant dream. Critics also sometimes suggest that the relatively extensive work that has been done on developing the global human rights regime may have deflected our collective attention away from other approaches to social justice that deserve greater emphasis and effort—such as a more intensive focus on development or inequality (see Chapter 13).

In this brief concluding chapter we argue that such limitations of the human rights project are real but not reasons to abandon it. Our goals are to appreciate (without overstating) what has been achieved and to provoke thoughtful reflection on the contemporary challenges ahead; on what more still needs to be—and can be—done. We take a birds-eye view of four dimensions of the global human rights project: the making of human rights law; the role of institutions; how human rights-related data is collected and assessed; and the state of global political leadership on human rights.

DOI: 10.4324/9781003373520-17

1 The Law-Making Process

As we have stressed throughout this book, human rights are international legal standards that are implemented *nationally*. Some might suggest that having thus discussed an irremediable flaw we simply stop the discussion.

This, though, would immediately raise the question of a preferable plausible alternative. And even if all we want to do is determine what might be better, we need a baseline assessment of the accomplishments, whatever they may be, of the current system.

Effective struggles for social justice require not only imagining a better future world but addressing the current world as it is. That, for better or worse, remains a legal and political system that is structured around sovereign states that retain near exclusive authority to make (national and international) law. Even when states choose to join supranational organizations or participate in international regulatory regimes, they rarely allow such institutions enforcement powers. (At the global level, the UN Security Council is the exception that proves the rule—but, in practice, only very rarely.)

States make international law. International human rights law is no exception. States negotiate the terms of human rights treaties, seeking consensus among their peers (both in order to avoid bias and to increase the number of those who agree to be bound). But after they sign the resulting treaty, which indicates an intention to ratify, the process of international law-making becomes a purely *domestic* process. And in nearly every country, the government (usually reflecting the will of the people) is willing to acknowledge international human rights obligations but unwilling to allow international implementation measures that go beyond largely unobtrusive monitoring.

The real choice, then, is between a system of national implementation of international human rights and nothing. And even most of the most cynical, we suspect, would not choose nothing.

Even unenforced obligations are obligations. And the fact that *this* injustice is not merely unjust but violates authoritative legal obligations *that the violator itself has accepted* transforms the meaning of the suffering and alters national and international political processes in favor of the victim.

This clearly is not enough. But it is much more than nothing. And, to repeat, there is no real alternative.

The unwillingness of states to accept *enforceable* international human rights obligations will similarly bedevil alternative political projects. There is no reason to believe that more than a handful of states that are unwilling to allow international enforcement of their existing international human rights obligations would allow international enforcement of, for example, global development or equality obligations. And in the case of human rights, we have several decades of successful work getting states to acknowledge a vast range of obligations. We can see no reason to start over with an alternative project that is likely to lead, at best, to roughly the same result.

In other words, the real object of criticism is international law itself—not (international) human rights law in particular. If one is to use international law as a mechanism for pursuing social justice, international human rights law is almost certainly at least as good as any politically plausible alternative.

But how good is that? A consensus assessment might be "not insignificant." But where should we put the emphasis in that formulation? Should we read it to mean that the achievements of the global human rights regime have been significant? Or merely not entirely insignificant? And if it tends toward the latter, has all the effort really been worth it?

The decisive answer to this question, it seems to us, is provided by the not merely continuing but increasing use of the language of human rights by victims of injustice and their advocates. Nonetheless, we would agree with critics that we should not overstate the achievements of international human rights law. And it most certainly has not been and cannot be *by itself* an adequate solution to the problems of human rights violations—let alone social justice more broadly. International human rights law is a resource of some limited value in the struggle for a more just world.

2 Institutions

In broad terms, we can identify *process* and *outcome* questions about existing mechanisms. For example, in the case of the Universal Periodic Review (UPR) (see Chapter 5, Section 1.1), we would want to consider the quality of both the inputs into the review—state reports, NGO observations, and UN system information—and the mechanisms by which this information is assessed, recommendations are formulated, and the conversation with the state under review pursued. (For example, does it really make sense for dozens of states to briefly state, in no particular order, scattered suggestions and observations?) But we would also want to know more about the impact of recommendations. What is the record of implementation? *How* are they implemented? (If laws are changed, how does this filter down to practice?) And what might be done to increase the impact of the review process?

Coordination between existing mechanisms also needs to be a matter of central concern. As we have noted above, this includes efforts already under way to streamline and standardize reporting processes, to better leverage the Office of the High Commissioner to support the work of the Human Rights Council, the treaty bodies, and the special procedures, and to integrate human rights into the work of other UN bodies. But coordination also needs to extend to relations between international human rights institutions and their national counterparts.

Nearly 120 countries have created national human rights institutions (NHRIs), more than three-quarters of which comply with the "Paris Principles"—standards on independence, investigatory authority, and financing.[2] Compliant NHRIs may participate in certain activities of the Human Rights Council. But much more could be done to use NHRIs as monitors of state behavior in reporting processes. And it seems likely that sustained international efforts to increase the independence, authority, and budgets of NHRIs could produce significant (if incremental) improvements in many countries.

Similar questions can be asked about the relations between international human rights institutions and (national and transnational) nongovernmental advocacy groups. NGOs have, over the past three decades, become much more active participants than they were during the Cold War. But more could be done to integrate them into the work of multilateral institutions. In particular, there seem to be untapped possibilities for international institutions to try to continue their promotional activities by working in a more coordinated way *through* NGOs. (Currently, NGOs largely pass information up to international institutions and participate in review processes. Much more might be done to use NGOs to continue an informal conversation after the formal review has been completed.)

Questions also need to be asked about funding levels for human rights institutions. What are the sources of funding? Is the pool shrinking or growing? What influence do funders have on the work that is done? A 2024 study published by the Human Rights Funders Network[3] examined the state of funding in 2020. We ae not aware, though, of more recent data. And there seems to be no mechanism for obtaining and disseminating it.

We also probably should ask whether new institutions are necessary. We suspect that the better path forward is improving the operation of existing institutions. Nonetheless, it would be dangerous simply to assume that we have all the institutions that we need (and that "the only problem" is getting them to work better).

3 Improving the Knowledge Base for Assessment

Reasoned assessment requires access to the relevant information. One of the more promising developments in recent decades has been a marked increase in the collection of raw empirical data relating to human rights. Given all the data available, the title of a 2019 report by the Universal Rights Group (URG) asked a bold question: "Is the global situation of human rights improving or deteriorating?"[4]

Their answer? *We simply do not know*, because "we need something we do not currently possess: global, comprehensive … and reliable empirical data tracking trends in national human rights performance." There is a lot of data. The URG report identifies, for example, ten indices that have been published and are regularly used to measure human rights performance, including the Freedom House Index, the Political Terror Scale, the Cingranelli–Richards Human Rights Data Project, and the Social and Economic Rights Fulfillment index developed by Sakiko Fukuda-Parr, Terra Lawson-Remer, and Susan Randolph to measure socioeconomic rights performance. In 2012, the Office of the UN High Commissioner for Human Rights published a study of the various data measurement models that the Unites Nations has used over the years, and a list of literally hundreds of indicators that *could* be used to measure human rights.

Nonetheless, there are still significant gaps in what is measured. There is no standardization in gathering and processing data. And different indicators are used by different indices to measure the same thing—which causes significant problems in comparing analyses and accumulating knowledge.

The Human Rights Measurement Initiative (HRMI),[5] which was launched in 2015, has thus attempted to create a comprehensive set of indicators to track human rights performance worldwide. They now have country-level metrics to measure five "quality of life" rights (food, education, health, housing, and work) and five "safety from the state" rights (freedom from the death penalty, extrajudicial execution, torture, disappearance, and arbitrary arrest and detention), and four "empowerment" rights (assembly and association, opinion and expression, political participation, and religion and belief). Because the metrics are common, there are standards for data collection, and standard analytical models, the HRMI is poised to finally be able to compare data cross nationally as well as measure change over time. While the HRMI database has entries for 203 countries, in 2025 only 19 of those have complete data for all three categories of rights (and the years for the latest data vary between categories). Most only cover one category (usually "safety" rights). Still, this is a (small) step in the right direction.

Our knowledge of remedies is even more limited and fragmentary. We do not even have much in the way of "best practices" guidelines.

Another important limitation on our knowledge is disciplinary. This book, as we noted at the outset, has been about the *politics* of human rights, written by two scholars of international relations. We both, however, also have interests in history and philosophy, which we have tried to draw on here. And we have drawn on the quite considerable body of international legal scholarship. But human rights—especially the effective enjoyment of human rights—is an inherently multidisciplinary endeavor that must draw not only on other social sciences but also the natural sciences (most obviously in the case of the right to health) and the humanities.

International law and international studies, however, are perhaps the only academic disciplines in which a subfield or specialty of human rights is widely recognized. What can be done to "mainstream" human rights in other disciplines? And how can knowledge from different disciplines not merely be brought to bear on one another but be integrated into broader and more penetrating analyses than those that focus, as in this book, on law and politics?

We have no idea how to provide productive answers to such questions. Nonetheless, we think it crucial to emphasize the importance of both improving what we know about human rights and bringing to bear many more ways of knowing.

4 Global Political Leadership

Given the focus of this book on *international* human rights, assessing the global human rights regime also requires attention to global political leadership for human rights.

Much has changed since the last edition of this book: the COVID-19 pandemic, which resulted in more than 7 million reported deaths (the actual toll is estimated to be between 19 and 32 million); Russia's full-scale invasion of Ukraine in 2022; the war in Gaza; the collapse of the Assad regime in Syria; and, for the second time, Donald Trump in the White House. During that time, many covers of *Foreign Affairs* magazine have led with titles like, "Decline and Fall: Can America Ever Lead Again?" (March 2021); "The Age of Uncertainty"

(September 2022); "The World Putin Made" (January 2023); "The Self-Doubting Superpower" (January 2024); "America Adrift" (October 2024); and "The Center Will Not Hold: How an Order Ends" (March 2025). And there are the specific challenges to human rights that we outlined in the introduction: the global crisis of democracy; the impunity of violators; global economic inequality and climate change; and the polarization over human rights within the global rights regime.

Global orders—even relatively stable ones—change over time. It is clear that the post-Cold War order under American leadership has faded. In their 2020 book *Exit from Hegemony: The Unravelling of the American Global Order*, Alexander Cooley and Daniel Nexon argue persuasively that the American-led order is being challenged at three levels simultaneously: "from above" (directly by China and Russia); "from below"—China and Russia are offering alternatives to American supplied "goods" such as security and access to economic resources and markets; and "from within"—by supporting transnational anti-democratic movements that are more favorable to their interests.

Others are more skeptical (or optimistic, depending on your perspective). International liberal theorist John Ikenberry has long argued that many normative and institutional elements of the liberal order that was established after World War II (including the human rights regime) have grown roots that are deep enough to withstand even the decline (or end) of American hegemony.

But Ikenberry probably did not anticipate that the architect and most powerful underwriter of the liberal order itself would *proactively* abandon that leadership. Perhaps the most bizarre example of this came in February 2025 at the 11th Emergency Special Session of the UN General Assembly, which has, since 2022, adopted eight resolutions on the ongoing war in Ukraine.[6] On the third anniversary of the Russian invasion, the United States voted *against* a resolution that repeated its finding of Russia as the aggressor in the conflict. In doing so, the United States sided with states such as Russia, Belarus, Hungary, Sudan, and North Korea.

What will this mean for the global human rights regime? What will be the impact of political leaders and movements, most notably in the Global North, that are downgrading their former support for global human rights—and in some cases even pushing back against international human rights norms?

Here the obvious first question is just how extensive, persistent, and powerful attacks on the global liberal order really are. In the last edition, we wondered whether this was a short-term problem largely restricted to the then-anomalous Trump presidency. As we outlined in Chapter 8, however, the actions of the second Trump administration with respect to human rights and humanitarian affairs (especially foreign aid and assistance) are unprecedented. Is nationalism and (often pseudo-) populism becoming increasingly common and respectable? In the Global North? In the Global South?

If the United States has truly abandoned its long-standing leadership role, are there possible alternatives? Europe? A North–South coalition? If there has traditionally been a sort of global division of labor on humanitarian leadership with the United States providing a great deal of the material resources for advancing human rights and humanitarianism and other states playing supportive roles especially with respect to normative and institutional development, what will be the impact of a significantly diminished resource base covered by a not insignificant number of smaller states with fewer resources to share, in absolute terms? And beyond resources, what about leadership? Will the long-term work of bolstering the human rights regime take a back seat to more pressing concerns?

If not, just how much difference is that likely to make?

Less pessimistically, the work of human rights norm development, monitoring, and protection moves forward. The UN Human Rights Council continues to meet; the UPR process marches forward; treaty monitoring bodies continue to assess states' human rights performance. Hundreds of NGOs continue their work on behalf of the global human rights project. Even in the face of the erosion of American leadership on human rights, the fact that human rights work goes on offer a test of Ikenberry's thesis.

The answers to these questions probably depend in significant measure on the "staying power" of international human rights norms and institutions. We will not try to predict the future. But we will conclude with a series of questions that pose possibilities—and ways of thinking about those possibilities.

Have human rights been sufficiently institutionalized—in the United Nations, national foreign policies, the activities of transnational advocacy groups, and the interests and self-understandings of citizens—that international action is likely to be sustained, at least in the short and medium run, without prominent global leadership? What, though, about the long run?

International relations theory may provide some analytical resources to address such questions. Are international institutions, as political realists often argue, largely the reflection of the preferences of their great power supporters? Or is there, as institutionalists argue, a certain "stickiness" to established international regimes?

Such stickiness is most likely when international regimes have altered not just the behavior of states but their understandings of who they are and what they value. Has the global human rights regime changed states (or merely changed their behavior)? If so, in what ways? And how significant are those changes for the future of human rights?

More broadly, have human rights become a deeply embedded part of the international society of states? Of transnational civil society? And if so, just how significant is that for the future prospects of international human rights?

What *are* the most likely futures of the global human rights regime? And just how much difference does the answer to this question make?

Suggested Reading

Kathryn Sikkink, *Evidence for Hope: Making Human Rights Work in the 21st Century* (Princeton University Press 2017) presents an argument for "hope without complacency." Chapters 1, 2, and 7 complement and extend the arguments we have made in this chapter.

Notes

1 Examples include Stephen Hopgood, *The Endtimes of Human Rights* (Ithaca, Cornell University Press 2013), Emily Hafner-Burton, *Making Human Rights a Reality* (Princeton, Princeton University Press, 2013), Eric Posner, *The Twilight of Human Rights Law* (Oxford, Oxford University Press, 2014); and Samuel Moyn, *Not Enough: Human Rights in an Unequal World* (Cambridge, Harvard/ Belknap, 2018). Rhoda E. Howard-Hassmann, "Review of Samuel Moyn, *Not Enough*," *Human Rights Quarterly* 41 (2) (2019): 515–527, provides a lively response to Moyn.

2 https://www.ohchr.org/sites/default/files/documents/countries/nhri/ganhri/ganhri-status-accreditation-chart.pdf.

3 https://www.hrfn.org/wp-content/uploads/2024/09/HRFN-Advancing-Human-Rights-2020-Full-Report.pdf.

4 www.universal-rights.org/urg-policy-reports/is-the-global-situation-of-human-rights-improving-or-deteriorating-making-the-case-for-the-empirical-measurement-of-human-rights-change/.

5 https://humanrightsmeasurement.org/.

6 Owing to Russia's permanent seat (and certain veto), the UN Security Council referred the Russian invasion of Ukraine to the General Assembly, under the 1950 "Uniting for Peace" resolution (377 V) that was adopted when the Soviet Union returned from its boycott of the UNSC several months after the Korean War broke out.

Appendix

Universal Declaration of Human Rights

United Nations General Assembly Resolution 217A (III), 10 December 1948

Whereas recognition of the inherent dignity and of the equal and inalienable rights of all members of the human family is the foundation of freedom, justice and peace in the world,

Whereas disregard and contempt for human rights have resulted in barbarous acts which have outraged the conscience of mankind, and the advent of a world in which human beings shall enjoy freedom of speech and belief and freedom from fear and want has been proclaimed as the highest aspiration of the common people,

Whereas it is essential, if man is not to be compelled to have recourse, as a last resort, to rebellion against tyranny and oppression, that human rights should be protected by the rule of law,

Whereas it is essential, to promote the development of friendly relations between nations,

Whereas the peoples of the United Nations have in the Charter reaffirmed their faith in fundamental human rights, in the dignity and worth of the human person and in the equal rights of men and women and have determined to promote social progress and better standards of life in larger freedom,

Whereas Member States have pledged themselves to achieve, in co-operation with the United Nations, the promotion of universal respect for and observance of human rights and fundamental freedoms,

Whereas a common understanding of these rights and freedoms is of the greatest importance for the full realization of this pledge,

Now, therefore,

The General Assembly

Proclaims this Universal Declaration of Human Rights as a common standard of achievement for all peoples and all nations, to the end that every individual and every organ of society, keeping this Declaration constantly in mind, shall strive by teaching and education to promote respect for these rights and freedoms and by progressive measures, national and international, to secure their universal and effective recognition and observance, both among the peoples of Member States themselves and among the peoples of territories under their jurisdiction.

Article 1. All human beings are born free and equal in dignity and rights. They are endowed with reason and conscience and should act toward one another in a spirit of brotherhood.

Article 2. Everyone is entitled to all the rights and freedoms set forth in this Declaration, without distinction of any kind, such as race, colour, sex, language, religion, political or other opinion, national or social origin, property, birth or other status.

Furthermore, no distinction shall be made on the basis of the political, jurisdictional or international status of the country or territory to which a person belongs, whether it be independent, trust, non-self-governing or under any other limitation of sovereignty.

Article 3. Everyone has the right to life, liberty and the security of person.

Article 4. No one shall be held in slavery or servitude; slavery and the slave trade shall be prohibited in all their forms.

Article 5. No one shall be subjected to torture or to cruel, inhuman or degrading treatment or punishment.

Article 6. Everyone has the right to recognition everywhere as a person before the law.

Article 7. All are equal before the law and are entitled without any discrimination to equal protection of the law. All are entitled to equal protection against any discrimination in violation of this Declaration and against any incitement to such discrimination.

Article 8. Everyone has the right to an effective remedy by the competent national tribunals for acts violating the fundamental rights granted him by the constitution or by law.

Article 9. No one shall be subjected to arbitrary arrest, detention or exile.

Article 10. Everyone is entitled to full equality to a fair and public hearing by an independent and impartial tribunal in the determination of his rights and obligations and of any criminal charge against him.

Article 11. 1. Everyone charged with a penal offence has the right to be presumed innocent until proved guilty according to law in a public trial at which he has had all the guarantees necessary for his defence.

2. No one shall be held guilty of any penal offence on account of any act or omission which did not constitute a penal offence, under national or international law, at the time when it was committed. Nor shall a heavier penalty be imposed than the one that was applicable at the time the penal offence was committed.

Article 12. No one shall be subjected to arbitrary interference with his privacy, family, home or correspondence, nor to attacks upon his honour and reputation. Everyone has the right to the protection of the law against such interference or attacks.

Article 13. 1. Everyone has the right to freedom of movement and residence within the borders of each state.

2. Everyone has the right to leave any country, including his own, and to return to his country.

Article 14. 1. Everyone has the right to seek and to enjoy in other countries asylum from persecution.

2. This right may not be invoked in the case of prosecutions genuinely arising from non-political crimes or from acts contrary to the purposes and principles of the United Nations.

Article 15. 1. Everyone has the right to a nationality.

2. No one shall be arbitrarily deprived of his nationality nor denied the right to change his nationality.

Article 16. 1. Men and women of full age, without any limitation due to race, nationality or religion, have the right to marry and to found a family. They are entitled to equal rights as to marriage, during marriage and at its dissolution.

2. Marriage shall be entered into only with the free and full consent of the intending spouses.

3. The family is the natural and fundamental group unit of society and is entitled to protection by society and the State.

Article 17. 1. Everyone has the right to own property alone as well as in association with others.

2. No one shall be arbitrarily deprived of his property.

Article 18. Everyone has the right to freedom of thought, conscience and religion; this right includes freedom to change his religion or belief, and freedom, either alone or in community with others and in public or private, to manifest his religion or belief in teaching, practice, worship and observance.

Article 19. Everyone has the right to freedom of opinion and expression; this right includes freedom to hold opinions without interference and to seek, receive and impart information and ideas through any media and regardless of frontiers.

Article 20. 1. Everyone has the right to freedom of peaceful assembly and association.

2. No one may be compelled to belong to an association.

Article 21. 1. Everyone has the right to take part in the Government of his country, directly or through freely chosen representatives.

2. Everyone has the right of equal access to public service in his country.

3. The will of the people shall be the basis of the authority of government; this will shall be expressed in periodic and genuine elections which shall be by universal and equal suffrage and shall be held by secret vote or by equivalent free voting procedures.

Article 22. Everyone, as a member of society, has the right to social security and is entitled to realization through national effort and international co-operation and in accordance with the organization and resources of each State, of the economic, social and cultural rights indispensable for his dignity and the free development of his personality.

Article 23. 1. Everyone has the right to work, to free choice of employment, to just and favourable conditions of work and to protection against unemployment.

2. Everyone, without any discrimination, has the right to equal pay for equal work.

3. Everyone who works has the right to just and favourable remuneration insuring for himself and his family an existence worthy of human dignity, and supplemented, if necessary, by other means of social protection.

4. Everyone has the right to form and to join trade unions for the protection of his interests.

Article 24. Everyone has the right to rest and leisure, including reasonable limitation of working hours and periodic holidays with pay.

Article 25. 1. Everyone has the right to a standard of living adequate for the health and well-being of himself and of his family, including food, clothing, housing and medical care and necessary social services, and the right to security in the event of unemployment, sickness, disability, widowhood, old age or other lack of livelihood in circumstances beyond his control.

2. Motherhood and childhood are entitled to special care and assistance. All children, whether born in or out of wedlock, shall enjoy the same social protection.

Article 26. 1. Everyone has the right to education. Education shall be free, at least in the elementary and fundamental stages. Elementary education shall be compulsory. Technical and professional education shall be made generally available and higher education shall be equally accessible to all on the basis of merit.

2. Education shall be directed to the full development of the human personality and to the strengthening of respect for human rights and fundamental freedoms. It shall promote understanding, tolerance and friendship among all nations, racial or religious groups, and shall further the activities of the United Nations for the maintenance of peace.

3. Parents have a prior right to choose the kind of education that shall be given to their children.

Article 27. 1. Everyone has the right freely to participate in the cultural life of the community, to enjoy the arts and share in scientific advancement and its benefits.

2. Everyone has the right to the protection of the moral and material interests resulting from any scientific, literary or artistic production of which he is the author.

Article 28. Everyone is entitled to a social and international order in which the rights and freedoms set forth in this Declaration can be fully realized.

Article 29. 1. Everyone has duties to the community in which alone the free and full development of his personality is possible.

2. In the exercise of his rights and freedoms, everyone shall be subject only to such limitations as are determined by law solely for the purpose of securing due recognition and respect for the rights and freedoms of others and of meeting the just requirements of morality, public order and the general welfare in a democratic society.

3. These rights and freedoms may in no case be exercised contrary to the purposes and principles of the United Nations.

Article 30. Nothing in this Declaration may be interpreted as implying for any State, group or person any right to engage in any activity or to perform any act aimed at the destruction of any of the rights and freedoms set forth herein.

Glossary

American exceptionalism is the belief that the United States is culturally and politically different from, and usually superior to, other countries. It can be traced to the colonial period and the biblical image of the city on the hill. In the area of human rights, it tends to be expressed in the common American view that the United States in some important sense defines human rights standards.

Amnesty exempts a person or group from legal liability for specified acts they may have committed. Amnesty policies are often pursued in countries undergoing a political transition after a period of intense human rights violations or abuses, ostensibly to move on from the past. They are widely condemned by human rights activists as promoting **impunity**—the knowledge that, no matter how serious the crimes that rulers may have committed, they will never be prosecuted for those crimes. Amnesty for genocide, war crimes, and crimes against humanity is widely considered to be contrary to international law.

Anarchy, the absence of political rule, is characterized by the lack of hierarchical relationships of superiority and subordination. In international relations, anarchy refers to the fact that there is no higher authority above states. Anarchy, however, need not involve chaos (absence of order). Thus, international relations have been called an anarchical society, a society in which order emerges from the interactions of formally equally sovereign states.

Apartheid, an Afrikaans term meaning "separateness," was the policy of systematic, official racial classification and discrimination in South Africa. Building on a long tradition of racial discrimination, white South African governments in the 1950s and 1960s developed an unusually extensive, highly integrated system of official discrimination, touching virtually all aspects of public life and many aspects of private life as well. The policy was officially renounced following a (whites-only) plebiscite in March 1992.

Civil and political rights are one of two principal classes of internationally recognized human rights. They provide protections against the state (such as rights to due process, habeas corpus, and freedom of speech) and require that the state provide certain substantive legal and political opportunities (such as the rights to vote and to trial by a jury of one's peers). They are codified in the International Covenant on Civil and Political Rights and in Articles 3–15 and 19–21 of the Universal Declaration of Human Rights (see Table 1.1).

Cold War is the term used for the geopolitical and ideological struggle between the Soviet Union and the United States following World War II. It began in earnest roughly in 1948, waxed and waned over the following forty years, and finally ended with the collapse of the Soviet bloc in 1989. See also **containment** and **détente**.

The United Nations Commission on Human Rights was created in 1946 as a subsidiary body of the UN Economic and Social Council (ECOSOC) as the UN's principal organ for the promotion and protection of human rights. Its members were representatives of UN member states, elected to the Commission by ECOSOC. It drafted the 1948 Universal Declaration of Human Rights, the two International Covenants and subsequent human rights treaties. In 2006, the Commission was disbanded and replaced by the **Human Rights Council**. See also **Human Rights Committee**.

The Committee on Economic, Social and Cultural Rights oversees the implementation and monitoring of the International Covenant on Economic, Social, and Cultural Rights (ICESCR). It is composed of 18 independent members serving in their personal professional capacity. It reviews state-party progress reports, deliberates and publishes general comments on interpretation of the Covenant, and is empowered to hear individual and group complaints of violations. See also **Human Rights Committee** and **Treaty Monitoring Bodies**.

The principle of achieving **consensus** has been part of the human rights culture of the United Nations since the 1970s. The idea was to move the organization away from the contentious politics of voting —where the goal is to simply achieve a numerical majority—to a more cooperative and inclusive process for drafting resolutions, programs, and policies. In practice, adoption by consensus is achieved when no one with a vote objects to such an adoption (although they may disagree with some part of it). If there is an objection, then a formal vote is taken.

Constructivism is a theoretical orientation that emphasizes the societal, socially constructed dimensions of international relations. Constructivism is regularly contrasted to **realism**, which stresses the pursuit of material interests in anarchy, and "rationalism," which focuses on developing models of how rational actors will respond to particular contexts of interaction.

The American policy of containment was a political, military, and economic strategy to thwart the expansionist tendencies of the Soviet Union during the Cold War. The core elements of the policy were first articulated by George Kennan, a US State Department diplomat posted in Moscow after World War II. Following the consolidation of Soviet influence in Eastern Europe immediately after the war, Kennan believed the most American prudent policy was to forestall further Soviet expansion (especially into Turkey, Southern Europe and Western Asia) through American military, economic, and political support to governments to keep them out of the Soviet sphere of influence. It explicitly rejected attempts by the United States to "roll back" Soviet power where it was already established, or attempts to reform the USSR from the outside. See also **détente**.

Contentious jurisdiction refers to the jurisdiction of a court or tribunal that is accepted by the parties to a dispute, which may be compulsory (for example, with the European Court of Human Rights) or voluntary. States that accept a court's contentious jurisdiction agree (in principle) to accept the judgment issued in any such case heard by the court.

Cosmopolitan and cosmopolitanism refer to a conception of international relations that views people first and foremost as individual members of a global political community (cosmopolis) rather than as citizens of states.

The Rome Statute of the International Criminal Court defines **crimes against humanity** as any number of acts committed as part of a widespread or systematic attack directed against a civilian population, in either time of war or peace. Examples include extermination, forcible transfer of a population, ethnic cleansing, torture, sexual slavery, and enforced disappearances. See Article 7 of the Rome Statute at www.icc-cpi.int/resource-library/documents/rs-eng.pdf.

Cultural relativism (see **relativism**, below).

Détente is a term used to describe the relaxation of tensions between the United States (and Western Europe) and the Soviet Union (associated with the **Cold War**) from the late 1960s through the early 1980s. Its hallmarks were several strategic arms control agreements and the Helsinki Final Act, which settled a variety of lingering post-World War II issues and problems between Western and Eastern Europe and placed human rights on the agenda of East-West relations.

Disappearances are a form of human rights violation that became popular in the 1970s. Victims, rather than being officially detained or even murdered by the authorities or semiofficial death squads, are "disappeared," taken to state-run but clandestine detention centers. Torture typically accompanies disappearance, and in some countries the disappeared have also been regularly killed.

Economic, social, and cultural rights are one of two classes of internationally recognized human rights. They guarantee socially provided goods and services (such as food, health care, social insurance, and education) and certain protections against the state (especially in family matters). They are codified in the International Covenant on Economic, Social, and Cultural Rights and in Articles 16–18 and 22–27 of the Universal Declaration of Human Rights (see Table 1.1).

Ethnic cleansing is the genocidal "purification" of the population of a territory through murder and forced migration. The term entered international political vocabularies to describe the strategy and practices of Serbian separatists in the former Yugoslavian republic of Bosnia-Herzegovina during the civil war of 1992–1995.

The four **Geneva Conventions** of 1949 (and their additional protocols of 1977 and 2005) form the basis of international humanitarian law in situations of armed conflict. They aim to protect those who are *hors de combat* (outside of combat) despite being in a combat zone. The First Convention protects soldiers who have been wounded or fall ill on land; the Second, those at sea. The Third Convention applies to soldiers who have surrendered or been captured (prisoners of war). The Fourth applies to civilians. The Conventions also set out the limitations and responsibilities of occupying powers with respect to civilian populations.

Genocide in the narrow, technical sense of the term, involves systematic killing and similar methods aimed at destroying, in whole or in part, a people (*genos*) or ethnic or religious group. In a looser sense of the term, it involves targeted mass political killing—politicide—directed against a group that may or may not be defined by common descent.

In international relations, **hegemony** is a form of leadership that is achieved in an otherwise anarchical system. It refers to the ability of a great power to shape relations through coercive and noncoercive means, both of which are crucial to the concept. Other states acquiesce in the leadership of the hegemon. Great Britain in the nineteenth century and the United States in the late twentieth and early twenty-first century are classic examples of hegemons.

Humanitarian intervention is intervention, usually involving the use of force, for humanitarian purposes, typically in situations of genocide, armed conflict, or severe humanitarian crisis.

Human rights, the rights that one has simply because one is a human being, are held equally and inalienably by all human beings. They are the social and political guarantees necessary to protect individuals from the standard threats to human dignity posed by the modern state and modern markets.

The Human Rights Committee is a body of eighteen independent experts created by the **International Covenant on Civil and Political Rights**. Its principal activities are reviewing periodic state reports on compliance with the Covenant and reviewing individual complaints of violations. See also **Committee on Economic, Social and Cultural Rights, treaty monitoring bodies, Commission on Human Rights,** and **Human Rights Council**.

The United Nations Human Rights Council was established by the UN General Assembly (in resolution 60/251) to replace the **Commission on Human Rights**. The Council is comprised of 47 member-states of the UN that serve staggered three-year terms. The Council conducts the ongoing **Universal Periodic Review** of all UN member-states human rights records and is the primary human rights policy-making organ of the UN.

An **intergovernmental organization**, often referred to as an international organization, is a treaty-based organization of states. Prominent global examples include the United Nations and the World Health Organization. The European Union is the most prominent regional example. Compare **nongovernmental organization**.

The International Bill of Human Rights is the informal name for the Universal Declaration of Human Rights and the **International Human Rights Covenants**, considered collectively as a set of authoritative international human rights standards. By virtue of resolution 52/136 of March 1998, the UN General Assembly seems to have added the 1986 Declaration on the Right to Development to the International Bill of Rights.

The International Human Rights Covenants comprise the International Covenant on Economic, Social, and Cultural Rights and the International Covenant on Civil and Political Rights, which were opened for signature in 1966 and entered into force in

1976. Along with the Universal Declaration of Human Rights, these are the central normative documents in the field of international human rights.

International humanitarian law is a body of law governing armed conflict. The Hague strand covers the laws of war itself: who can legally wage it, how it is declared, and the laws of surrender and armistice. The Geneva strand—codified especially by the four **Geneva Conventions**—limits the legal use of force to protect those who are outside of combat, and therefore not belligerents. International humanitarian law has also codified many violations as constituting crimes: genocide, war crimes, and crimes against humanity.

An **international regime** is a set of principles, norms, rules, and decision-making procedures accepted by states (and other relevant international actors) as binding in an issue area. Many international regimes include formal institutions or organizations that are established by treaty or agreement. However, the notion of a regime points to patterns of international governance that are not necessarily limited only to a single treaty or organization.

Internationalist and **internationalism** refer to a conception of international relations that stresses both the centrality of the state and the existence of social relations among those states. See also **society of states**.

Intervention as the term is used in international law and relations means coercive interference, usually involving the threat or use of force, against the sovereignty, territorial integrity, or political independence, or any matters essentially within the domestic jurisdiction, of a state.

The **like-minded countries** are a group of about a dozen small- and medium-sized primarily Western countries, including Canada, the Netherlands, and the Nordic countries. They often act in concert in international organizations and generally pursue foreign policies that are more "liberal" than those of the United States, Japan, or the larger Western European countries. The like-minded countries particularly emphasize development issues, and they have tried to play an intermediary role between the countries of the Global South and the larger Northern countries.

Mainstreaming is a process within (especially) the United Nations to incorporate what have traditionally been thought of as "specialty" concerns (such as gender or human rights) into the wider work of the United Nations. Thus, human rights are not merely the concern of the UN Human Rights Council or the treaty monitoring bodies but also are incorporated into the work of development, environmental, or security-related agencies as well.

A **nongovernmental organization** is a private association of individuals or groups that engages in political activity. International NGOs (INGOs) carry on their activities across state boundaries. The most prominent human rights INGOs include Amnesty International, Human Rights Watch, and the Minority Rights Group. In some areas, especially international relief, NGOs are frequently referred to as private voluntary organizations. Domestically, they often are referred to as civil society organizations.

Nonintervention is the international obligation not to interfere in matters that are essentially within the domestic jurisdiction of a sovereign state. This duty is correlative to the right of sovereignty and expresses the principal practical implications of sovereignty, viewed from the perspective of other states.

An **Optional Protocol** is an set of rules or procedures added to an existing treaty. Being optional, states can decide whether to be bound to its provisions without prejudice to the obligations contained in the parent treaty. Nearly all of the major international human rights treaties have one or more such protocols, establishing additional procedures (e.g., petition mechanisms) or addressing a specific human rights issue (e.g., the abolition of the death penalty or child exploitation and trafficking).

Peacekeeping involves the use of lightly armed multilateral forces to separate previously warring parties. Peacekeeping is distinguished from collective security enforcement by a limited mandate, an effort to maintain neutrality, and reliance on the consent of the parties in whose territory peacekeepers are placed.

Quiet diplomacy is the pursuit of foreign policy objectives through official channels, without recourse to public statements or actions. A standard mechanism for pursuing virtually all foreign policy goals, it became a political issue in the United States in the late 1970s and 1980s, when conservative critics of the policy of the Carter administration and defenders of the policy of the Reagan administration argued that US international human rights policy toward "friendly" (anticommunist) regimes should in most cases be restricted *solely* to quiet diplomacy.

Realism (Realpolitik) is a theory of international relations that stresses the absence of international government (that is, the presence of international **anarchy**) and the centrality of egoism in human motivation, thus requiring states to give priority to power and security in international relations and to exclude considerations of morality from foreign policy.

A **relativist** believes that values are not universal but are a function of contingent circumstances. **Cultural relativism** holds that morality is significantly determined by culture and history. Radical cultural relativism sees culture as the source of all values.

When states ratify human rights treaties, they may attach a **reservation** to a provision of the treaty indicating that the ratifying state does not intend to be bound by that provision. These are different than "declarations" and "understandings," whose intention it is to interpret a provision or to declare some limitation to the effect of the provision in national law. Unless a treaty (human rights or otherwise) expressly prohibits reservations, they usually are permitted. However, the Human Rights Committee (in its General Comment 24) has interpreted any reservation that significantly contradicts the "object and purpose" of the treaty itself to be invalid.

The **society of states** conceptualizes "the international community" as a largely contractual community whose principal members are states. See also **internationalism**.

To be **sovereign** is to be subject to no higher authority. International relations over the past three centuries have been structured around the principle of the **sovereignty** of territorial states.

Statist and **statism** (also "pluralism") refer to a theory of international relations that stress the centrality of sovereign states. Realism is usually associated with a statist theory of international relations.

Thomism is the philosophical tradition founded by Thomas Aquinas, It plays a central role in Catholic moral and ethical theory.

A **treaty** is an agreement between states that creates obligations on those states. Treaties—sometimes also called "conventions" or "covenants"—are one of the two principal sources of international law, along with custom (regularized patterns of action that through repeated practice have created expectations and thus acquired an obligatory character). The two most important international human rights treaties are the International Covenant on Economic, Social, and Cultural Rights and the International Covenant on Civil and Political Rights.

Treaty monitoring bodies is the term of art used for the various committees created under the International Human Rights Covenants and other international human rights treaties to monitor state compliance. See also **Committee on Economic, Social and Cultural Rights** and **Human Rights Committee**.

The United Nations is the premiere international multilateral organization. Its Charter was adopted by the fifty countries that were allied against Nazi Germany and Japan in the waning days of World War II, in June 1945. Today its membership is nearly universal, at 193 countries. The UN has powers and responsibilities with respect to maintaining international peace and security, protecting human rights, and promoting economic and social development. The organization oversees hundreds of specialized agencies, funds, and programs as well as coordinating its activities with other **international organizations**.

The Universal Declaration of Human Rights is a 1948 UN General Assembly resolution that provides the most authoritative statement of international human rights norms. See also **International Human Rights Covenants** and **International Bill of Human Rights**.

Universalism is the belief that moral values such as human rights are fundamentally the same at all times, in all places, or across some particular "universe" of application. It is the opposite of **relativism**.

Utilitarianism is a moral theory (most closely associated with Jeremy Bentham and John Stuart Mill) that holds that the right course of action is that which maximizes the balance of pleasure over pain. This is the most common form of "consequentialist" ethics, which judges behavior on the consequences of acts rather than their inherent character.

The Vienna Declaration and Programme of Action is the most recent comprehensive statement of the United Nations' standards and goals surrounding human rights. The Declaration and Programme of Action were drafted by governments with significant input from human rights NGOs and other civil society groups at the 1993 World Conference on Human Rights, following the end of the Cold War. It reiterates the universality and indivisibility of all human rights and especially emphasizes the rights of women and of children. It is considered authoritative insofar as it was adopted by **consensus**.

Index

Note: Page numbers followed by "n" denote endnotes.